From Inkmarks to Ideas

Reading is one of the most sophisticated demonstrations of human pattern recognition and symbolic processing skill. Skilled readers effortlessly comprehend written text at rates of at least 300 words per minute, despite the complex interactions between perceptual, cognitive and memory processes required for effective comprehension. Understanding how we achieve this remarkable feat has been a focus of investigation since the birth of experimental psychology. Over the last two decades, visual word recognition has been at the forefront of developments in cognitive science. This book brings together many of the most influential contributors to these developments to reflect on current issues in the cognitive science of lexical processing and the methods required for further progress. The first section focuses on computational models. Written words provide a fertile context for large-scale modelling and the domain of lexical retrieval has become a test-bed for evaluating competing theoretical frameworks. The later sections draw upon cognitive psychology, linguistics, philosophy, computer science and neuroscience to elaborate critical theoretical issues and to develop novel research tools.

From Inkmarks to Ideas provides advanced students and researchers with a comprehensive overview of the critical theoretical and empirical controversies in current research on the cognitive science of lexical processing and reading.

Sally Andrews is Professor of Cognitive Psychology and Head of the School of Psychology at the University of Sydney, Australia. She is a Fellow of the Australian Academy of Social Sciences and a member of the Australian Research Council's College of Experts. She has published influential papers that have established "benchmark" phenomena that are used to evaluate current computational models of visual word recognition.

From Inkmarks to Ideas

Current issues in lexical processing

Edited by Sally Andrews

Psychology Press
Taylor & Francis Group
HOVE AND NEW YORK

First published 2006 by Psychology Press,
27 Church Road, Hove, East Sussex, BN3 2FA

Simultaneously published in the USA and Canada
by Psychology Press
270 Madison Avenue, New York, NY 10016

Psychology Press is an imprint of the Taylor & Francis Group, an informa business

Typeset in Times by RefineCatch Limited, Bungay, Suffolk
Printed and bound in Great Britain by
TJ International Ltd, Padstow, Cornwall
Cover design by Design Deluxe

British Library Cataloguing in Publication Data
A catalogue record for this book is available from the British Library

Library of Congress Cataloging in Publication Data
From inkmarks to ideas : current issues in lexical processing / edited by Sally Andrews.
p. cm.
Includes bibliographical references and index.
ISBN 1-84169-607-2
1. Lexicology–Psychological aspects. 2. Reading, Psychology of.
3. Written communication–Data processing. I. Andrews, Sally, 1953–
P326.5.P75F76 2006
401′.9–dc22
2006006622

ISBN13: 978–1–84169–607–2

ISBN10: 1–84169–607–2

Contents

Plates, tables, and figures, including captions

Plate

Tables

Figures

Contributors

Sally Andrews, School of Psychology, University of Sydney, NSW 2006, Australia. Email: sallya@psych.usyd.edu.au

David A. Balota, Department of Psychology, Washington University, St Louis, MO 63130, USA. Email: dbalota@artsci.wustl.edu

Anne Castles, School of Behavioural Science, University of Melbourne, Victoria 3010, Australia. Email: acastles@unimelb.edu.au

Max Coltheart, Macquarie Centre for Cognitive Science, Macquarie University, NSW 2109, Australia. Email: max@maccs.mq.edu.au

Chris Davis, School of Behavioural Science, University of Melbourne, Victoria 3010, Australia. Email: cwd@unimelb.edu.au

Colin J. Davis, Department of Experimental Psychology, University of Bristol, 8 Woodland Road, Bristol BS8 1TN, UK. Email: Colin.Davis@bristol.ac.uk

Kenneth I. Forster, Department of Psychology, University of Arizona, Tucson, AZ 85721, USA. Email: kforster@u.arizona.edu

Jukka Hyönä, Department of Psychology, University of Turku, FIN–20014 Turku, Finland. Email: hyona@utu.fi

Christopher T. Kello, Department of Psychology, George Mason University, 4400 University Drive, Fairfax, VA 22030, USA. Email: ckello@gmu.edu

Jeesun Kim, Graduate School of Education, Sejong University, Seoul, South Korea. Email: jeesun@unimelb.edu.au

Gary Libben, Department of Linguistics, 4–36 Assiniboia Hall, University of Alberta, Edmonton, Alberta, T6G 2E7 Canada. Email: gary.libben@ualberta.ca

Maryellen C. MacDonald, Department of Psychology, W. Brogden Hall, 1202 West Johnson Street, Madison, WI 53706–1696, USA. Email: mcmacdonald@wisc.edu

Kate Nation, Department of Experimental Psychology, South Parks Road, Oxford OX1 3UD, UK. Email: kate.nation@psy.ox.ac.uk

Karalyn Patterson, MRC Cognition and Brain Sciences Unit, 15 Chaucer Road, Cambridge CB2 2EF, UK. Email: karalyn.patterson@mrc-cbu.cam.ac.uk

David C. Plaut, Department of Psychology, Carnegie Mellon University, 5000 Forbes Avenue, Pittsburgh, PA 15213–3890, USA. Email: plaut@cmu.edu

Alexander Pollatsek, Department of Psychology, University of Massachusetts, Amherst, MA 01003, USA. Email: pollatsek@psych.umass.edu

Kathleen Rastle, Department of Psychology, Royal Holloway, University of London, Egham, Surrey TW20 0EX, UK. Email: Kathy.Rastle@rhul.ac.uk

Keith Rayner, Department of Psychology, University of Massachusetts, Amherst, MA 01003, USA. Email: rayner@psych.umass.edu

Erik D. Reichle, Department of Psychology, University of Pittsburgh, 210 South Bouquet Street, Pittsburgh, PA 15260, USA. Email: reichle@pitt.edu

Mark S. Seidenberg, Department of Psychology, University of Wisconsin, Madison WI 53706, USA. Email: seidenberg@wisc.edu

Marcus Taft, School of Psychology, University of New South Wales, NSW 2052, Australia. Email: m.taft@unsw.edu.au

Melvin J. Yap, Department of Psychology, Washington University, St Louis, MO 63130, USA.

Plate A Presenters at the Sydney Workshop on Words, December 2003. Standing (L–R): Gary Libben, Anne Castles, David A. Balota, Christopher T. Kello, Alexander Pollatsek, Kathleen Rastle, Keith Rayner, Mark S. Seidenberg, Marcus Taft, Colin J. Davis, Karalyn Patterson, Chris Davis. Seated (L–R): Max Coltheart, Sally Andrews, Kenneth I. Forster.

Acknowledgements

The publishers and editor wish to thank the following for permission to reprint copyright materials in this book.

The American Psychological Association for:
Figure 7 from Coltheart, M., Rastle, K., Perry, C., Langdon, R., & Ziegler, J. C. (2001). DRC: A dual route cascaded model of visual word recognition and reading aloud. *Psychological Review, 108*, 204–256.
Appears in this book in Figure 3.1, and in modified form as Figure 1.2.
Figure 1 from Seidenberg, M. S., & McClelland, J. L. (1989). A distributed, developmental model of word recognition and naming. *Psychological Review, 96*, 523–568.
Appears in this book in Figure 3.1.
Figures 2 and 3 from Murray, W. S., & Forster, K. I. (2004). Serial mechanisms in lexical access: The rank hypothesis. *Psychological Review, 111*, 721–756.
Appear in this book as Figures 5.5 and 5.6 respectively.
Figure 10 from Balota, D. A., Cortese, M. J., Sergent-Marshall, S. D., Spieler, D. H., & Yap, M. J. (2004). Visual word recognition of single-syllable words. *Journal of Experimental Psychology: General, 133*, 283–316.
Appears in this book in Figure 10.4.

The Cognitive Science Society for:
Figure 2 from Kello, C. T., Sibley, D. E., & Plaut, D. C. (2005). Dissociations in performance on novel versus irregular items: Single-route demonstrations with input gain in localist and distributed models. *Cognitive Science, 29*, 627–654.
Appears in this book as Figure 3.3.
Figure 1 from Steyvers, M., & Tenenbaum, J. B. (2005). The large-scale structure of semantic networks: Statistical analyses and a model of semantic growth. *Cognitive Science, 29*, 41–78.
Appears in this book as Figure 10.2.

Elsevier for:
Figure 1 from Cortese, M. J., Balota, D. A., Sergent-Marshall, S. D., & Buckner, R. L. (2003). Sublexical, lexical, and semantic influences in spelling: Exploring the effects of age, Alzheimer's disease and primary semantic impairment. *Neuropsychologia*, *41*, 952–967.
Appears in this book as Figure 10.5.

Preface

Sally Andrews
University of Sydney, Australia

Reading is one of the most significant achievements of the human mind and among the most critical cognitive skills required in modern societies. Our ability to translate from inkmarks on a page to the rich, sophisticated meanings conveyed by texts demonstrates both the efficiency of human pattern-recognition skills and the power of our symbolic processing capabilities. The educated adult reader of English can identify over 50,000 words and can process and comprehend the meaning of texts at a rate of at least 300 words per minute. This incredible efficiency is achieved even though words are composed from a limited array of letters, and are therefore necessarily confusable with each other, and despite the essentially arbitrary relationships between the visual forms of words and their meanings. In spite of the complexity of the perceptual and cognitive operations required to achieve the task of reading, it occurs effortlessly and the reader usually has no awareness of the operations required to identify words, only of the final outcome—comprehension of the text.

Visual word recognition and reading have been a focus of psychological investigation since psychology's birth as a scientific discipline (Cattell, 1886). Huey (1908/1968) claimed that understanding the processes involved in skilled reading would be the "acme of psychologists' achievements" because it would provide insight into one of the most remarkable feats of the human mind. The vast amount of evidence collected about a variety of aspects of reading behaviour over the intervening century indicates that cognitive psychologists have responded to Huey's (1908/1968) challenge and successfully described many of the processes involved in reading. They have also used this evidence to make specific and influential recommendations about how to teach reading (e.g. Adams, 1990; Rayner, Foorman, Perfetti, Pesetsky, & Seidenberg, 2002). However, word recognition remains an area of intense investigation, suggesting that the accumulated evidence has not resolved its mystery. As a gross indication of the intensity of this interest, the keyword phrases "lexical access" and "word recognition" retrieve 3773 and 3808 documents respectively from the Psycinfo database for 1985–2004. This is fewer than the number of papers referring to the highly ubiquitous concepts of "short-term memory" (5302) and "working memory" (5603) but considerably more than the number dealing with the apparently more general domains of "semantic memory" (1327) and "episodic memory" (915).

There are a number of reasons why reading, particularly visual word recognition, has remained a central focus of research in experimental psychology. Most obviously, learning to recognize words is crucial to achieving literacy. Although questions remain about the precise relationship between the skills required to identify isolated words and those underlying reading comprehension (e.g. Adams, 1990; Jackson & Coltheart, 2001; Rayner et al., 2002), most theories of both reading and speech perception assume that "words are where the action is" (Cole & Jakimik, 1978) in the sense that identification of individual words, however it is achieved, provides the basis for comprehension. This consensus view is exemplified by Perfetti's (1991) "restricted interactive" model of reading comprehension, which assumes that, although semantic and syntactic information can, in principle, interact with the results of sensorily driven analysis to achieve word identification, skilled readers identify most words automatically on the basis of perceptual features without any influence from higher linguistic levels. Lexical retrieval is, therefore, "minimally constrained by semantic context" (Perfetti, 1991) and functionally, if not structurally, modularized from the processes involved in comprehension (Posner & Carr, 1992).

The assumption of functional modularity has important applied and methodological implications. Instructionally, it implies that methods of teaching reading should train automatic word identification skills (e.g. Adams, 1990; Perfetti, 1991; Rayner et al., 2002). Methodologically, assuming that lexical retrieval and comprehension processes operate independently both justifies investigations of the processes involved in identifying isolated words and validates the relevance of these processes to reading comprehension: if lexical retrieval operates in the same way for words in or out of context, it is better to investigate it in isolation than in the presence of contaminating effects of context; and if comprehension uses the products of lexical retrieval, then word recognition is a legitimate and essential focus of research directed toward understanding reading comprehension.

A second reason for the intensive interest in word recognition is that word identification tasks provide a vehicle for investigating a variety of other cognitive processes. A noteworthy recent demonstration is the widespread application of the Stroop (1935) paradigm to investigate the memory structures and processes underlying various psychopathological disorders (e.g. Mogg, Bradley, Dixon, Fisher, Twelftree, & McWilliams, 2000). The interpretation of such research is parasitic upon theories of lexical retrieval: differential Stroop interference for emotionally relevant words is of interest only because it is assumed to indicate preferential access to the concepts associated with these words. Such interpretations often acquire a life of their own and survive long past the theories that initially motivated them. For example, despite a variety of theoretical and empirical challenges to the claim that Stroop effects index automatic word identification (e.g. Kahneman & Treisman, 1983; MacLeod, 1991), this assumption is uncritically accepted in much of the cognitive psychopathological literature.

An increasingly wide array of the tasks used to investigate word identification are being co-opted for use in investigations of other psychological phenomena in domains such as social cognition (e.g. Bargh & Pietromonaco, 1982; Kay & Jost, 2003), cognitive ageing (e.g. Balota & Ferraro, 1996), and experimental psychopathology (e.g. Matthews & MacLeod, 2002). Word recognition tasks have also served as a major vehicle in recent neuroimaging investigations of cognitive processing (Fiez, Balota, Raichle, & Petersen, 1999; Posner & Carr, 1992) both because the well-specified theoretical accounts of lexical processing provide an effective basis for functional interpretation of neuroimaging data and because written words can be relatively easily presented under a variety of conditions.

A third reason for the intensity of research interest in word identification is the insight it provides into pattern recognition and memory retrieval more generally. Investigations of word recognition have played a central role in the development and evaluation of a range of issues that are fundamental to cognitive theorizing in general as well as being of specific relevance to understanding linguistic processing and reading. Written words are discrete stimuli with clearly definable attributes that can be relatively easily measured, and, in their printed form, words provide a very tractable stimulus domain in which variables such as legibility, frequency, and ambiguity can be easily controlled and manipulated. But as well as being tractable, words are complex. They have a wide range of attributes and a complex, but definable, similarity structure—and there are lots of them. Thus, visual word recognition provides an eminently suitable domain in which to develop computational models and a fertile "test-bed" for investigating the psychological validity of different frameworks for understanding symbolic processing more generally.

Indeed, visual word identification has been one of the major domains used to investigate the psychological validity of computational implementations of a variety of theoretical frameworks. McClelland and Rumelhart's (1981) seminal, large-scale computational implementation of a system embodying principles of parallel activation, the interactive activation (IA) model, used four-letter words as the stimulus domain. Seidenberg and McClelland's (1989) similarly pioneering application of parallel-distributed processing (PDP) learning and performance mechanisms in a large, naturalistic domain used English monosyllabic words as the target vocabulary. Capitalizing on the IA implementation and advances in computing power, Coltheart computationally implemented the highly influential dual-route model of word naming that he had been conceptually elaborating and evaluating since the 1970s (Coltheart, 1978; Coltheart, Curtis, Atkins, & Haller, 1993).

These three computational implementations and their subsequent extensions (e.g. Coltheart, Rastle, Perry, Langdon, & Ziegler, 2001; Grainger & Jacobs, 1996; Harm & Seidenberg, 1999; Kello & Plaut, 2003; Plaut, McClelland, Seidenberg, & Patterson, 1996) represent explicit instantiations of very different sets of conceptual principles about memory representation and retrieval that are relevant to a variety of domains apart from word recognition. In addition to its crucial importance in theories of language acquisition (e.g. Pinker, 1991), the distinction between "rules" and "associational networks" that constitutes a critical difference between dual-route and IA frameworks is relevant to theories of categorization and skill in a variety of task domains (e.g. Kruschke, 1992; Nosofsky, Palmeri, & McKinley, 1994). Similarly, the distinction between localist and distributed knowledge representations that critically differentiates IA and PDP frameworks has pervasive implications for almost every domain of cognitive psychology (e.g. Page, 2000; Smolensky, 1989). Comparisons of the various models of word recognition have therefore provided evidence that has been used to evaluate both the validity and the significance of the supposed "paradigm shift" provided by neural network or PDP models of cognitive processing more generally (Elman, Bates, Johnson, Karmiloff-Smith, Parisi, & Plunkett, 1996; Forster, 1994; Seidenberg, 1994).

The development of computational models has also forced specification of a range of issues about visual word recognition itself that remained unclear in conceptual presentations of the underlying theories. Implementing a theory in computational form requires the modeller to make decisions about issues that were not specified at all in the theory. The original models have been subject to a variety of modifications both on grounds of principle and to address limitations in the models' fit with empirical data. The more refined predictions generated by explicit computational models have also spawned a variety of new empirical questions that have stimulated research designed to provide the more fine-grained constraints necessary to discriminate between these more precisely specified models. The search for more constraining data has also led to the development of a variety of new empirical paradigms and methods of data analysis.

Current issues in lexical processing

The existence of fully specified computational implementations of a range of different conceptual frameworks creates a new theoretical landscape for the study of word recognition. On the face of it, the existence of explicit models should allow definitive resolution of theoretical debate: we should be able to find out which model is right by directly testing them against empirical data. In practice, a range of theoretical and empirical arguments remain. This is partly because of deep philosophical differences in what constitutes an adequate explanation of word recognition and reading. Some of these are elaborated in the early chapters of this volume. It is also because, despite the enormous increases in computational power available for large-scale modelling, it remains impossible to implement fully the massively parallel processing that is conceptually assumed by some current frameworks. Current models therefore remain relatively impoverished implementations of the theories they are designed to test.

Current research is also fuelled by changes in the nature of what we want to know. With the increasing specificity of theories and models, we have "upped the ante" on what constitutes a complete understanding of reading. Many current controversies are not so much about what readers do as about why they behave in this way. The body of data to be explained is also increasing as researchers develop new methodologies to address the more refined questions generated by the models.

The chronometric methods of cognitive psychology have provided a rich body of evidence about the factors influencing visual word identification, a database that now serves as the principal benchmark for evaluating the relative validity of current conceptual and computational models. As many of the chapters in this collection demonstrate, in the hands of linguistically and experimentally sophisticated researchers, such methods continue to provide a rich source of evidence that is being very effectively used to constrain and refine theoretical models. They are, however, limited in a variety of ways that have led to the search for alternative methodologies and empirical approaches that better capture the functional context of on-line reading.

The present collection of papers has been assembled in the context of this new theoretical and empirical environment. The chapter authors have all made significant contributions to the existing theoretical and/or empirical literature on visual word recognition and contributed to shaping the focus of current research. The group met in Sydney, Australia, in December 2003, to participate in the Sydney Workshop on Words with the goals of assessing the current state of knowledge about lexical processing and word recognition, identifying current controversies, and determining a research agenda and set of strategies appropriate to the new theoretical context. The chapters are modified versions of presentations made at the workshop that have been shaped and refined by the extended and robust discussion that occurred during and following the workshop.

To reflect the broad themes, contributors were asked to draw upon their own research on lexical processing to address the broad questions:

- What do we know?
- What do we need to know?
- How can we find out?

The chapters fall into two broad groups that adopt two different approaches to the current theoretical context. The approach reflected in the first set of chapters focuses on the theoretical models themselves by explicitly developing and evaluating well-specified conceptual frameworks, usually implemented in computational form. The other approach, represented in the second set of chapters, responds to the challenge provided by increasingly precise theories by developing a richer empirical database that can be used to discriminate between the increasingly refined predictions of current models.

Theories of lexical processing: Computational models and mechanisms

The chapters in this section provide a variety of perspectives on current theoretical models and their computational implementation. In the chapters by *Rastle and Coltheart* and *Seidenberg and Plaut*, the proponents of the two most influential computational models of the last 20 years, the dual-route cascaded (DRC) and PDP frameworks, each presents the principles and rationale of their own approach to computational modelling and the role it plays in theory development and validation. Both also summarize their views about the strengths and weaknesses of the alternative approach. Together, the chapters provide insight into a range of epistemological issues that are the source of current controversy.

Drawing on both DRC and PDP models, *Kello* describes his recent progress toward a new computational model, the junction model, which implements a novel "single-route" architecture in which orthography is mapped onto representations mediating between phonology and semantics. The model is grounded in PDP principles, but shares the DRC model's assumption of localist lexical representations. Evidence taken to support the independent lexical and sublexical pathways of the DRC framework is attributed to variations in "input gain" that give rise to distinct lexical and sublexical processing modes. Kello also demonstrates an approach to tackling the processing of multisyllabic words, a crucial step for the next generation of computational models. Although still in its early stages, the junction model provides a glimpse of the sort of developments that will occur in computational models of word recognition in the hands of the new generation of cross-disciplinarily trained cognitive scientists.

Taft also describes a new model, the localist-cum-distributed (LCD) framework, which follows the general architectural and processing assumptions of the IA model but provides a more precise specification of the nature and organization of orthographic, phonological, and semantic knowledge. Unlike the authors of the earlier chapters, Taft is not convinced that computational implementation of the model is necessary, or even desirable, because it requires decisions that are not part of his theory. He argues that a concrete conceptual description of the form he provides allows generation of new hypotheses. The chapter reviews a substantial body of evidence that he has collected to evaluate and refine the LCD framework.

Rather than presenting a complete model, *Forster* discusses the general principle of parallel activation that is critical to virtually all current computational frameworks. Despite the ubiquity of the notion of parallel activation,

Forster argues that there are a number of empirical phenomena that present major challenges for theoretical frameworks that rely on this mechanism. In the final section of the chapter, he sketches a new model that he is in the process of implementing, which combines parallel activation with the serial processing assumptions of his "search model" (Forster, 1976). He argues that such hybrid approaches may ultimately prove necessary to accommodate current evidence about lexical processing.

The final chapter in this section reports on a computationally implemented model, but one with a very different approach and focus than those reported in the first three chapters. *Rayner, Reichle, and Pollatsek* describe E-Z Reader, a mathematical model that predicts patterns of eye movements during sentence and text reading. Following a review of evidence demonstrating fine-grained features of eye movement control, the chapter describes the development and evaluation of E-Z Reader (Reichle, Pollatsek, Fisher, & Rayner, 1998; Reichle, Rayner, & Pollatsek, 2003), which assumes that lexical retrieval processes play a critical role in the coordination of eye movements during reading. The complexity of these processes and their reliance on simultaneous processing of a variety of sources of information presents challenges to models of word recognition that are capable of processing only a single word at a time.

Models, methods and measures: Converging approaches for investigating word lexical processing

The second section of this collection comprises chapters that discuss and report on empirical procedures directed toward evaluating current theoretical issues. The chapters describe a wide variety of methodological approaches to investigating word recognition. Many contributors report convergent evidence from different approaches to shed light on the distinctions between different theoretical frameworks.

The chapters draw on data obtained from a variety of paradigms and populations to address three broad themes. The first two are concerned with the acquisition and representation of orthographic knowledge (*Castles & Nation; C. J. Davis*). The next three consider the broader cognitive architecture of the lexical system and the relationships between lexical processing and the attentional and cognitive demands of different word recognition tasks (*Davis & Kim; Balota & Yap; Libben*). The final set of chapters goes beyond single word processing to consider morphological processing, discourse processing, and sentence reading (*Pollatsek & Hyönä; Patterson & MacDonald; Andrews*).

Castles and Nation focus on the development of orthographic knowledge. They review the available developmental evidence for clues as to exactly how children make the transition to the fluent orthographic processing that characterizes skilled reading. They conclude that the processes involved in orthographic learning are inadequately specified in most current models of word recognition, and identify a number of foci for further research. *C. J. Davis* focuses on orthographic processing in skilled readers and reviews theory and evidence about how skilled readers code the identity and order of letters in a word. He concludes that the letter-coding schemes incorporated in most computational models of visual word recognition are incompatible with the empirical evidence and describes the spatial coding scheme employed in his self-organising lexical acquisition and recognition (SOLAR) model, which accurately simulates the human data.

Davis and Kim focus on the long-standing problems associated with isolating the processes involved in performing word-identification tasks, arguing that any attempt to identify isolable, "elementary" processes needs to consider the complexities of how these processes are modulated by task context and general cognitive mechanisms, such as attention. They use a variety of clever modifications of the masked priming paradigm, along with comparisons of different orthographies, to investigate the interaction between perceptual and cognitive processes in word-recognition tasks. They conclude in favour of a stable perceptual component of lexical processing that, when appropriately assessed, is remarkably invulnerable to higher-level task demands. *Balota and Yap* are also concerned with the interactions between lexical and cognitive processes. They first summarize the results of their recent database approach to exploring the relative contributions of the highly correlated measures of orthographic, phonological, and semantic attributes to performance in lexical decision task (LDT) and naming tasks. This is complemented by investigation of how word-recognition performance changes with both normal and pathological effects of ageing and the application of neuroimaging methods to determining the neural and cognitive mechanisms underlying these changes. This wide variety of methodological approaches is used to flesh out their proposal of a flexible lexical processor that interacts with the attentional mechanisms to tailor processing to the specific demands of the task context.

The next two chapters move beyond the monosyllabic words that dominate the research reported in earlier chapters to consider how multisyllabic words are processed. *Libben* focuses on morphological processing of complex words. On the basis of a combination of linguistic and cross-linguistic analyses, he reports empirical investigations of people's explicit and implicit sensitivity to morphological ambiguities both in and out of sentence context. Paralleling the conclusions about flexibility drawn by Balota and Yap and Davis and Kim, Libben concludes in favour of a "hungry lexicon" that activates all potential morphological parsings and allows readers to "select" those that are most functionally relevant. *Pollatsek and Hyönä* report comparisons of the effects of morphological structure on English and Finnish, using eye-movement methodologies. As well as investigating the processing of multisyllabic words, this method provides more refined insight into the time course of processing various word attributes than is possible from the single-word studies discussed in earlier chapters.

Patterson and MacDonald also move away from the investigation of single words to explore discourse processing in brain-injured patients. They systematically analyse the discourse produced by patients with semantic dementia in a complex, but structured, picture description task in order to evaluate the relative independence of lexical, phonological and syntactic processing.

In the final chapter, I (*Andrews*) attempt to reconcile some of the controversies that emerge from the theoretical and empirical issues discussed in the previous chapters by arguing for a "lexicalist" perspective that focuses on the functions of lexical processing rather than on fine-grained issues about lexical structure. I argue that debate about the grain size of lexical representations should not obscure consideration of how lexical information is used to achieve readers' goals: comprehension and action. The initial outcomes of a research programme using repetition blindness in sentence contexts are summarized to exemplify a method of investigating how lexical retrieval contributes to reading comprehension.

In combination, the chapters in this volume provide a state-of-the-art summary of current theories and methods of investigating lexical processing as seen by some of the most influential researchers in the field. They provide insight into the questions and issues that are currently exciting debate among "werd nerds", as lexical processing researchers are sometimes called. The workshop that provided the basis for this book was filled with robust discussion that has continued through the process of collecting these papers. The workshop has also resulted in new research projects, both among the original participants and in collaboration with others. I thank the workshop participants for their active engagement in the event and its aftermath, and the Faculty of Science, University of Sydney, which funded it. I am also sincerely grateful to Anna Woollams, Rachel Bond, Martin Daly, and Suzanne Borgwaldt for all of their contributions to the workshop and the evolution of this book.

Sally Andrews
December 2005

References

Adams, M. (1990). *Beginning to read: Thinking and learning about print*. Cambridge, MA: MIT Press.

Balota, D. A., & Ferraro, F. R. (1996). Lexical, sublexical, and implicit memory processes in healthy young, healthy older adults, and in individuals with dementia of the Alzheimer's type. *Neuropsychology*, *10*, 82–95.

Bargh, J. A., & Pietromonaco, P. (1982). Automatic information processing and social perception: The influence of trait information presented outside of conscious awareness on impression formation. *Journal of Personality and Social Psychology*, *43*, 437–449.

Cattell, M. (1886). The time it takes to see and name objects. *Mind*, *2*, 63–85.

Cole, R. A., & Jakimik, J. (1978). Understanding speech: How words are heard. In G. Underwood (Ed.), *Strategies of information processing*. Hillsdale, NJ: Lawrence Erlbaum Associates, Inc.

Coltheart, M. (1978). Lexical access in simple reading tasks. In G. Underwood (Ed.), *Strategies of information processing*. New York: Academic Press.

Coltheart, M., Curtis, B., Atkins, P., & Haller, H. (1993). Models of reading aloud: Dual-route and parallel-distributed-processing approaches. *Psychological Review, 100*, 589–608.

Coltheart, M., Rastle, K., Perry, C., Langdon, R., & Ziegler, J. (2001). DRC: A dual route cascaded model of visual word recognition and reading aloud. *Psychological Review, 108*, 204–256.

Davis, C., & Forster, K. I. (1994). Masked orthographic priming: The effect of prime-target legibility. *Quarterly Journal of Experimental Psychology, 47A*, 673–697.

Elman, J. L., Bates, E. A., Johnson, M. H., Karmiloff-Smith, A., Parisi, D., & Plunkett, K. (1996). *Rethinking innateness*. Cambridge, MA: MIT Press.

Fiez, J. A., Balota, D. A., Raichle, M. E., & Petersen, S. E. (1999). Effects of lexicality, frequency, and spelling-to-sound consistency on the functional anatomy of reading. *Neuron, 24*, 205–218.

Forster, K. (1994). Computational modeling and elementary process analysis in visual word recognition. *Journal of Experimental Psychology: Human Perception and Performance, 20*, 1292–1310.

Forster, K. I., & Davis, C. (1984). Repetition priming and frequency attenuation in lexical access. *Journal of Experimental Psychology: Learning, Memory, and Cognition, 10*, 680–698.

Grainger, J., & Jacobs, A. M. (1996). Orthographic processing in visual word recognition: A multiple read-out model. *Psychological Review, 103*, 518–565.

Harm, M. W., & Seidenberg, M. S. (1999). Phonology, reading acquisition and dyslexia: Insights from connectionist models. *Psychological Review, 106*, 491–528.

Huey, E. B. (1968). *The psychology and pedagogy of reading*. Cambridge, MA: MIT Press. (Original work published in 1908)

Jackson, N., & Coltheart, M. (2001). *Routes to reading success and failure*. Hove, UK: Psychology Press.

Kahneman, D., & Treisman, A. (1983). Changing views of attention and automaticity. In R. Parasuraman & R. Davies (Eds.), *Varieties of attention*. New York: Academic Press.

Kay, A. C., & Jost, J. C. (2003). Complementary justice: Effects of "poor but happy" and "poor but honest" stereotype exemplars on system justification and implicit activation of the justice motive. *Journal of Personality and Social Psychology, 85*, 823–837.

Kello, C. T., & Plaut, D. C. (2003). Strategic control over rate of processing in word reading: A computational investigation. *Journal of Memory and Language, 48*, 207–232.

Kruschke, J. K. (1992). The ALCOVE model: an exemplar-based connectionist model of category learning. *Psychological Review, 99*, 22–44.

MacLeod, C. M. (1991). Half a century of research on the Stroop effect: An integrative review. *Psychological Bulletin, 109*, 163–203.

Matthews, A., & MacLeod, C. (2002). Induced processing biases have causal effects on anxiety. *Cognition and Emotion, 16*, 331–354.

McClelland, J. L., & Rumelhart, D. E. (1981). An interactive activation model of context effects in letter perception. I. An account of basic findings. *Psychological Review*, *88*, 375–407.

Mogg, K., Bradley, B. P., Dixon, C., Fisher, S., Twelftree, H., & McWilliams, A. (2000). Trait anxiety, defensiveness and selective processing of threat: An investigation using two measures of attentional bias. *Personality and Individual Differences*, *28*, 1063–1077.

Nosofsky, R. M., Palmeri, T. J., & McKinley, S. C. (1994). Rule-plus-exception model of classification learning. *Psychological Review*, *101*, 53–79.

Page, M. P. (2000). Connectionist modeling in psychology: A localist manifesto. *Behavioral and Brain Sciences*, *23*, 443–512.

Perfetti, C. A. (1991). Representations and awareness in the acquisition of reading competence. In L. Rieben & C. A. Perfetti (Eds.), *Learning to read: Basic research and its implications* (pp. 33–44). Hillsdale, NJ: Lawrence Erlbaum Associates, Inc.

Pinker, S. (1991). Rules of language. *Science*, *253*, 530–535.

Plaut, D. C., McClelland, J. L., Seidenberg, M. S., & Patterson, K. (1996). Understanding normal and impaired word reading: Computational principles in quasi-regular domains. *Psychological Review*, *103*, 56–115.

Posner, M. I., & Carr, T. H. (1992). Lexical access and the brain: Anatomical restraints on cognitive models of word recognition. *American Journal of Psychology*, *105*, 1–26.

Rayner, K., Foorman, B. R., Perfetti, C. A., Pesetsky, D., & Seidenberg, M. S. (2002). How should reading be taught? *Scientific American*, *286*, 84–91.

Reichle, E. D., Pollatsek, A., Fisher, D. L., & Rayner, K. (1998). Toward a model of eye movement control in reading. *Psychological Review*, *105*, 125–157.

Reichle, E. D., Rayner, K., & Pollatsek, A. (2003). The E-Z Reader model of eye-movement control in reading: Comparisons to other models. *Behavioral and Brain Sciences*, *26*, 445–526.

Seidenberg, M. S. (1994). Language and connectionism: the developing interface. *Cognition*, *50*, 385–401.

Seidenberg, M. S., & McClelland, J. L. (1989). A distributed, developmental model of word recognition and naming. *Psychological Review*, *96*, 523–568.

Smolensky, P. (1989). On the proper treatment of connectionism. *Behavioral and Brain Sciences*, *11*, 1–74.

Stroop, J. R. (1935). Studies of interference in serial verbal reactions. *Journal of Experimental Psychology*, *18*, 643–662.

Taft, M. (1991). *Reading and the mental lexicon*. Hillsdale, NJ: Lawrence Erlbaum Associates, Inc.

Part I

Theories of lexical retrieval: Computational models and mechanisms

1 Is there serial processing in the reading system; and are there local representations?

Kathleen Rastle
Royal Holloway, University of London, UK
Max Coltheart
Macquarie University, Australia

There is wide agreement that the goal of any cognitive theory of lexical processing must be to describe the mental architectures and processing components that enable the transformation and retransformation of information across three broad domains of knowledge: orthography, phonology, and semantics. There is also a degree of consensus that processing within and between these broad domains of knowledge can be understood in terms of a triangle with connections between each domain,[1] as indicated in Figure 1.1. This triangle framework is a venerable one, dating back at least to Baron (1977; see Coltheart, 2005).

This diagram does not, of course, present a satisfactory theory of lexical processing, because it makes only the barest of commitments—for example, that both semantic and orthographic knowledge can be accessed directly from phonology. Rather, the diagram provides a framework from which we can work to formulate more precise characterizations of each transformation. For example, what exactly are the mental architectures and processing components that enable the transformation of phonology to semantics (i.e. spoken word comprehension), or the transformation of semantics to phonology (i.e. spoken word production)? It is in formulating these more

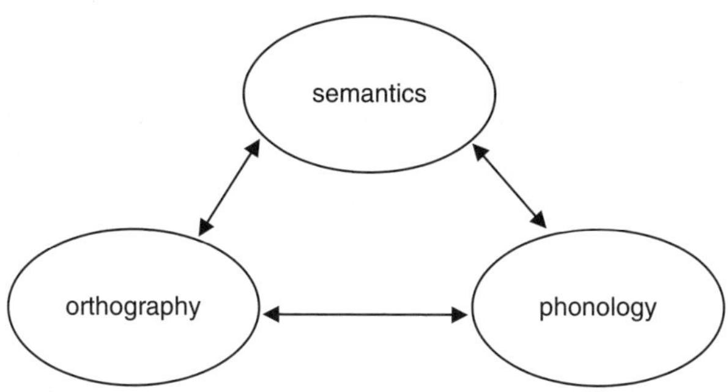

Figure 1.1 The "triangle framework" of lexical processing.

specific characterizations of lexical processing that theoretical commitments are made and hence theoretical disagreements are generated. In this chapter, we consider just one of the computational transformations that occurs within the triangle framework—the derivation of phonology from orthography (i.e. reading aloud).

Two perspectives on print-to-sound translation

Our discussion begins with an idea originating some 30 years ago (e.g. Baron, 1977; Coltheart, 1978; Forster & Chambers, 1973; Marshall & Newcombe, 1973)—the idea that skilled reading aloud involves two procedures, a lexical dictionary look-up procedure required for the correct reading aloud of exception words (e.g. *pint*), and a nonlexical rule-based procedure required for the correct reading aloud of nonwords (e.g. *vib*). This dual-route theory was supported by numerous lines of behavioural and neuropsychological evidence, and proved highly influential for much of the 1970s and 1980s. However, empirical data that seemed difficult to reconcile with early dual-route theories plus a growing dissatisfaction with the lack of specificity in these theories (see Humphreys & Evett, 1985) saw a turn away from them and a turn toward the alternative perspective being offered by Seidenberg and McClelland (1989; hereafter SM89). These authors had developed a computational model of reading aloud, based on parallel-distributed-processing (PDP) principles, which differed radically from the dual-route theory that had dominated the past decade: This model was argued to simulate the reading aloud of exception words and nonwords in a single procedure without reference to rules or to a lexicon of known words. Although SM89 was later shown to provide an inadequate account of nonword reading (Besner, Twilley, McCann, & Seergobin, 1990), it provided the foundation for a range of PDP models of reading aloud (Plaut, McClelland, Seidenberg, & Patterson,1996; Harm & Seidenberg, 2004) influential in modern theoretical debate. The years following SM89 also saw the rise of the dual-route cascaded (DRC) model, a computational instantiation of the dual-route theory of reading (Coltheart et al., 1993, 2001; Coltheart & Rastle, 1994; Rastle & Coltheart, 1999) that has provided a counterpoint to the PDP models on a range of theoretical issues. The DRC model is represented in Figure 1.2.

Modern theoretical debate in the area of reading aloud has considered two fundamental differences between the DRC model and the PDP models. The first difference has to do with the nature of *processing* in the orthography-phonology transformation: is it entirely parallel, or are there forms of processing which operate serially? The second theoretical distinction has to do with the nature of *representation* in the reading aloud system: are representations distributed or local? PDP and DRC modellers not only offer different answers to these questions but also propose fundamentally different methods for reaching these answers. PDP modellers argue that the orthography-phonology transformation is accomplished solely through parallel processing, and that

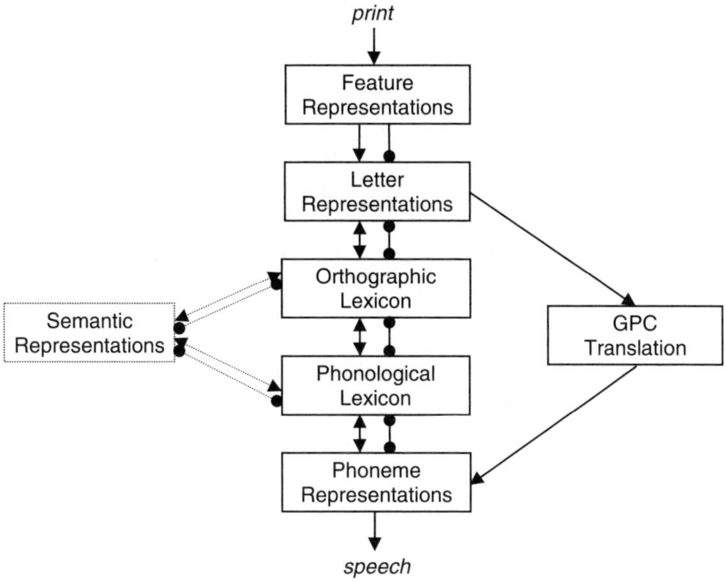

Figure 1.2 The dual-route cascaded model of visual word recognition and reading aloud (reprinted with permission from Coltheart et al., 2001). Dashed lines indicate components of the model that have not yet been implemented.

the representations in the reading aloud system are distributed. In contrast, DRC modellers argue that the orthography-phonology transformation is characterized by both parallel and serial processing (while the lexical procedure of the DRC model operates fully in parallel, the nonlexical procedure operates serially, letter-by-letter, from left-to-right across the stimulus), and that the representations in the reading system are local. Further, while these theoretical commitments were derived by DRC modellers by inference from evidence, they were derived by the PDP modellers through faith, that is, via a set of a priori "principles" that govern the development of all PDP models of cognition and stipulate that all processing must be parallel and that all representations must be distributed. In short, PDP modellers make a priori *assumptions* about the nature of representation and processing in the reading system; DRC modellers *infer* representational and processing characteristics of the reading system through the analysis of behavioural data.

In this chapter, we address both of the areas of theoretical debate (that is, the nature of processing and the nature of representation) outlined above. With respect to the processing issue, we review a set of phenomena that suggests strongly that the orthography-to-phonology transformation is accomplished in part by a process that operates in a serial, letter-by-letter manner. With regard to the representation issue, we review facts about the lexical decision task that are very difficult to reconcile with the view that all representations within the reading aloud system are distributed, and we also point out ways in which some defects of PDP models have been specifically attributed to a wholesale commitment to distributed representation. We further demonstrate that the DRC model provides a natural account of all of the phenomena that we discuss—a fact that should come as no surprise given the evidence-based manner in which this model was developed.[2] In contrast to the DRC model, we argue that the PDP models offer no coherent account of these phenomena. Indeed, it seems to us that these phenomena pose serious and possibly even insurmountable challenges to PDP models of reading, as long as these models maintain their a priori commitments to parallel processing and distributed representation.

Serial nonlexical phonological assembly

Eight well-established phenomena point to the existence of a nonlexical phonological assembly procedure that operates in a serial, left-to-right, manner: the position of irregularity effect (Coltheart & Rastle, 1994; Cortese, 1998; Rastle & Coltheart, 1999; Roberts, Rastle, Coltheart, & Besner, 2003); the position of bivalence effect (Havelka & Rastle, 2005); the position-sensitive Stroop effect (Bibi, Tzelgov, & Henik, 2000; Coltheart, Woollams, Kinoshita, & Perry, 1999); the length by lexicality effect (Weekes, 1997); the length by language effect (Perry & Ziegler, 2002; Ziegler, Perry, Jacobs, & Braun, 2001); the exaggerated length effect in surface dyslexia (Gold et al., 2005); the whammy effect (Joubert & Lecours, 1998; Rastle & Coltheart, 1998); and the onset effect observed in masked form priming (Forster & Davis, 1991; Kinoshita, 2003). The DRC model, with its left-to-right phonological assembly procedure, provides a clear account of each of these phenomena. The PDP models, by contrast, offer no account of this body of evidence.

The position of irregularity effect

In their early development of the DRC model, Coltheart and Rastle (1994) asked whether nonlexical phonological assembly operates in parallel or serially, from left-to-right across the letter string. They developed a prediction based on the well-known spelling-sound irregularity disadvantage on reading aloud performance, an effect attributed to competing outputs of lexical and nonlexical procedures (e.g. Forster & Chambers, 1973; Paap & Noel, 1991). Coltheart and Rastle (1994) reasoned that a dual-route model in which nonlexical phonological assembly operates in parallel predicts no effects of the position in an irregular word at which the irregularity occurs, because all letters are translated to phonemes at the same time. Conversely, a dual-route model in which nonlexical phonological assembly operates serially predicts that the effect of irregularity should be modulated by the position of the irregularity in the word: Early spelling-sound irregularities (e.g. *ch*ef) should be more detrimental to reading aloud performance than late spelling-sound irregularities (e.g. gl*ow*). Coltheart and Rastle (1994) found solid evidence for the serial version of nonlexical phonological assembly. Relative to regular control words, the cost of spelling-sound irregularity decreased monotonically and linearly over the position in the word at which the irregularity occurred. They argued from this evidence that the transformation of orthography to phonology is accomplished, in part, by a serially operating phonological assembly procedure.

Coltheart and Rastle's (1994) position of irregularity effect has now been replicated several times with monosyllabic stimuli controlled on a range of variables (Cortese, 1998; Rastle & Coltheart, 1999; Roberts et al., 2003). Such replication has been valuable because it has enabled actual simulations of the effect with the available models of reading aloud—all of which are currently restricted to monosyllabic stimuli. These simulations have consistently demonstrated that the DRC model—as a consequence of its serial phonological assembly procedure—provides a clear account of the position of irregularity effect. In contrast, simulations with the available parallel models have usually revealed a failure to account for the position of irregularity effect (see Coltheart et al., 2001). Zorzi (2000), however, was able to simulate the position of irregularity effect reported by Rastle and Coltheart (1999) with a fully parallel model (Zorzi et al., 1998), thus calling into question a serial interpretation of the effect. Zorzi (2000) was able to simulate this effect because of an inadvertent confound in Rastle and Coltheart's (1999) materials between grapheme-phoneme consistency and position of irregularity, as words consisting of early irregularities are more inconsistent than words consisting of later irregularities.[3] To illustrate, though both CHEF and GLOW are irregular, the CH→/S/ correspondence in CHEF occurs far more infrequently ("chaise" being the only other exemplar) than does the OW→/O/ correspondence in GLOW (which also occurs, for example, in "blow", "flow", and "slow").

The issue of consistency and position of irregularity appears to have been put to rest (at least temporarily) by Roberts et al. (2003), who reported a position of irregularity effect on reading aloud, using a set of stimuli tightly controlled on grapheme-phoneme consistency. Roberts et al. (2003) reported that of the models currently available, only the DRC model could simulate their human data. Neither the data reported in this final study nor its conclusions—that the translation from orthography to phonology is accomplished, in part, by a serially operating phonologically assembly system—have been challenged. Furthermore, Havelka and Rastle (2005) have recently reported a position of bivalence effect on Serbian reading (described below), which is analogous to the position of irregularity effect and which precludes an explanation in terms of consistency.

The position of bivalence effect

The Serbian language is written in two alphabets, Roman and Cyrillic, each of which is perfectly feed-forward (i.e. spelling-to-sound) and feedback (i.e. sound-to-spelling) consistent. Each alphabet comprises three types of letters: (1) unique letters (n=19) occur in only one alphabet, thus providing two graphemic interpretations (one in each alphabet) of a single phoneme; (2) common letters (n=7) are shared by each alphabet and map onto the same phoneme in both alphabets; and (3) ambiguous letters (n=4) are shared by each alphabet but map onto different phonemes in each alphabet. These letter types are used in the formation of two types of words: (1) unique words comprising common and unique letters, which can be read only in one alphabet; and (2) bivalent words comprising common and ambiguous letters, which have two possible pronunciations depending on the alphabet in which the letter string is interpreted. Bivalent words are typically meaningful only in one alphabet, and are pronounceable nonwords (with a different pronunciation of the ambiguous letters) in the other alphabet. These bivalent words are read aloud more slowly and less accurately than matched unique words (Lukatela, Lukatela, Carello, & Turvey, 1999). This result is analogous to the regularity effect on reading aloud: It arises on a dual-route theory because the nonlexical route yields two pronunciations for bivalent words, one of which competes with the correct lexical pronunciation.

Havelka and Rastle (2005) reasoned that a Serbian dual-route model in which nonlexical phonological assembly operates in parallel predicts no effects of the position in a bivalent word at which the ambiguous letter occurs—for the reason that all letters are translated to phonemes at the same time. Conversely, a Serbian dual-route model in which nonlexical phonological assembly operates serially predicts that the effect of bivalence should be modulated by the position of the ambiguous letter in the word: Words with early ambiguities should be read aloud more slowly and less accurately relative to matched unique controls than words with late ambiguities. Havelka and Rastle (2005) observed exactly this result when they compared bivalent words with initial and final or penultimate ambiguities to matched unique controls. The cost of initial ambiguity was 117 ms while the cost of final/penultimate ambiguity was 37 ms.

This manipulation directly addresses the concerns regarding consistency that have arisen with regard to the position of irregularity effect. Serbian bivalent words are inconsistent because they map to more than one pronunciation. However, the four ambiguous letters that create these words are equally inconsistent, since each of them has only a single pronunciation in Roman and a single pronunciation in Cyrillic. Furthermore, analysis of the *Frequency Dictionary of Serbian Language* (Kostić, 1999) reveals that there is no difference in the frequency with which ambiguous letters occur in initial and final/penultimate positions of Serbian words (Jelena Havelka, personal communication, 2004). Thus, there is no sense in which words with initial ambiguities could be more inconsistent than words with final or penultimate ambiguities. Havelka and Rastle (2005) asserted that these data constitute strong evidence for a serially operating phonological assembly procedure in reading aloud. While the DRC model offers a natural explanation for this phenomenon, the set of models that operate solely in parallel offer no account of this phenomenon.

The whammy effect

A dual-route model in which nonlexical phonological assembly operates in a serial, left-to-right manner makes an interesting prediction with regard to the reading aloud of nonwords with multiletter graphemes, such as the graphemes *oo* and *ph* in the nonword *fooph* (Rastle & Coltheart, 1998). If letters are converted to phonemes one at a time in the nonlexical route, then nonwords with multiletter graphemes (e.g. *fooph*) should be read aloud more slowly than nonwords in which every grapheme is a single letter (e.g. *frelp*). This prediction is easily understood by considering the manner in which a serially operating nonlexical route generates a pronunciation for the stimulus *fooph*. After translation of the letter F to /f/, the nonlexical route translates the letter O to /O/, yielding /fO/. While activation for this second phoneme is rising, the nonlexical route gets to the next letter O and discovers that it is actually part of the multiletter grapheme OO. The nonlexical route revises the second phoneme of the stimulus to /u/, yielding /fu/. However, by this time, activation for the incorrect /O/ phoneme has been allowed to rise, and therefore competes with the activation of the correct /u/ phoneme. The same problem occurs as the nonlexical route translates the letters PH. Rastle and Coltheart (1998) used the word "whammy" to describe the competition resulting from the letter-by-letter translation of a complex grapheme. Rastle and Coltheart (1998) observed that human reading aloud latencies were longer for nonwords that contained multiletter graphemes (e.g. *fooph*) than for nonwords that did not (e.g. *frelp*)—an effect that was mirrored perfectly by the DRC model with its serially operating phonological assembly procedure. This effect has also been observed in French readers (Joubert & Lecours, 1998).

In contrast, none of the available parallel models produce a convincing simulation of the whammy effect (Coltheart et al., 2001). The nature of this effect—whether it genuinely implicates serial phonological assembly—has been called into question on two fronts, however. First, the attractor network of Plaut et al. (1996) yielded a near-successful simulation of the whammy effect (p=.058). If the PDP model does in fact yield a whammy effect, once again differences in consistency between the two sets of nonwords provide a potential explanation for this marginal success. While complex graphemes can map reliably onto particular phonemes (e.g. PH→/f/), their individual constituents map onto different phonemes when presented out of context (e.g. P→/p/, H→/h/). Further analysis of this network is needed to determine definitively whether it can simulate the whammy effect, and, if it can, what is it about the model that is responsible for the effect. Second, a disadvantage in recognizing words and nonwords with complex graphemes is also revealed in tasks that do not require phonological assembly—namely, perceptual identification using the luminance increasing procedure (Rey & Schiller, 2005;

Rey, Ziegler, & Jacobs, 2000). Although this demonstration does not rule out the possibility that the source of the whammy effect is serial phonological assembly (or, indeed, that these are two separate effects), further research is needed to demonstrate that the DRC model produces the whammy effect in reading aloud for the same reason that it is revealed in human readers.

The length by lexicality effect

A dual-route model in which nonlexical phonological assembly operates in a serial, letter-by-letter manner makes a clear prediction: There should be an effect of length (i.e. number of letters) on reading aloud that is particularly apparent for nonwords (Weekes, 1997). Weekes (1997) examined this prediction using a multiple regression approach, which afforded a means to control the natural confound that exists between length and neighbourhood size. He found an interaction between length and lexicality: Reading aloud latency increased as the number of letters in the stimulus increased, but only for nonwords. Weekes (1997) interpreted these findings as strong evidence for a dual-route model in which nonlexical phonological assembly operates in a serial, left-to-right manner. Simulations have revealed that the DRC model provides a sufficient account of the length by lexicality effect. Further, the model explains a massive 40% of the variance in Weekes' (1997) nonword reading aloud latencies.

In contrast, none of the available parallel models produce a convincing simulation of Weekes' (1997) length by lexicality interaction (Coltheart et al., 2001). Some authors (Zorzi, 2000; see also Perry & Ziegler, 2002) have, however, argued that the length by lexicality effect may actually constitute a form of the consistency by frequency interaction—and therefore may not reflect serial phonological assembly at all. This argument is based on two premises: (a) longer letter strings are typically more inconsistent than shorter letter strings (because they contain multiletter vowels such as "ough"); and (b) inconsistencies in low-frequency words (of which nonwords are an extreme case) are particularly detrimental to performance. In general, then, longer stimuli should be more difficult to read aloud than shorter stimuli, particularly when they do not correspond to well-known words. While we cannot exclude this possibility, we would wonder why a network such as that developed by Plaut et al. (1996) can produce the consistency by frequency interaction but not the length by lexicality interaction (see Coltheart et al., 2001). Fortunately, a more direct refutation of this possibility is now available in research on the length by language effect (Perry & Ziegler, 2002; Ziegler et al., 2001) described below.

The length by language effect

Ziegler et al. (2001; see also Perry & Ziegler, 2002) conducted an experiment that compared the size of the length effect across English and German.

Stimulus materials comprised words and nonwords that were cognates in the two languages (e.g. English: *tea*, *loud*, *storm*; German: *tee*, *laut*, *sturm*). One nice thing about using cognates is that they preclude an interpretation of a length by language interaction in terms of early visual processing or articulatory processing—arguments that PDP modellers have often pursued with regard to serial effects (e.g. Kawamoto, Kello, Jones, & Bame, 1998; Plaut, 1999; see Havelka & Rastle, 2005, for a discussion). Ziegler et al. (2001) reasoned that if the length effect arises because of increasing inconsistency with greater length, then German should show a *smaller* length effect than English because German is more spelling-sound consistent than English. This prediction was verified by Perry and Ziegler (2002), who implemented English and German parallel models of reading aloud based on the connectionist dual-process model of Zorzi et al. (1998). Simulations revealed, as expected, that the German model showed a smaller length effect (across words and nonwords combined) than the English model. The human data revealed the opposite effect, however, the size of the German length effect being greater than the size of the English length effect. These data would appear to refute an explanation of the length effect in terms of increasing inconsistency with increasing length.

Perry and Ziegler (2002) also tested English and German DRC models on their stimuli, and found, somewhat surprisingly, that (as in the human data) the German model showed a larger length effect than the English model. Why are the DRC models able to simulate the larger length effect for German than English? Perry and Ziegler (2002) traced this effect to an interaction between DRC's serial phonological assembly procedure and its application of German context-sensitive rules called "super rules", which account for a great deal of German spelling-sound regularity. Consider the English and German nonword GACK. The English DRC phonological assembly procedure translates this stimulus to phonology letter by letter and encounters no whammies. The German DRC phonological assembly procedure also translates this stimulus letter by letter, but encounters an extensive whammy because of a context-sensitive rule that "vowels are long unless followed by two or more consonants". Thus, an incorrect vowel sound is allowed to rise in the German translation of GACK until the entire stimulus has been translated—a powerful whammy indeed. The effect of this whammy increases with increasing length (for example, with three-letter words, it occurs only in vowel–consonant–consonant (VCC) stimuli; with four-letter words, it occurs in CVCC and VCCC stimuli; Perry & Ziegler, 2002), and that is why the DRC model produces a greater length effect for German than for English. We have no guarantee, of course, that the DRC model produces the length by language effect for the same reason that human readers show this effect. However, we can guarantee that the parallel models provide no account of this effect, since these models make exactly the wrong prediction about its direction.

The exaggerated length effect in surface dyslexia

Surface dyslexia is an acquired disorder of reading characterized by relatively intact regular word and nonword reading in the face of extremely poor exception word reading. The dual-route account of surface dyslexia involves a lesion to the lexical route (such as a lesion that reduces the accessibility of orthographic lexical entries; see Coltheart et al., 2001), so that processing along the nonlexical route dominates the reading aloud computation. Such a lesion results in regularization errors for irregular words (such as pronouncing "pint" as if it rhymed with "mint"). If the nonlexical procedure operates in a serial manner, such a lesion should also result in an exaggerated length effect on reading aloud latencies *that extends to regular words*. PDP models of reading do not make this prediction, since the computation of orthography to phonology in those models occurs solely in parallel.

Gold et al. (2005) investigated this issue by studying length effects in healthy controls, patients with dementia of the Alzheimer's type (who were not semantically impaired), and patients with semantic dementia and surface dyslexia (who were semantically impaired). All performed at ceiling on regular word reading accuracy. The mean differences between short-word and long-word response times (RTs) for regular words were 8.5 ms for the healthy controls, 8.5 ms for the Alzheimer's patients, and 73 ms for the patients with semantic dementia and surface dyslexia. This result provides good evidence for the dual-route account of reading in surface dyslexia, as well as further strong evidence for the presence of a serial processing component within the human reading system: "the group by length interaction is more easily accommodated within dual route than connectionist models. . . . Connectionist models have a more difficult time accounting for the increased length effect observed in SD [semantic dementia] latencies because they do not contain a serial processing component. Rather, orthographic, phonological and semantic components of words are processed in parallel" (Gold et al., 2005, pp. 842–843).

The position-sensitive Stroop effect

Coltheart et al. (1999) conducted an experiment to examine evidence for serial phonological assembly, capitalizing on the phonological Stroop effect in order to avoid the types of issues faced in related studies. Subjects were presented with coloured words, to which they were instructed to name the colour. Target words shared either their initial or final phonemes with the colour name (e.g. RAT or BAD printed in red), and responses to these words were compared with responses to control words that shared no phonemes with the colours in which they were printed. Coltheart et al. (1999) reasoned that a serially operating phonological assembly system would predict a benefit of phonemic overlap on colour naming that is larger when the phonemic overlap is early than when it is late. Conversely, a phonological assembly system that operates solely in parallel predicts a main effect of phonemic overlap but no effect of the position of phonemic overlap. Coltheart et al. (1999) reported clear evidence in favour of serial phonological assembly, and demonstrated that the DRC model with a rudimentary semantic system could produce a close simulation of the effect. One particularly desirable aspect of this experiment is that it comprises a within-target comparison (e.g. the participant says "red" in both initial and final conditions). Therefore, it is difficult to see how an argument from a consistency standpoint could be lodged, as has been lodged with regard to related effects such as the position of irregularity effect.

Bibi et al. (2000) conducted a similar investigation in Hebrew, in which words are read from right to left. They presented stimuli in three conditions for colour naming: (a) a *neutral* condition in which the stimulus was a row of identical letters in a particular colour; (b) a *congruent* condition in which the stimulus was either a printed colour name printed in that particular colour, or a word that differed by one letter from the printed colour name; and (c) an *incongruent* condition in which the stimulus was a printed colour name printed in a different colour, or a word that differed by one letter from this printed colour name. Results showed a significant *congruency effect* (neutral – congruent) when the printed stimulus was a complete colour name. However, when the stimulus differed by one letter from the congruent colour name, the size of the congruency effect depended on the position of the mismatching letter in the printed stimulus: The congruency effect increased in size as the mismatching letter moved further to the left in the right-to-left sequence. Results also showed a significant incongruity effect (neutral – incongruent) when the printed stimulus was a complete colour name. However, when the stimulus differed by one letter from the incongruent colour name, the size of the incongruity effect depended on the position of the mismatching letter in the printed stimulus: The incongruity effect increased in size as the mismatching letter moved further to the left in the right-to-left sequence. These data parallel the English findings of Coltheart et al. (1999) nicely, and provide very good evidence for right-to-left serial processing of Hebrew.

Masked onset priming

Forster and Davis (1991) reported that when a briefly presented (50–60 ms) masked prime and a subsequently presented target shared their initial letter, target naming was faster than when target and prime shared no letters: this is the masked onset priming effect. This priming effect occurs irrespective of the lexicality of the prime and target (Kinoshita, 2000); it is based not on shared initial letters across prime and target but on shared initial phonemes (Kinoshita, 2003); and, crucially, it arises only if prime and target share the *initial* phoneme. Sharing all phonemes bar the first produces no priming (Kinoshita, 2000).

The DRC model offers a natural account of this masked onset priming effect (see Coltheart et al., 2001). Early on in the processing of a letter string by the DRC model, activation of the phoneme level is produced only via the nonlexical route. Since that route operates from left to right, the first phoneme of the prime will be activated just by the nonlexical route. Suppose that the prime duration is such that before the nonlexical procedure can move on to the second letter of the prime, the prime is terminated and replaced by the target. This means that when target processing begins there is already some activation at the phoneme level—activation of the first phoneme of the prime. If so, there will be facilitation of target phoneme activation if target and prime share the same initial phoneme and inhibition (via competition based on lateral inhibition) if they do not: thus, a masked onset priming effect will occur.

If the prime were being processed in parallel rather than from left to right (as PDP models would have it), these masked onset priming results would seem inexplicable. In particular, consider the prime–target pairs *mof* SIB (zero-phoneme overlap), *suf* SIB (one-phoneme overlap), and *sif* SIB (two-phoneme overlap). PDP accounts can explain the basic finding of faster response latencies for *suf* SIB than for *mof* SIB, since the former pair is more similar than the latter pair. However, these accounts also predict more priming when there are two phonemes in common between prime and target (*sif* SIB) than when there is only one (*suf* SIB), but these conditions do not differ. Now compare *mof* SIB (zero-phoneme overlap) and *mib* SIB (two-phoneme overlap): a PDP account predicts priming here, but none is observed. Finally, compare *suf* SIB (one-phoneme overlap) with *mib* SIB (two-phoneme overlap). Priming occurs with the one-letter-in-common condition, yet there is no priming with the two-letters-in-common condition. All of these results were reported by Kinoshita (2000). Clearly, all that matters here is the identity of the initial phoneme of the prime; a parallel processing model has no explanation for this set of results.

Local and distributed representations

It is quite possible that, in some cognitive domains, people use distributed representations to do cognitive processing in that domain, whereas in other domains they rely exclusively on local representations. So we will not seek here to say anything at all general about the issue of distributed versus local representation. Instead, we will focus on just one cognitive domain—reading—and will address the following issue: does the human reading system use local representations, or are all its representations distributed? And we will narrow our scope even further: we will consider only computational models of reading. This is worth doing because any computational model of reading, since it has to be expressed explicitly, must make an explicit commitment to a particular degree of distributed representation; and, in fact, computational models of reading vary enormously in the degree to which they employ distributed representation, from not at all, through partly (representations at some levels are distributed, but those at other levels are local) to fully (there are no local representations in the model).

The first PDP model of reading (Seidenberg & McClelland, 1989) was completely committed to distributed representation: neither letters, graphemes, phonemes, nor words were represented locally. One deficiency of this model was that it "was much worse than skilled readers at pronouncing orthographically legal nonwords (Besner, Twilley, McCann & Seergobin, 1990)" (Plaut, 1997, p. 769). Plaut (1997) blamed this deficiency on the SM89 model's wholesale commitment to distributed representation: "Plaut et al. (1996) demonstrated that network implementations of the phonological pathway can learn to pronounce regular and exception words, and yet also pronounce nonwords as well as skilled readers, if they use more appropriately structured orthographic and phonological representations (based on graphemes and phonemes)" (Plaut, 1997, p. 769). All subsequent PDP models of reading have had local representations at the input and output levels, so none of them are fully distributed models.

However, although all of the post-SM89 PDP models have local representations of letters or graphemes and of phonemes or phonetic features, none have gone so far as to have local representations of *words*. The consistent use of distributed word representations in these models has made the lexical decision task of critical importance, as argued by Plaut (1997):

> The distinction between words and nonwords is of fundamental importance to the lexical system, and many researchers incorporate this distinction into their models by representing words as explicit structural entities such as logogens or localist word units. Such units provide a natural account of how skilled readers can accurately distinguish written words from nonwords in lexical decision (LD) tasks. Given that the current distributed approach to lexical processing does not contain word-specific representations, it becomes important to establish that distributed models can, in fact, perform lexical decision accurately and that, in doing so, they are influenced by properties of the words and nonwords in the same way as human readers. (Plaut, 1997, p. 785).

Thus, we next consider how well models of reading in which words are represented in distributed fashion can explain how human readers perform the visual lexical decision task.

Distributed representations and lexical decision

The first of the PDP models of reading, the SM89 model, was applied to the task of lexical decision, but its treatment of lexical decision was not very successful. As noted by Plaut (1997, p. 787), SM89 yielded a rate of false positives to nonwords far higher than that seen with human subjects, and the orthographic error scores for words and nonwords generated by the model and used for its lexical decisions did not bear any relationship to human lexical decision accuracy and latency for these items. Hence Plaut (1997, p. 787) concluded, "These negative findings concerning Seidenberg and McClelland's implemented model call into question the more general claim that words can be distinguished from nonwords by a distributed system lacking word-specific representations." The next three PDP models of reading, those described in Plaut et al. (1996), were not applied to the lexical decision task. However, Plaut (1997) did describe a model based on PDP principles that was applied to the lexical decision task.

Plaut's (1997) model consisted of units in three bodies of knowledge: 200 semantic units, 108 grapheme units, and 61 phoneme units. Units in these three bodies of knowledge were connected to each other via three sets of hidden units: 1000 hidden units connected grapheme units to semantic units, 1000 hidden units connected semantic units to phoneme units, and 100 hidden units connected grapheme units to phoneme units. When a word or nonword is presented to this trained network, a measure called *stress* can be computed for each semantic unit. The value of stress is a measure of the absolute distance that the input drives the semantic unit away from its resting level of 0.5 (up toward 1.0 or down toward 0.0). The value of stress is zero when a unit's activation is 0.5 and approaches 1.0 as the unit's activation approaches 1.0 or 0.0. The average stress value of the semantic units tends to be lower for a nonword than for a word. Thus, a criterion applied to stress values might allow the trained model to discriminate between words and nonwords.

We consider two issues here. The first is whether this method of performing the lexical decision task via consultation of the semantic level of PDP models can in fact result in accurate lexical decision performance. The second is whether this approach to lexical decision offers a reasonable account of how human readers perform the visual lexical decision task.

The obvious way to evaluate the first issue is to present the trained network with all of the words in its training set plus an equal number of orthographically comparable nonwords, compute semantic stress for all of these items, and determine the percentage of correct performance of the model when an optimal criterion for distinguishing the words from the nonwords is applied to the stress values. Plaut (1997) did just this. The words presented to the trained network for lexical decision were 1800 words extracted from the 2998 words of the network's training set. The nonwords were 591 pronounceable monosyllabic nonwords with orthographic bodies drawn from real words. The decision rule "Respond YES if average stress is greater than 0.955" produced correct responses to 1773/1800 words and 582/591 nonwords (an overall error rate of 1.5%). This result demonstrates that systems which do not have local representations can nevertheless perform the lexical decision task accurately.

The second issue is whether this PDP approach offers a plausible account of how human readers perform the lexical decision task. We know a great deal about the factors that affect YES and NO latencies when human readers perform this task, so one could evaluate the PDP approach by studying whether the RTs of a PDP model performing the lexical decision task are affected by the same factors in the same manner. However, neither the modelling work of Plaut (1997) nor that of Harm and Seidenberg (2004), which also investigated the use of semantic stress in modelling lexical decision, simulated lexical decision times. Rather, these modellers simulated asymptotic lexical decision accuracy. Thus, we do not know whether the PDP approach to lexical decision is capable of simulating RT data from the literature on human lexical decision.

However, we can approach this issue in a more general way. In these PDP approaches to lexical decision, and also that of Plaut and Booth (2000), lexical decision depends entirely upon consulting the semantic system. Is that how human readers perform the task? We do not think so, because neuropsychological evidence indicates that human readers can perform the lexical decision task with high accuracy even when they cannot be relying on the semantic system to do this task.

If visual lexical decision requires consultation of the semantic system to be performed accurately, then all patients with impaired semantic systems might be expected to be impaired at visual lexical decision. But, as discussed by Coltheart (2004), some are not. Patient JO (Lambon Ralph, Ellis, & Sage, 1998; Lambon Ralph, Sage, & Ellis, 1996) was poor at a variety of semantic tasks but 100% correct at visual lexical decision. Patient DC (Lambon Ralph, Ellis, & Franklin, 1995), also semantically impaired, was well within the normal accuracy range on visual lexical decision (117/120 correct). Patient SA (Ward, Stott, & Parkin, 2000), also semantically impaired, nevertheless scored 113/120 on visual lexical decision. Patient EM (Blazely, Coltheart, & Casey, 2005) showed exactly the same pattern—poor at any task requiring semantics but excellent at visual lexical decision (103/106 correct).

Now, it might be argued that visual lexical decision requires less accurate access to semantics than do the tasks typically used to assess semantics, such as picture–word matching. So perhaps these four patients had a degree of semantic impairment that was sufficient to compromise tests of semantics but not severe enough to compromise visual lexical decision. However, this explanation does not seem a viable one. Blazely et al. (2005) reported results from two patients with semantic dementia, EM (mentioned above) and PC. On various tests of semantic processing, EM consistently performed less accurately than PC, indicating that EM was at least as semantically impaired as PC and probably more so. Yet EM was very accurate at visual lexical decision (103/106) whereas PC was impaired (80/106; significantly worse than EM). These results indicate that if the semantic system is required for accurate visual lexical decision, then PC's semantic system was sufficiently impaired to compromise visual lexical decision. However, EM was at least as semantically impaired as PC and thus should not have been normal at visual lexical decision. But she was.[4]

Thus, we contend that human readers can perform the visual lexical decision task perfectly without needing to consult semantics. That does not mean that intact readers' lexical decision performance is not influenced by semantics: semantic priming of lexical decision and effects on lexical decision of various semantic properties of words such as imageability or semantic ambiguity show that there is semantic influence on lexical decision. However, the task can be performed perfectly even when this semantic influence is not available.

Plaut (1997) emphasized that he was not claiming that consultation of semantics was the *only* method human readers used to perform the lexical decision task. If nonwords and words are sufficiently orthographically or phonologically distinct, then consultation of orthography or phonology might suffice. But that does not eliminate the problem, because it predicts that when words and nonwords are closely matched on such properties, the reader will have to use semantics, and that does not seem to be so. For example, in the materials given to the semantically impaired patients JO, DC, SA, and EM described above, words and nonwords did not differ in bigram or trigram frequency (Coltheart, 2004), so these orthographic properties could not be used to perform the visual lexical decision task accurately; nor could semantics, yet all four patients performed the task with normal accuracy. Thus, even if PDP models can perform visual lexical decision accurately when they can consult a simulated semantic system, the models are not offering an adequate account of how human readers perform this task, because human readers can do so without needing to consult their semantic systems.

The most recent PDP work on visual lexical decision, described by Harm and Seidenberg (2004), briefly explores the possibility of using a measure of *orthographic* stress rather than semantic stress as a basis for lexical decision by PDP models, and also explores the use of a measure of orthographic distance. However, they do not report the accuracy of lexical decision performance that can be achieved by the use of either of these two measures. Furthermore, what is simulated in this work is asymptotic performance of the model, not lexical decision latency. But most important is the fact that these two orthographic measures are computed from an orthographic representation of the stimulus that is regenerated from its semantic representation. As such, this way of doing lexical decision still relies on the semantic system and so would by impaired if the semantic system were impaired. Hence, to offer this as an account of how human readers perform the lexical decision task is open to the objection discussed above—that semantically impaired patients can perform the visual lexical decision task with normal accuracy.

A few more words on "principles"

In this introduction to this chapter, we explained that one main difference between the approach taken in developing the DRC model of reading and the approach taken in developing the PDP models of reading has to do with "principles". DRC modellers take an evidence-based approach to theoretical development, relying on behavioural and neuropsychological results to guide the construction of their models; PDP modellers take a faith-based approach to theoretical development, relying on certain a priori principles to guide the construction of their models. This distinction was also considered by *Seidenberg and Plaut* (this volume), who cast it in terms of "data-driven" versus "theory-driven" modelling. Models that are "theory-driven", in the view of these authors, are those that are grounded in a set of a priori principles. Further, and perhaps not surprisingly, these authors argue that the extent to which a model holds fast to such principles provides a primary criterion for judging its adequacy. They write, "a model needs to explain phenomena in a principled way. That is, the explanation for the phenomena should derive from biological, computational, or behavioural principles that have some independent justification" (p. 32).

Seidenberg and Plaut (this volume, p. 26) to assert that one problem for the DRC approach is that the model "can fit specific data patterns without capturing the principles that govern the phenomena at a biological, computational, or behavioural level". In contrast, they (p. 26) argue that PDP models are able to avoid certain problems faced by the DRC model "by being grounded in a set of more completely specified and constrained computational principles". Two major principles of the PDP approach are specified by the first and second letters in the acronym PDP: regardless of what domain of cognition is being modelled, the first principle is that models should use *P*arallel processing, and the second principle is that models should use *D*istributed representations. That is why we focused in this chapter on (a) whether all of the processing that goes on in the human reading system *is* parallel and (b) whether all the representations present in the human reading system *are* distributed.

In our view, the many lines of evidence we have cited in this chapter concerning serial processing in reading demonstrate beyond doubt that the human reading system violates the principle of parallel processing. Further, as for the principle of distributed representation, even the PDP models themselves violate this principle. Only in the first PDP model of reading (Seidenberg & McClelland, 1989) were all of the representations distributed. Indeed, *Seidenberg and Plaut* (this volume, p. 42) write, "SM89 was interesting but ultimately limited by its phonological representation; PMSP96 largely fixed the phonological problem." But this fix was accomplished *by abandoning the view that phonological representations in the reading system are distributed*: each unit in the phonological system of the PMSP96 model represents a single phoneme, and each phoneme of the language is represented by just one unit. That is, a system of local representations. What is more, the principle of distributed representation was abandoned elsewhere in the model. In SM89 orthographic representations were distributed, but in PMSP96 they too are local: each unit in the orthographic system represents a grapheme, and each of the graphemes of the language is represented by just one unit. Every subsequent version of the triangle model (Harm & Seidenberg, 1999, 2001, 2004) uses local representations of orthography and of phonology. So what has happened to the principle of distributed representation? All that remains of it in these models is that *whole words* do not have local representations; and we argue in this chapter that this makes it very difficult for these models to explain how unimpaired readers perform the visual lexical decision task (and even more difficult to explain how it can be that performance on this task can sometimes be intact in people with severe impairments of the semantic system).

It seems very clear to us that in the case of reading there is a conflict between what the principles say the reading system *must be* like and what the data say the reading system *is* like. So much for the principles, is our view. But the view of PDP modellers seems to be different: "Models are judged not only with respect to their ability to account for robust findings in a particular domain but also with respect to considerations that extend well beyond any single domain. These include the extent to which the same underlying computational principles apply across domains"; and "The primary goal is not to implement the model that fits the most possible data" (*Seidenberg & Plaut*, this volume, pp. 41 and 42). The implication is that it does not matter, for example, how strong the evidence is that there is serial processing in the human reading system; a model of reading in which all of the processing occurs in parallel may nevertheless be preferred because it conforms to the principles.

Some may wonder, at this point, where these principles about the nature of cognitive processing come from in the first place. A major source seems to be considerations about the brain:

> The PDP approach starts from a very different assumption—namely, that the nature of cognitive processing is shaped and constrained in fundamental ways by properties of the underlying neural substrate . . . hypotheses are supported by computational demonstrations that models embodying the supposed principles are, in fact, consistent with the relevant behavioural (and neuroscientific) data. (*Seidenberg & Plaut*, this volume, p. 35)

But, surely, this confuses software with hardware. One can implement a parallel algorithm on a serial computer, and one can implement a serial algorithm on a parallel computer: the hardware does not constrain the software. From slogans such as "the brain is massively parallel" one cannot infer that the mind never does serial processing. If there are facts about the brain which indicate that the DRC approach to reading is misguided and the PDP approach to reading is correct, what are some of these facts?

Conclusions

Our chapter has considered the PDP approach to modelling reading, focusing on both the *P* and the *D* in PDP. We described eight different phenomena observed in studies of reading aloud by human readers that provide strong evidence for the view that the human reading system includes a processing component which operates serially; we believe this evidence rules out the view that processing in the human reading system occurs entirely in parallel. With respect to the view that representation in the human reading system is entirely distributed, we noted that no PDP model of reading after the SM89 model has used entirely distributed representation: all of these models have local representations at input and local representations at output. The representations of *words* in these models, though, are distributed, and we argued that this feature of the models makes it very difficult for them to offer an account of how the visual lexical decision task is done, especially by neuropsychological patients with severe semantic impairments.

In contrast to PDP models, models that use local representations and that include a serially operating mechanism that converts orthography to phonology (such as the DRC model; Coltheart et al., 2001) are compatible with the evidence we cite concerning serial effects in human reading, and also offer a tenable approach to explaining how human readers, neuropsychologically intact or neuropsychologically impaired, perform the visual lexical decision task.

Acknowledgements

We are grateful to Sally Andrews, Dave Balota, Derek Besner, and Ken Forster for helpful comments on an earlier draft of this chapter.

References

Baron, J. (1977). Mechanisms for pronouncing printed words: use and acquisition. In D. LaBerge & S. J. Samuels (Eds.), *Basic processes in reading: Perception and comprehension*. Hillsdale, NJ: Lawrence Erlbaum Associates, Inc.

Besner, D., Twilley, L., McCann, R. S., & Seergobin, K. (1990). On the connection between connectionism and data: Are a few words necessary? *Psychological Review*, *97*, 432–446.

Bibi, U., Tzelgov, J., & Henik, A. (2000). Stroop effect in words that differ from color words in one letter only. *Psychonomic Bulletin Review*, *7*, 678–683.

Blazely, A., Coltheart, M., & Casey, B. (2005). Semantic dementia with and without surface dyslexia. *Cognitive Neuropsychology*, *22*, 695–717.

Coltheart, M. (1978). Lexical access in simple reading tasks. In G. Underwood, (Ed.), *Strategies of information processing*. London: Academic Press.

Coltheart, M. (2004). Are there lexicons? *Quarterly Journal of Experimental Psychology*, *57A*, 1153–1171.

Coltheart, M. (2005). Modelling reading: The dual-route approach. In M. J. Snowling & C. Hulme (Eds.), *The science of reading*. Oxford: Blackwell.

Coltheart, M., Curtis, B., Atkins, P., & Haller, M. (1993). Models of reading aloud: Dual-route and parallel-distributed-processing approaches. *Psychological Review, 100*, 589–608.

Coltheart, M., & Rastle, K. (1994). Serial processing in reading aloud: Evidence for dual-route models of reading. *Journal of Experimental Psychology: Human Perception and Performance, 20*, 1197–1211.

Coltheart, M., Rastle, K., Perry, C., Langdon, R., & Ziegler, J. (2001). DRC: A dual route cascaded model of visual word recognition and reading aloud. *Psychological Review, 108*, 204–256.

Coltheart, M., Woollams, A., Kinoshita, S., & Perry, C. (1999). A position-sensitive Stroop effect: Further evidence for a left-to-right component in print-to-speech conversion. *Psychonomic Bulletin and Review, 6*, 456–463.

Cortese, M. J. (1998). Revisiting serial position effects in reading. *Journal of Memory and Language, 39*, 652–665.

Forster, K. I., & Chambers, S. (1973). Lexical access and naming time. *Journal of Verbal Learning and Verbal Behaviour, 12*, 627–635.

Forster, K. I., & Davis, C. (1991). The density constraint on form-priming in the naming task: Interference effects from a masked prime. *Journal of Memory and Language, 30*, 1–25.

Gold, B. T., Balota, D. A., Cortese, M. J., Sergent-Marshall, S. D., Snyder, A. Z., Salat, D. H., et al. (2005). Differing neuropsychological and neuroanatomical correlates of abnormal reading in early-stage semantic dementia and dementia of the Alzheimer type. *Neuropsychologia, 43*, 833–846.

Harm, M., & Seidenberg, M. S. (2004). Computing the meanings of words in reading: Cooperative division of labor between visual and phonological processes. *Psychological Review, 111*, 662–720.

Harm, M. W., & Seidenberg, M. S. (1999). Phonology, reading acquisition and dyslexia: Insights from connectionist models. *Psychological Review, 106*, 491–528.

Harm, M. W., & Seidenberg, M. S. (2001). Are there orthographic impairments in phonological dyslexia? *Cognitive Neuropsychology, 18*, 71–92.

Havelka, J., & Rastle, K. (2005). The assembly of phonology from print is serial and subject to strategic control: Evidence from Serbian. *Journal of Experimental Psychology: Learning, Memory, and Cognition, 31*, 148–158.

Humphreys, G. W., & Evett, L. J. (1985). Are there independent lexical and non-lexical routes in word processing? An evaluation of the dual route theory of reading. *Behavioral and Brain Sciences, 8*, 689–739.

Jared, D. (1997). Spelling-sound consistency affects the naming of high-frequency words. *Journal of Memory and Language, 36*, 505–529.

Joubert, S., & Lecours, A. R. (1998). The effect of graphemic parsing in nonword reading. *Brain and Cognition, 37*, 97–99.

Kawamoto, A. H., Kello, C. T., Jones, R., & Bame, K. (1998). Initial phoneme versus whole-word criterion to initiate pronunciation: Evidence based on response latency and initial phoneme duration. *Journal of Experimental Psychology: Learning, Memory, and Cognition, 24*, 862–885.

Kinoshita, S. (2000). The left-to-right nature of the masked onset priming effect in naming. *Psychonomic Bulletin and Review, 7*, 133–141.

Kinoshita, S. (2003). The nature of masked onset priming effects in naming: A review. In S. Kinoshita & S. J. Lupker (Eds.), *Masked priming: The state of the art* (pp. 223–238). Hove, UK: Psychology Press.

Kostić, D. (1999). *Frekvencijski recnik savremenog srpskog jezika* [Frequency dictionary of contemporary Serbian language]. Yugoslavia: Institute for Experimental Phonetics and Speech Pathology and Laboratory for Experimental Psychology, University of Belgrade.

Lambon Ralph, M., Ellis, A. W., & Franklin, S. (1995). Semantic loss without surface dyslexia. *Neurocase, 1*, 363–369.

Lambon Ralph, M., Ellis, A. W., & Sage, K. (1998). Word meaning blindness revisited. *Cognitive Neuropsychology, 15*, 389–400.

Lambon Ralph, M. A., Sage, K., & Ellis, A. W. (1996). Word meaning blindness: A new form of acquired dyslexia. *Cognitive Neuropsychology, 13*, 617–639.

Law, S.-P., Wong, W., & Chiu, K. M. Y (2005). Preserved reading aloud with semantic deficits: Evidence for a non-semantic lexical route for reading Chinese. *Neurocase, 11*, 167–175.

Lukatela, G., Lukatela, K., Carello, C., & Turvey, M. T. (1999). Effects of frequency and phonological ambiguity on naming Serbo-Croatian words. *European Journal of Cognitive Psychology, 11*, 1–16.

Marshall, J. C., & Newcombe, F. (1973). Patterns of paralexia: A psycholinguistic approach. *Journal of Psycholinguistic Research, 2*, 175–199.

Paap, K. R., & Noel, R. W. (1991). Dual-route models of print to sound: Still a good horse race. *Psychological Research, 53*, 13–24.

Perry, C., & Ziegler, J. C. (2002). On the nature of phonological assembly: Evidence from backward masking. *Language and Cognitive Processes, 17*, 31–59.

Plaut, D. C. (1997). Structure and function in the lexical system: Insights from distributed models of word reading and lexical decision. *Language and Cognitive Processes, 12*, 767–808.

Plaut, D. C., & Booth, J. R. (2000). Individual and developmental differences in semantic priming: Empirical and computational support for a single-mechanism account of lexical processing. *Psychological Review, 107*, 786–823.

Plaut, D. C., McClelland, J. L., Seidenberg, M. S., & Patterson, K. (1996). Understanding normal and impaired word reading: Computational principles in quasi-regular domains. *Psychological Review, 103*, 56–115.

Rastle, K., & Coltheart, M. (1998). Whammies and double whammies: The effect of length on nonword reading. *Psychonomic Bulletin and Review, 5*, 277–282.

Rastle, K., & Coltheart, M. (1999). Serial and strategic effects in reading aloud. *Journal of Experimental Psychology: Human Perception and Performance, 25*, 461–481.

Rey, A., & Schiller, N. O. (2005). Graphemic complexity and multiple print-to-sound associations in visual word recognition. *Memory and Cognition, 33*, 76–85.

Rey, A., Ziegler, J. C., & Jacobs, A. M. (2000). Graphemes are perceptual reading units. *Cognition, 75*, B1–B12.

Roberts, M. A., Rastle, K., Coltheart, M., & Besner, D. (2003). When parallel processing in visual word recognition is not enough: New evidence from naming. *Psychonomic Bulletin Review, 10*, 405–414.

Seidenberg, M. S., & McClelland, J. L. (1989). A distributed, developmental model of word recognition and naming. *Psychological Review, 96*, 523–568.

Ward, J., Stott, R., & Parkin, A. J. (2000). The role of semantics in reading and spelling: Evidence for the "summation hypothesis". *Neuropsychologia, 38*, 1643–1653.

Weekes, B. S. (1997). Differential effects of number of letters on word and non-word naming latency. *Quarterly Journal of Experimental Psychology, 50A*, 439–456.

Ziegler, J. C., Perry, C., Jacobs, A. M., & Braun, M. (2001). Identical words are read differently in different languages. *Psychological Science, 12*, 379–384.

Zorzi, M. (2000). Serial processing in reading aloud: No challenge for a parallel model. *Journal of Experimental Psychology: Human Perception and Performance, 26*, 847–856.

Zorzi, M., Houghton, G., & Butterworth, B. (1998). Two routes or one in reading aloud? A connectionist dual-process model. *Journal of Experimental Psychology: Human Perception and Performance, 24*, 1131–1161.

Notes

1 We say a "degree" of consensus, because not all investigators believe that every connection exists. For example, a strong phonological theorist of written word comprehension would deny that there is a direct connection between orthography and semantics.

2 It should be noted that neither serial processing nor local representations are *required* by dual-route theories in general. For example, the model of Seidenberg and McClelland (1989) has neither serial processing nor local representations and yet those authors correctly observed that "Ours is a dual route model" (Seidenberg & McClelland, 1989, p. 559). The DRC model has these properties not because the properties are required by the general dual-route approach but because they appear to be required by the evidence (the point of our chapter is to document this evidence). In other words, the claim that the reading system involves serial processing and local representations is not an article of faith or an a priori assumption, but an inference from behavioural data.

3 It may be useful at this stage to remind readers of the distinction between regularity and consistency. Regularity is always a categorical variable: a word is regular if its pronunciation is generated correctly by a set of rules that relates spelling to sound. These rules typically relate graphemes to phonemes (e.g. Coltheart et al., 2001; Rastle & Coltheart, 1999), but could, in principle, apply to other grain sizes (such as relating bodies to rimes). The spelling-sound consistency of a word is defined by its relationship not to a set of rules but to other words in the language. Though consistency was initially defined as a categorical variable relating to a single grain size (a letter string is inconsistent if its body has at least two pronunciations in the set of words possessing that body) (Glushko, 1979), more recent research (e.g. Jared, 1997; Plaut et al., 1996; Rastle & Coltheart, 1999; Zorzi, 2000) has defined it as a continuous variable that can operate at multiple grain sizes (such as the body, the antibody, and the grapheme). For example, one could compute the body consistency of a particular stimulus by relating the number of words that have the same pronunciation of the orthographic body of the stimulus to the total number of words that possess that orthographic body.

4 This pattern of preserved lexical decision with impaired semantics has even been reported in some Chinese patients, leading Law, Wong, and Chiu (2005, p. 174) to conclude that "observations of [patients] YKM, LJG and CML seem to lend support to localist models, which assume the existence of word form representations in the mental lexicon."

2 Progress in understanding word reading: Data fitting versus theory building

Mark S. Seidenberg
University of Wisconsin, USA
David C. Plaut
Carnegie Mellon University, USA

Computational modelling is a tool that can be used in different ways for different purposes. There are several distinct styles of modelling research in cognitive science and neuroscience, with differing goals, methods, and evaluation criteria. Nowhere is this clearer than in the area of lexical processing in reading, in which computational models have played a prominent role for over 25 years.

In this chapter, we examine two contrasting approaches to computational models of reading, the dual-route approach developed by Max Coltheart and his colleagues, and the parallel distributed processing (PDP) approach developed by ourselves, James L. McClelland, and others. These approaches have spawned a series of implemented models (including Coltheart, Curtis, Atkins, & Haller, 1993; Coltheart, Rastle, Perry, Langdon, & Ziegler, 2001; Harm & Seidenberg, 1999, 2004; Plaut, 1997; Plaut, McClelland, Seidenberg, & Patterson, 1996; Seidenberg & McClelland, 1989, among others). The usual way this research is assessed is by examining individual models with respect to factors such as their fidelity to behavioural data, the breadth of the behavioural phenomena addressed, the limitations of the model, and so on. Our primary goal in this chapter is not to evaluate individual models but rather to examine more basic foundational assumptions of the two approaches. They differ fundamentally with respect to these assumptions, including what models are for, how they are developed, and how they are to be evaluated. Of course, these differences greatly complicate the task of comparing models. Dual-route models are constructed with specific desiderata in mind, some of which are not shared by the other approach, and they necessarily come out "ahead" if those criteria are used in comparing models. The same is true for the PDP models. If all fruits are judged on the basis of what makes a good apple, then apples are necessarily the best fruit. This is unsatisfying if only some of the criteria also apply to oranges.

Our goal is to clarify the differences between the approaches and how they affect the interpretation of specific models. We will argue that the more important consideration at this stage in the development of the field is between the alternative approaches, not individual models. The questions that end up mattering are ones such as, which approach raises the most interesting questions? Is better able to relate behaviour to its brain basis? Can explain individual variation in reading ability or style? Offers theoretically meaningful links between reading and other aspects of cognition? Our claim is that other questions, such as which model has been applied to the broader range of experimental paradigms and tasks, or how good a fit has been achieved to the results of specific behavioural studies, are currently somewhat less important. The latter questions already presuppose a commitment to a particular approach, but the basis for making such a commitment is what needs to be examined. One set of questions involves assessing which approach is on a trajectory toward answering basic questions; the other set is more focused on keeping score about the intermediate products of the research programmes.

It will not surprise readers to learn that, in our view, the results of this analysis favour the PDP approach. But convincing readers of this conclusion is far less important to us than facilitating a deeper understanding of the nature of the disagreement. There is no doubt that the dual-route approach has served a highly valuable function by orienting researchers to important research questions, and generating testable hypotheses that promoted numerous empirical studies over a multiyear period. Moreover, the competition between the approaches has advanced the understanding of the theoretical and empirical issues considerably. In our assessment, however, the implemented dual-route models—particularly the 2001 attempt to expand the range of phenomena to which the dual-route cascaded (DRC) model was applied—exposed some fundamental limitations of the approach.

DRC is an example of a bottom-up, data-fitting approach to modelling that has a long history in cognitive science. The limitations of this approach have been widely discussed in the literature, dating from at least Newell's famous "Twenty Questions" chapter (1973). The basic problem with the bottom-up approach is that a model can fit specific data patterns without capturing the principles that govern the phenomena at a biological, computational, or behavioural level. "Fitting the data", then, tells us more about the flexibility of a style of modelling than about the questions that motivated the research in the first place. To be clear, the PDP approach is not wholly immune from these problems either, because it also involves detailed comparisons between models and data, and not all aspects of all models are equally well motivated. However, it largely avoids them by being grounded in a set of more completely specified and constrained computational principles. The emphasis in the PDP approach is not on capturing every empirical data point in a single model but rather on providing a framework for addressing issues that will continue to be the focus of attention for the foreseeable future: how the brain achieves the computations that underlie reading; the relationship between reading and other capacities; the bases of differences (across individuals and writing systems) in reading, and how such differences interact with brain injury; and the causes of developmental dyslexia, understood at genetic, neurophysiological, and behavioural levels.

The dual-route approach

The term "dual-route model" is ambiguous and a source of confusion for many researchers (Coltheart, 2000; Harm & Seidenberg, 2004). The term can refer either to dual (visual versus phonological) mechanisms for accessing the meanings of words from print (which Coltheart terms "DR-M models") or dual (lexical versus sublexical) mechanisms for computing the pronunciations of words (which Coltheart terms "DR-P models"). Although Coltheart (1978) discussed the issue of visual versus phonological processes in reading, most subsequent research focused on the DR-P idea (e.g. Coltheart, Davelaar, Jonasson, & Besner, 1977; Paap & Noel, 1991; Patterson, Marshall, & Coltheart, 1985), and that is our focus here. The dual-route theory was initially developed by means of informal information-processing models (sometimes called "box and arrow" models), of which there were multiple variants (see Coltheart, Sartori, & Job, 1987; Patterson et al., 1985, for examples).

Computational versions of the DR-P model were eventually developed after critiques of the informal modelling approach (e.g. Seidenberg, 1988) and the development of connectionist models of word reading (e.g. McClelland & Rumelhart, 1981; Seidenberg & McClelland, 1989).

Coltheart et al. (2001) presented considerable background concerning the origins of their approach and its fundamental assumptions. They link their models to nineteenth-century "diagram makers" such as Lichtheim (1885), and emphasize the continuity between the informal (e.g. Coltheart et al., 1977) and computational versions of the dual-route model. Principal features of the approach include the commitment to a version of the modularity hypothesis (Fodor, 1983; Coltheart, 1999), to theorizing pitched at the level of the "functional architecture" of the cognitive system (Shallice, 1988), and to identifying the modules of the functional architecture primarily through studying brain-injured patients.

Several other important components of the approach should also be noted. First, Coltheart et al. (2001) emphasize the data-driven character of their modelling, endorsing Grainger and Jacobs' (1998, p. 24) view that "in developing algorithmic models of cognitive phenomena, the major source of constraint is currently provided by human behavioral data". Second, they view models as cumulative: each model improves upon the previous one by adding to the phenomena covered by a previous version. Thus, the 2001 version of the DRC is said to account for the same facts as the 1999 version but also many others. The models are described as "nested" with respect to data coverage. Again they quote Grainger and Jacobs (1998): "[I]n other sciences it is standard practice that a new model accounts for the crucial effects accounted for by the previous generation of the same or competing models." Finally,

Coltheart and colleagues emphasize fidelity to behavioural data as the principal criterion for evaluating models (see also *Rastle & Coltheart*, this volume). Models are designed to simulate data patterns, and a model is valid unless disconfirmed by making an incorrect prediction. So, for example, in justifying their use of an interactive-activation (IA) model as a component of DRC, the authors note that the McClelland and Rumelhart IA model had not been "refuted" by any behavioural data; thus, there was no empirical reason to abandon it.

Having described the rationale behind their approach and motivated major parts of their model's architecture, Coltheart et al. (2001) turned to applying the model to a large number of phenomena. The most noteworthy feature of the research was the application of a single model to more than 20 empirical phenomena involving word and nonword reading. The breadth of the data coverage led Coltheart and colleagues to conclude that "the DRC model is the most successful of the existing computational models of reading" (p. 204).

Comments on the approach

As already noted, the technique of fitting models to data has a long history in psychology. Other prominent examples from the not-too-distant past include Sternberg's (1969) serial search model; Smith, Shoben, and Rips' (1974) model of semantic categorization; Collins and Loftus' (1975) spreading activation model of semantic memory; Clark's (1969) deductive reasoning model; Ratcliff's (1978) diffusion model of memory retrieval; Massaro's (1989) fuzzy logical model of perception; and so on. The methodology in this research was roughly as follows: behavioural data were collected in the service of addressing a general question such as "how do people retrieve information from memory?" or "how are categories organized in memory?" The data derived from a small number of laboratory tasks such as probe verification ("is this stimulus a member of a prespecified target set?"), statement verification ("is a canary a bird?"), and probe recognition ("is this stimulus new or old?"). The researcher then developed a model that rationalized various facets of the data, such as why some statements are more difficult to verify than others. The models were usually presented informally (in words or figures), although some models were implemented as computer simulations for additional precision and clarity. The models were mainly tools for developing explicit accounts of the types of procedures and knowledge representations that give rise to overt performance.

These models were developed out of a vocabulary of representations and processes loosely drawn from flowcharting. Thus, there would be data structures (such as propositions) and operations upon them, such as encoding, comparing, testing conditions, decision making, and so on. The inventory of elements out of which a model could be constructed was large, providing considerable flexibility and descriptive power. A model could then be developed which fit some interesting empirical phenomenon (for example, why it is easier to decide that a canary is a bird than an animal).

The DRC models were developed in a similar fashion. Over a multiyear period, researchers had collected a large body of data in the service of addressing basic questions such as how people read words aloud (naming) or decide whether a string of letters is a word (lexical decision). Informal models were then constructed to fit these data. The models were built out of constructs, such as rules (for pronouncing letter strings), lexical nodes, activation levels, spreading activation, and so on, that were carried over from earlier accounts of word reading. These concepts were employed because they closely matched intuitions about reading and language, and because they were available as part of the information-processing vocabulary of the era. Eventually, the models were implemented as computer simulations that reproduced behavioural effects, such demonstrations being taken as evidence that the model was correct, especially when a single model could be applied to a large number of findings derived from several tasks.

Coltheart et al. (2001) termed this approach "Old Cognitivism" (in contrast to the more recent PDP paradigm). Although they correctly situated their research within this older tradition, they did not discuss long-standing critiques of it. The basic problem is that the strategy of accounting for the most data possible is not itself sufficiently powerful to converge on a satisfactory theory in cognition. Rather, what happens is this: The researcher has a certain favoured vocabulary of elements out of which to construct a model that accounts for target behavioural data. There is also considerable freedom to introduce new types of representations, processing mechanisms, assumptions about the time course of processing, parameter settings, and so on (see, for example, the discussion in Seidenberg, 1988, of how boxes are added to such models). Considerable resources are therefore available for model construction. The elements of the model are configured in response to empirical data; that is the essence of the methodology. This procedure does not guarantee, or even promote, converging on theoretical generalizations that explain the phenomena.

This assertion seems rather harsh; how can it be evaluated? One way is to ask of any given model whether it accounts for data other than those that were used in constructing it. If a model instantiates relevant general principles, it should accommodate other data of a similar kind. If the model merely fits selected target data, there is no guarantee that it will generalize; and if it does not, this is a telltale sign that the model has failed to capture the general principles that underlie the behaviour. In our view, the DRC model—particularly the 2001 version—is subject to this criticism.

The DRC 2001 model was configured to fit the results of studies illustrating a variety of phenomena concerning word and nonword reading. For each phenomenon (such as regularity effects, frequency by regularity interaction, consistency effects, nonword naming, pseudohomophone effects, and so on), the authors fit the results of a key experiment or two demonstrating the effect. For example, the frequency by regularity experiment was one by Paap and Noel (1991), the consistency experiment was one by Jared (1997), and the pseudohomophone experiments were from McCann and Besner (1987) and Taft and Russell (1992). In each case, of course, one might choose other experiments addressing the same phenomenon. For example, the frequency-by-regularity interaction can also be assessed with studies such as Jared (1997); Seidenberg (1985); Seidenberg, Waters, Barnes, and Tanenhaus (1984); Taraban and McClelland (1987); Waters and Seidenberg (1985); and others. Consistency effects can be assessed with respect to studies such as Cortese and Simpson (2000); Jared (2002); Jared, McRae, and Seidenberg (1990); and Seidenberg et al. (1984). If one examines the results across a set of studies on one issue, it often turns out that the behavioural effect in question consistently replicates across studies, but not in DRC. In other words, DRC's fit to the data is rather better for the study presented in Coltheart et al. (2001) than for other exemplars.[1]

To illustrate, a number of studies have reported that words with inconsistent spelling-sound correspondences yield longer naming latencies than words with consistent correspondences (e.g. Cortese & Simpson, 2000; Glushko, 1979; Jared, 1997, 2002; Seidenberg et al., 1984; Waters & Seidenberg, 1985). A word such as GAVE is inconsistent because the pattern –AVE is pronounced differently in HAVE. Inconsistent words are theoretically important because they are rule governed and therefore should pattern with words such as MUST, which have no close inconsistent neighbours. The weights in a PDP model reflect the net effects of exposure to a large corpus of words. Other factors being equal, inconsistent words such as GAVE should take longer to read aloud than a more consistent words such as MUST, even though both are "rule governed". This effect was first reported by Glushko (1979); subsequent studies showed that it is larger for lower frequency words and for younger readers. Consistency effects therefore provide evidence to support a model which represents degrees of consistency in the mapping from spelling to sound, rather than rule-governed forms and exceptions (Seidenberg & McClelland, 1989). However, Coltheart et al. (2001) suggested that consistency effects arise from other, confounding factors, and showed that DRC simulated the results of a study by Jared (1997) (Figure 2.1). Thus, consistency effects seemed to be less of a problem for the dual route approach than some had thought.[2]

Consistency effects have been reported in several other studies; how does DRC fare with respect to these findings? Consider Glushko's (1979) original study comparing regular words (e.g. MUST), exception words (e.g. HAVE), and inconsistent words (e.g. MINT). As Figure 2.2 indicates, the study yielded a regularity effect (regular words faster than irregular) but also a consistency effect (inconsistent words longer than regular). The DRC model, tested on the same words, reproduces the regularity effect, but not the consistency effect (Figure 2.3). Jared (2002) manipulated both regularity (rule-governed words versus exceptions) and consistency (consistent versus

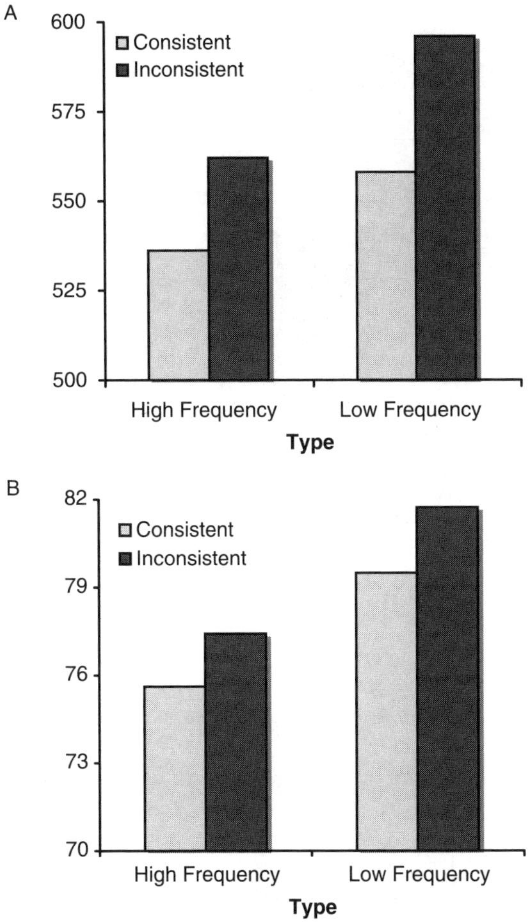

Figure 2.1 (A) Results of Jared's (1997) study of consistency effects. (B) DRC model simulation of the same study.

inconsistent spelling patterns) in a factorial design. The behavioural results and DRC's performance on the same items are presented in Figure 2.3. The behavioural data yielded a consistency effect (consistent < inconsistent) but no effect of regularity. The simulation yielded a regularity effect (regular < exception) but no effect of consistency. There are similar differences between the behavioural and simulation results in other studies of consistency effects.

Thus, the DRC model does not capture the consistency effects observed across different studies in different laboratories. The methodology used in developing DRC results in overfitting: The model is closely tailored to the results of specific experiments and is less successful when assessed against other studies. Would one really want to conclude that a model captures a phenomenon if it adequately reproduces the results of one study, but not

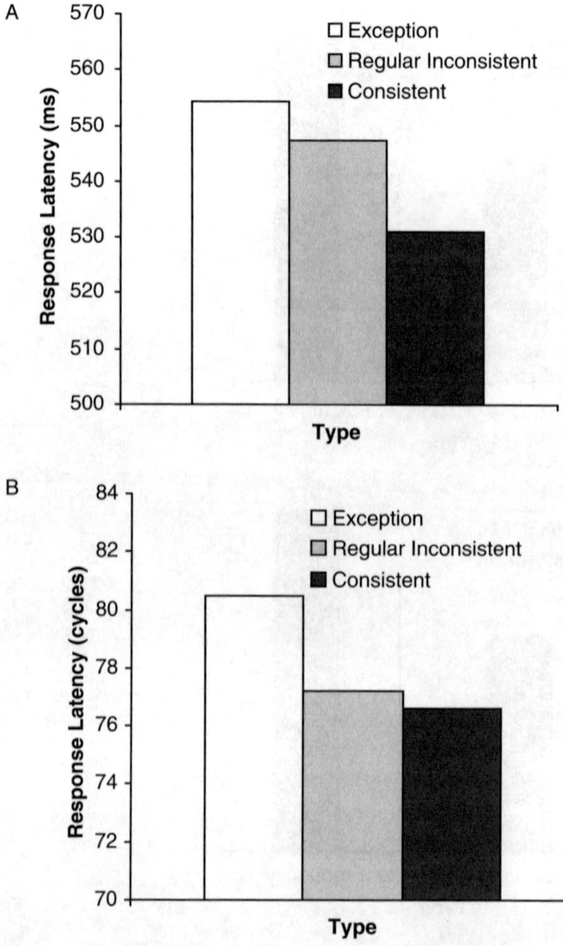

Figure 2.2 (A) Glushko's (1979) study of regular (rule-governed), regular inconsistent, and exception word naming. Latencies for regular inconsistent words fall between regular words and exceptions. (B) DRC model simulation using the same words. Regular inconsistent words do not differ from regulars.

others that yielded the same pattern of results (e.g. using different stimulus items)? One could just as well conclude that the model failed to simulate the phenomenon.

One might further hold that a model needs to explain phenomena in a principled way. That is, the explanation for the phenomena should derive from biological, computational, or behavioural principles that have some independent justification and thus are not merely introduced in response to the data at hand. Judged by these additional criteria, DRC does not fare well either. DRC's core commitments were introduced as ways of rationalizing

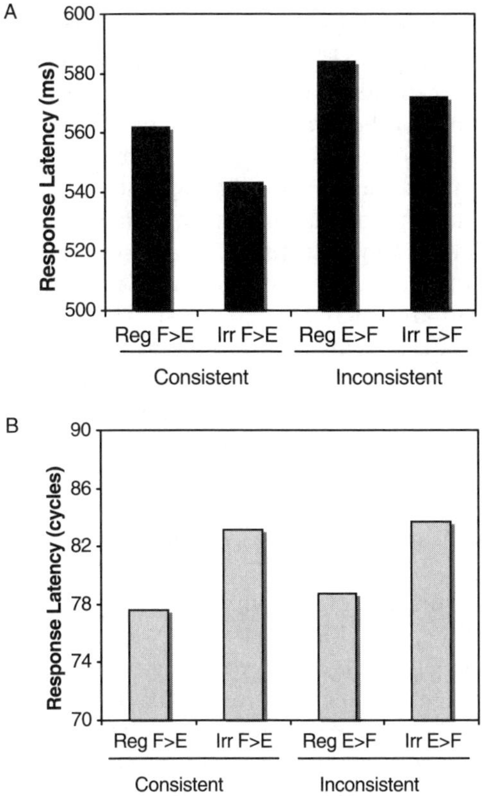

Figure 2.3 (A) Results of Jared's (2002) study of regularity and consistency effects. F = friends, E = enemies. Words with more friends than enemies are regular; words with more enemies than friends are exceptions. The results indicate a reliable effect of consistency and no effect of regularity. (B) Dual-route cascaded simulation of this study. The results show a reliable effect of regularity but not consistency.

data about reading, not because they were independently motivated by other concerns. They were largely inherited from the informal models of the precomputational era that relied heavily on intuitions about reading: for example, the "lexical entries" of the 1970s became the "localist representations of words" in the DRC models.

We have noted that DRC-type models are built out of a large inventory of modelling elements. There is little constraint on what can be included in a model to allow it to fit data successfully. It might therefore seem that the DRC model merely needs some additional modification in order to fix the generalization problem identified above. For example, interactive-activation models (one component of DRC) have a large number of parameters governing the flow of activation between and within units. (Coltheart et al., 2001, Table 1, p. 218, list 31 such parameters, which do not include seven additional parameters introduced to model lexical decision.) Each of these parameters can take on a large number of values. Hence, the space of IA models defined by these parameters is huge. Perhaps fixing the model is just a matter of searching this space more systematically to find a set of parameters that yields good fits to a broader range of behavioural results, or of adding additional components to the model. Indeed, it is common lore that complex models with large numbers of parameters can "fit any data"; all that is required is sufficient skill and stamina to find the right combination.

It turns out that DRC-type models do not actually behave this way. Rather, developing a model to fit a set of data has the opposite effect: it makes it more difficult to modify the model to accommodate additional data. The results described by Coltheart et al. (2001) are closely tied to the parameter settings that were used. We have not explored all possible combinations of parameter settings, but it is clear from experimentation with the model that it is very difficult to find a different parameter set that yields better results than the ones reported. Although better fits might be achieved, one assumes that if the authors had been able to find such a set, they would have reported it. In fact, the model's performance is brittle insofar as it does not perform as well with many other parameter settings.

Further complications arise from altering parameters to account for additional phenomena. For example, in Coltheart et al. (2001), the standard parameters failed to exhibit the facilitatory effect of neighbourhood size on word-naming latencies observed empirically by Andrews (1989, 1992) and by Sears, Hino, and Lupker (1995). In order to get the DRC to exhibit this effect, Coltheart and colleagues eliminated lateral inhibition within both the orthographic and phonological lexicons, and reduced feed-forward letter-to-word inhibition. Even so, while this yielded a main effect of neighbourhood size, it still failed to produce the interaction of neighbourhood size and word frequency as observed by Andrews (1992) and Sears et al. (1995). Moreover, these new parameter values create problems with respect to other phenomena. For example, the new parameter regime introduced to produce neighbourhood effects compromises the ability of the model to exhibit consistency effects. Whereas the original parameters produced a weak but reliable effect of consistency for Jared's (1997, experiment 1) stimuli (and no errors), the new parameters produce relatively high error rates (10–16% across conditions) and no reliable consistency effect.

This behaviour is characteristic of DRC. Changing parameters may allow the model to fit better the results of an individual experiment. However, it is then essential to examine the effects of these parameter changes on *other* aspects of the model's behaviour, which Coltheart et al. (2001) did not report. In practice, changing parameters to fit specific results has the effect of moving the behavioural mismatch somewhere else. One leak is patched but others spring up elsewhere because the underlying problem has not been addressed.

This analysis is further borne out by developments since the publication of the 2001 version of DRC. Coltheart and colleagues have presented additional data and arguments favouring the DRC model, primarily focused on atypical cases of developmental or acquired dyslexia with patterns of impaired reading that are said to contradict one or another aspect of the PDP theory (e.g. Blazely, Coltheart, & Casey, 2005; Coltheart, in press). The interpretation of such case studies is highly controversial, particularly double dissociations (see Dunn & Kirsner, 2003; Juola & Plunkett, 2000; Plaut, 1995; Van Orden, Pennington, & Stone, 2001). The more important point, however, is that Coltheart and colleagues' analyses of these cases are not tied to their implemented model. They wish to argue that certain patterns of behavioural impairment are consistent with their model (and not the PDP approach); however, these arguments are not coupled to simulations of the cases in question.

On our analysis, the successes of the 2001 version of DRC are so tightly bound to particular parameter values and other implementation-specific features that it should be difficult to extend it to other phenomena, including these case studies. The net result is that the most recent arguments in favour of the dual-route approach have the same form as in the precomputational modelling era. We are back to arguments of the 1980s from double dissociations and patterns of "selective" impairment. It is almost as though the models (and the insights about the interpretation of such cases that emerged from them) had never occurred.

The PDP approach

All cognitive processes, including word reading, are ultimately implemented in terms of changes in patterns of neural activity in the brain. Traditional cognitive modelling, of the sort exemplified by the DRC model, assumes that this fact places little if any constraint on the nature of the computations performed by the brain, thereby licensing the introduction of any types of cognitive mechanisms thought capable of fitting behavioural data.

The PDP approach starts from a very different assumption—namely, that the nature of cognitive processing is shaped and constrained in fundamental ways by properties of the underlying neural substrate. The goal is to formulate a set of computational principles that capture how neural activity gives rise to cognition. In pursuing this goal, the mechanisms that are available for modelling are extremely limited and must ultimately be grounded in emerging insights from neuroscience. Note, however, that neuroscientific investigation per se does not directly identify the relevant principles, because not all properties of the brain are equally relevant to understanding cognition. Thus, the PDP approach puts forth *hypotheses* about which properties are central and which are peripheral. These hypotheses are supported by computational demonstrations that models embodying the proposed principles are, in fact, consistent with the relevant behavioural (and neuroscientific) data. Similarly, the limitations of a model can suggest ways in which existing principles need to be modified, supplemented, or replaced. In this way, an individual model need not be interpreted as a proposed "solution" that is somehow correct or incorrect on the basis of its fit to data. Rather, modelling as an enterprise can be a means of exploring the validity and implications of a set of hypotheses for how cognitive processes are implemented in the brain. It is the underlying hypotheses, rather than the models per se, which collectively constitute a theory of a given domain.

The principles at the core of PDP modelling are well known: cooperative and competitive interactions among simple, neuron-like processing units; different types of information represented by distributed patterns of activity over different groups of units, with similarity reflected by pattern overlap; knowledge encoded as weights on connections between units; and learning as gradual adjustment of connection weights based on the statistical structure among inputs and outputs, often via internal ("hidden") representations. Although this list is certainly not exhaustive—for instance, it makes no mention of intrinsic variability or recurrent connectivity—it conveys the essence of the approach.

Of particular note is the emphasis on learning. Although it is sometimes possible to hand-specify connection weights for small networks that employ localist representations (that is, one unit per entity, as in the lexical route of the DRC model), this quickly becomes infeasible for networks with distributed representations and tens, if not hundreds, of thousands of connections. More to the point, hand-specifying representations, even if possible, would undermine one of the most interesting aspects of the approach—the ability to use a general learning procedure to acquire knowledge that gives rise to effective representations and processes. This property—lacking in many traditional cognitive models including the DRC—is critical for two reasons. The first is that it allows the approach to make direct contact with developmental data on the acquisition of cognitive skills, which can be essential to improving pedagogical practice and elucidating mature mechanisms in adults (e.g. Harm & Seidenberg, 1999; Thomas & Karmiloff-Smith, 2003). The second reason is that the nature of the representations and processes developed through learning, when analyzed and understood thoroughly, can give rise to novel and interesting hypotheses about cognitive and neural representations in the brain (Plaut & McClelland, 2000).

A major attraction of the PDP approach is that the same computational principles are brought to bear not only across development, skilled performance, and breakdown after brain damage, but also across the full range of perceptual, cognitive, and motor domains. One consequence is that the mechanisms available for modelling are not introduced solely in response to the data from a particular domain, but are constrained to be broadly consistent with applications in other domains. Of course, developing any specific model involves combining the domain-general principles with domain-specific assumptions about the tasks to be performed and the way in which relevant inputs and outputs are represented. For instance, a simulation of reading aloud must, at the very least, specify a corpus of text for reading acquisition as well as representations for visual or orthographic input and phonological or articulatory output. Ideally, these domain-specific assumptions are supported by independent evidence, but they can also be taken as additional hypotheses that are subject to evaluation and revision. Thus, it is often informative to develop and examine a range of models that vary in particular ways, in order to clarify what specific properties lead to its ability (or inability) to account for behavioural findings, and the extent to which these derive from domain-specific or domain-general assumptions. In this way, PDP models are like experiments—a means of testing hypotheses by exploring the consequences of particular factors that influence performance.

Finally, it is important to emphasize that, like all models, PDP models are approximations of the representations and processes that underlie human cognition. These approximations are of two kinds. The first concerns the nature of the inputs and outputs of a model. No model implements the entire processing stream from sensory receptors to muscle contractions. Models must incorporate assumptions about the form of input representations generated by earlier, upstream processes, and about how the model's output representations are used by later, downstream processes to produce behaviour. Most word-reading models assume static orthographic input representations and static phonological output representations, but, clearly, these assumptions ignore the complex, temporal nature of early visual processes (including eye movements e.g. Rayner, 1998; Reichle, Pollatsek, & Rayner, 1998) and later articulatory processes (e.g. Browman & Goldstein, 1990; Plaut & Kello, 1999). Although omitting these processes may limit the ability of implemented models to address some order and length effects (see *Rastle & Coltheart*, this volume), such effects do not pose fundamental challenges to the more general framework.

The second kind of approximation concerns simplifications within the implementation itself. Not every principle plays a critical role in explaining every phenomenon. Some models make simplifications for reasons of computational efficiency. For example, a feed-forward network is far less computationally demanding to simulate than a fully recurrent version and provides an adequate approximation in some contexts, even though it lacks the interactivity that plays a major role in many PDP accounts. Other simplifications are made for expository purposes. For instance, *Rastle and Coltheart* (this volume) portray Plaut et al.'s (1996) use of localist units for graphemes and phonemes as inconsistent with the principle of distributed representation. However, the simulations were focused on the implications of distributed representation at the level of words and nonwords, and coding graphemes and phonemes as patterns of activity, although straightforward computationally, would have obscured the importance of condensing spelling-sound regularities.[3] Finally, some simplifications provide a means of hypothesis testing. A given model may incorporate only a subset of the relevant principles in order to evaluate whether that subset is sufficient. In this way, modelling is no different than empirical work: no experiment on word recognition examines all factors that influence processing; rather, studies are designed to provide clear evidence about individual factors and their interactions.

Comments on the approach

The PDP approach to cognitive modelling in general, and word reading in particular, carries with it a number of implications that are worth spelling out in detail. The first and most obvious is that the development of a model is subject to several constraints, only one of which is fitting specific behavioural findings. The result is that, in the short run, specific PDP models may not match particular empirical findings or account for as much variance in empirical data as approaches for which data fitting is the primary goal.

In fact, it would be difficult for PDP modelling to do as well even if data fitting were a goal of the approach. The reason relates to the notion of a *parameter*. In the DRC, a parameter (e.g. letter-to-word inhibition) is a theoretically unconstrained numeric value that can be manipulated independently of other parameters and whose consequences for performance can be evaluated relatively directly. As a result, it is possible to "search" parameter space by running the model repeatedly until a set of parameter values is found that optimizes the fit between model and human performance. The process becomes more computationally demanding when the number of parameters is large and a broad range of data must be fit, but the basic character of the process is unchanged.

The situation is very different for PDP modelling for a number of reasons. First, many of the numeric values within a simulation—most obviously, the connection weights—are not under the direct control of the modeller but are derived algorithmically, and thus do not constitute parameters in any real sense. Second, some of the values that can be directly manipulated, such as those that govern learning and some aspects of network architecture, turn out to have relatively little impact on the nature of what is learned, other than to speed up or slow down the process (as long as the values are within reasonable ranges). Other properties of the models that vary, such as the numbers of units or layers, have broad consequences that are interpretable with respect to behaviour and thus are theoretically relevant.

There are, of course, many aspects of the design of a simulation that ultimately affect its match to behavioural data, but the degree to which these can be optimized is severely constrained by the reliance on learning. Training a large PDP simulation on a complex, realistic task can take days if not weeks on modern-day computing hardware. At this time scale, it is simply infeasible to rerun the simulation a large number of times in order to "search" for parameter values that optimize its fit to data. In practice, small-scale simulations are run to refine general aspects of a simulation, and then multiple runs of the early stages of learning by the full-scale simulation are carried out in order to improve the ability of the model to learn the training corpus. Note, however, that what the model is directly trained to do (generate correct pronunciations of words) is only a small aspect of how it is evaluated empirically. Rather, models are evaluated largely against incidental consequences of learning, such as the relative rates of acquisition of different types of stimuli, differences in the processing time required to generate word pronunciations, accuracy and error types in pronouncing novel stimuli, or performance after different types of damage. The ways in which design decisions affect these aspects of performance are generally complex and often difficult to anticipate, further limiting the modeller's ability to fit data directly.

None of these comments should be taken to imply that the relationship between model and human performance is not important to the development of PDP models. To the contrary, success at accounting for empirical findings remains the primary means by which a model is evaluated. What must be clarified, however, is what exactly should be taken as the findings against which models should be judged, and what kinds of comparisons between model and human data are informative for understanding the cognitive and neural processes underlying reading.

It should be clear from our earlier discussion of overfitting by the DRC that we consider it unwise to place undue theoretical weight on the quantitative fit of a model to data from any individual empirical study. The results of a single study include large amounts of variance due to a variety of factors other than those under investigation. Even attempts at direct replication that vary only subjects or items often succeed only partially, or reproduce statistical effects but not the quantitative relationship among condition means. Robust behavioural findings that have been replicated across a number of studies provide a more appropriate basis for evaluating models.

Although testing a model with the same stimuli as used in a behavioural study provides a powerful means of comparing the two, care must be taken not to overinterpret the quantitative fit without clear measures of the reliability and precision of the findings themselves. This point is all the more important when considering item-level correlations between model performance and behavioural data from large corpora (e.g. Balota, Cortese, & Sergent-Marshall, 2004; Spieler & Balota, 1997). Even setting aside idiosyncratic aspects of experimental set-up and subject population, the factors that give rise to the most systematic item variance may not be those that are the most important to understand theoretically (Seidenberg & Plaut, 1998). For example, it is well known that word frequency has a strong impact on naming latencies. In PDP models, the influence of frequency on performance is indirect: it determines how often a word is presented during training, which in turn determines how strongly the word's spelling-sound correspondence influences weight values. Although knowledge of all words is superimposed within the same set of weights, the impact that individual words had during training nonetheless leads to faster and more accurate processing. The DRC model lacks a procedure for learning from word presentations, and so (log) frequency is directly stipulated in terms of the resting activation of word units, which, in turn, directly influence processing time. It is thus entirely unsurprising that the DRC model captures more frequency-related variance than PDP models (Coltheart et al., 2001), but in doing so, it provides no insight into the basis for such effects in people. Conversely, sometimes factors that account for little item-level variance within a large corpus can nonetheless lead to significant theoretical insight. For instance, the distinction between regularity (whether a word's pronunciation adheres to grapheme-phoneme correspondence rules) and consistency (the degree to which a word's pronunciation agrees with those of similarly spelled words) plays a major role in distinguishing dual-route from PDP approaches, but the amount of response time (RT) variance attributable to either factor is tiny on either account.

The argument for the importance of not overinterpreting individual behavioural experiments applies with equal force to the interpretation of single-case studies in cognitive neuropsychology and their implications for models. Such cases appear to be highly informative because they may produce behavioural effects that are larger and more dramatic than the corresponding effects in the normal population (for example, surface dyslexic patients make errors in pronouncing exception words for which normal subjects are merely slower) or, in some instances, they exhibit effects that are not observed in normals (such as semantic errors in single-word reading by deep dyslexic patients). The standard assumption in interpreting such cases is that all individuals share a common cognitive architecture, so that any observed deviation from control subjects is due solely to the effects of the lesion. This stance is, of course, belied by well-established individual differences in cognitive performance within the normal population in virtually every cognitive domain (see chapters in Boyle & Saklofske, 2004, for overviews). Of immediate relevance is individual variation in tasks such as word and nonword naming (e.g. Andrews & Scarratt, 1998). Zevin and Seidenberg (2006) illustrate how such individual differences can be explained in connectionist networks. The same model was run different times, corresponding to different subjects. Each model was exposed to somewhat different training examples, corresponding to small differences in reading experience. The different models produced different pronunciations for nonwords such as MOUP and WALF, as observed in people (Andrews & Scarratt, 1998; Seidenberg et al., 1994). Hence, the standard assumption underlying the interpretation of the naming performance of brain-injured patients—that there are no relevant premorbid individual differences—is contradicted by the Zevin and Seidenberg (2006) data.

The problem of interpreting single cases is exacerbated by the tendency of neuropsychologists to study (or report) only extreme cases of performance rather than the full distribution of observed cases. Moreover, the alternative of carrying out group analyses of large patient groups is also problematic due to individual differences in lesion characteristics and in the distribution of cognitive processes in the brain (Caramazza, 1986). Perhaps the best compromise is offered by a case series approach, in which behavioural effects are replicated across a series of patients with common aetiology (e.g. Lambon Ralph, Patterson, & Graham, 2003; Patterson et al., 2006; Rogers,

Lambon Ralph, Hodges, & Patterson, 2004; Woollams, Lambon Ralph, Hodges, & Patterson, 2005). On this perspective, atypical findings from single-case studies (e.g. Blazely et al., 2005; Derouesne & Beauvois, 1985) must be viewed with scepticism until replicated in the context of studies that assess a broader range of impaired performance, and theories or models that explain how the full range of cases arises.

Conclusions

The dual-route and PDP approaches to understanding word reading are both supported by explicit computational simulations, but the roles that these simulations play in theory development in the two cases is strikingly different. The DRC model of Coltheart et al. (2001) continues the long tradition of a bottom-up, data-driven approach to modelling: A model is designed to account for specific behavioural findings, and its match to those findings is the sole basis for evaluating it. These models aspire to what Chomsky (1965) called "descriptive adequacy". The PDP approach is different. The models are only a means to an end. The goal is a theory that explains behaviour (such as reading) and its brain bases. The models are a tool for developing and exploring the implications of a set of hypotheses concerning the neural basis of cognitive processing. Models are judged not only with respect to their ability to account for robust findings in a particular domain but also with respect to considerations that extend well beyond any single domain. These include the extent to which the same underlying computational principles apply across domains, the extent to which these principles can unify phenomena previously thought to be governed by different principles, the ability of the models to explain how behaviour might arise from a neurophysiological substrate, and so on. The models (and the theories they imperfectly instantiate) aspire to what Chomsky termed "explanatory adequacy". The deeper explanatory force derives from the fact that the architecture, learning, and processing mechanisms are independently motivated (such as by facts about the brain) rather than introduced in response to particular phenomena.[4]

The data-fitting approach appears to be better suited to capturing the results of individual studies, because that is the major goal of the approach. DRC thus seems satisfying because it accords with the intuition that accounting for a broad range of behavioural phenomena is always a good thing. Examining DRC more closely, however, suggests two fundamental problems with this strategy. First, the extent to which a model developed in this manner actually fits the data is questionable; fitting the results of one study but not others out of a series is problematic, as are parameter changes that fix one problem but create others. The long list of phenomena that DRC is said to account for needs to be assessed in light of these considerations. The second problem is that the short-term strategy of fitting models to data may in fact contravene the longer-term goal of uncovering fundamental principles. To use an economic metaphor, moves that maximize short-term profits (that is, fitting more data) may conflict with achieving longer-term economic growth (addressing additional phenomena) and prosperity (converging on the correct theory).

Whereas the DRC approach is data driven, the PDP approach is more theory driven because the models derive from a set of principles concerning neural computation and behaviour. The models are responsive to data insofar as they need to capture patterns that reflect basic characteristic of people's behaviour, particularly with regard to phenomena, such as consistency effects, that distinguish between theories, given their current states of development. The primary goal is not to implement the model that fits the most possible data; rather, it is to use evidence provided by the model, in conjunction with other evidence (such as about brain organization or neurophysiology, or about other types of behaviour) to converge on the correct theory of the phenomena.

The PDP approach to modelling is frustrating to some because there is no single simulation that constitutes *the* model of the domain. The models seem like a moving target: SM89 was interesting but ultimately limited by its phonological representation; PMSP96 largely fixed the phonological problem but introduced the idea that the orth:sem:phon pathway also contributes to pronunciation, something SM89 had not considered. Harm and Seidenberg (1999) used yet another phonological representation and focused on developmental phenomena; Harm and Seidenberg (2004) implemented both orth:sem and orth:phon:sem parts of the triangle but focused on data concerning activation of meaning rather than pronunciation, etc. Each model shares something with all of the others, namely the computational principles discussed above, but each model differs as well. Where, then, is the integrative model that puts the pieces all together?

The answer is, there is none and there is not likely to be one. The concept of a complete, integrative model is a non sequitur, given the nature of the modelling methodology—particularly the need to limit the scope of a model in order (a) to gain interpretable insights from it and (b) to complete a modelling project before the modeller loses interest or dies. The goal of the enterprise, as in the rest of science, is the development of a general theory that *abstracts away from* details of the phenomena to reveal general, fundamental principles (Putnam, 1973). Each model serves to explore a part of this theory-in-progress.

The proponents of DRC view these issues differently. In addition to the data-driven tenet, they emphasize that modelling should be "cumulative", with each successive model addressing the same phenomena as previous models, and new ones as well. Thus each model is a superset of the preceding ones. Here two questions arise. The narrow one is whether the dual-route framework is actually cumulative in the described sense. The second is whether *any* science proceeds in this manner. At first glance, the 2001 version of the DRC appears to be an extension of the 1993 version. In actuality, a variety of changes were made to parameter values and processing assumptions that render the relationship between the models far more complicated than the "nested" idea suggests. Certainly the two models share core assumptions about the nature of lexical versus sublexical processing, but they differ in the details of how these are implemented. Nor are the models strictly cumulative with respect to the empirical phenomena addressed: for example, the DRC models have used versions of the McClelland and Rumelhart (1981) interactive-activation model as the "lexical" component, and Coltheart et al. (2001) emphasize this genealogy. However, they did not develop DRC by first showing that it accounted for the same phenomena as the IA model (concerning, for example, word superiority effects) and then go on to show that it accounted for others as well.

This situation is not all that different from the relationship among successive versions of the triangle model (Harm & Seidenberg, 1999, 2004; Plaut et al., 1996; Seidenberg & McClelland, 1989): they share a common set of assumptions concerning the architecture of the reading system and basic learning mechanisms, and differ in specific (but important) implementational details. Like DRC, the models address different but overlapping sets of behavioural phenomena and thus are not strictly cumulative.

Whether science proceeds in the cumulative, nested manner described by Grainger and Jacobs (1998) and endorsed by Coltheart et al. (2001) has been strongly questioned, in different ways, by Kuhn (1962) Feyerabend (1975), Lakatos (1970), and many others. Even within the narrower confines of cognitive psychology, it is hard to point to a single example of a series of models that were developed in this strictly cumulative manner. By contrast, it is easy to identify cases in which researchers have developed a series of models that share common principles but differ in detail and address overlapping but nonidentical phenomena (e.g. Roger Ratcliff's diffusion models and John Anderson's ACT models). In short, science does not conform to an incremental, cumulative pattern, and neither has the development of the dual-route model.

Finally, *Rastle and Coltheart* (this volume) disparage the exploration of general principles characteristic of the PDP approach as a matter of "faith" and instead endorse modelling on the basis of "inference from evidence". The first of these assertions reflects confusion about our models, and the second confusion about their own. As we noted above, the "principles" that underlie the PDP approach are hypotheses about behaviour and its brain bases. These principles could be proved wrong (via normal scientific methods), in which case they would (and inevitably will) be modified. Whether the principles are correct is thus a question of fact, not an assertion of faith. The second assertion—that models should be developed wholly in response to data—does not accurately characterize the development of scientific theories in general or DRC in particular. Unless science is construed as random fact gathering in the manner of Francis Bacon, empirical studies are invariably conducted in a theoretical context. How did reading researchers decide that it was important to look at words with regular versus irregular pronunciations?

Words do not come labelled as "regular" or "irregular"; the distinction already assumes a nascent theory of the relationships between spelling and sound. In practice, science involves working back and forth between theory and data, with theories guiding what data to gather and the data feeding back on development of the theory. What Rastle and Coltheart apparently mean is that it is valid to introduce an element into a theory (or model) in response to specific findings. We have argued that this is ill-advised for many reasons. Such elements are literally ad hoc: "for the particular end or case at hand without consideration of wider application" (*Merriam-Webster Dictionary*). This leads to the over-fitting problem discussed above, a failure to capture generalizations *within* the target domain. It also leads to failures to capture generalizations that hold *across* domains—aspects of knowledge representation, learning, and processing that are not specific to reading at all. That reading exists at all is due to the fact that it exploits capacities that evolved for other purposes. Hence our emphasis on looking for principles that govern perception, cognition, learning, and their brain bases. Advances in understanding these principles can then facilitate understanding specific tasks such as reading.

Computational modelling has contributed significantly to our understanding of word reading, but considerable work remains to be done. Even basic issues, such as how spelling-sound knowledge is represented and applied, and its relation to lexical and semantic knowledge, remain unresolved. In such a context, it is premature to focus on the degree to which existing models fit specific empirical findings. Rather, the greatest progress will come from a broader perspective that attempts to integrate the study of word reading into the more general enterprise of elucidating the neural basis of cognitive processes. In this regard, the PDP approach to modelling—quite apart from the strengths and limitations of existing models—has much to offer.

Acknowledgements

The authors are grateful to Karalyn Patterson, Marcus Taft, and Sally Andrews for comments on an earlier version.

References

Andrews, S. (1989). Frequency and neighborhood effects on lexical access: Activation or search? *Journal of Experimental Psychology: Learning, Memory, and Cognition*, *15*, 802–814.

Andrews, S. (1992). Frequency and neighborhood effects on lexical access: Lexical similarity or orthographic redundancy? *Journal of Experimental Psychology: Learning, Memory, and Cognition*, *18*, 234–254.

Andrews, S., & Scarratt, D. R. (1998). Rule and analogy mechanisms in reading nonwords: Hough dou peapel rede gnew wirds? *Journal of Experimental Psychology: Human Perception and Performance*, *24*, 1052–1086.

Balota, D. A., Cortese, M. J., & Sergent-Marshall, S. D. (2004). Visual word recognition of single-syllable words. *Journal of Experimental Psychology: General, 133*, 283–316.

Blazely, A. M., Coltheart, M., & Casey, B. J. (2005). Semantic impairment with and without surface dyslexia: Implications for models of reading. *Cognitive Neuropsychology*, *22*, 695–717.

Boyle, G. J., & Saklofske, D. H. (2004). *Psychology of individual differences* (Vols 1–4). Thousand Oaks, CA: Sage.

Browman, C. P., & Goldstein, L. (1990). Representation and reality: Physical systems and phonological structure. *Journal of Phonetics*, *18*, 411–424.

Caramazza, A. (1986). On drawing inferences about the structure of normal cognitive systems from the analysis of patterns of impaired performance: The case for single-patient studies. *Brain and Cognition*, *5*, 41–66.

Chomsky, N. (1965). *Aspects of the theory of syntax*. Cambridge, MA: MIT Press.

Clark, H. H. (1969). Linguistic processes in deductive reasoning. *Psychological Review*, *85*, 59–108.

Collins, A. M., & Loftus, E. F. (1975). A spreading-activation theory of semantic processing. *Psychological Review*, *82*, 407–428.

Coltheart, M. (1978). Lexical access in simple reading tasks. In G. Underwood (Ed.), *Strategies of information processing* (pp. 151–216). London: Academic Press.

Coltheart, M. (1999). Modularity and cognition. *Trends in Cognitive Sciences*, *3*, 115–120.

Coltheart, M. (2000). Dual routes from print to speech and dual routes from print to meaning: Some theoretical issues. In A. Kennedy, R. Radach, J. Pynte, & D. Heller (Eds.), *Reading as a perceptual process*. Oxford: Elsevier.

Coltheart, M. (2004). Brain imaging, connectionism, and cognitive neuropsychology. *Cognitive Neuropsychology*, *21*, 21–25.

Coltheart, M. (in press). Acquired dyslexias and the computational modeling of reading. *Cognitive Neuropsychology*.

Coltheart, M., Curtis, B., Atkins, P., & Haller, M. (1993). Models of reading aloud: Dual-route and parallel distributed processing approaches. *Psychological Review*, *100*, 589–608.

Coltheart, M., Davelaar, E., Jonasson, J., & Besner, D. (1977). Access to the internal lexicon. In S. Dornic (Ed.), *Attention and performance VI* (pp. 535–555). Hillsdale, NJ: Lawrence Erlbaum Associates, Inc.

Coltheart, M., Rastle, K., Perry, C., Langdon, R., & Ziegler, J. (2001). DRC: A dual route cascaded model of visual word recognition and reading aloud. *Psychological Review*, *108*, 204–256.

Coltheart, M., Sartori, G., & Job, R. (1987). *The cognitive neuropsychology of language*. Hove, UK: Lawrence Erlbaum Associates, Ltd.

Cortese, M. J., & Simpson, G. B. (2000). Regularity effects in word naming: What are they? *Memory and Cognition*, *28*, 1269–1276.

Derouesne, J., & Beauvois, M. F. (1985). The "phonemic" stage in the non-lexical reading process: Evidence from a case of phonological alexia. In K. E. Patterson, M. Coltheart, & J. C. Marshall (Eds.), *Surface dyslexia*. Hove, UK: Lawrence Erlbaum Associates Ltd.

Dunn, J. C., & Kirsner, K. (Eds.) (2003). Forum on "What can we infer from double dissociations". *Cortex*, *39*, 129–202.

Feyerabend, P. (1975). *Against method*. London: Verso.

Fodor, J. A. (1983). *The modularity of mind: An essay on faculty psychology*. Cambridge, MA: MIT Press.

Glushko, R. J. (1979). The organization and activation of orthographic knowledge in reading aloud. *Journal of Experimental Psychology: Human Perception and Performance*, *5*, 674–691.

Grainger, J., & Jacobs, A. M. (1998). On localist connectionism and psychological science. In J. Grainger & A. M. Jacobs (Eds.), *Localist connectionist approaches to human cognition* (pp. 1–38). Mahwah, NJ: Lawrence Erlbaum Associates, Inc.

Harm, M. W., & Seidenberg, M. S. (1999). Phonology, reading acquisition, and dyslexia: Insights from connectionist models. *Psychological Review*, *106*, 491–528.

Harm, M. W., & Seidenberg, M. S. (2004). Computing the meanings of words in reading: Cooperative division of labor between visual and phonological processes. *Psychological Review*, *111*, 662–720.

Jared, D. (1997). Spelling-sound consistency affects the naming of high-frequency words. *Journal of Memory and Language*, *36*, 505–529.

Jared, D. (2002). Spelling-sound consistency and regularity effects in word naming. *Journal of Memory and Language*, *46*, 723–750.

Jared, D., McRae, K., & Seidenberg, M. S. (1990). The basis of consistency effects in word naming. *Journal of Memory and Language*, *29*, 687–715.

Juola, P., & Plunkett, K. (2000). Why double dissociations don't mean much. In G. Cohen, R. Johnston, & K Plunkett (Eds.), *Exploring cognition: Damaged brains and neural networks* (pp. 111–172). New York: Psychology Press.

Kuhn, T. (1962). *The structure of scientific revolutions*. Chicago: University of Chicago Press.

Lakatos, I. (Ed.) (1970). *Criticism and the growth of knowledge*. Cambridge: Cambridge University Press.

Lambon Ralph, M. A., Patterson, K., & Graham, N. (2003). Homogeneity and heterogeneity in mild cognitive impairment and Alzheimer's disease: A cross-sectional and longitudinal study of 55 cases. *Brain*, *126*, 2350–2362.

Lichtheim, L. (1885). On aphasia. *Brain*, *7*, 433–484.

Marshall, J. C., & Newcombe, F. (1973). Patterns of paralexia: A psycholinguistic approach. *Journal of Psycholinguistic Research*, *2*, 175–199.

Massaro, D. W. (1989). Testing between the TRACE model and the fuzzy logical model of speech perception. *Cognitive Psychology*, *21*, 398–421.

McCann, R., & Besner, D. (1987). Reading pseudohomophones: Implications for models of pronunciation assembly and the locus of word-frequency effects in naming. *Journal of Experimental Psychology: Human Perception and Performance*, *13*, 14–24.

McClelland, J. L., & Rumelhart, D. E. (1981). An interactive activation model of context effects in letter perception. I. An account of basic findings. *Psychological Review*, *88*, 375–407.

Newell, A. (1973). You can't play 20 questions with nature and win. In W. G. Chase (Ed.), *Visual information processing* (pp. 283–308). New York: Academic Press.

Paap, K., & Noel, R. W. (1991). Dual route models of print to sound: Still a good horse race. *Psychological Research*, *53*, 13–24.

Patterson, K. E., Marshall, J. C., & Coltheart, M. (1985). *Surface dyslexia: Neuropsychological and cognitive studies of phonological reading*. Hove, UK: Lawrence Erlbaum Associates Ltd.

Patterson, K., Lambon Ralph, M. A., Jefferies, E., Woollams, A., Jones, R., Hodges,

J. R., et al. (2006). "Pre-semantic" cognition in semantic dementia: Six deficits in search of an explanation. *Journal of Cognitive Neuroscience*, *18*, 169–183.

Plaut, D. C. (1995). Double dissociation without modularity: Evidence from connectionist neuropsychology. *Journal of Clinical and Experimental Neuropsychology*, *17*, 291–321.

Plaut, D. C. (1997). Structure and function in the lexical system: Insights from distributed models of word reading and lexical decision. *Language and Cognitive Processes*, *12*, 765–805.

Plaut, D. C., & Kello, C. T. (1999). The emergence of phonology from the interplay of speech comprehension and production: A distributed connectionist approach. In B. MacWhinney (Ed.), *The emergence of language* (pp. 381–415). Mahwah, NJ: Lawrence Erlbaum Associates, Inc.

Plaut, D. C., & McClelland, J. L. (2000). Stipulating versus discovering representations: Commentary on M. Page, Connectionist modeling in psychology: A localist manifesto. *Behavioral and Brain Sciences*, *23*, 489–491.

Plaut, D. C., McClelland, J. L., Seidenberg, M. S., & Patterson, K. E. (1996). Understanding normal and impaired word reading: Computational principles in quasi-regular domains. *Psychological Review*, *103*, 56–115.

Putnam, H. (1973). Reductionism and the nature of psychology. *Cognition*, *2*, 131–146.

Ratcliff, R. (1978). A theory of memory retrieval. *Psychological Review*, *85*, 59–108.

Rayner, K. (1998). Eye movements in reading and information processing: 20 years of research. *Psychological Bulletin*, *124*, 372–422.

Reichle, E. D., Pollatsek, A., & Rayner, K. (1998). Toward a model of eye movement control in reading. *Psychological Review*, *105*, 125–157.

Rogers, T. T., Lambon Ralph, M. A., Hodges, J. R., & Patterson, K. (2004). Natural selection: The impact of semantic impairment on lexical and object decision. *Cognitive Neuropsychology*, *21*, 331–352.

Sears, C. R., Hino, Y., & Lupker, S. J. (1995). Neighborhood size and neighborhood frequency effects in word recognition. *Journal of Experimental Psychology: Human Perception and Performance*, *21*, 876–900.

Seidenberg, M. S. (1985). The time course of phonological code activation in two writing systems. *Cognition*, *19*, 1–10.

Seidenberg, M. S. (1988). Cognitive neuropsychology and language: The state of the art. *Cognitive Neuropsychology*, *5*, 403–426.

Seidenberg, M. S., & McClelland, J. L. (1989). A distributed, developmental model of word recognition and naming. *Psychological Review*, *96*, 523–568.

Seidenberg, M. S., & Plaut, D. C. (1998). Evaluating word-reading models at the item level: Matching the grain of theory and data. *Psychological Science*, *9*, 234–237.

Seidenberg, M. S., Plaut, D. C., Petersen, A. S., McClelland, J. L., & McRae, K. (1994). Nonword pronunciation and models of word recognition. *Journal of Experimental Psychology: Human Perception and Performance*, *20*, 1177–1196.

Seidenberg, M. S., Waters, G. S., Barnes, M. A., & Tanenhaus, M. K. (1984). When does irregular spelling or pronunciation influence word recognition? *Journal of Verbal Learning and Verbal Behavior*, *23*, 383–404.

Shallice, T. (1988). *From neuropsychology to mental structure*. Cambridge: Cambridge University Press.

Smith, E. E., Shoben, E. J., & Rips, L. J. (1974). Structure and process in semantic memory: A featural model for semantic decisions. *Psychological Review*, *81*, 214–241.

Spieler, D. H., & Balota, D. A. (1997). Bringing computational models of word naming down to the item level. *Psychological Science*, *8*, 411–416.

Sternberg, S. (1969). The discovery of processing stages: Extensions of Donders' method. *Acta Psychologica*, *30*, 276–315.

Taft, M., & Russell, B. (1992). Pseudohomophone naming and the word frequency effect. *Quarterly Journal of Experimental Psychology: Human Experimental Psychology*, *45A*, 51–71.

Taraban, R., & McClelland, J. L. (1987). Conspiracy effects in word recognition. *Journal of Memory and Language*, *26*, 608–631.

Thomas, M. S. C., & Karmiloff-Smith, A. (2003). Connectionist models of development, developmental disorders and individual differences. In R. J. Sternberg, J. Lautrey, & T. Lubart (Eds.), *Models of intelligence: International perspectives* (pp. 133–150). Washington, DC: American Psychological Association.

Van Orden, G., Pennington, B. F., & Stone, G. O. (2001). What do double dissociations prove? *Cognitive Science*, *25*, 111–172.

Waters, G. S., & Seidenberg, M. S. (1985). Spelling-sound effects in reading: Time course and decision criteria. *Memory and Cognition*, *13*, 557–572.

Woollams, A., Lambon Ralph, M. A., Hodges, J. R., & Patterson, K. (2005). *SD-squared: On the association between semantic dementia and surface dyslexia*. Paper presented to the Experimental Psychology Society meeting, April 2005.

Zevin, J. D., & Seidenberg, M. S. (2006). Simulating consistency effects and individual differences in nonword naming: A comparison of current models. *Journal of Memory and Language*, *54*, 145–160.

Notes

1 Note that we are not asserting that a model has to be tested against every study of a given phenomenon that has appeared in the literature. Experiments often yield varying results, for a variety of reasons. Some studies are clear outliers, insofar as they fail to replicate, or are contradicted by, multiple other studies. Some studies yield results that may be valid but have not been replicated, and so their status is unclear. It is appropriate to omit outliers and unclear cases in testing a model. However, it would not be appropriate to select studies on the basis of whether a model simulates them correctly or not. The safest strategy is to focus on robust phenomena that have replicated in multiple studies.

2 Coltheart et al.'s simulation of Jared's (1997) study is problematic. They asserted that consistency effects in studies such as hers were due to two confounding factors: the inconsistent words included some items that DRC treats as exceptions, and included more words that create "whammies", temporary misapplications of rules based on a left-to-right pass through the word. However, when the suspect items are removed, the consistency effect remains in Jared's data, but not in the DRC simulation.

3 The concept of "localist representation" engenders some confusion. A representation is localist or distributed only with respect to a specific set of entities. For example, in McClelland and Rumelhart's interactive activation model, the representations at the letter level are localist with respect to letters but distributed with respect to words; the same is true of DRC. A PDP model such as that of Harm and Seidenberg (2004) used localist representations of letters in orthography, but distributed representations for words in orthography, phonology, and semantics. The contrast is not between models employing localist versus distributed representations, since all of the above models include both. Rather,

DRC is committed to the narrower claim that there are localist representations of *words*.

4 The usefulness of the distinction between descriptive and explanatory adequacy is distinct from questions concerning the extent to which Chomsky's own theories achieve these goals.

3 Considering the junction model of lexical processing

Christopher T. Kello
Department of Psychology, George Mason University, USA

The work presented in this chapter arose from two questions that may at first appear unrelated: should we accept the premise that skilled word reading is supported by lexical and sublexical routes of processing, and how can we model the learning of orthographic and phonological representations for multisyllabic words? The field as a whole has answered "yes" to the first question, but is mostly silent with regard to the second. Here I will consider an alternative to lexical and sublexical routes, one in which these are modes of processing instead of components of processing. My colleagues and I have pursued this idea by exploring theories of lexical processing in which orthographic, phonological, and semantic codes are all mediated by one level of representation. In our pursuit, we were forced to confront the long-standing problem of modelling multisyllabic words. This chapter is an account of our efforts that have recently culminated in the junction model of lexical processing.

The story begins with yet another question: how does speech fit into theories of word reading? It is only common sense that written language processes are built upon spoken language processes. Spoken language takes precedence in all senses of the word. It is during speech acquisition that the phonological, morphological, and semantic structures of words are learned. These structures are learned as a bridge between speech signals (acoustic, optical, and articulatory) and the rest of the language system. When orthographic structures are introduced, they must be learned in a way that fits with the bridge already in place.

So how are orthographic inputs mapped onto spoken language processes in current theories of word reading? An answer can be found in diagrams of the two major current frameworks, shown in Figure 3.1. In the dual-route cascaded (DRC) model (Coltheart, Curtis, Atkins, & Haller, 1993; Coltheart, Rastle, Perry, Langdon, & Ziegler, 2001), orthographic inputs connect with the spoken language system via two routes of processing, one lexical and the other sublexical. The sublexical processes break down the orthographic forms of words into sequences of graphemes, and a rule is used to essentially map each grapheme onto a corresponding phoneme. Phonemes would presumably be learned during spoken language acquisition, and should therefore be

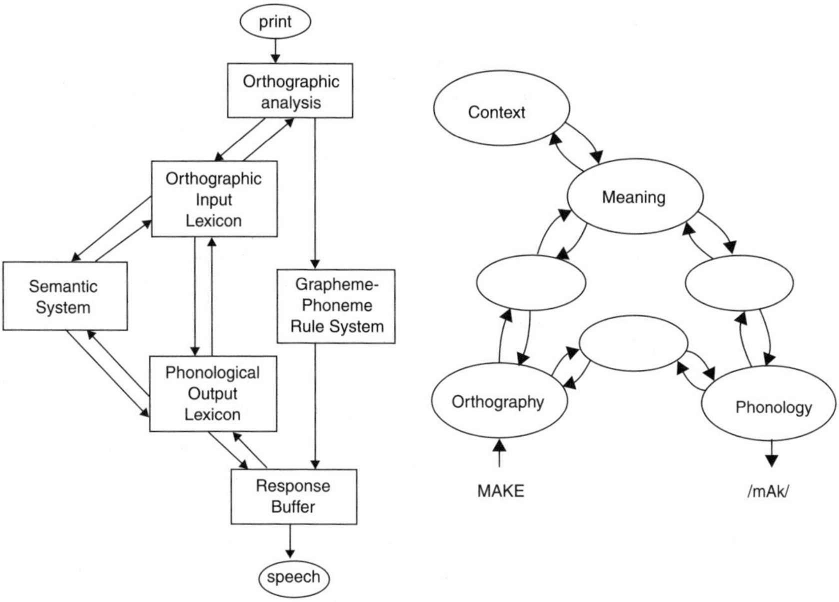

Figure 3.1 Diagrams of two theories of the lexical processing system. The one on the left is taken from Coltheart et al. (2001), and the one on the right is taken from Seidenberg and McClelland (1989); both are reprinted with permission. Lexical and sublexical routes of processing can be found in both theories.

considered as part of the spoken language system. The lexical processes associate each orthographic word form as a whole with semantic and phonological representations that would also be learned during spoken language acquisition.

The answer is similar for the triangle framework of lexical processing (Plaut, McClelland, Seidenberg, & Patterson, 1996; Seidenberg & McClelland, 1989). Orthographic inputs are mapped onto phonological and semantic representations via two corresponding sets of hidden units. The orthography-phonology mapping is sublexical in nature because in most languages there tend to be systematic relations between orthographic and phonological units that are smaller than the word. The orthography-semantics mapping is lexical in nature because the relation between orthographic units and meaning is mostly unsystematic within individual morphemes (thus, in English, the letter "d" bears no relation to the meaning of DOG).

Why is it hypothesized in these frameworks that orthographic inputs connect with the spoken language system via two separate routes, one lexical and the other sublexical? One reason is historical: researchers at one time believed that the functions performed by skilled readers required these two routes. On the one hand, skilled readers can pronounce words like PINT and HAVE even though they do not conform to the systematic relations between orthography and phonology. This ability suggests that a lexical route is necessary to store the pronunciations of such irregular words individually. On the other hand, skilled readers can give plausible pronunciations for nonwords like PILT and HOVE. This ability suggests that a sublexical route is necessary to assemble novel pronunciations from grapheme-phoneme correspondences or the like.

As it turns out, the ability to read aloud both irregular words and nonwords does not necessarily require a lexical and sublexical route. Glushko (1979) explained how lexical representations might be used to generate nonword pronunciations via a process of analogy. For instance the pronunciation of PILT might be computed as a blend of words like SILT and PILL. Such an analogy model would be able to generate pronunciations for both irregular words and nonwords via a single route of processing. Seidenberg and McClelland (1989) then showed how a single level of distributed representation in a connectionist model can be used to generate pronunciations for both kinds of items.

These demonstrations are valuable in delineating the space of viable theories, but most researchers still believe that orthographic inputs are connected to the spoken language system via two routes. The main reason is evidence for the dissociation of lexical and sublexical processes. This evidence has most notably come from surface versus phonological dyslexia in their acquired forms. Surface dyslexia is characterized by poor reading of irregular words with relatively intact reading of nonwords (Behrmann & Bub, 1992). Phonological dyslexia is characterized as the opposite, thereby forming a double dissociation (Funnell, 1983). Double dissociations are usually interpreted as evidence for separable processes, and this dissociation is no exception. How could surface and phonological dyslexia occur without a lexical route and a sublexical route? The question seems hard to answer, not to mention other arguments for lexical and sublexical routes that have been made on the basis of evidence for strategic control of the two routes (Monsell, Patterson, Graham, Hughes, & Milroy, 1992; Zevin & Balota, 2000).

Considering a shared-route architecture

The idea of lexical and sublexical routes appears to have good empirical support. But let us again consider the interface of orthography with the spoken language system. Does it make good sense for orthography to interface along these two routes? The core competency of spoken language is to map between sound and meaning. We can probably all agree that processes and representations are learned during spoken language acquisition to support this mapping. Reading requires a mapping to sound and meaning. What if orthography interfaced with the representations that mediate sound and meaning (Figure 3.2), rather than with sound and meaning themselves?

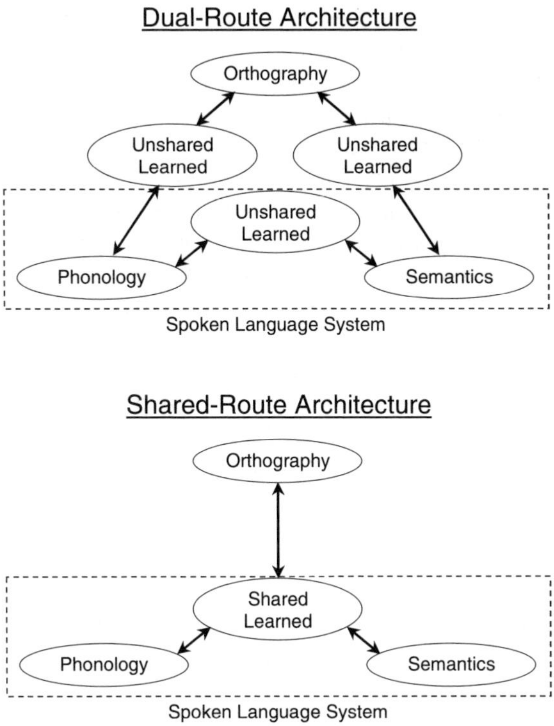

Figure 3.2 Diagrams comparing dual-route and shared-route architectures. The well-known triangle model is used to illustrate the theoretical commitments that apply more generally to dual-route architectures. The shared-route architecture is implemented in this chapter as the junction model of lexical processing. The outlined portions represent the spoken language parts of these architectures, which are presumably in place prior to the development of the written language parts.

This idea has a certain efficiency to it. To start with, only one route of processing would be needed between orthography and the spoken language system. The loss of a route seems more efficient in principle, but there is a more specific advantage in this case. Orthographic inputs would be interfaced with what may be construed as morphological representations, because morphology is at the intersection of phonology and semantics (Plaut & Gonnerman, 2000). If so, morphological structure would not need to be duplicated across two routes, as it is with lexical and sublexical routes. Having two routes leads to the duplication of morphology because the relation between semantics and phonology is structured similarly to that between semantics and orthography.

So far so good, but there is an obvious question. What about the evidence for a dissociation between lexical and sublexical processes? Does this evidence already rule out a shared-route architecture? Not necessarily. For one thing,

Patterson and her colleagues have proposed that surface and phonological dyslexia may be explained by damage to semantic and phonological representations, respectively (Patterson & Hodges, 1992; Patterson & Marcel, 1992). The logic of this idea can be seen in the fact that, in the dual-route architecture, one terminal of the lexical route is semantics, and one terminal of the sublexical route is phonology. The idea has been criticized on the grounds that surface and phonological dyslexias do not always coincide with semantic and phonological impairments (Coltheart, 1996), but there have been counterarguments (Patterson & Lambon Ralph, 1999). It is fair to say that the debate is undecided, which means that the shared-route verdict remains undecided.

The shared-route architecture gains even more credibility when we consider a second way to account for the lexical/sublexical dissociation. Kello and his colleagues (Kello, 2003; Kello, Sibley, & Plaut, 2005a; Sibley & Kello, 2004) recently showed how lexical and sublexical processing can be two modes of a single processing route. A control parameter termed "input gain" was manipulated in a series of demonstration models with only one route of processing. The single route was mediated by either localist or distributed representations. Input gain had the effect of scaling the net inputs to processing units. For both kinds of representation, low and high levels of input gain shifted the models between *regularity-based* and *item-based* modes of processing, respectively.

These modes resulted in a clear double dissociation, as shown in Figure 3.3. The models were given a mapping task for a corpus of items that mostly but not entirely conformed to a simple rule (the identity mapping). Mapping accuracy is plotted as a function of input gain for regular trained items (those conforming to the identity mapping), irregular trained items (those not conforming to the identity mapping), and untrained items. The pattern of results was the same for both localist and distributed models. At low input gain, performance was near perfect for regular and novel items, but nearly all of the irregular items were "regularized", that is, incorrectly given the identity mapping. This performance profile is analogous to the defining characteristics of surface dyslexia. At high input gain, performance was highly accurate for all trained items, but poor for novel items. This profile is analogous to the defining characteristics of phonological dyslexia.

Input gain caused a double dissociation for both localist and distributed representations because it affected the scope of knowledge that was brought to bear on the mapping task. At low input gain, each input pattern was mapped according to a wide range of trained items with similar patterns. Irregularities were essentially averaged out of the mapping. At high input gain, each input pattern was mapped according to a much smaller range of similar items, hindering the generalization that relies on regularities spanning across multiple items.

Input gain demonstrates a mechanism by which lexical (item-based) and sublexical (regularity-based) processing may be two modes of operation in a

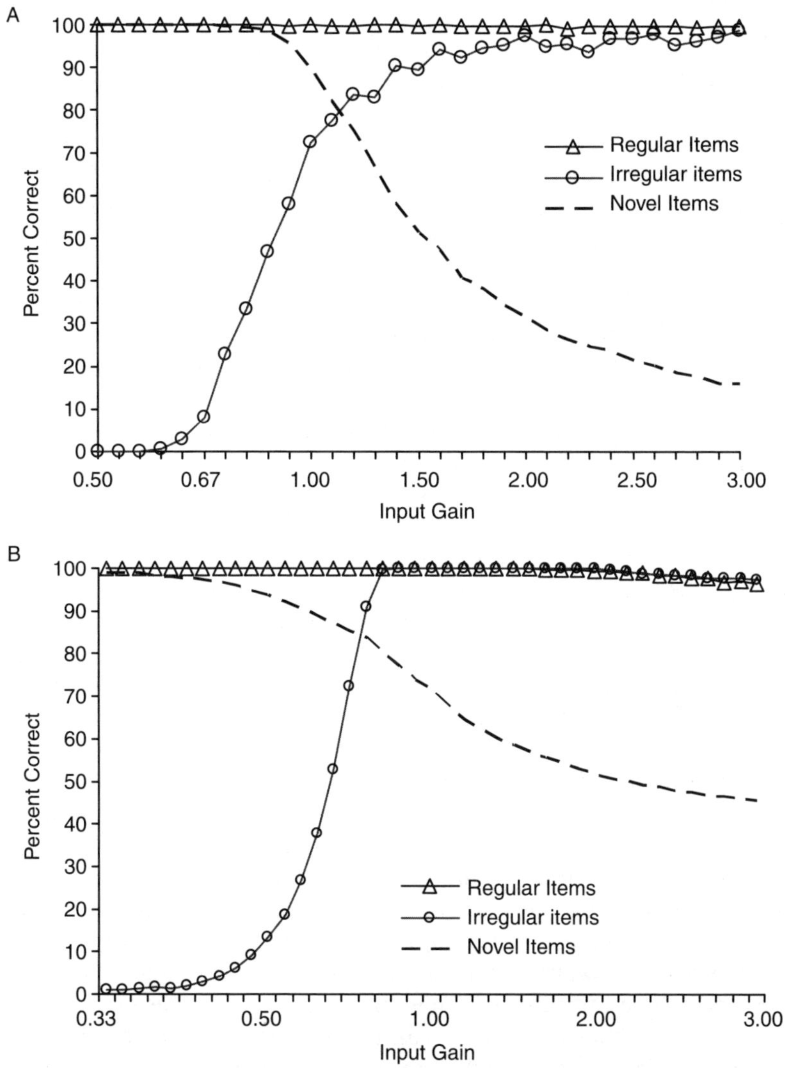

Figure 3.3 Performance of localist (A) and distributed (B) models as a function of item type and input gain (reprinted with permission from Kello et al., 2005a).

shared-route architecture. Surface and phonological dyslexia could therefore result from trauma or developmental abnormalities that restrict the flexibility of processing to a single mode. While there are well-established neural correlates to input gain (Fellous & Linster, 1998), there are currently no data to determine whether such correlates may play a role in surface or phonological dyslexia.

A hint of evidence in tempo naming

At this point in the argument, we can say that there are principled reasons for considering a shared route of processing between orthography, phonology, and semantics. We can also say that a shared-route architecture is at least viable in the face of dissociations between lexical and sublexical processes. But is there any evidence in favour of such a route? In fact, the idea was pursued in the first place because of observed naming errors that were readily accommodated by a shared-route architecture, but not by dual-route architectures.

The naming errors came from the tempo-naming task that was introduced by Kello and Plaut (Kello, 2004; Kello & Plaut, 2000). In this task, an audiovisual metronome is used to control the amount of time between the onset of a letter string and the initiation of a naming response. The metronome is played for a set number of beats on each trial, and a letter string is displayed on the final beat. Participants are instructed to name the letter string such that their response is timed with what would be the next beat of the metronome. Feedback is given at the end of each trial to indicate whether the response was initiated early or late relative to the metronome. Fast tempos can be used to induce a speed/accuracy trade-off because they reduce the amount of time between stimulus onset and the cue to respond.

Numerous experiments have shown that fast tempos lead to four basic categories of errors: articulatory errors (e.g. slurs and mis-starts), regularizations (e.g. PINT pronounced to rhyme with MINT), lexicalizations (e.g. BOARD pronounced as a similar word like BROAD), and nonword errors (e.g. STINT pronounced as a similar nonword like STIT). The question is, which kinds of errors should become more prevalent under time pressure, given a separation of lexical and sublexical routes? To answer this question, Kello and Plaut (2000) ran simulations of the tempo-naming task with the triangle and DRC models of lexical processing. They found that both models generated a comparable increase in both regularization and lexicalization errors under time pressure. The time pressure caused by faster tempos was simulated by sampling the models' outputs at earlier points in the time course of processing relative to stimulus onset. In another simulation, Kello and Plaut (2003) found the same result for the triangle model when time pressure was simulated by increasing the rate of processing.

The tempo-naming experiments have yielded a different result. As tempos increase, the rate of regularization errors has been shown to remain constant while the rates of other types of errors, including lexicalization errors, increase. The lack of an increase in regularization errors means that time pressure in the tempo-naming task does not lead to a misapplication of sublexical spelling-sound correspondences. But this is precisely what happened when time pressure was implemented in the triangle and DRC models. So the question now becomes, how can time pressure be implemented in a model of lexical processing such that it does not lead to a misapplication of spelling-sound correspondences?

One possible answer can be found by delving into the reason behind the effect of time pressure in the triangle model. As mentioned earlier, the mapping between orthography and phonology is much more systematic (due to spelling-sound correspondences) than the mapping between semantics and either orthography or phonology, at least in English. Distributed representations are more adept at processing systematic mappings than arbitrary mappings. This is because, by default, similar inputs generate similar distributed representations, and similar distributed representations generate similar outputs. As a result of this adeptness, the relatively direct mapping between orthography and phonology is computed more quickly in the triangle model, compared with the same mapping that is mediated by semantics (Van Orden, Bosman, Goldinger, & Farrar, 1997). The consequence is that spelling-sound correspondences represented in the direct mapping lead to increases in regularization errors when time pressure is simulated.

One way to avoid the increases in regularization errors is to simply remove the direct mapping from orthography to phonology. The shared-route architecture does this by essentially combining the route from orthography to phonology with the route from orthography to semantics. Kello and Plaut (2003) reported a simulation of the shared-route architecture to show that it could in fact provide a closer account of the observed errors in tempo naming than the triangle model. They also showed that the shared-route architecture can account for the hallmark effects of printed frequency and spelling-sound regularity in word reading. It should be mentioned that the dual-route architecture may ultimately be reconciled with the tempo-naming data, but the point here is that it was the challenge of the tempo-naming data that led us to reconsider the dual-route architecture.

Large-scale modelling and the problem of multisyllabic words

I have now laid out the logical, empirical, and computational arguments in favour of a shared-route architecture. These arguments may not sway a proponent of dual-route architectures, but they should at least provide justification for further pursuit. The model presented by Kello and Plaut (2003) was a good start, but it was small (a corpus of 470 words) in comparison to the DRC and triangle models that have been reported. The precedent set by these models calls for a large-scale simulation of the shared-route architecture. The term "large-scale" in the domain of lexical processing currently refers to models that contain roughly between 3000 and 8000 words.

But if we fully embrace the notion that large-scale simulations provide strong tests of theories of lexical processing, we must go beyond the extant models because they are restricted to processing monosyllabic words. One might at first think that the inclusion of multisyllabic words is only a matter of scaling up the current models, but in fact we are forced to confront a fundamental issue that was heretofore marginalized: how does one represent variable-length sequences of letters or sounds? Moreover, how are such representations learned? Current models provide inadequate answers to the first question, and no answers to the second question.

The representation of multisyllabic word forms is difficult because it engenders a binding problem (Rosenblatt, 1961; von der Malsburg, 1981) in which sounds or letters must be bound to their positions in the word form. Information must be learned and represented about elements with respect to their positions, as well as independently of their positions. Slot-based codes have been used in most models, but these engender the alignment and dispersion problems that were explained by Plaut et al. (1996). The "Wickelfeatures" that were used by Seidenberg and McClelland engender a different set of problems (see Pinker & Prince, 1988). Perhaps a scheme of representation can be engineered to overcome the known problems of orthographic and phonological representation (for instance, see *C. J. Davis*, this volume), but ultimately one must come to grips with the fact that these representations are learned, not engineered.

This fact aside, it is important to recognize the progress that has been made with the extant models using engineered representations of monosyllabic words. There were and still are many theoretical questions for which the problem of multisyllabic words can be put off until a later date. It also must be noted that there have been very few data on multisyllabic words to test the models against. However, the recent development of the Elexicon database has drastically changed the size of the playing field (Balota et al., 2002). The database currently contains lexical-decision and word-naming data for over 30,000 English words, and most of these words are multisyllabic. These data constitute a vast source of evidence for testing models of lexical processing, but they cannot fully be put to use until the problem of multisyllabic words is addressed.

The upcoming junction model is a first-pass effort at testing the shared-route architecture against the Elexicon database. In this model, the learning of multisyllabic words was accomplished by drawing upon earlier modelling work by Plaut and Kello (1999). They introduced a theory of phonological development in which the phonological representations of words are learned in the service of speech comprehension, production, and imitation. The theory was implemented in a connectionist model in which phonological representations were learned through three language tasks: (1) the integration of variable-length acoustic sequences into fixed-width representations, and the use of those fixed-width representations to (2) activate semantic knowledge (i.e. speech comprehension) and (3) generate variable-length sequences of articulatory outputs (i.e. speech production).

The means of learning multisyllabic word forms lies in this model's ability to learn fixed-width representations of variable-length sequences. Mono- and multisyllabic word forms vary widely in their numbers of letters and sounds. By converting such variable-length sequences into fixed-width representations, a model can leverage the benefits of distributed representation and processing. Such representations would provide a common basis for relating word forms of different lengths, and for generalizing to novel word forms of varying lengths. Information about letters and sounds would be learned both within and across their positions in orthographic and phonological word forms.

Kello and his colleagues (Kello, Sibley, & Colombi, 2004; Kello, Sibley, Plaut, & Elman, submitted, 2005b) recently provided a proof-of-concept that the methods developed by Plaut and Kello (1999) can indeed be used to learn representations of both mono- and multisyllabic word forms. The basic innovation was to extend the simple recurrent network architecture (SRN) (Elman, 1990; Jordan, 1986) to learn fixed-width representations in the dual service of both encoding and decoding variable-length sequences. SRNs have been used most often in models of language processing to learn the transitional probabilities of sequences by training them to predict each subsequent element from previous elements. While transitional probabilities can be used naturally as assays of grammatical learning (Christiansen, Allen, & Seidenberg, 1998; Cleeremans, Servan-Schreiber, & McClelland, 1989), they do not translate directly into a method for learning fixed-width representations. The problem is that the task of learning transitional probabilities requires the network to hold *only* enough information about a sequence to predict its next element. Thus, there is no pressure to encode or decode an entire sequence.

The *sequence encoder* developed by Kello and his colleagues creates the necessary pressure by coupling two SRNs in order to simulate what is essentially the imitation of variable-length sequences (Figure 3.4). An encoder SRN is trained to generate a fixed-width representation of a given sequence, and a decoder SRN is trained to regenerate that sequence from the fixed-width representation. At the beginning of training, representations generated by the encoder SRN are mostly arbitrary, and the decoder SRN is pressured

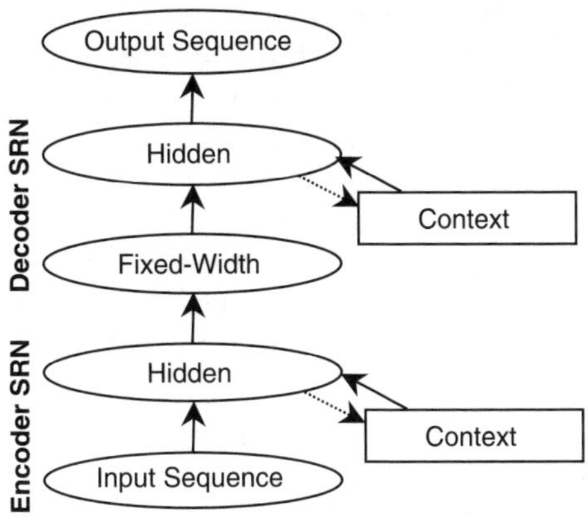

Figure 3.4 Diagram of the sequence encoder architecture.

to reproduce the input sequences from these arbitrary representations. As learning progresses, weight changes in the encoder SRN adapt the fixed-width representations to error signals that come from the decoder SRN. At the same time, weight changes in the decoder SRN adapt to the fixed-width representations that are generated by the encoder SRN.

Simulations with small, artificial sets of sequences have shown that the sequence encoder is capable of learning to encode and decode variable-length sequences (Kello et al., 2004; submitted, 2005b). Learning also generalized very well to novel sequences. Analyses showed that the elements of a sequence were represented both with and without respect to their positions, where position is defined either in terms of rank order or relative to other elements in the sequence. Moreover, large-scale models have been built to learn orthographic and phonological representations for nearly 75,000 English words. These models were shown to generalize very well to legal pseudowords: 82% of over 71,000 phonological pseudoword forms were processed correctly, and 76% of over 74,000 orthographic pseudoword forms were processed correctly. Generalization to illegal nonwords was only 18% and 23%, respectively, which indicates that learning was shaped by the structures of English word forms. This shaping was also seen in that the errors made by the sequence encoder tended to create legal word forms. Space limitations prohibit a more detailed discussion of the sequence encoder, but the brief overview given here is meant only to motivate the sequence encoder's use in the upcoming model of lexical processing.

The last kind of representation to consider is semantics. At first, it may not be clear whether the sequence encoder is appropriate for simulating the learning of semantic representations, but it would be if one views such representations as being formed at the junction of perception and action. For instance, consider how the semantic aspects of a word like BAT are grounded in our experiences with bats and batting. It is plausible to hypothesize that, at some level of abstraction, our perceptual representations of bats and batting have structure that is systematically related to our action representations of bats and batting, e.g., the shape and weight of a bat captures something about how bats are perceived, as well as how they are acted upon. The principle of perception/action junctions would lead one to hypothesize representations that capture the common ground between perception and action that exists for any given concept denoted by a word. This idea has much in common with Gibson's affordances (Gibson, 1979). If one goes on to say that even abstract concepts are grounded in experience, the idea also has much in common with Lakoff and Johnson's conceptual metaphors (Lakoff & Johnson, 1980), and the recent movement toward embodied cognition (Wilson, 2002).

As appealing as the idea may sound, there are many questions that remain to be answered. What would the sequences of perceptual inputs and action outputs consist of? How would one handle polysemy and the contextual flexibility of meaning? Could this embodied idea cover even the most abstract aspects of semantics? And so on. In the upcoming model, these questions are set aside by using semantic representations built from textual co-occurrence statistics as proxies for junction representations. While one could raise questions about the validity of using textual co-occurrences to derive semantic representations (see Harm & Seidenberg, 2004), they are at least sufficient approximations given the current knowledge of lexical semantics.

Putting it all together: A large-scale pilot of the junction model

We now have the motivation and means of implementing a large-scale model of lexical processing according to a shared-route architecture. The model presented here was built from a corpus of 45,273 English words, and tested against response times for over 30,000 of those words. The simulated response times were compared against response times in the Elexicon database (Balota et al., 2002). The proportions of explained variance are benchmarked against regression models with word frequency, length, and articulatory factors as the predictors. Results from the pilot model are also benchmarked against results from Plaut et al.'s (1996) simulations and the DRC model of word recognition (Coltheart et al., 2001). The chapter closes with a discussion of how the pilot model can be improved and extended to more fully address the range of phenomena relevant to lexical processing.

Model architecture

The junction model implemented here is diagrammed in Figure 3.5. The orthographic, phonological, and semantic representations were first constructed separate from each other, and then bound by a set of mediating

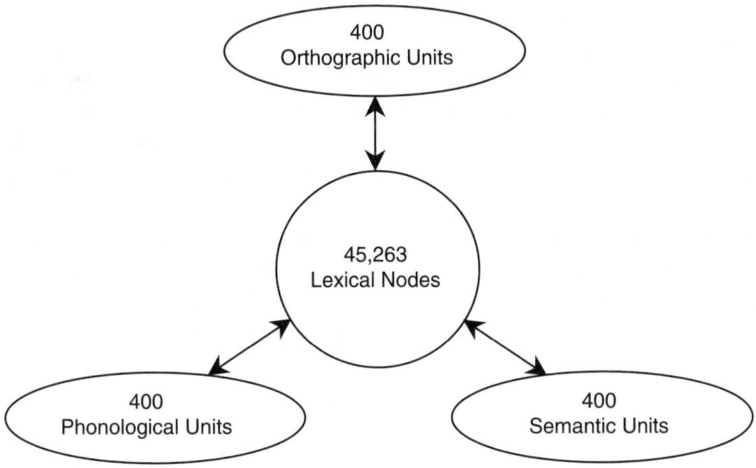

Figure 3.5 Architecture of the junction model. Arrows denote full connectivity.

representations. The pilot model was constructed piecemeal in order to simplify matters. The theory actually calls for spoken language acquisition to be simulated as the learning and binding of phonological and semantic representations. Then the learning of orthographic representations would be gradually integrated with the spoken language system. For the sake of simplicity, this developmental side to the model was not implemented here, but is planned for future simulations.

Orthographic, phonological, and semantic representations

Sequence encoders were used to learn an orthographic and a phonological representation for each of the 45,263 words in the training corpus. The training corpus comprised the intersection of the Carnegie Mellon University (CMU) pronunciation dictionary, the COALS database of word co-occurrences (Rohde, Gonnerman, & Plaut, in preparation, 2006), and the Microsoft spelling dictionary. The orthographic and phonological representations were learned with two pairs of sequence encoders, one pair for orthography and one pair for phonology. The orthography pair learned to encode and decode sequences of capital letters that comprised English words. The phonology pair learned to encode and decode sequences of phonemes. Each letter was coded by a pattern of 10 binary features, such as "has a left vertical line" and "has a curve". Each phoneme was coded by 10 phonetic features, such as frication and voicing, plus two additional features to code for lexical stress on vowels.

The pairs were used to create two hierarchical models of two stages each. The first stage was used to learn to encode and decode sequences of letters or phonemes into vowel groups that roughly corresponded to syllables. The second stage was used to learn to encode and decode sequences of vowel groups into words, using 400 hidden units for the fixed-width representations. This two-stage method was used to reduce the number of elements that any one sequence encoder was required to process. The two-stage method was a simplification that helped make progress toward the larger effort of building a large-scale model of lexical processing. As mentioned earlier, more recent work with sequence encoders has shown that orthographic and phonological representations of words can be learned in a single stage (Kello et al., submitted, 2005b).

At the end of training, the sequence encoders could correctly encode and decode over 99% of the trained words. Two 400-bit codes were learned for each word, one orthographic code and one phonological code. The similarity structure of these codes is crudely illustrated in Figure 3.6. Six example words are listed along with their closest neighbours, three for orthography and three for phonology. Neighbours are listed in order of similarity as measured by the number of bits in common with each example word. The neighbours illustrate how similarity of the orthographic and phonological codes was driven by the overlap in letters or phonemes, semi-independently of their position.

	Orthography			Phonology		
	Deterministic	**Jumping**	**Lice**	**Board**	**Hat**	**Institutionalization**
Most Similar	determination	jumped	lace	bored	sat	institutionalizes
	determinate	jumpers	vice	born	haut	institutionalizing
	determining,	jumper	malice	borne	hath	institutionalize
	determinative	bumping	device	bourn	seat	internationalization
	determinations,	jumpy	nice	brought	set	institutionalized
	determinable	ramping	sluice	bard	height	institutionally
	determinedly	slumping	police,	barred	head	constitutionality
	determinism,	lumping	face	bared	heat	institutional
	determines	tamping	dice	gored	half	counterrevolutionary
	determined	thumping	rice,	gourd	shad	internationalism
	determinants	pumping,	mice	mort	sec	unconstitutionally
	determine	camping	slice	barn	heath	internationalized
	paternalistic	stumping,	licorice	guard	haute	antidiscrimination
	determinist	scrimping,	loci	marred	site	extraterritoriality
	determinant	jumbo	solace,	morgue	sight	industrialization
	mechanistic	dumping	pace,	bread	shit	denationalization
	hedonistic	stomping	mace	bred	sheet	constitutional
	pessimistic,	lamping	vide	chord	had	constitutionally
Less Similar	opportunistic			cord	cite	interdisciplinary
						recapitalization

Figure 3.6 Illustration of the similarity structure of the orthographic and phonological representations learned by the sequencer models. Three example words for orthography are shown along with three example words for phonology, and below each example is a word list ordered from most similar to less similar.

Finally, one semantic representation was generated for each of the 45,273 words. Each representation was a 400-bit pattern derived from the COALS method of compiling co-occurrence statistics for words in texts (Rohde et al., in preparation, 2006). The method is similar to latent semantic analysis (Landauer & Dumais, 1997), and the statistics were culled from numerous and various text sources on the Internet. As noted earlier, the statistical extraction of co-occurrence statistics was a proxy for what would ideally be implemented as semantic junctions.

Mediating lexical nodes

This part of the pilot model may lead to some confusion and controversy without careful explanation. The defining aspect of the shared-route architecture is that a single level of representation is used to mediate the mapping between orthography, phonology, and semantics. In precursors to the junction model (Kello, 2003; Kello & Plaut, 2003), this mediating level of representation was learned by back-propagating error that was incurred in mapping among the three types of codes. Back-propagation is a versatile learning algorithm, but it has certain biases and limitations. One of its biases is that systematic mappings are learned more easily (fewer training epochs and/or hidden units) than unsystematic mappings. This bias works in favour of learning the mapping between orthography and phonology, but not between semantics and either orthography or phonology. All of these mappings must be supported by the mediating level of representation. In the precursor models, the bias was overcome by using a sufficient number of hidden units, and training for a sufficient number of epochs. But the corpus of words that was learned in those models was relatively small at 470 words. Using back-propagation to learn the mediating representations for over 45,000 words would take a prohibitive amount of time and computing power.

The alternative used in the current pilot model was to create lexical nodes and assign each one to represent one word in the corpus. Lexical nodes have no inherent bias in computing systematic versus unsystematic mappings. Because they can be prespecified, no training is required in order to use them. Theoretically, the use of lexical nodes in the pilot model makes it clear that the mediating level of representation in the shared-route architecture is a lexicon of sorts (see *Andrews*, this volume; *Taft*, this volume). This point is true regardless of whether the mediating level comprises lexical nodes or more distributed representations. But in using lexical nodes do we forfeit the benefits of learning and generalization that are conferred by distributed representations? The short answer is no.

The longer answer starts with the fact there are established algorithms for learning localist codes, such as the one developed by Grossberg in adaptive resonance theory (Grossberg, 1980). Such an algorithm will be used in future implementations, after other issues are worked out in earlier implementations. As for generalization, Kello et al. (2005a) showed how nonwords could, in principle, be processed by lexical nodes in the junction model. The simple idea is that the orthographic representation for a given nonword will be similar to the orthographic representations for similarly spelled words. This similarity gradient can be reflected in the activations of localist units (depending on their activation function), thereby creating a distribution of activation over the localist nodes for any given nonword. This distribution may in turn activate an appropriate phonological representation for the nonword, provided that the mapping is set up appropriately. Future work will extend the junction model along these lines to address issues of learning and nonword processing.

Connectivity and processing

Each localist node was bidirectionally connected to each of 1200 sigmoidal processing units, one unit per bit of orthography (400), phonology (400), and semantics (400). The activation of each localist node was computed by the normalized exponential function,

$$o_j = \frac{e^{\beta I_j + \gamma L_j}}{\sum_k e^{\beta I_k + \gamma L_k}} \tag{1}$$

This function caused the nodes to compete for activation, with o_j being an exponential function of support for word j. Support was summed from two sources, with the strength of each one scaled by the free parameters β and γ. One source was activation of the distributed units, and the other was activation of the neighbouring words. Support from distributed units was given by

$$I_j = \sum_i w_{ji} a_i \tag{2}$$

where w_{ji} was the connection weight from distributed unit i to localist node j, and a_i was the activation of distributed unit i. Each w_{ij} was set equal to +1 or −1 in accordance with the sign of bit i in the pattern for word j. This type of connectivity meant that support increased as the correlation increased between the pattern of activation over the distributed units, and the incoming weight vector.

Support from neighbouring words was given by a novel, Hebbian-like input,

$$L_j = o_j \sum_n o_n \tag{3}$$

where the o_n were activations of all the neighbours of word j. Neighbours of word j were all other words that shared at least 280 out of 400 bits in their orthographic, phonological, or semantic patterns. This neighbourhood support was "self-scaled" (i.e. scaled by o_j) to ensure that support was maximal when activations were evenly distributed in a neighbourhood, and minimal when either o_j or the sum of neighbour activations went to zero. Neighbourhood support provided cooperative interactions among words, and the balance of cooperation and competition was controlled by the ratio of β to γ.

The activation of each distributed unit was computed as a sigmoid bounded by (−1,+1),

$$a_i = \tanh(\alpha I_i + \tau E_i) \tag{4}$$

There were two sources of net input into the distributed units, scaled by the free parameters α and τ. One source came from activations of the localist nodes,

$$I_i = \sum_j w_{ij} o_j \tag{5}$$

where w_{ij} was the connection weight from localist unit j to distributed unit i, and o_j was the activation of localist node j. Each w_{ij} was set equal to $+f_{ij}$ or $-f_{ij}$, where f_{ij} was the log frequency of occurrence of word j in the COALS database, and its sign was set in accordance with the sign of bit i in the pattern for word j. Given that the o_j were normalized to one, each I_i was an average of the w_{ij}, weighted by the o_j.

The other source of input into the distributed units, E_i, was external to the model. It came from environmental inputs such as letters seen or sounds heard. In the current simulations, the only external input was orthographic, in order to simulate the standard tasks of word naming or lexical decision. The E_i were set to –1 or +1 in accordance with the orthographic bit pattern of a given input word. The influence of internal and external inputs to the distributed units was balanced by the α and τ free parameters, respectively.

Unit and node activations were computed in discrete time. The distributed units were used to index the model's response to an orthographic input. The model's readiness to respond was measured by the degree to which unit activations were near their asymptotes. This response measure was implemented by the response probability function

$$p(t) = E[(a^t_j)^2] \tag{6}$$

where the probability of a response at time step t was equal to the mean square activation value across all phonological units. The phonological units constituted a generic response measure that could be used to simulate both naming response times and lexical decision response times. These tasks differ in important ways, but this simplified response measure was adequate for the pilot model.

The probability of a response over time is illustrated in Figure 3.7 for three example word inputs. The probability response function given by equation (6) allowed for these response distributions to be calculated after only a single presentation of each word to the model. The graphs show that response distributions for individual items are positively skewed, and that items with faster response times also have less variation in their response times. These distributional characteristics were a natural consequence of the model architecture, and they are consistent with the distributional characteristics of real response times to words.

Model tests

The model's free parameters were fit against the mean naming response times for 30,894 words that were collected as part of the Elexicon database (Balota

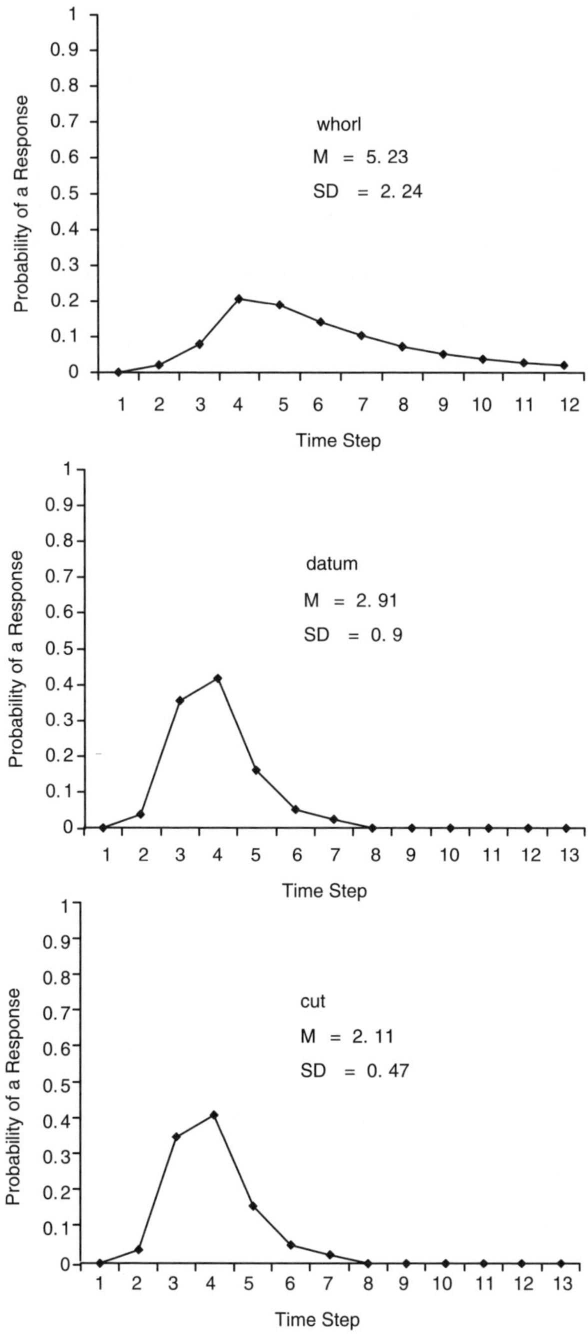

Figure 3.7 Probability density functions of the model response times for three individual words, with means (M) and standard deviations (SD) shown.

et al., 2002; *Balota & Yap*, this volume). This set comprised the full intersection of the model's lexicon with the data available in the Elexicon database at the time of simulation. Model performance was mostly the same for a wide range of parameter values, indicating that model fit was not crucially dependent on any particular set of values. It is well known that the articulatory characteristics of a naming response have a large effect on naming response times (Kessler, Treiman, & Mullennix, 2002; Rastle & Davis, 2002). It is also well known that the length of a word has large effects on naming response times and lexical decision response times (Balota, Cortese, Sergent-Marshall, Spieler, & Yap, 2004). The current model cannot be held accountable for these effects because it does not have a mouth or eyes. Therefore, the effect of articulatory characteristics of the initial phoneme was partialled out of the Elexicon mean naming response times, and the effect of length was partialled out of the Elexicon mean naming and lexical decision response times. The following analyses were conducted on the resulting response time residuals.

The histogram of normalized model response times is graphed in Figure 3.8, along with the normalized response time residuals for word naming and lexical decision data from the Elexicon database. The graph shows a close fit between the simulated and empirical distributions, particularly with respect to positive skew. It is important to note that there were no parameters to directly control the shape of the model response time distribution. Moreover, the parameter values were not adjusted with respect to the response time distribution; they were instead adjusted to maximize the variance in naming response times explained by the model (see next).

In Figure 3.9, the model response times are compared against the Elexicon response times for naming. The model accounted for 18.4% of the variance in naming residuals, and the parameter values were adjusted to maximize this percentage. By comparison, log frequency accounted for 16.6% of the variance when it was regressed against the response time residuals. To determine

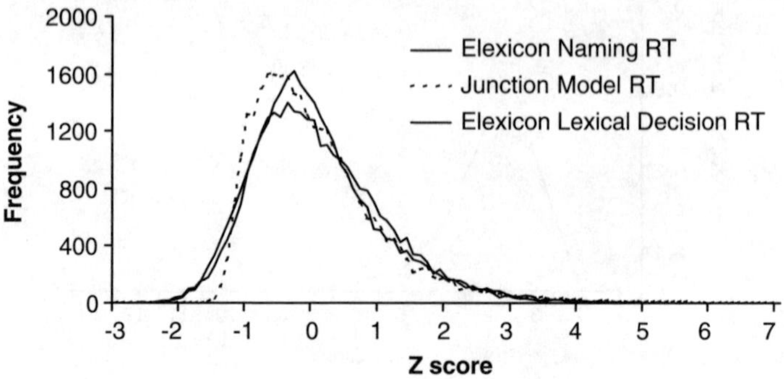

Figure 3.8 Normalized histograms of mean response times (RT) from the junction model, and from mean response time residuals from the naming data and lexical decision data in the Elexicon database.

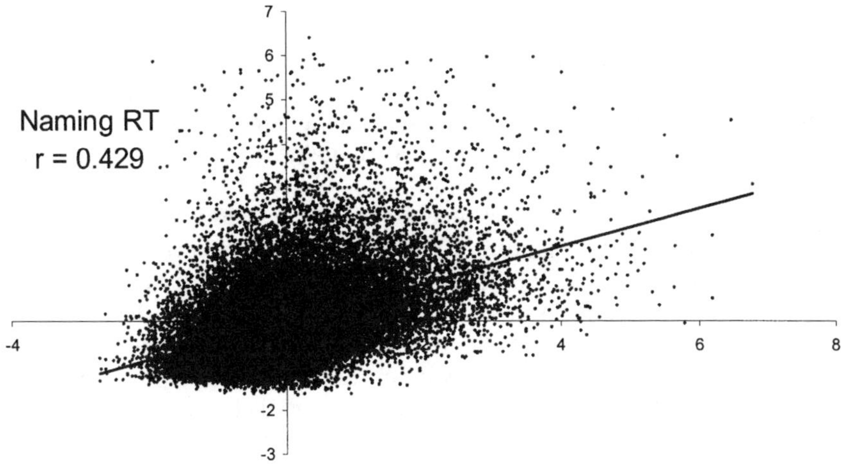

Figure 3.9 Model mean response times (RT) plotted against the naming response time residuals from the Elexicon database, in normalized coordinates.

why the model accounted for this additional variance, log frequency was partialed out of both the model response times and the response time residuals: the model still accounted for 2.6% of the remaining variance. This 2.6% was solely attributable to the competitive and cooperative interactions among words.

In Figure 3.10, the model response times are plotted against the Elexicon response time residuals for lexical decision, in normalized coordinates. The

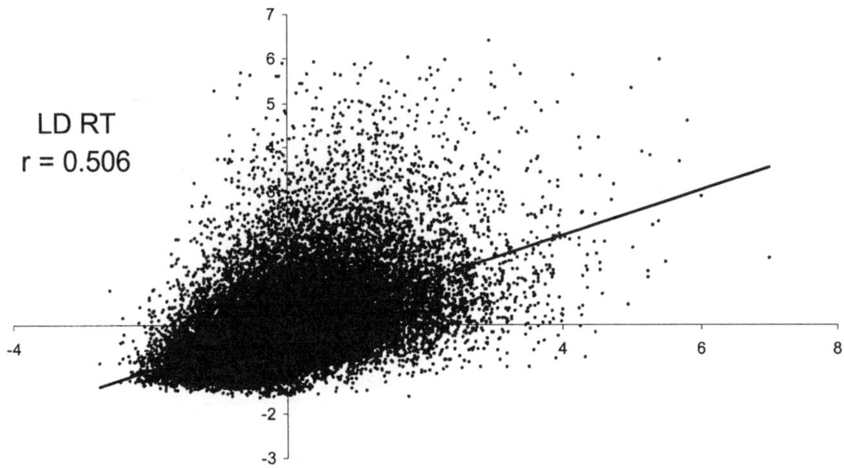

Figure 3.10 Model mean response times plotted against the lexical decision response time (LD RT) residuals from the Elexicon database, in normalized coordinates.

model accounted for 24.7% of the variance in response time residuals, even though the parameter values were not adjusted with respect to these residuals. Log frequency accounted for about the same amount of variance (24.8%). When frequency was removed from the model and from the residuals, the model still accounted for 2.4% of the remaining variance. As with naming response times, this 2.4% was solely attributable to the competitive and cooperative interactions among words.

In addition to mean response times for each item, the Elexicon database provides the standard deviations of response times. As shown in Figure 3.5, the model naturally predicts both the means and standard deviations of item response times. The model's predictions were tested against the database. The model accounted for 7.8% of the item variance in standard deviations for naming, and 5.2% for lexical decision. By comparison, log frequency accounted for 8.2% and 5.9%, respectively. The slightly higher percentages for log frequency mean that the model's ability to account for item standard deviations was primarily due to the way that word frequency had its effect on processing.

Finally, the large-scale junction model was also compared against the two currently dominant models of lexical processing, the triangle (Plaut et al., 1996) and DRC (Coltheart et al., 2001) models of lexical processing. The PMSP and DRC response times were subjected to the same analyses as the junction model response times, and comparisons are shown in Table 3.1. The junction model clearly outperformed the other two models (PMSP simulation 4 performed so well because word frequency was more directly reflected in performance than with the other PMSP simulations). The DRC comparison is somewhat fair because both models are engineered, and the DRC model has 31 free parameters, which are 26 more than the junction model. The PMSP comparison is less fair because the mappings between orthography and phonology were learned in the PMSP model, but not in the junction model. In making either comparison, one must bear in mind that nonword processing was not addressed in the current implementation of the junction model. This will be an important point of comparison in future work that will address nonword processing by incorporating the most recent sequence encoders that support good generalization.

Table 3.1 Proportions of variance in naming response times accounted for by the junction model, compared with the Dual-Route Cascaded (DRC) and Plaut et al. (1996) PMSP models

DRC comparison *n = 5190*		*PMSP comparisons* *n = 2808*				
Junction	DRC	Junction	Sim 1	Sim 2	Sim 3	Sim 4
12.2%	5.1%	14.7%	5.2%	4.1%	2.1%	11.9%

Sim: simulation.

General discussion

It is time to revisit the questions that started off the chapter. First, should we accept the premise that skilled word reading is supported by lexical and sublexical routes of processing? As it stands, the junction model is computational evidence that we should not accept this premise, at least not without more distinguishing evidence. Second, how can we model the learning of orthographic and phonological representations for multisyllabic words? The sequence encoder provides a way, and in doing so, it opens the door to very large-scale models of lexical processing that simulate performance for both mono- and multisyllabic items. The perennial need for such models was heightened when Spieler and Balota (1997) made the well-taken point that item-level performance is an important source of evidence for theories of lexical processing. They showed that the PMSP and DRC models accounted for little variance in performance measures for monosyllabic items, not to mention the fact that they do not simulate performance on multisyllabic items. Balota and his colleagues then upped the ante by providing performance measures for over 30,000 words in the Elexicon database.

The junction model implemented here represents a significant step toward a very large-scale model of lexical processing. The results were encouraging, but more steps lie ahead. Most immediately, the model needs to be extended to address issues of learning and nonword processing, as discussed earlier. These extensions are necessary precursors to embarking on the task of addressing the wide range of results that exist in the literature on lexical processing. For instance, the model will need to be tested on a number of hallmark findings from word naming and lexical decision experiments. It will also need to be tested against a variety of findings from priming and blocking experiments (see *Davis & Kim*, this volume; *Balota & Yap*, this volume). And crucially, it will need to be tested against the data on lexical acquisition and impairments (see *Castles & Nation*, this volume).

These tasks are daunting but doable. The pilot model has already shown that lexical-decision and word-naming data can be simulated. Previous work on the simulation of priming in connectionist models, both weight-based and activation-based, could be incorporated into the junction model. With regard to impairments, performance errors may be generated from noise or damage to units or connections, as in all connectionist models. They may also come from aberrant settings chosen on the basis of specific hypotheses about control parameters of the lexical system. For instance, competition among the localist nodes could be increased by increasing the β parameter, which is equivalent to the input gain parameter in the localist simulations reported by Kello et al. (2005a). Those simulations indicated that high levels of input gain should cause the large-scale model to exhibit a selective impairment in nonword reading, akin to phonological dyslexia. Low levels of input gain should cause a selective impairment in exception word reading.

With regard to acquisition, the localist nodes would need to be formed, and their weight vectors learned, in coordination with the learning of junction representations. This coordination could be implemented by running two learning algorithms that interact with each other. For instance, back propagation in the sequence encoder could be used to learn junction representations, and the developing junctions could be fed as inputs to a localist learning algorithm. In turn, the localist nodes could bias the mapping that is learned by the sequence encoder. All of these ideas are specific enough to be implemented and tested against empirical data.

In closing, I would like to indulge in a bit of pontification. Computational models of language and cognition serve a number of interrelated purposes (see *Seidenberg & Plaut*, this volume). Broadly speaking, the principle of junctions provides a way to think about cognitive representations that emerge from the demands of perception and action. The principle of junctions is made more tangible by theoretical constructs such as distributed coding and pattern formation in the confluence of competitive and cooperative interactions. These constructs come from the connectionist and complex systems frameworks, which carry with them formalisms for computational modelling. The models are implementations of the constructs, and thereby provide the most tangible incarnation of the principles.

Computational models allow for rigorous tests of the constructs and principles, but they also serve as a wellspring for new ideas. For instance, it was the computational work with input gain that led to the idea that junction representations could be mediated by localist nodes, and still provide a basis for explaining nonword generalization and acquired dyslexia. The use of localist nodes distinguishes the junction model from the PDP "triangle" models at the level of construct, but these models share the principles of distributed coding. Moreover, it was work on the sequencer architecture that allowed us to apply the construct of distributed coding to represent multisyllabic words. The interplay of principles, constructs, and models has driven and will continue to drive progress on the junction model of lexical processing.

Acknowledgements

The author thanks Sally Andrews and Kathy Rastle for comments on an earlier draft of this chapter. The work was funded by awards from NIH and NSF, and does not reflect the views of NSF. Correspondence should be addressed to Christopher Kello, Department of Psychology, George Mason University, 4400 University Drive, Fairfax, VA 22030, USA, ckello@gmu.edu

References

Balota, D. A., Cortese, M. J., Hutchison, K. A., Neely, J. H., Nelson, D., Simpson, G. B., et al. (2002). *The English Lexicon Project: A web-based repository of descriptive and behavioral measures for 40,481 English words and nonwords.* http://elexicon.wustl.edu: Washington University. Accessed December 2005.

Balota, D. A., Cortese, M. J., Sergent-Marshall, S. D., Spieler, D. H., & Yap, M. (2004). Visual word recognition of single-syllable words. *Journal of Experimental Psychology: General, 133*, 283–316.

Behrmann, M., & Bub, D. (1992). Surface dyslexia and dysgraphia: Dual routes, single lexicon. *Cognitive Neuropsychology, 9*, 209–251.

Christiansen, M. H., Allen, J., & Seidenberg, M. S. (1998). Learning to segment speech using multiple cues: A connectionist model. *Language and Cognitive Processes, 13*, 221–268.

Cleeremans, A., Servan-Schreiber, D., & McClelland, J. L. (1989). Finite state automata and simple recurrent networks. *Neural Computation, 1*, 372–381.

Coltheart, M. (1996). Phonological dyslexia: Past and future issues. *Cognitive Neuropsychology, 13*, 749–762.

Coltheart, M., Curtis, B., Atkins, P., & Haller, M. (1993). Models of reading aloud: Dual-route and parallel-distributed-processing approaches. *Psychological Review, 100*, 589–608.

Coltheart, M., Rastle, K., Perry, C., Langdon, R., & Ziegler, J. (2001). DRC: A dual route cascaded model of visual word recognition and reading aloud. *Psychological Review, 108*, 204–256.

Elman, J. L. (1990). Finding structure in time. *Cognitive Science, 14*, 179–211.

Fellous, J.-M., & Linster, C. (1998). Computational models of neuromodulation. *Neural Computation, 10*, 771–805.

Funnell, E. (1983). Phonological processes in reading—new evidence from acquired dyslexia. *British Journal of Psychology, 74*, 159–180.

Gibson, J. J. (1979). *The ecological approach to visual perception.* Boston: Houghton Mifflin.

Glushko, R. J. (1979). The organization and activation of orthographic knowledge in reading aloud. *Journal of Experimental Psychology: Human Perception and Performance, 5*, 674–691.

Grossberg, S. (1980). How does a brain build a cognitive code? *Psychological Review, 87*, 1–51.

Harm, M. W., & Seidenberg, M. S. (2004). Computing the meanings of words in reading: Cooperative division of labor between visual and phonological processes. *Psychological Review, 111*, 662–720.

Jordan, M. I. (1986). *Serial order: A parallel distributed processing approach* (No. 8604 ICS Technical Report): University of California at San Diego, La Jolla, CA.

Kello, C. T. (2003). The emergence of a double dissociation in the modulation of a single control parameter in a nonlinear dynamical system. *Cortex, 39*, 132–134.

Kello, C. T. (2004). Control over the time course of cognition in the tempo-naming task. *Journal of Experimental Psychology: Human Perception and Performance, 30*, 942–955.

Kello, C. T., & Plaut, D. C. (2000). Strategic control in word reading: Evidence from speeded responding in the tempo-naming task. *Journal of Experimental Psychology: Learning, Memory, and Cognition, 26*, 719–750.

Kello, C. T., & Plaut, D. C. (2003). Strategic control over rate of processing in word reading: A computational investigation. *Journal of Memory and Language, 48*, 207–232.

Kello, C. T., Sibley, D. E., & Colombi, A. (2004). Using simple recurrent networks to learn fixed-length representations of variable-length strings. In *Proceedings of the AAAI Symposium on Compositional Connectionism*. Washington, DC.

Kello, C. T., Sibley, D. E., & Plaut, D. (2005a). Dissociations in performance on novel versus irregular items: Single-route demonstrations with input gain in localist and distributed models. *Cognitive Science*, *29*, 627–654.

Kello, C. T., Sibley, D. E., Plaut, D., & Elman, J. L. (2005b). *Learning representations of linguistic sequences*. Manuscript submitted for publication.

Kessler, B., Treiman, R., & Mullennix, J. (2002). Phonetic biases in voice key response time measurements. *Journal of Memory and Language*, *47*, 145–171.

Lakoff, G., & Johnson, M. (1980). *Metaphors we live by*. Chicago: University of Chicago Press.

Landauer, T. K., & Dumais, S. T. (1997). A solution to Plato's problem: The latent semantic analysis theory of acquisition, induction, and representation of knowledge. *Psychological Review*, *104*, 211–240.

Monsell, S., Patterson, K. E., Graham, A., Hughes, C. H., & Milroy, R. (1992). Lexical and sublexical translation of spelling to sound: Strategic anticipation of lexical status. *Journal of Experimental Psychology: Learning, Memory, and Cognition*, *18*, 452–467.

Patterson, K., & Hodges, J. R. (1992). Deterioration of word meaning: Implications for reading. *Neuropsychologia*, *30*, 1025–1040.

Patterson, K., & Lambon Ralph, M. A. (1999). Selective disorders of reading? *Current Opinion in Neurobiology*, *9*, 235–239.

Patterson, K., & Marcel, A. (1992). Phonological alexia or phonological alexia? In J. Alegria, D. Holender, J. Morais, & M. Radeau (Eds.), *Analytic approaches to human cognition* (pp. 259–274). Amsterdam: Elsevier.

Pinker, S., & Prince, A. (1988). On language and connectionism: Analysis of a parallel distributed processing model of language acquisition. *Cognition*, *28*, 73–193.

Plaut, D. C., & Gonnerman, L. M. (2000). Are non-semantic morphological effects incompatible with a distributed connectionist approach to lexical processing? *Language and Cognitive Processes*, *15*, 445–485.

Plaut, D. C., & Kello, C. T. (1999). The emergence of phonology from the interplay of speech comprehension and production: A distributed connectionist approach. In B. MacWhinney (Ed.), *The emergence of language* (pp. 381–415). Mahwah, NJ: Lawrence Erlbaum Associates, Inc.

Plaut, D. C., McClelland, J. L., Seidenberg, M. S., & Patterson, K. (1996). Understanding normal and impaired word reading: Computational principles in quasi-regular domains. *Psychological Review*, *103*, 56–115.

Rastle, K., & Davis, M. H. (2002). On the complexities of measuring naming. *Journal of Experimental Psychology: Human Perception and Performance*, *28*, 307–314.

Rohde, D. L. T., Gonnerman, L., & Plaut, D. C. (in preparation, 2006). *An improved model of semantic similarity based on lexical co-occurrence*.

Rosenblatt, F. (1961). *Principles of neurodynamics: Perceptions and the theory of brain mechanisms*. Washington, DC: Spartan Books.

Seidenberg, M. S., & McClelland, J. L. (1989). A distributed, developmental model of word recognition and naming. *Psychological Review*, *96*, 523–568.

Sibley, D. E., & Kello, C. T. (2004). Dissociations between regularities and irregularities in language processing: Computational demonstrations without separable processing components. In K. Forbus, D. Gentner & T. Regier (Eds.), *Proceedings of the Twenty-Sixth Annual Conference of the Cognitive Science Society* (pp. 1249–1254). Hillsdale: NJ: Lawrence Erlbaum Associates, Inc.

Spieler, D. H., & Balota, D. A. (1997). Bringing computational models of word naming down to the item level. *Psychological Science*, *8*, 411–416.

Van Orden, G. C., Bosman, A. M. T., Goldinger, S. D., & Farrar, W. T. I. V. (1997). A recurrent-network account of reading, spelling, and dyslexia. In J. W. Donahoe & V. P. Dorsel (Eds.), *Neural-network models of cognition: Biobehavioral foundations. Advances in psychology* (pp. 522–538). Amsterdam: North-Holland/Elsevier.

von der Malsburg, C. (1981). The correlation theory of brain function. *MPI Biophysical Chemistry, Internal Report, 81–2*. Reprinted in E. Domany, J. L. van Hemmen, & K. Schulten (Eds.), *Models of neural networks II* (1994). Berlin: Springer.

Wilson, M. (2002). Six views of embodied cognition. *Psychonomic Bulletin and Review*, *9*, 625–636.

Zevin, J. D., & Balota, D. A. (2000). Priming and attentional control of lexical and sublexical pathways during naming. *Journal of Experimental Psychology: Learning, Memory, and Cognition*, *26*, 121–135.

4 A localist-cum-distributed (LCD) framework for lexical processing

Marcus Taft
School of Psychology, University of New South Wales, Australia

In 1991, I authored a monograph entitled *Reading and the Mental Lexicon*, which surveyed the evidence on what was known at that time about the storage and retrieval of words in lexical memory within the reading context. In the course of doing this, my conceptualization of the lexical processing system evolved considerably from the search framework that had guided my earlier work (e.g. Taft & Forster, 1975, 1976). Like most others in the field, I found the most fruitful approach to be an activation-based model, and my theorizing since that time has centred upon an evolution and expansion of that framework. In this chapter, I will present my most recent conceptualization along with a few examples of how it has helped to provide a concrete way of thinking about a range of specific issues. The primary focus will be on the relationship between orthography and phonology, since this has been the most prominent issue in the literature on visual lexical processing, but the way in which the proposed model incorporates the important issues of syllabic and morphemic processing will also be outlined. The purpose of the model is to provide a useful framework for organizing one's thoughts about all aspects of lexical processing, with particular emphasis on the recognition of visually presented words.

The model has both distributed and localist features. The representations of form (i.e. orthography and phonology) are distributed in the sense that the units of activation correspond to sublexical components of a word, and not to the whole word itself, but they are localist in the sense that the identity of these sublexical units is made explicit. The units that represent functional information (i.e. meaning and syntax) are seen as being feature-based and hence are also distributed, though it must be said that these are ill-specified in the model (as in most models). The localist orientation of the model particularly emerges in the guise of a unit that brings together a set of distributed form units with the relevant set of distributed functional units. I refer to this mediating unit as the "lemma", following the terminology borrowed from the word-production literature by Baayen, Dijkstra, and Schreuder (1997) in their discussion of word recognition. Because each word is represented by a lemma, it is the lemma representation that is equivalent to the "lexical entry".

Thus, the lexical entry is neither a form unit nor a meaning unit, but something that integrates the two levels.

In models that are entirely distributed (e.g. Plaut, McClelland, Seidenberg, & Patterson, 1996; Seidenberg & McClelland, 1989), the formal and functional units activated by the presented word are mediated by a set of hidden units rather than a single lemma. The sort of model presented in this chapter is meant to be more a concrete framework for helping one think about lexical processing than something designed for implementation in a computerized simulation. As such, the metaphor of a localist lemma has an advantage over a description in terms of hidden units in that it allows a clearer depiction of the nature of lexical processing and representation. In fact, I see lemmas as providing a way of capturing the correlation between form and function (see Taft, 2003), and this means that they will vary in their strength depending upon that correlation. Such a notion is equivalent to variations in the tuning of "basins of attraction" as described in the distributed model of Plaut et al. (1996). However, while the brain may work in a distributed fashion, the model presented in this chapter is not meant to be a facsimile of the lexical processing system, but rather a metaphor that allows us to envisage in more concrete terms how words are represented and retrieved in reading and speech. It is for this reason that I have adopted a localist orientation. By doing so, a range of different issues—from phonological involvement in reading to the representation of morphological structure—can be readily embraced within the one framework. A depiction of such a "localist-cum-distributed" (LCD) model is found in Figure 4.1.

The LCD model

Figure 4.1 illustrates what is essentially the same model as that presented in my 1991 book (p. 81), the only differences being that lemmas replace units previously called "concepts" and, for the sake of explication, the different levels of sublexical form units are simplified and shown within the same box. The hierarchical activation of sublexical form units is a feature of the model. The assumption is made that the final consonant(s) of a monosyllabic word (i.e. the "coda", such as the D of HEAD, or the NCH of LUNCH) go together with the vowel to form a unit of representation. This sublexical unit is called the "body" when referring to orthography (e.g. EAD or UNCH), and the "rime" when referring to phonology (e.g. /ɛd/ or /ʌnč/), and such units have been shown to be important in lexical processing (e.g. Andrews & Scarratt, 1998; Bowey, 1990; Kay & Marcel, 1981; Taraban & McClelland, 1987; Treiman, 1983, 1986; Treiman & Chafetz, 1987; Treiman & Zukowski, 1988). So, when a letter string (e.g. HEAD) is visually presented, activation passes from the grapheme units (H, EA, and D) to the relevant body unit (EAD), and, in combination with activation from the unit representing the consonantal onset (H), the appropriate lemma is activated (i.e. the lexical entry).

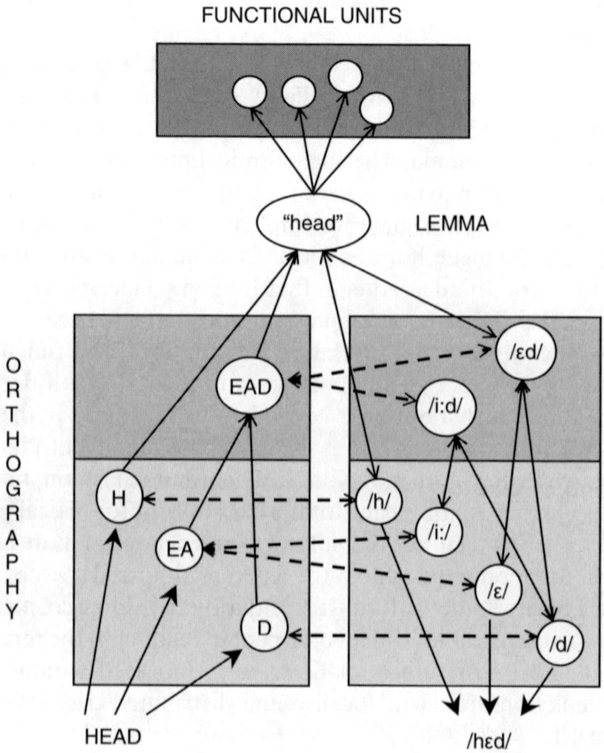

Figure 4.1 The localist-cum-distributed (LCD) model illustrating the pathways involved in recognizing and naming the word HEAD.

Another important feature of the LCD framework is that activation can pass directly between sublexical orthographic units and sublexical phonological units. When naming is required, the pronunciation is constructed from the phoneme units that are activated via the grapheme-phoneme links, guided by activation feeding down from the rime units that have been activated via the body-rime links. Importantly, the choice of phonemes is also guided by information passing down from the lemma, that is, lexical information. This is necessary because there is frequently more than one phoneme activated by a grapheme and more than one rime activated by a body, and such ambiguity needs to be resolved.

We see this in Figure 4.1, where the grapheme EA will activate both /i:/ and /ɛ/, which will then be in competition with each other. If there were no activation passing down from the higher levels, the pronunciation given to the grapheme would be the phoneme that is most strongly (i.e. frequently) associated with that grapheme (being /i:/ in the case of EA). However, information *is* passed down from the higher levels, namely, from the lemma unit mediated by the rime unit. That is, the body EAD also activates more than one unit (i.e. the rimes /iːd/ and /ɛd/), again with strength of activation being determined by the frequency of pronunciation (/ɛd/ being more common than /iːd/). The competition between rime units is ultimately resolved through lemma activation which, in the case of HEAD, supports the /ɛd/ rime unit over the /iːd/ rime unit (while the reverse would be true if the presented word were BEAD). So we see that phonological output is based on the integration of both sublexical and lexical information.

LCD's relationship to other models

The LCD approach draws upon a number of features found in other models. The idea that activation passes through a hierarchy of sublexical units has been around for a long time (e.g. Shallice & McCarthy, 1985; Shallice, Warrington, & McCarthy, 1983), as has the specification of linked body and rime units (e.g. Patterson & Morton, 1985). The involvement of units representing onset, vowel, and coda has also been incorporated into several computational models of visual lexical processing, both localist (e.g. Jacobs, Rey, Ziegler, & Grainger, 1998) and distributed (e.g. Plaut et al., 1996). The LCD model integrates all these features into a single framework.

The idea that orthography and phonology are linked to meaning via the same set of mediating units (i.e. the lemma level) has also been suggested elsewhere. Frost (1998) entertained such a possibility, but rejected it on the grounds of redundancy inasmuch as it added nothing to the orthographic and phonological lexical representations. However, this is only true if the orthographic and phonological systems include whole-word representations, which is not the case in the LCD model. A unit such as a lemma is necessary to draw together the relevant sublexical form units to represent a whole word. The junction model proposed by *Kello* (this volume) also incorporates the idea that orthography and phonology are linked to meaning via a shared set of units. In Kello's model, orthography and phonology are associated with each other only through this mediating level, whereas the LCD model also includes direct links between orthography and phonology at the sublexical level. In that sense, the LCD framework provides a dual-route account of the relationship between spelling and sound. However, it differs from the standard dual-route account represented by the dual-route cascaded (DRC) model advocated by M. Coltheart, Rastle, Perry, Langdon, and Ziegler (2001).

In the DRC model, sublexical processing is a separate system from lexical processing, with the former being a set of rules that represent the most frequent grapheme-to-phoneme correspondences (i.e. GPC rules, as in EA → /iː/). Grapheme-to-phoneme correspondences are also captured in the LCD model, but in a probabilistic manner (i.e. EA activates /iː/ more strongly than /ɛ/). Thus, the LCD account has the advantage of flexibility, while being able to handle the same dissociations between lexical and sublexical processing that are the bread and butter of the DRC model (see M. Coltheart, Curtis, Atkins,

& Haller, 1993; M. Coltheart et al., 2001). For example, surface dyslexia can be characterized by a dysfunction of the links from orthography to phonology via the lemma, leading to pronunciations based on sublexical information only (e.g. pronouncing HEAD as /hi:d/); and phonological dyslexia can be characterized by a dysfunction of the sublexical links, leading to difficulties in pronouncing pseudowords (e.g. NESH), which do not possess a lemma and hence can be named only via sublexical links.

In addition, the standard finding (e.g. Andrews, 1982; Seidenberg, Waters, Barnes, & Tanenhaus, 1984) that low-frequency irregular words take longer to name than frequency-matched regular words (e.g. THREAT taking longer to name than THROAT) is handled in terms of irregular words encountering competition at the sublexical levels (e.g. the phoneme /i:/ competing with the less common phoneme /ɛ/, and the rime /i:t/ competing with the less common rime /ɛt/). Adjudication between the sublexical competitors comes from lexical information passed down from the lemma, a unit whose activation is influenced by word frequency. So, when the irregular word is of high frequency, such lexical information is rapidly recruited, and, therefore, no delay in naming is observed.

There is also one result that is problematical for the DRC account, but which is perfectly compatible with the LCD framework. This is the finding, originally reported by Glushko (1979), that the naming of words with inconsistently pronounced bodies is delayed even when the word itself has a regular pronunciation. For example, CHEAT takes longer to name than CHESS even though the pronunciation of both words follows GPC rules and is hence regular. The delay arises from the fact that the body –EAT has more than one pronunciation (i.e. /i:t/ and /ɛt/), while –ESS does not. Because both pathways of the DRC model generate the same output for inconsistent regular words like CHEAT, there should be no delay in naming. On the other hand, the same sublexical competition that occurs for irregular words will take place in the LCD model for inconsistent regular words; therefore, the observed consistency effect is predicted. That is, resolution of the correct phonological output for CHEAT needs the rime unit /i:t/ to triumph over the competing rime unit /ɛt/.

Thus, by incorporating a form of dual-route architecture, the LCD model is not only able to handle the evidence presented in favour of DRC, but can also explain other findings. What will now be described are further aspects of processing that involve associations between orthography and phonology for which the LCD model also helps to provide an understanding.

Pseudoword naming

In the LCD framework, pseudoword naming can be influenced by top-down information, primarily information that feeds down to the phoneme units from the rime units (with the potential for some influence from lemmas that might be weakly activated via orthographic overlap with the pseudoword).

Thus, the pronunciation of NESH is supported by activation coming down to the phoneme level from the rime unit /ɛš/ activated through the body unit ESH. In contrast, the pronunciation of a pseudoword whose body does not exist in English (e.g. JENK) must rely solely on grapheme-phoneme links without support from the higher-level body-rime activation. This means that naming times to pseudowords whose body exists (e.g. NESH, STAIL) should be faster than those to pseudowords whose body does not exist (e.g. JENK, GRAIP) when their general similarity to real words is matched (in terms of both the number of one-letter-different neighbours and homophony). I have recently observed such an outcome ("existing body": 650 ms and 7.0% errors; "non-existing body": 678 ms and 13.8% errors), a result that would be hard for a model to handle if it did not incorporate the importance of the body as a unit of processing (such as the DRC model).

Also consistent with the LCD model is the finding of Andrews and Scarratt (1998) that the pronunciation of a nonword is influenced by the phonological characteristics of its body. For example, the letter "I" is given a long pronunciation (i.e. /aɪ/) more often in HILD (as in MILD, WILD, and CHILD) than in HINK. Overlying this, however, is the finding that pronunciations based on individual graphemes are generally preferred (as in HILD being more often pronounced with a short "I" than a long "I" because the former is the most common pronunciation of "I"). In terms of the LCD model, this means that, while there is activation passing down from the body-rime level to the grapheme-phoneme level, the pronunciation settled upon at the phoneme level is only weakly influenced by this activation when there is no lemma providing top-down support.

However, information at the body-rime level can be made more influential by preactivating the body-rime links. Kay and Marcel (1981) and Taraban and McClelland (1987) showed that a nonword with a potentially irregular pronunciation (e.g. JEAD) is given that pronunciation more often when preceded by an irregular word sharing its body (e.g. HEAD). In other words, if the –EAD → /ɛd/ link is strengthened through recent use, then the pronunciation of a nonword containing –EAD is more likely to be given an /ɛd/ pronunciation. Note that the priming seems to arise from the strengthening of body-rime links rather than strengthening of the rime units alone, because Kay and Marcel (1981) found no increase in irregular pronunciations when the prime word shared its rime with the nonword, but not its body (e.g. SHED–JEAD).

Feedback phonology

Another feature of the LCD framework is that the sublexical links between orthography and phonology are bidirectional. So, not only is there "feed-forward phonology" where activation passes from orthography to phonology, but also "feedback phonology" (Stone, Vanhoy, & Van Orden, 1997) where activation rebounds from phonology back to orthography. There is increasing evidence that feedback phonology plays a role when a letter string is visually presented. For example, lexical decision responses to pseudowords like WICE are longer than those to pseudowords like SICE (Taft, 1982). Both have the same phonological relationship to a real word (i.e. WISE and SIZE respectively), but confusion of WICE with WISE can arise from feedback phonology (i.e. –ICE → /aɪs/ → –ISE), whereas SICE will never be confused with SIZE because /aɪs/ cannot be transcribed as –IZE. This finding implies that sublexical phonology is automatically activated when a word is processed visually, resulting in resonance between orthography and phonology such that there is a rebound back to orthography. Stone et al. (1997) reach the same conclusion from their related finding that visual lexical decisions are more difficult to make when a rime is associated with more than one body. Thus, recognition of RINSE is affected by the fact that its rime /ɪns/ can also be spelt as the body –INCE, which competes with the correct body –INSE. This is in contrast to a word like SLANG, whose rime can be spelt in only the one way. Again, the LCD framework provides a natural account for the resonance that can occur between sublexical orthographic and phonological units.

Pseudohomophone judgement

Most research into the translation of orthography into phonology has made use of the naming task. This makes sense inasmuch as it provides a direct measure of the conversion from print to sound. However, another task also taps into the translation of orthography into phonology and, in so doing, elaborates upon the lexical processing system. Instead of requiring overt output from the generated phonological representation, this task requires that the lexical status of the generated phonological representation be identified. In other words, participants must decide whether a visually presented letter string is pronounced identically to a real word. Although this task can be used to examine real-word stimuli (requiring a judgement of whether there is a homophonic partner, as in SALE being homophonic with SAIL), it is most productively employed with pseudowords as stimuli. This is the "pseudohomophone judgement task" (also called the "phonological lexical decision task"; e.g. McCann, Besner, & Davelaar, 1988; Unsworth & Pexman, 2003), because it requires participants to decide whether a pseudoword is homophonic with a real word (as it is in the case of STAIL and WIZE).

The most straightforward way of making a pseudohomophone judgement would seem to be the following. Orthography is converted into phonology sublexically (giving /steɪl/ from STAIL and /zaɪt/ from ZITE) and then, rather than the generated output being overtly articulated, it is established whether the output corresponds to a lexical representation (e.g. "yes" for /steɪl/ and "no" for /zaɪt/). In the LCD model, this would entail the activation of a lemma via the sublexical phonological units.

There is one very clear result, however, that suggests that the task is not performed simply by accessing lexical information directly from phonology. Specifically, the orthographic similarity of the pseudoword with its homophonic base word affects the ease with which its homophony is recognized. For example, SKREAM is easier to identify as being a homophone of the word SCREAM than is SKREME, while SKEME is easier to identify as being homophonic with SCHEME than is SKEAM (Taft, 1982). Thus, the orthographic similarity of the pseudohomophone to the target word has greater impact than the unusualness of orthographic structure (e.g. –EME being a rarer letter combination than –EAM).

If it were possible to directly determine the lexical status of a phonological representation generated from a visually presented letter string, the orthographic characteristics of the homophonic target word should be irrelevant. That is, both SKREAM and SKREME would be recoded as /skri:m/ and SKEAM and SKEME would be recoded as /ski:m/, meaning that the only potential difference between the members of each pair should be the ease of recoding as determined by the unusualness of orthographic structure. Because the factor of orthographic similarity turns out to be more important, however, we need to establish from where its effects might arise.

Taking SKREAM versus SKREME as an example, the LCD framework offers a straightforward explanation. The lemma for SCREAM is normally activated via the onset SCR– and the body –EAM. When either SKREAM or SKREME is presented, the appropriate onset unit will be partially activated, but the appropriate body unit will be fully activated only in the former case. Thus, activation of the relevant lemma will gain more support from the orthographic system in the case of SKREAM than SKREME. Of course, a nonhomophonic item like SPREAM would provide exactly the same orthographic activation as SKREAM, so a pseudohomophone judgement cannot be made on the basis of orthography alone. However, feedback phonology can contribute to the activation of the homophonic word inasmuch as the onset unit SCR– will be more activated by SKR– than SPR– via the K→ /k/ → C pathway.

Note that an orthographic similarity effect has also been reported in relation to homophone confusions in a semantic judgement task (V. Coltheart, Patterson, & Leahy, 1994). For example, it is hard to classify DEAR as being a nonanimal because it is confusable with its orthographically similar homophone DEER, whereas a nonanimal classification is not so difficult for WAIL because of its orthographic dissimilarity to its homophone WHALE. While such a result could be explained in terms of confusions arising within the orthographic processing system (i.e. in line with the LCD explanation above), V. Coltheart et al. (1994) point out that it could alternatively have arisen from confusion when the orthography associated with the lexical representation, activated purely through phonology, is ultimately checked against the spelling of the presented letter string. Such a trivial explanation for the orthographic similarity effect is circumvented in the pseudohomophone judgement task because there is no spelling check required. That is, unlike a semantic judgement, a pseudohomophone judgement does not require that a decision be made about the actual letter string that is presented, only about its pronunciation. Thus, it would be counterproductive to conduct a spelling check.

For this reason, the finding of orthographic similarity effects in the pseudohomophone judgement task is particularly instructive. The implication is that the orthographic route to the lexical representation (i.e. the lemma) is clearly important in a task that explicitly requires a phonological judgement, and this flies in the face of claims that the primary route from a visual stimulus to its meaning is via the phonological system (e.g. Frost, 1998; Van Orden, 1987). Here we have a task that would seem to be best carried out via the phonological system, yet orthographic information is unquestionably involved in making the response. Moreover, this orthographic influence is hard to overcome: When the orthographic similarity between the pseudohomophone and its base word is very low, it is extremely hard to detect their homophony at all when the task is performed silently. For example, I have found very high error rates in detecting the homophony of items like FOAN and SEEJ even though there is little difficulty in naming them.[1] If it were easy to get from orthography to the lemma (or to meaning) via phonology, it should not matter if the orthographic system has difficulty gaining direct access to the lemma for the homophonic target: The judgement of homophony should then be based purely on the phonological representation, which ought to be sufficient information on which to make the response.

The fact that phonological information is not called upon even as a default, leads to the controversial speculation that the phonological system does not actually allow access to the lexical representation at all. That is, the phonological pathway that is involved in visual word recognition might allow only top-down activation, such that the arrows leading from the lemma to the phoneme level in Figure 4.1 are actually unidirectional, with no information passing from phonology up to the lemma level (see also Taft & van Graan, 1998). According to this account, the act of reading involves not only a different type of phonological representation from that used in spoken word recognition, but also a different phonological system altogether. The spoken word system must obviously gain access to meaning, so the only way to get from the printed word to meaning would be by uttering the word aloud (or perhaps subvocally) via the phonological system and then accessing meaning through the input system specialized for speech recognition.

We see, then, that the LCD framework is flexible enough to allow speculation about the nature of the lexical processing system, but constrained enough to have considerable explanatory power. Unlike other models that are designed to perform particular tasks (mostly print-to-sound conversion), LCD embraces all aspects of lexical processing. The framework can be adopted not only in considerations of print-to-sound conversion, but also in relation to the processing of orthographic and morphemic structure, and we now turn to these other areas of lexical processing.

Lexical and morphemic representation

Lemmas capture the correlation between form (i.e. orthography and/or phonology) and function (i.e. meaning and/or grammatical role). In other words, when form-based features (e.g. the letter combination C + A + T) are repeatedly associated with a specific function (e.g. referring to a "furry creature that says miaow"), this constancy in the environment emerges through the development of a lemma that links together the representations of the relevant formal features and the representations of the relevant functional features. The strength of the lemma depends on how consistent the form–function relationship is against the background of varying contexts. From this description, it is apparent that individual words are represented by individual lemmas, because a word corresponds to a formal structure that is associated with a recurring constellation of functional features.

Note that it is possible for a form unit to be associated with more than one constellation of functional features and, if so, more than one lemma will develop for that form. For example, the ambiguous word PORT is associated with a "harbour" meaning and a "drink" meaning. Therefore, having two separate lemmas for each meaning allows stronger form–function correlations to be captured than if there were a single lemma trying to span the two meanings.

However, not all lemmas represent free-standing words. A "bound morpheme" is a form unit that is found only sublexically, but is associated with consistent functional information. Such a unit will therefore develop its own lemma, with a strength that depends on an interplay between the variety of environments in which the sublexical unit occurs and the constancy of meaning within those environments. If the same meaning is upheld in a variety of environments (e.g. the VENGE of REVENGE, AVENGE, VENGEANCE, and VENGEFUL), the lemma that captures the association between that meaning and the recurring form will be strongly developed, though not as strongly as a free-standing word, whose environment is even more variable. This is why VENGE is clearly considered to be a morpheme, even though it does not stand on its own as a word. When the form–function correlation is weaker, however, the mediating lemma will be more weakly tuned, and the linguistic status of the sublexical unit as a morpheme is thus more controversial. For example, the words CONCEIVE, PERCEIVE, DECEIVE, and RECEIVE have a certain amount of shared meaning, but it is hard to define what that overlap is. Therefore, the sublexical unit CEIVE may well develop a lemma, but one that is quite weakly represented, and some may even argue that it is not a morpheme at all.

Prefixes and suffixes will also develop their own lemmas, again with varying degrees of strength depending on the consistency of their function. So, the prefix UN– will be strongly represented, being consistently associated with a "negative" function, while the prefix PER– will be more weakly represented. In fact, some linguistically definable affixes may never develop a lemma at all if the meaning of the words in which they occur are sufficiently diverse in meaning (the SE– of SECEDE, SECRETE, SEDUCE, SELECT, SEDATE, etc.).

To gain insight into the representation of lemmas, it is instructive to examine a situation where both bound morphemes and free-standing words (i.e. free morphemes) have the same formal structure. The Chinese logographic script provides such an opportunity (Taft, 2003) because single characters can represent both free and bound morphemes. Many Chinese characters are only ever found within two-character compound words, and when the set of words in which the same character occurs are semantically related, a lemma should develop for that recurring character (just like VENGE in English). It turns out that Chinese readers often classify such bound characters as free morphemes, though to a lesser extent than genuine free-standing words that never participate in compounding (Taft, 2003). On the other hand, these two types of morpheme are equally recognized as being an existing Chinese character, which is a form-based judgement. In other words, both types of character are represented within the orthographic system in the same way, but they differ in terms of their lemma representation (and hence their morphemic status) by virtue of the different contexts in which they are found. A free morpheme has a stronger lemma representation than a bound morpheme because the contexts in which the latter occur are more constrained than those in which the former can occur.

It is important to note, though, that not all sublexical form units that are consistently associated with the same function in different contexts can be considered morphemes. Take, for example, GRA– in the semantically related words GRASP, GRAB, and GRAPPLE. No lemma will develop here because GRA does not correspond to any unit of representation within the orthographic system (being an onset plus vowel). On the other hand, one could argue that the –ASH of CLASH, SMASH, CRASH, BASH, DASH, SLASH, FLASH, etc., should form a lemma because it is represented as a body unit that is consistently associated with the meaning "sharp action". However, –ASH may not develop a lemma (and hence not be considered a morpheme) simply because the remaining letters are not systematically associated with any function (e.g. the onset CL or SM).

To examine the impact of having both orthographic and semantic overlap, Rastle, Davis, Marslen-Wilson, and Tyler (2000) conducted a study that looked at cases of unsystematic form overlap between semantically related masked prime and target pairs (e.g. GRASP–GRAB, FROST–FREEZE, BRUNCH–LUNCH). No facilitation was observed, suggesting that there is no shared representation between such words (although what happens in the explicit case of overlapping bodies, such as BRUNCH–LUNCH or CRASH–SMASH, is still unknown).

While few would argue that GRA or UNCH are morphemes, Taft and Kougious (2004) present evidence that certain types of sublexical units can develop lemmas even when their status as a morpheme is dubious. The word

VIRUS would be considered by few people to be a suffixed word, though VIRAL might be. However, most would accept that these two words are morphemically related, and this essentially means that VIR should be treated as a bound morpheme in both words. In support of this view, Taft and Kougious (2004) demonstrated facilitation of lexical decision times when the target and the masked prime were words of this type (e.g. VIRUS–VIRAL, DONATE–DONOR), in contrast to words of similar orthographic overlap that were not semantically related (e.g. FUTILE–FUTURE). It was proposed that when the onset-plus-body of the first part of a word (e.g. VIR–) recurs in association with the same meaning, it develops a lemma. There is also a lemma for each of the words that include that component (i.e. VIRUS and VIRAL), being activated via the sublexical lemma (i.e. VIR). The remaining letter combination (e.g. –US, –AL) may or may not also have its own lemma (developed through syntactic association), but if it does not, it will have an orthographic representation that feeds directly to the whole-word lemma. This is depicted in Figure 4.2 (where, for ease of understanding, the only form representations shown are orthographic ones).

Recognizing polymorphemic words

As can be seen in Figure 4.2, hierarchical lemma activation is being proposed, with the lemma for VIRUS being activated through the lemma for VIR. Similarly, if REVENGE were presented, its lemma would be activated via the lemma for VENGE. We can then ask what happens when the presented word

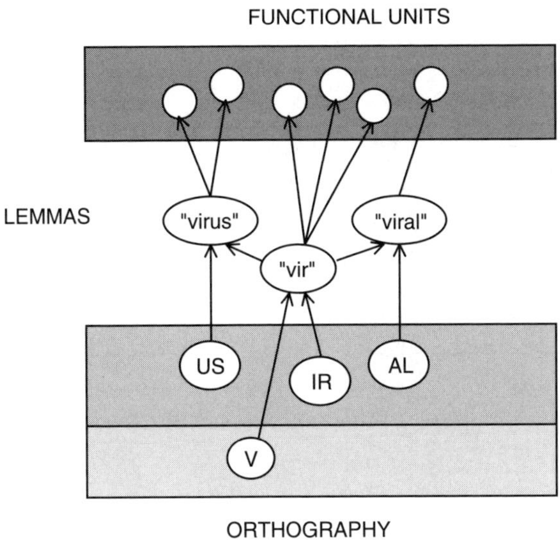

Figure 4.2 The lemma representation of two semantically related words that share a sublexical orthographic unit.

is polymorphemic with a stem that is a free-standing word (e.g. CATS, FEATHERY). Is there a "polymorphemic lemma" that is activated via the lemma that exists for the monomorphemic stem? My argument is that no polymorphemic lemma need exist if the function of that polymorphemic word is entirely predictable from the function of its constituents (e.g. inflected words like CATS), but, otherwise, it must exist in order to capture what is unique about the word (see Taft, 2004).

To clarify, semantic and syntactic information associated with the lemma for CAT will provide everything one needs to know about its combination with the plural suffix (indeed, a dictionary would not bother listing CATS). On the other hand, a word like FEATHERY is associated with more information than merely "being like a feather" (e.g. the emphasis is on the texture of a feather rather than its shape). So, what I propose is that all polymorphemic words, be they inflected or derived, are decomposed into their constituent morphemes. Inflected words (e.g. CATS, FAILED) are then recognized through an on-line recombination of their stem and affix as based on functional information (Taft, 2004), whereas other polymorphemic words (e.g. FEATHERY, FAILURE, REPLACE) are recognized when the whole-word lemma is activated via the individual stem and affix lemmas (see Taft & Ardasinski, in press, for evidence in the case of prefixed words). Figure 4.3 illustrates this contrast between the representations of inflected words (using FAILED as the example) and derived words (with FAILURE as the example).

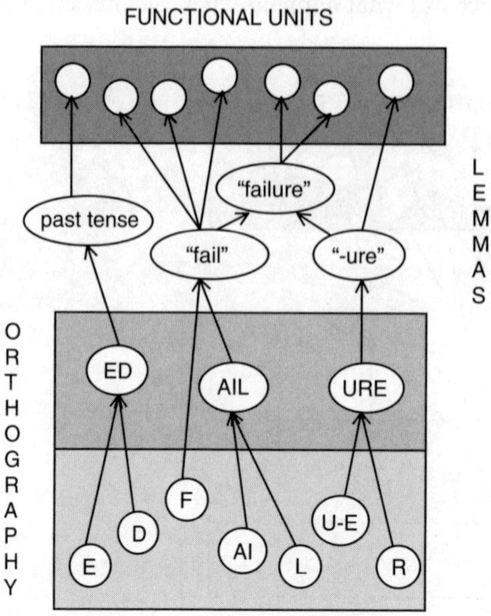

Figure 4.3 The lexical representation of an inflected word (FAILED) and a derived word (FAILURE) according to an obligatory decomposition account framed within the localist-cum-distributed model.

No lemma exists for FAILED because this word means nothing more than the meaning associated with the lemma for FAIL in combination with the past-tense function of –ED. On the other hand, there must be a lemma for FAILURE in order to capture the way in which that word conveys more than the meaning of FAIL combined with the nominalizing function of the –URE suffix. For example, some uses of FAIL cannot be nominalized (e.g. "He failed to understand" can be nominalized as "He had a failure to understand", but "He failed to reply" cannot be nominalized as "He had a failure to reply"). Moreover, a lemma for FAILURE provides the knowledge that FAIL is nominalized by combining it with –URE (rather than, say, –MENT or –AGE). As can be seen in Figure 4.3, the word FAILURE is recognized only after it is decomposed into FAIL and URE via the matching of orthographic units. Thus, there is obligatory decomposition for derived words, despite the existence of a lemma representation for the whole word.

A more popular theory of morphological processing, however, is a dual-pathways account that states that whole-word access and morphological decomposition work in parallel with the successful pathway depending on the nature of the polymorphemic word being recognized (e.g. Baayen, Dijkstra, & Schreuder, 1997; Bertram, Schreuder, & Baayen, 2000; Burani & Caramazza, 1987; Schreuder & Baayen, 1995). Within the LCD framework, this amounts to saying that whole-word lemmas can be activated directly from form units without the mediation of constituent lemmas. However, it still means that decomposition is taking place inasmuch as affixes are treated separately from stems within the form units. To make the stronger claim that the whole-word pathway involves no decomposition at all (the typical dual-pathways view), there would need to be an orthographic representation of the whole word that can be activated directly from the graphemic level of representation. Such a form-based lexical representation is not a part of the LCD model, so the LCD framework is not compatible with the strongest version of the dual-pathways account.

The finding that evidence for stem processing disappears under certain circumstances (which is the basis for the dual-pathways account) is the greatest challenge to the obligatory decomposition idea. Taft (2004) explains how such results might be handled by obligatory decomposition, largely on the grounds that difficulties at the recombination stage for particular types of words could potentially counteract any advantages those words might benefit from during stem activation. However, it must be acknowledged that interactions of stem-processing effects with word length using eye-movement measures, as reported by *Pollatsek and Hyönä* (this volume), do remain to be dealt with. The argument will require a case-by-case determination of whether the lack of stem-processing effects for short words can be explained in terms of the decomposition and recombination stages both taking place within a single eye fixation.

Polysyllabic words

I argued earlier that monosyllabic morphemes are recognized via their body units (see Figures 4.1 and 4.3). As can also be seen in Figure 4.2, the polysyllabic word VIRUS is activated through two orthographic units, IR and US, where the former is the body of the unit shared with VIRAL. It would then be parsimonious to suggest that a polysyllabic word is recognized via the same subsyllabic units involved in the recognition of a monosyllabic word. For example, the lemma for MEADOW might be activated through the same body unit as HEAD (i.e. –EAD) along with a body unit corresponding to its second syllable (i.e. –OW). Such an idea is consistent with the finding (Taft, 1992) that nonword pronunciations are biased by the prior presentation of the body of their first syllable (e.g. MEADOW–JEAD), and not by the presentation of their onset-plus-vowel (e.g. JEALOUS–JEAD). While not saying anything about the fate of the second syllable, this result implies that the body of the first syllable is treated as if it were the body of a monosyllabic word.

If that is the case, it is necessary to establish what the boundary of the first orthographically defined syllable is. What I have suggested over many years (Taft, 1979, 1986, 1987, 1992, 2001, 2002) is that the first orthographically defined syllable maximizes the size of its coda, and I termed this unit the basic orthographic syllabic structure (*BOSS*). So, the *BOSS* of THUNDER is THUND and the *BOSS* of VIRUS is VIR, even though the first spoken syllables are THUN and VI, respectively (minimizing the coda). The primary technique used to support this position was to show faster lexical decision times when a word was physically split according to its *BOSS* (e.g. with a gap, such as THUND ER) than when split according to its corresponding spoken syllable (e.g. THUN DER). The more recent studies (Taft, 2001, 2002) went on to suggest that this was actually the case only for better adult readers and that, if anything, poorer readers favoured the syllable division.

Within the LCD framework, the difference between good and poor readers could arise from the latter having a less efficient representation of orthography (i.e. having units that are not optimally informative because of their minimal coda), or it could arise from the latter using a less sophisticated phonological system, namely, one that is based more closely on the spoken form of the word than on the phonological equivalent of the orthographic representation. So, if phonological units connect directly to orthographic units (e.g. –UND → /ʌnd/), then better readers will not be able to directly activate the correct spoken syllable structure (i.e. /θʌn-də/) from their orthographic units if the coda is optimized (giving /θʌnd-ə/ rather than /θʌn-də/). Instead, they would need to resyllabify the phonological representation when generating any spoken output. Poorer readers, on the other hand, would be able to output the correct syllabification directly from their phonological representation. If this is so, it would imply that proficient reading relies more upon an optimal representation of orthography than upon an optimal representation of surface phonology.

Conclusions

As outlined in this chapter, the LCD model provides a useful way of framing our understanding of issues such as phonological activation in reading, polysyllabic word recognition, and morphological processing. Few, if any, other single models have been as all-embracing as this, with their focus being on specific domains of lexical processing. The main reason for the narrower focus of other models has probably been their quest for computational simulation where such an endeavour would be too complex if they were to stray beyond a single domain. There is no computational version of the LCD model, but I would argue that this does not limit the understanding of how the model works and how it incorporates a wide range of research findings.

The aim of the model is to provide a concrete framework for understanding how words are processed, as exemplified by Figures 4.1–4.3, in which the representation of actual words is identified explicitly. The way in which any word might be represented and activated could be similarly illustrated, and, in so doing, comparisons can be readily made between different types of words, as, indeed, Figure 4.3 shows in relation to inflected versus derived words. It is not difficult to extrapolate from such depictions of the lexical processing system what they would predict in relation to the ease of responding to different types of words (see, for example, Taft & Ardasinski, in press, for predictions regarding the comparison of inflected and derived words based on the structure proposed in Figure 4.3).

It is arguable whether it would be an advantage or disadvantage to go further and implement a computational version of the LCD model. Clearly, there are those who would only trust a model that has been computationally implemented, because the physical generation of simulation data depends on all aspects of the model having been made to function successfully. All the decisions that need to be made at every point of an implemented model must have been confronted and successfully resolved. On the other hand, the problems that need to be resolved when implementing a model are often peripheral to its central focus, and it is for this reason that I have eschewed implementation.

To illustrate, in setting up a computational model of the mapping of print to sound, decisions need to be made about the coding at input of the individual letters in relation to their position in the word and whether to restrict the input to a certain type of stimulus (e.g. monosyllabic words). In so doing, one needs either to choose the most expedient solution (in which case the decision is arbitrary and atheoretical) or to explore thoroughly the options (in which case the research endeavour moves away from its *raison d'être*). If the former, the computational model verges on the meaningless because all components of processing are integral to generating the simulation data, and quite different output would arise if different solutions to the peripheral problems of implementation are chosen. By not constraining the LCD model with a computational implementation, the essential aspects of how different types of words might plausibly be stored in and retrieved from lexical memory can be readily conceptualized, and the purpose of this chapter has been to provide a demonstration of how the model does this in relation to orthographic, phonological, and morphological processing.

Acknowledgement

The research reported in this paper was supported by a grant to the author from the Australian Research Council.

References

Andrews, S. (1982). Phonological recoding: Is the regularity effect consistent? *Memory and Cognition, 10*, 565–575.

Andrews, S., & Scarratt, D. R. (1998). Rule and analogy mechanisms in reading nonwords: Hough dou peapel rede gnew wirds? *Journal of Experimental Psychology: Human Perception and Performance, 24*, 1052–1086.

Baayen, R. H., Dijkstra, T., & Schreuder, R. (1997). Singulars and plurals in Dutch: Evidence for a parallel dual route model. *Journal of Memory and Language, 37*, 94–117.

Bertram, R., Schreuder, R., & Baayen, R. H. (2000). The balance of storage and computation in morphological processing: The role of word formation type, affixal homophony, and productivity. *Journal of Experimental Psychology: Learning, Memory, and Cognition, 26*, 489–511.

Bowey, J. A. (1990). Orthographic onsets and rimes are functional units of reading. *Memory and Cognition, 18*, 419–427.

Burani, C., & Caramazza, A. (1987). Representation and processing of derived words. *Language and Cognitive Processes, 2*, 217–227.

Coltheart, M., Curtis, B., Atkins, P., & Haller, M. (1993). Models of reading aloud: Dual-route and parallel-distributed-processing approaches. *Psychological Review, 100*, 589–608.

Coltheart, M., Rastle, K., Perry, C., Langdon, R., & Ziegler, J. (2001). DRC: A dual route cascaded model of visual word recognition and reading aloud. *Psychological Review, 108*, 204–256.

Coltheart, V., Patterson, K., & Leahy, J. (1994). When a ROWS is a ROSE: Phonological effects in written word comprehension. *Quarterly Journal of Experimental Psychology: Human Experimental Psychology, 47A*, 917–955.

Frost, R. (1998). Toward a strong phonological theory of visual word recognition: True issues and false trails. *Psychological Bulletin, 123*, 71–99.

Glushko, R. J. (1979). The organization and activation of orthographic knowledge in reading aloud. *Journal of Experimental Psychology: Human Perception and Performance, 5*, 674–691.

Jacobs, A. M., Rey, A., Ziegler, J. C., & Grainger, J. (1998). MROM-P: An interactive-activation, multiple read-out model of orthographic and phonological processes in visual word recognition. In J. Grainger & A. M. Jacobs (Eds.), *Localist connectionist approaches to human cognition* (pp. 147–188). Mahwah, NJ: Lawrence Erlbaum Associates, Inc.

Kay, J., & Marcel, A. J. (1981). One process, not two, in reading aloud: Lexical analogies do the work of nonlexical rules. *Quarterly Journal of Experimental Psychology, 33A*, 397–414.

McCann, R. S., Besner, D., & Davelaar, E. (1988). Word recognition and identification: Do word-frequency effects reflect lexical access? *Journal of Experimental Psychology: Human Perception and Performance, 14*, 693–706.

Patterson, K. E., & Morton, J. (1985). From orthography to phonology: An attempt at an old interpretation. In K. E. Patterson, J. C. Marshall, & M. Coltheart (Eds.), *Surface dyslexia*. Hove, UK: Lawrence Erlbaum Associates Ltd.

Plaut, D. C., McClelland, J. L., Seidenberg, M. S., & Patterson, K. (1996). Understanding normal and impaired word reading: Computational principles in quasi-regular domains. *Psychological Review, 103*, 56–115.

Rastle, K., Davis, M. H., Marslen-Wilson, W. D., & Tyler, L. K. (2000). Morphological and semantic effects in visual word recognition: A time-course study. *Language and Cognitive Processes, 15*, 507–537.

Schreuder, R., & Baayen, R. H. (1995). Modeling morphological processing. In L. B. Feldman (Ed.), *Morphological aspects of language processing* (pp. 131–154). Hillsdale, NJ: Lawrence Erlbaum Associates, Inc.

Seidenberg, M. S., & McClelland, J. L. (1989). A distributed, developmental model of word recognition and naming. *Psychological Review, 96*, 523–568.

Seidenberg, M. S., Waters, G. S., Barnes, M. A., & Tanenhaus, M. K. (1984). When does irregular spelling or pronunciation influence word recognition? *Journal of Verbal Learning and Verbal Behavior, 23*, 383–404.

Shallice, T., & McCarthy, R. (1985). Phonological reading: From patterns of impairment to possible procedures. In K. E. Patterson, J. C. Marshall, & M. Coltheart (Eds.), *Surface dyslexia*. Hove, UK: Lawrence Erlbaum Associates Ltd.

Shallice, T., Warrington, E. K., & McCarthy, R. (1983). Reading without semantics. *Quarterly Journal of Experimental Psychology, 35A*, 111–138.

Stone, G. O., Vanhoy, M., & Van Orden, G. C. (1997). Perception is a two-way street: Feedforward and feedback phonology in visual word recognition. *Journal of Memory and Language, 36*, 337–359.

Taft, M. (1979). Recognition of affixed words and the word frequency effect. *Memory and Cognition, 7*, 263–272.

Taft, M. (1982). An alternative to grapheme-phoneme conversion rules? *Memory and Cognition, 10*, 465–474.

Taft, M. (1986). Lexical access codes in visual and auditory word recognition. *Language and Cognitive Processes, 1*, 49–60.

Taft, M. (1987). Morphographic processing: The BOSS re-emerges. In M. Coltheart (Ed.), *Attention and performance, XII*. Hove, UK Lawrence Erlbaum Associates Ltd.

Taft, M. (1991). *Reading and the mental lexicon*. Hove, UK: Lawrence Erlbaum Associates Ltd.

Taft, M. (1992). The body of the BOSS: Subsyllabic units in the lexical processing of polysyllabic words. *Journal of Experimental Psychology: Human Perception and Performance, 18*, 1004–1014.

Taft, M. (2001). Processing of orthographic structure by adults of different reading ability. *Language and Speech, 44*, 351–376.

Taft, M. (2002). Orthographic processing of polysyllabic words by native and non-native English speakers. *Brain and Language, 81*, 532–544.

Taft, M. (2003). Morphological representation as a correlation between form and meaning. In E. Assink & D. Sandra (Eds.), *Reading complex words*. Amsterdam: Kluwer.

Taft, M. (2004). Morphological decomposition and the reverse base frequency effect. *Quarterly Journal of Experimental Psychology, 57A*, 745–765.

Taft, M., & Ardasinski, S. (in press). Obligatory decomposition in reading prefixed words. *The Mental Lexicon*.

Taft, M., & Forster, K. I. (1975). Lexical storage and retrieval of prefixed words. *Journal of Verbal Learning and Verbal Behavior, 14*, 638–647.

Taft, M., & Forster, K. I. (1976). Lexical storage and retrieval of polymorphemic and polysyllabic words. *Journal of Verbal Learning and Verbal Behavior, 15*, 607–620.

Taft, M., & Kougious, P. (2004). The processing of morpheme-like units in monomorphemic words. *Brain and Language, 90*, 9–16.

Taft, M., & van Graan, F. (1998). Lack of phonological mediation in a semantic categorization task. *Journal of Memory and Language, 38*, 203–224.

Taraban, R., & McClelland, J. L. (1987). Conspiracy effects in word pronunciation. *Journal of Memory and Language, 26*, 608–631.

Treiman, R. (1983). The structure of spoken syllables: Evidence from novel word games. *Cognition, 15*, 49–74.

Treiman, R. (1986). The division between onsets and rimes in English syllables. *Journal of Memory and Language, 25*, 476–491.

Treiman, R., & Chafetz, J. (1987). Are there onset- and rime-like units in printed words? In M. Coltheart (Ed.), *Attention and performance, XII*. Hove, UK: Lawrence Erlbaum Associates Ltd.

Treiman, R., & Zukowski, A. (1988). Units in reading and spelling. *Journal of Memory and Language, 27*, 466–477.

Unsworth, S. J., & Pexman, P. M. (2003). The impact of reader skill on phonological processing in visual word recognition. *Quarterly Journal of Experimental Psychology: Human Experimental Psychology, 56A*, 63–81.

Van Orden, G. C. (1987). A ROWS is a ROSE: Spelling, sound, and reading. *Memory and Cognition, 15*, 181–198.

Note

1 The homophonic words are *phone* and *siege* respectively. Note that the difficulty in judging the homophony of SEEJ cannot be explained in terms of its unusual orthographic structure because naming responses should then be difficult as well.

5 Five challenges for activation models

Kenneth I. Forster
University of Arizona, USA

Virtually all current theories of visual word recognition are based on some version of a parallel activation model. Some are explicitly based on the original interactive activation model proposed by McClelland and Rumelhart (1981), which was itself based on ideas developed in the earlier logogen model (Morton, 1970), and before that, the Pandemonium model of pattern recognition (Selfridge, 1959). Foremost among these models are the dual-route cascaded (DRC) model (Coltheart, Rastle, Perry, Langdon, & Ziegler, 2001), MROM (Grainger & Jacobs, 1996), and BIA (Dijkstra & Van Heuven, 2002). Others are based on the parallel distributed processing (PDP) connectionist approach, such as Seidenberg and McClelland's "single"-route model (Seidenberg & McClelland, 1989), Plaut (1997), and *Kello*'s junction model (this volume). Although these models differ in their basic assumptions and approach (e.g. whether word units exist), there is universal agreement on the basic algorithm that subserves the process of lexical access, namely, parallel activation.

It is my belief that the parallel activation assumption has become so dominant, so ingrained in our thinking, that it may soon begin to have a stultifying effect. The basic validity of this approach has become so accepted that it has slipped into the background, where it is shielded from close examination. If we think of a theory as a way of viewing the world around us, the danger is that we get to see only the phenomena that our theory lets us see. Newly discovered phenomena that do not readily fit within the framework of the model may be ignored, and new ideas about information-processing mechanisms may be rejected out of hand.

The object of this paper is to attempt to redress this situation, and to promote a more "free market" approach to theory construction. To this end, I will outline five challenges for activation models. Each challenge consists of a recently discovered phenomenon that does not readily fit into an activation mould. It is not claimed that these phenomena cannot be explained in activation terms, but it is hoped that the effort necessary to achieve this will stimulate new growth.

From my perspective, the essence of the parallel model is the assumption that the input stimulus is compared with the lexical representations of every word in the mental lexicon simultaneously. The amount of activation in each word unit is a function of the resting level of the unit, plus the degree of orthographic overlap with the input. The alternative to a parallel model is to propose that the comparison is made only for a limited subset of the lexicon, and is carried out in a serial fashion, with goodness-of-fit scores being assigned to lexical representations one at a time, instead of all at once. Essentially, a search path is defined through a subset of the entire lexicon, such that if the input corresponds to a word, the lexical entry for that word will be included in the search set. The search through this set is conducted in a serial fashion, and is frequency ordered, so that the first entry scanned is the entry for the highest-frequency word in the set, and the last entry to be scanned is the entry for the lowest-frequency word in the set. This corresponds to the critical assumptions in the so-called bin model of lexical access (Forster, 1976, 1989).

For each of the challenges, I will claim that that the phenomena are more consistent with a model that includes a serial component than with a parallel activation model. My hope is that when the dust settles, we will begin to see that the different approaches have crept a little closer.

Challenge 1: Is word recognition incremental?

The first challenge concerns the nature of the activation process itself. In a parallel activation model with localist representations (that is, for each word, there is a word unit), activation in the word units accumulates gradually over time. All other things being equal, the activation level in the correct word unit will be greater than in any other unit at all stages of processing. As time progresses, the difference in activation level between the correct unit and all other units will steadily increase, but, theoretically, the relative activation levels could be used to identify the stimulus with better than chance accuracy at any point in time, although obviously, with less reliability at earlier points in time.

This capacity is in stark contrast with the capacities of a search model. Prior to the point in time when a matching entry is first contacted, there is absolutely no evidence to indicate which word best matches the input, nor is there any indication about whether the input is more likely to be a word or a nonword. For a search model, there is no sense in which recognition could be described as incremental. Although a logogen-type model has parallel incremental activation, this model suffers the same fate—prior to a logogen reaching threshold, there is no information about whether the input is likely to be a word or not. However, in cascaded models such as DRC and MROM, there is no threshold, and the decision that the input is a word is made whenever the activation level in a particular word unit reaches a criterion level. It is even possible that reasonably accurate decisions can be made prior to this point. Obviously, if the activation in a particular word unit is approaching criterion at a rapid rate, the chances are that it is a word. However, there are limits on the capacity of a network to observe its own state, and it is difficult to arrange matters so that the activation levels in all word units and their rate of change can be individually monitored (see Challenge 2).

This problem is overcome by postulating the existence of a global activation index. This index represents summed activation over all word units, and gives an overall measure of the activity in the lexical network. As proposed by Grainger and Jacobs in MROM, there are two methods by which lexical decisions can be made. One is to respond positively whenever activation in a word unit reaches a certain level (the *M* criterion), and the other is to respond positively if the activation in the global activation index reaches a certain level (the Σ criterion). Fast lexical decisions could be based on the global activation index, since the strongest contribution to this index comes from a word unit that matches the input exactly. Thus, the activation level in the global index increases at a more rapid rate when the input is a word rather than a nonword, and therefore better than chance accuracy in a lexical decision task could be attained long before any word unit reaches criterion. This index performs an important function in models such as DRC and MROM, enabling these models to explain why lexical decisions are longer for nonwords that have a word as a neighbour (e.g. Coltheart, Davelaar, Jonasson, & Besner, 1977), and why low-frequency words with many neighbours are responded to more rapidly than words with few neighbours (Andrews, 1997).

For present purposes, the important issue is whether there is direct evidence for or against the existence of such an index. If it can be shown that decisions in a lexical decision task can be based on global activation, this is an important result, because the class of models that could provide such an index is very limited. This capacity of the global activation index to predict the likelihood that a word unit will reach criterion at some future point in time depends on the fact that the input is compared with all word units simultaneously, and that activation builds up more rapidly in a word unit that matches the input exactly. This capacity cannot be duplicated in a serial model, and hence this seems like an important area for further investigation. However, with one exception, it appears that there has been no effort to test experimentally whether such an index exists. The one exception is a paper by Jacobs, Graf, and Kinder (2003), who used signal detection analysis to demonstrate that lexical decisions are based on a smooth, incremental accumulation of evidence, rather than a discrete, all-or-nothing process typical of threshold models (and search models). The argument is based on the work of Yonelinas (1994), who was concerned with episodic recognition and the role that familiarity might play in that process. The evidence supporting an incremental process is that the receiver operating characteristics (ROC) for lexical decision under data-limited conditions (very brief, masked presentation) show a curvilinear relationship between the probability of a hit and the probability of a false alarm. When the probabilities are converted to *z*-scores, the result is a linear plot with a slope of 1. This is the result obtained by Jacobs et al. (2003), although the results obtained by Paap, Chun, and Vonnahme (1999) in a similar study were less clear.

The connection between these results and the existence of a global activation index is of course rather indirect, and depends on a number of assumptions. Further, the data being analysed are essentially guesses about the possible lexical status of a heavily masked stimulus. However, there is a more direct approach that involves time-limited rather than data-limited decisions. As pointed out by Dennis Norris (personal communication), in a speeded lexical decision task, where a very short response deadline is imposed, subjects are forced to respond earlier than they would normally; yet decisions are still more accurate for high-frequency words than for low-frequency words. This result fits nicely with the assumption of incremental growth of activation. Even after a short interval, the global activation index will be higher for words than for nonwords (because of the strong contribution from a matching word unit), and will also be higher for high-frequency words than for low-frequency words (because high-frequency word units have higher resting levels of activation). This result also fits a logogen-type model with thresholds, provided we assume that subjects can lower the thresholds on all word units when the task demands a rapid response. However, this result is problematic for a serial search model because prior to locating the matching entry, nothing at all would be known about the lexical status of the input, and hence it is difficult to explain how anything other than chance performance could be achieved with an early deadline.

This seems quite devastating for a search model. However, the existence of a frequency effect is problematic only if the deadline is set so early that not even high-frequency words can be accessed in the time allowed. If this is not the case, it would be quite possible for subjects to be above chance in discriminating high-frequency words from nonwords, but at chance for low-frequency words. Interestingly, it is not so clear that this situation is entirely compatible with a parallel activation model. This can be seen if we consider the growth function of global activation in DRC shown in Figure 5.1 (these data were kindly supplied by M. Coltheart). These curves were based on the 60 highest-frequency words in the DRC lexicon, the 60 lowest-frequency words, and 120 nonwords matched with the words on length and number of neighbours. The important point to note is that no matter where the response deadline is placed, there will always be a difference between the activation levels for low-frequency words and nonwords. Obviously, discrimination accuracy will be poorer with very early deadlines (e.g. deadline A), because the differences in global activation are smaller and presumably subject to greater variability. However, it is not unreasonable to expect better than chance performance on low-frequency words as well as high-frequency words.

So now we have an interesting hypothesis to test. If a short response deadline is used, so that decisions must be made via a global activation index, performance should theoretically be above chance for both high- and

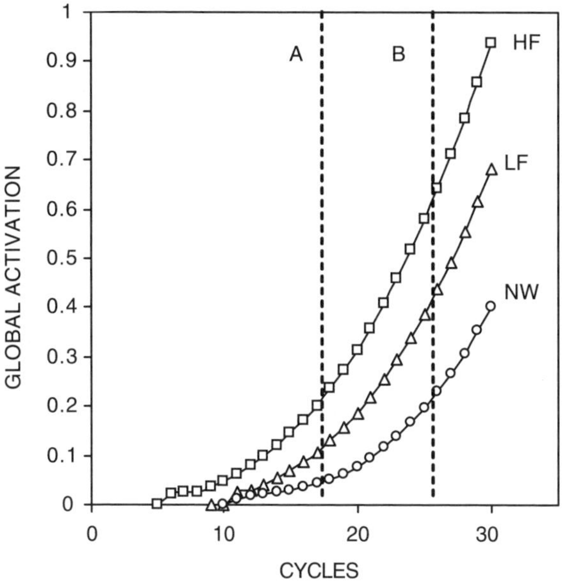

Figure 5.1 Growth of global activation over time for high-frequency words (HF), low-frequency words (LF), and nonwords (NW). The dotted vertical lines represent two examples of response deadlines.

low-frequency words, no matter where the deadline is placed, provided that it is not so early that the differences in the global activation values are so small as to be unreliable. The same reasoning does not apply to a search model. The fact that high-frequency words can be accurately classified could simply mean that there was sufficient time for the search to find a matching entry (recall that in the bin model, the search process compares the input with the entries for high-frequency words first), but there would be no implication that low-frequency words should also be above chance. That would depend on how long it took to find the relevant entry. So it would be quite possible to find a situation in which low-frequency words were at chance, but high-frequency words were above chance.

The predictions for nonwords are a little different. Under normal conditions, a "No" decision would not be made until sufficient time had been allowed for even the lowest-frequency word to be accessed. But if an earlier deadline has been imposed, there is no clear basis for making a decision, and hence the subject is forced to guess. So under these conditions, performance on nonwords could never be better than chance.[1] This is not true for judgements based on a global activation index. If the index is very low, subjects should decide that it is more likely to be a nonword. If it is relatively high, it is more likely to be a word. Therefore, if the deadline is long enough to produce above chance accuracy for words, we should expect to find above chance accuracy for nonwords as well.

The first experiment testing these predictions was carried out in our laboratory by David Lent. The stimuli consisted of 50 high-frequency words (above 75 per million in the Kucera-Francis count), 50 randomly chosen low-frequency words (3–8 per million), and 100 orthographically legal nonwords. All items were 4–6 letters in length. Subjects were asked to classify the item as a word or not, and were told they must respond before the item was erased from the screen. This occurred after 500 ms. Trials on which a response was not made before the deadline were discarded. The dependent variable was therefore accuracy on the trials where a response was made before the deadline. As it turned out, subjects varied in their ability to cope with the deadline. Some were able to operate at a high level of accuracy. For them, the deadline was too long, and for present purposes, these individuals do not contribute useful data. Instead we restricted our analysis to those subjects who were unable to perform above chance on the low-frequency words (above chance being defined as greater than 65% correct, which is equivalent to a binomial probability value of .016). Seven out of the eleven subjects tested fell into this category. Their data are shown in Table 5.1.

As shown in Table 5.1, the mean percentage correct for these subjects was 81.8% for high-frequency words, which differed from chance, $t(6) = 10.92$, $p < .001$. Every subject achieved a better than chance level of performance (65%) in this condition. As would be expected, mean performance on low-frequency words (52.4%) did not differ from chance, $t(6) = 1.08$, $p > .05$. This was also true for performance on nonwords (55.1%), $t(6) = 0.84$, $p > .05$. For the four subjects who performed above chance for low-frequency words, the mean percentages correct for high-frequency words, low-frequency words, and nonwords were 86.5%, 76.2%, and 45.5%, respectively. It is of interest to note that, despite being well above chance on words, they were slightly below chance on nonwords.

Such a pattern of results is completely compatible with the assumptions of

Table 5.1 Mean number of correct decisions reached before the deadline for high-frequency words (HF), low-frequency words (LF), and nonwords (NW) for seven subjects failing to score significantly above chance for LF words

Subject	*HF*	*LF*	*NW*
1	73.4	42.9	44.1
2	91.4	48.3	28.9
3	73.3	50.0	58.8
4	76.2	52.9	68.8
5	84.4	55.3	73.3
6	90.7	58.1	65.8
7	82.9	59.0	46.2
Mean	81.8	52.4	55.1
t	10.92	1.08	0.84
p	< .001	.32	.43

the search model. For the seven individuals at chance for low-frequency words, the deadline was long enough to allow them to find a matching entry for most high-frequency words, but not for low-frequency words. Since insufficient time was allowed to access the entries for low-frequency words, there was also no way to generate an accurate decision for nonwords, and hence these individuals were at chance for both. For the four individuals who performed above chance on low-frequency words, the deadline was long enough for them to access most high-frequency words and some low-frequency words. However, because there was insufficient time to access *all* low-frequency words, it was impossible to classify the input as a nonword, and hence subjects were still forced to guess.[2] This approach is reasonable if subjects are defining nonwords by exclusion (i.e. *X* is a nonword if and only if it is not a member of the set of words).

In contrast, these results are not so favourable for an activation model, if it assumed that these fast decisions are based on a global activation index. The growth curves shown in Figure 5.1 suggest that if there was sufficient time for the global activation index to reliably signal the presence of a high-frequency word, it should have been able to signal the presence of a low-frequency word as well, since the curve for nonwords is clearly lower than the curve for low-frequency words. One possibility is that for these subjects, the deadline was positioned so that the global activation for low-frequency words was in a region of uncertainty, as shown in Figure 5.2. Under these circumstances, it would be reasonable to expect subjects to respond at random. However, the global activation value for nonwords is still well below the uncertain region, which ought to lead to above chance performance for nonwords. Yet this was not the case. Even more surprising is the fact that this was also true for the subjects who were above chance on both sets of words. For these subjects, the deadline would have been located further to the right in Figure 5.2, where the difference in activation between words and nonwords would have been even greater.

An alternative interpretation is that decisions about the high-frequency words were not based on the global activation index, but instead were based on the fact that unit activation levels for these words actually reached criterion. If high-frequency words reached criterion very early, before the global activation for low-frequency words had fully developed, one could explain chance performance on low-frequency words. However, the earliest point at which high-frequency words reached a criterion of 0.70 was cycle 36, and by that stage, the global activation for low-frequency words was well above zero.

What is needed here is a way of explaining the poor performance on nonwords. Perhaps for some subjects (unlike DRC), the global activation functions for low-frequency words do not reliably diverge from nonwords until relatively late, with the result that at the point of testing, the difference in global activation is not sufficient to produce accurate decisions. One way to test whether this alternative is worth pursuing is to manipulate another variable that contributes to the global activation index, namely, N, the number of

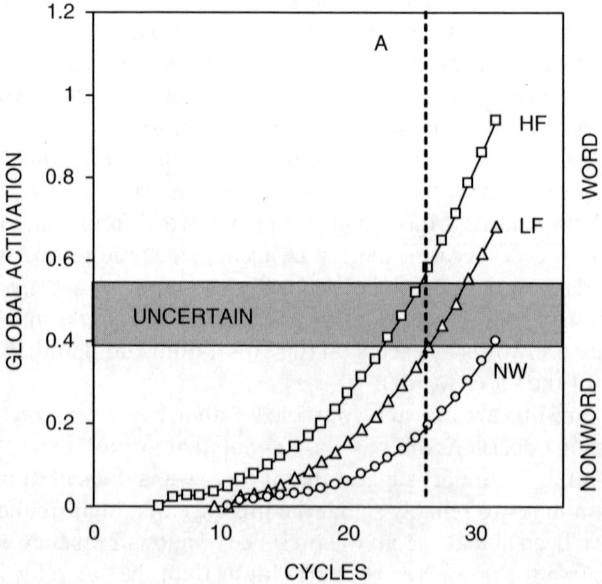

Figure 5.2 Growth of global activation over time for subjects showing chance performance on low-frequency (LF) words. The shaded area represents the region of uncertainty, and the dotted, vertical line A represents the imposed deadline. In this example, the deadline is assumed to be set at the point when the global activation produced by a low-frequency word is equivocal. HF: high frequency; NW: nonwords.

neighbours. Words that overlap orthographically with the input will generate activation, which will contribute to the global activation level. This situation is illustrated in Figure 5.3, which plots the global activation levels in DRC for high-N items (more than six neighbours) and low-N items (fewer than six neighbours). As is evident from this figure, N makes a contribution to global activation, but lexicality makes a stronger contribution. So if it is assumed that the reason that some subjects are at chance on both low-frequency words and nonwords is that lexical status exerts too small an influence on global activation early in processing, then it should also be the case that N has no effect as well.

The next experiment was carried out in our laboratory by Zachary Wolff. It is basically a repetition of the first, but now the items vary in the number of neighbours. Target items consisted of 60 words and 60 nonwords; half were high N (eight or more neighbours), and half were low N (one or fewer neighbours). Half of the words were high frequency (Kucera & Francis ≤ 80) and half were low frequency (Kucera & Francis ≤ 20). All items were 4–6 letters in length. Ten subjects were tested with a response deadline of 450 ms. Once again, we consider only the data from individuals who were at chance (below 65% correct) on low-frequency

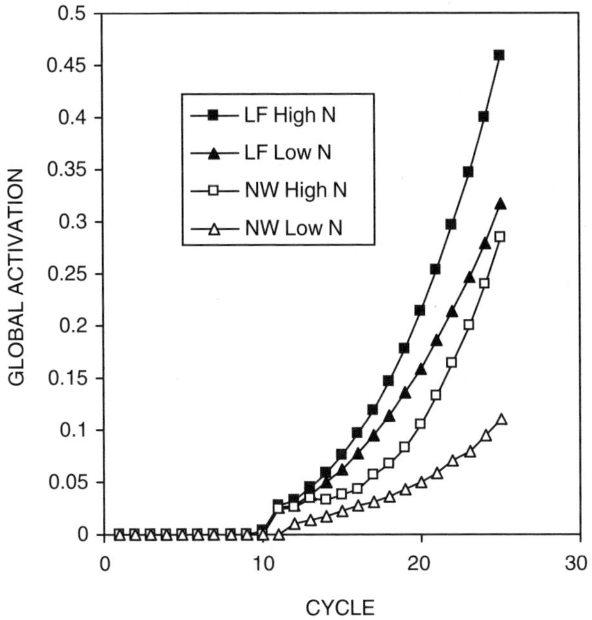

Figure 5.3 Growth of dual-route cascaded global activation for low-frequency (LF) words and nonwords (NW) for high-N items (more than six neighbours) and low-N items (fewer than seven neighbours).

Table 5.2 Mean percentage of correct decisions for high-frequency words (HF), low-frequency words (LF), and nonwords (NW) varying in number of neighbours (N)

	HF	*LF*	*NW*
Low N	69.6	38.9	58.0
High N	78.2	59.6	46.3
Mean	73.9	49.2	52.2

words. Seven subjects fell into this category. The means for these subjects are shown in Table 5.2.

Once again, we see that performance for these selected subjects on high-frequency words is well above chance, $t(6) = 3.29$, $p < .01$, but performance on both low-frequency words and nonwords did not differ from chance ($p > .05$). The critical comparisons involving the effect of N showed that for high-frequency words, there was no significant effect (8.6%), $t(6) = 0.94$, $p > .05$, but for low-frequency words, there was a strong effect (20.7%), $t(6) = 5.14$, $p = .001$, with performance being much better for high-N words. There was also a sizeable effect in the reverse direction for nonwords (11.7%), but this proved not to be reliable, $t(6) = 1.66$, $p > .05$.

These results make it very difficult to argue that the poor performance of the at-chance subjects on low-frequency words is due to a negligible difference in global activation between low-frequency words and nonwords. The reason is that there could not be an effect of N on global activation without there also being an effect of lexicality. Therefore, subjects who are sensitive to N should also be sensitive to lexical status. But for low-frequency words, they are not. Of course, this argument would have less force if N had a far greater impact on global activation than lexicality. This is not the case, as shown in the DRC global activation curves in Figure 5.3, where it can be seen that low-frequency words generate higher global activation levels than nonwords both when N is high and when it is low (although at later cycles, high-N nonwords are clearly catching up to low-N low-frequency words).

The relative impact of lexicality and N is best seen when we analyze the effects of these variables on global activation for low-frequency words and nonwords as a function of processing cycle. The items were divided into high-N and low-N groups (ignoring lexicality) by a median split on N, and the N effect was defined as the difference between the mean global activation for the high-N group and the mean global activation for the low-N group. The items were also divided into word and nonword groups, and the lexicality effect was defined as the difference between the mean global activation for the words and the nonwords. Early in processing there is no global activation, so both effects will be zero; both effects should increase monotonically after some particular processing cycle is reached.

What is critical for the DRC interpretation is that the N effect should move above zero on an earlier processing cycle than the lexicality effect. This would explain the performance of subjects whose lexical decision performance with low-frequency words and nonwords is affected by N, but not by lexicality. Figure 5.4 shows that this does not happen with the DRC model. Both the N effect and the lexicality effect are zero up to and including cycle 10, and they first rise above zero on the same cycle, that is, cycle 11. So an effect of N on global activation in the absence of an effect of lexicality could not be simulated with DRC's standard parameter set; yet some subjects do show this effect.

Clearly, if these results hold up to closer scrutiny, major changes in the global activation approach to lexical decision will have to be made. Should the same be said for a search approach? After all, N effects are not easily explained with such a model. However, it is possible to argue that when subjects are forced to respond before a matching entry has been located, they use whatever information has already been extracted from the stimulus. If we assume that the initial stage of word recognition involves the recognition of sublexical constituents such as syllables, bodies, onsets, etc. (e.g. Forster & Taft, 1994; Taft & Kougious, 2004), then high-N words (and nonwords) are more likely to contain high-frequency, familiar sublexical units than are low-N words. This could induce a bias toward a "Yes" response. Normally, this bias would be overridden by information derived from lexical sources, but under these speeded conditions, only high-frequency words are accessed

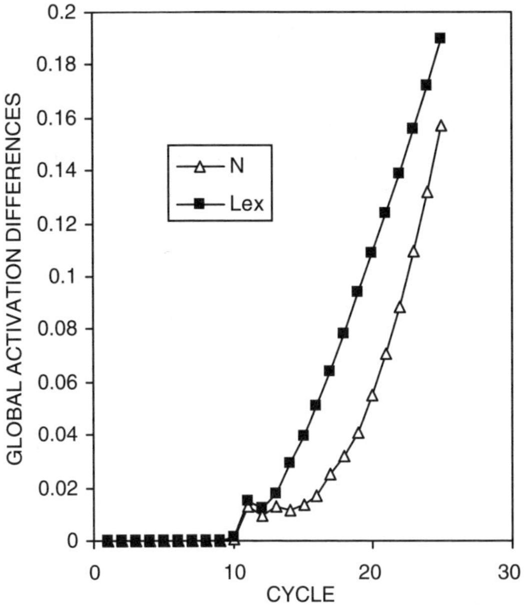

Figure 5.4 Differences in dual-route cascaded global activation due to lexicality (Lex) (LF words–nonwords) and N (high-N items–low-N items).

quickly enough to override this bias. Hence, there is virtually no effect of N on responses to high-frequency words, but there is a strong effect for low-frequency words and a reverse effect for nonwords.

It will not go unnoticed that this pattern of results duplicates the effects observed by Andrews (1997) with standard lexical decision (that is, faster responses for high-N low-frequency words, but no effect of N for high-frequency words). The important thing about the present results is that the same effects are observed when subjects are operating at chance levels (that is, without the benefit of lexical input), which suggests that response bias may be involved in the effects observed by Andrews (1997).

Challenge 2: How are decisions made in a parallel system?

How does a parallel network model arrive at a "Yes" decision in a lexical decision experiment? Coltheart et al. (2001) are very clear on this point. In DRC, a "Yes" decision is made whenever the activation level in any word unit reaches a criterion level. A similar assumption is made in MROM. This seems straightforward enough, until we ask how the system knows when a unit reaches the required level. In the logogen model, this problem is solved by having a threshold, such that a logogen fires when its threshold is reached, and this acts as a signal for the decision system. In essence, each logogen is given the responsibility for deciding whether it has reached criterion, and generating a signal when it has. But in DRC there is no such threshold mechanism, because activation is assumed to be cascaded (that is, activation is always passed forward regardless of the activation level). However, not having a threshold mechanism makes the task of deciding whether any unit has reached criterion more complicated. In fact, it appears that the only way to determine whether any unit has reached a given activation level would be to scan the word units one at a time, comparing the activation level in each unit with the criterion level. This process would have to be repeated after each update cycle. Obviously, much of the advantage of a parallel activation process would be lost, since a scan across the units would be required after each cycle. Thus, it appears that a threshold mechanism is a critical component for the decision process.

We can think of this type of threshold as a *decision* threshold. When the threshold is reached, the system has in a sense made its decision about which word unit matches the input best, and activation levels in all other units are reset. Models based on the IA model do not operate in this way, although they do employ thresholds elsewhere; for example, there is a threshold that determines when letter-to-word inhibition, or word-to-word inhibition is generated. However, there is no threshold that serves as a signal that a matching word unit has been found. In fact, threshold mechanisms are not generally thought of as being compatible with a cascaded system. Normally, the purpose of a threshold is to prevent transmission of activation to other units if the threshold has not been reached. However, the opposite assumption applies in the case of a cascaded system, so that, for example, activation is passed from the word level to phonological and semantic levels in a continuous fashion.

The motivation for a cascaded system is clear. For example, in a semantic categorization task, nonwords that are neighbours of words take longer to reject (e.g., *turple* in an animal categorization task), but only if they are neighbours of an exemplar (Forster & Hector, 2002). The same is true for words (Rodd, 2004). If semantic activation was prevented until a matching word unit had been found, such interference effects would be difficult to explain. Nevertheless, the cascading assumption raises problems in explaining how tasks such as lexical decision are carried out. Of course, one solution would be to propose that the system has a threshold mechanism just for decision purposes, but is fully cascaded nevertheless, although this is somewhat ad hoc. This solution is not without its problems, since humans did not evolve in order to be able to do lexical decision tasks quickly. The more general point is that we need to pay careful attention to the process by which information about the state of the network is transmitted to higher-level decision processes. There are limits to a network's ability to observe its own state, and these limits may have implications for what a network can and cannot do.

As for PDP models with distributed representations, it is still not clear whether the capacity for lexical decision is present, since there are no word units. Instead, a word is simply a pattern of activation across orthographic, phonological, and semantic units. The question then arises, what is a nonword? Is it also a pattern of activation across orthographic, phonological, and semantic units? If so, how is one to tell whether the input is a word or not? One might consult a list of the possible patterns that exist in the language, but this makes the model equivalent to a dictionary look-up. Perhaps the answer is that nonwords do not generate recognizable patterns. However, nonwords obviously do generate a pattern of activation across orthographic and phonological units (since PDP models are designed to be able to pronounce nonwords). But what would happen to the semantic units? Is it possible to argue that nonwords do not generate activity in the semantic layer? This seems unlikely. The experimental evidence indicates that nonwords that are neighbours of words generate sufficient activation in the semantic layer to affect decision making in a semantic categorization task (e.g. Forster & Hector, 2002). Plaut (1997) has proposed an index of activity in the semantic layer called *stress*, which enables a PDP model to make reasonably accurate lexical decisions (nonwords produce slightly less activity than words), although it is not clear what this model would predict as far as latencies are concerned. Moreover, as argued by *Rastle and Coltheart* (this volume), it is doubtful that lexical decisions are made at a semantic level, since patients with impaired semantic systems are nevertheless unimpaired at visual lexical decision.

Challenge 3: Parallel processing of multiple inputs

In a masked priming experiment, the SOA between the prime and the target is usually 60 ms or less. The usual method of simulating these effects with models based on the interactive activation model is to present the prime for 2–5 cycles, and then to replace it with the target (e.g. Van Heuven, Dijkstra, Grainger, & Schriefers, 2001). This means that the target interrupts the processing of the prime very early on, and any further processing of the prime is terminated. Strong letter-to-word inhibition would mean that activation produced by the prime would be quickly suppressed, depending on the degree of orthographic overlap between the prime and target. Initially, the activation produced by the target merges with the pattern produced by the prime, but eventually the target takes complete control. If the two patterns of activation are very similar, processing of the target is facilitated. If they are very different, processing of the target is inhibited.

Similar accounts of priming are offered in attractor-based models (e.g. Rueckl, 2002). Word recognition is described as traversing a trajectory in a high dimensional state space from some random starting point to the attractor basin for the target word. The distance travelled is a measure of access time. When a prime is introduced, the system travels initially in the direction of the prime, but when this is replaced by the target, the direction of travel changes toward the target. If the prime and target are similar either in form or meaning, their attractor basins will be located near each other; therefore moving in the direction of the prime also means moving in the direction of the target, and therefore total travel time is reduced. However, if the prime and target are located in quite different regions, travel time will be increased.

An important point to note about both of these accounts is that processing of the prime is not completed. However, there are reasons for thinking that it must be. For example, strong masked cross-language priming is obtained for translation-equivalent words (e.g. Gollan, Forster, & Frost, 1997; Grainger & Frenck-Mestre, 1998; Jiang & Forster, 2001). In order for *chien* to prime *DOG*, surely it must be the case that the processing of *chien* is virtually completed, so that the appropriate set of semantic features (and only those) are activated. Similar arguments apply in the case of congruence effects in a semantic categorization task with masked primes. For example, when subjects are asked to categorize words according to whether they are animal names or not, slower "No" responses are obtained for items such as *turkey-WALNUT* than for items such as *sponge-WALNUT*, indicating that subjects must be categorizing the prime as well as the target (Forster, 2004, experiment 3). It is hard to imagine that this could be possible with only very preliminary processing of the prime. Similar arguments apply in the case of masked semantic priming (e.g. Perea & Gotor, 1997).

The obvious response to these arguments would be to conclude that the primes must be fully processed within 50–60 ms. However, the problem with this response is that evidence from eye movements and event-related potentials indicates that lexical access takes about 200 ms (Sereno, Rayner, & Posner, 1998). A possible counter to this conclusion is the evidence discussed by *Rayner, Reichle, and Pollatsek* (this volume), which shows that reading is unimpaired when words are removed after 60 ms. This fact might be taken as evidence that lexical access is completed within 60 ms, but, equally, it may simply mean that 60 ms viewing time is sufficient to *initiate* access, but not to complete it. Thus, on balance, it seems reasonable to conclude that processing of the prime is not in fact terminated by the target, but continues on after target onset, with both words being processed in parallel.

However reasonable this solution might seem, it is problematic for parallel activation models. For example, in an attractor model, the system cannot be moving in two directions at once—it cannot continue to move toward the location of the prime while it is also moving toward the location of the target (unless, of course, the prime is the same word as the target). Similarly, in an interactive activation model, activation from the letter units of the target would quickly suppress activation in the word units originally activated by the prime, and hence processing of the prime would effectively terminate.

Search models face the same problem—the system cannot follow two different search paths at the same time, and therefore the search for the prime would have to be abandoned when the target is presented, and a new search launched for the target. However, in this case, there is a relatively simple solution, and that is to propose that the system has two separate search engines that can independently search the same set of lexical entries. This would obviously speed up processing. For example, in reading a sentence, the system could begin processing an upcoming word in the periphery while still processing the currently fixated word, giving rise to the so-called preview effect (Rayner, Balota, & Pollatsek, 1986; *Rayner, Reichle, & Pollatsek*, this volume). A possible problem for such a system might be keeping the results of the two searches distinct. For example, in the entry-opening model of lexical access (Forster, 1999; Forster & Davis, 1984), the search process marks entries that are close matches as possible candidates, but if two searches are carried out at the same time, there is the obvious problem of deciding which candidate belongs to which stimulus. This might seem like a design defect, but it nevertheless provides a very convenient way to explain masked form priming. That is, the initial search for the prime marks the entry for the target as a candidate, and this initiates preprocessing of that entry, saving time when the search for the target encounters the same entry.

There appears to be no comparable solution available for a parallel activation model. One might try to solve the problem by having duplicate networks, so that the prime activates word units in the first network, while the target activates word units in the second, but this is not exactly a parsimonious solution. It would also make it difficult to explain priming, since the word unit activated by the prime would be quite distinct from the word unit activated by the target, even if the prime and target were the same.

Another possibility is to propose a buffered input system, such that the target stimulus is placed in a buffer until processing of the prime has been completed. However, this would predict that the prime delays processing of the target by as much as 150 ms (200 minus the stimulus onset asynchrony (SOA)). That is, responses to a target word preceded by an unrelated prime would be 150 ms slower than responses to a target word preceded by no prime at all. While there is no published evidence on such a comparison, our own unpublished data suggest that the delay is more like 15 ms. Hence, this alternative is not particularly attractive.

Thus, it seems that the only recourse for a parallel activation approach is to claim that 50–60 ms is sufficient time for the prime to be processed to a stage sufficient to produce translation priming, semantic priming, and congruence effects. Obviously, this is not sufficient time to complete the processing of the prime, but with a cascaded activation network, it might be sufficient to weakly activate the semantic features associated with the prime, but perhaps not very clearly, because the semantic features of every neighbour of the prime would also be activated to some degree. Nevertheless, this might be enough to produce a priming effect, since the activation levels in at least some of the semantic units for the target will have been boosted by the prime, and the fact that many other semantic feature units are also active may be quite irrelevant. In other words, maybe the processing of the prime does not have to be very precise.

This approach would also predict that masked priming effects should be observed for pairs such as *fable–CHAIR* when they are presented under the same conditions that produce priming for pairs such as *table–CHAIR* (e.g. a relatively long SOA, such as 60–67 ms). The reasoning here is that *fable* must activate the semantic feature units appropriate for the word *table* because these words are neighbours. The closest example to this is the claim that masked priming effects occur for pairs such as *towed–FROG* (Drieghe & Brysbaert, 2002; Lukatela & Turvey, 1994), where the prime is a homophone of a word that is semantically related to the target. Whether one could also observe priming when the prime is an orthographic neighbour of a word that is semantically related to the target (e.g. *tead–FROG*) is not so clear. A further prediction would be that masked cross-language priming should be observed even when the prime is not a translation of the target, but is merely semantically similar. For example, in an English-French experiment, a translation-equivalent pair such as *horse–CHEVAL* might not produce any more priming than *donkey–CHEVAL*. Interpreted in terms of Rueckl's (2002) metaphor for priming in attractor-based models, which describes priming as resulting from the fact that the prime drives the system state closer to the state required for the target, this would mean that the system does not have to actually reach the attractor basin for the translation prime. All that is necessary is that the prime moves the system closer to the location of the target word, and *horse* and *donkey* might do this equally well. Clearly, these are interesting hypotheses that need to be thoroughly tested.

Challenge 4: How to model semantic categorization

In a semantic categorization task, subjects are asked to classify words according to their meaning; for example, is it the name of animal? The question arises as to how this task should be modelled in a network model. As proposed by Carreiras, Perea, and Grainger (1997), the most obvious procedure would be to directly monitor activation levels in the appropriate semantic feature units. When the activation level reaches a criterion level, a "Yes" decision is made. The speed of response will be influenced by the frequency of the word, and its typicality. For nonexemplars, however, the activation in the semantic feature units will fail to reach criterion, and after a suitable time has elapsed, a "No" decision could be made.

One advantage of this procedure is that it can account of selective interference effects from neighbours. As shown by Forster and Hector (2002), nonwords in an animal categorization experiment take longer to reject when they have an animal name as a close neighbour (e.g. *turple*), but there is no interference when the neighbours are not animal names (e.g. *cishop*). This finding contrasts with the results in a lexical decision experiment, where all neighbours cause interference. The difference is that in a semantic categorization task, the category makes it possible to selectively monitor just one or two feature units, so that activation in category-irrelevant feature units is simply ignored. This is not possible in a lexical decision task, where all feature units would have to be monitored.

The disadvantage of this procedure is that it predicts no frequency effect for nonexemplars, since a "No" decision is based on the expiration of a deadline. Although this was the result originally obtained by Balota and Chumbley (1984), subsequent work has shown that there is a strong frequency effect for nonexemplars (Forster & Shen, 1996; Monsell, Doyle, & Haggard, 1989; for an alternative view, see Balota & Chumbley, 1990). A possible reason for these conflicting results is that the studies obtaining a frequency effect used a single, broad category with a large number of exemplars, whereas Balota and Chumbley used multiple categories, each of which was fairly narrow. Recently, the importance of category size has been confirmed (Forster, 2004). When small categories are used (e.g. month, farm animal), there is no effect of frequency for nonexemplars, but when a broader category is used (e.g. animal), the frequency effect returns.

This effect of category size complicates the issue. One might have argued that whenever a frequency effect for nonexemplars is observed, it means that feature monitoring was not possible. In these cases, the decision system simply waits until an appropriate word unit reaches criterion (setting aside the problems raised in challenge no. 3), and then checks to see whether the appropriate features have been activated. But if this was the procedure used with the animal category, no word unit would reach criterion when a nonword such as *turple* is presented. A "No" decision would be based on the fact that the input was not a word, and therefore no interference would occur.

These findings make perfect sense if we resurrect the notion of category search originally put forward by Landauer and Freedman (1968). In this model, the decision is reached by comparing the input with a list of exemplars. If a match is found, a "Yes" decision is made, and if no match is found, a "No" decision is made. In either case, a decision is made without access to the lexicon proper. This would then explain the absence of frequency effects for nonexemplars when a small category is used. However, very large categories cannot be searched exhaustively, so that a failure to find a match does not guarantee that the input is not an exemplar. In this case, the decision is delayed until lexical access has been completed, explaining why the frequency effect returns for large categories.

It is often the case that one can translate explanations expressed in one model into the terms appropriate for another, but it is not so easy here. One might follow Jared and Seidenberg's (1991) suggestion that the use of a small category allows for the possibility that all members of the category are preactivated, but it is hard to see how that would help nonexemplars. A suggestion made by Max Coltheart (personal communication) that would explain how a frequency effect could be obtained for nonexemplars is that the resting level for each semantic feature unit is set at 0.5, and activation is either driven up toward 1.0 or down toward zero, depending on whether the input word is coded for that feature. The speed with which this happens would be influenced by frequency. So, in an animal categorization task, a high-frequency nonexemplar would drive activation levels down to zero faster than a low-frequency nonexemplar.

An obvious problem with such a proposal is that each word has to be coded for every feature that it does *not* possess, although in network models, rich interconnectivity of units is not generally considered to be a drawback. However, this proposal runs into trouble with small categories, where no frequency effect is observed. To explain this effect, one might argue that such a mechanism is not available for small categories, so that, although words can be coded as "not an animal", they cannot be coded as "not a month". Without any additional support, this solution seems somewhat ad hoc.

An alternative proposal (actually, the reverse of the previous proposal) is to suggest that only certain types of semantic feature units can be effectively monitored. For example, there may be no single feature unit that is activated by all animal names, and hence there may be too many features units to monitor effectively. So, failing to detect any semantic indicator of "animal-ness" is not conclusive evidence that the input is not an animal name, and hence the decision system must wait until lexical processing is complete, and the final semantic pattern can be read off. This would produce a frequency effect. But for small categories, there may be a single feature unit that would reliably indicate the presence of an exemplar, and hence "No" decisions will be based on the failure of this unit to be activated. Under these circumstances, no frequency effect would be expected.

Which kind of system does best with respect to these issues is not easily decided. A search model could obviously be extended to handle the notion of category search, but since it is necessarily noncascaded, the selective interference generated by nonwords such as *turple* is difficult to interpret. On the other hand, parallel models are forced into a number of seemingly arbitrary assumptions about when semantic feature monitoring is possible and when it is not. Clearly, there is room for improvement in both camps.

Challenge 5: The frequency effect is really a rank effect

The effect of word frequency on lexical decision times is usually assumed to be logarithmic; that is, response times (RTs) change as a function of log frequency rather than absolute frequency. This captures the fact that quite large changes in frequency at the high end of the frequency spectrum produce very little change in RT, whereas small changes at the low end produce very large changes in RT. However, there is no particular theoretical reason for choosing a logarithmic function—it is just that this is the way the data look.

Activation models such as MROM and DRC accommodate the frequency effect by postulating differences in resting levels of activation. High-frequency words have higher resting levels, and this is why they reach criterion faster than low-frequency words—they start from a higher level, but otherwise there is no difference in the rate at which activation increases. Clearly, this proposal is not in any way constrained by architectural or processing assumptions. The precise mathematical function relating resting levels to frequency could be anything that the data demanded.

This is not true for a search model. What is important is that the entries are searched in order of frequency of occurrence. This predicts that access time should be a linear function of *rank* in a frequency-ordered list; that is, it is relative frequency that is important, not absolute frequency.

One can immediately see that if this is true, it will produce a function that has approximately the right properties. The difference in access time between a word in first position and a word in second position will be the same as the difference in access time between a word in second-last position and a word in last position, assuming a constant search rate. However, the difference in frequency between the first and second words will be very large, whereas the difference between the last two will be very small.[3]

In fact, the rank hypothesis provides a very good fit to the data (Murray & Forster, 2004), as shown in Figure 5.5. Each data point represents the mean lexical decision time for 36 words drawn at random from a narrow frequency band. The rank of each word was determined from the ranking of the word in the Kucera and Francis count (1986). Also shown are the same data plotted as a function of log frequency. Although the difference between the R^2 values is not great, there was a significant nonlinear residual in the log plots (but not in the rank plot). This is due to the fact that the log function

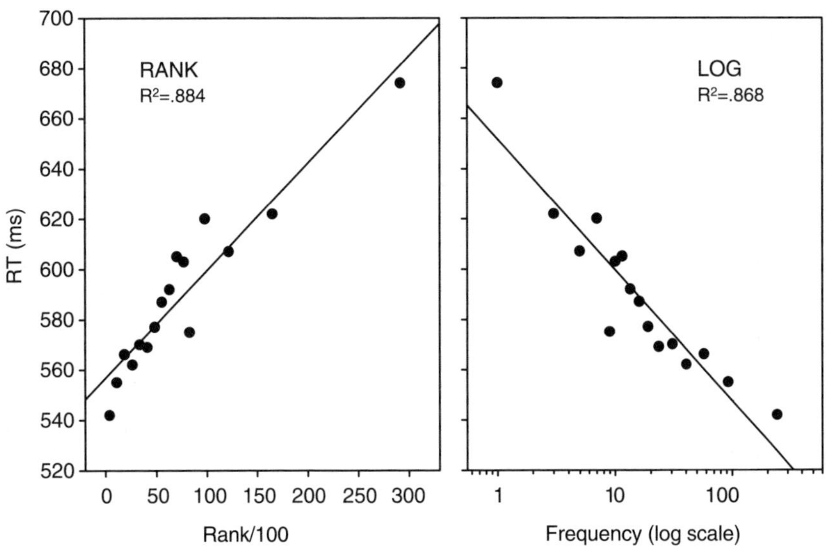

Figure 5.5 Mean lexical decision times as a function of rank (left panel) and log frequency (right panel). (Reprinted with permission from Murray & Forster, 2004.) RT: response time.

underestimates RT at low frequencies, and overestimates RT at high frequencies. Exactly the same feature was noted by Balota, Cortese, Sergent-Marshall, Spieler, and Yap (2004).

Unexpectedly, rank also turns out to be a very effective predictor of error rates in lexical decision, as shown in Figure 5.6. Here it is very clear that rank is superior to log frequency, so much so that one would have to reject the log function as a satisfactory fit. Why should error rates be so closely linked to rank? One suggestion is that one can think of the search path as a linked list, in which each lexical entry in the sequence contains a pointer to the next entry. In order to locate a matching entry, each step in the search path must be executed correctly. If any error occurs, the search will fail, leading to an incorrect decision.[4] Obviously, the longer the search path, the greater the probability that such an error will occur before the correct entry is reached. Since rank is an index of the length of the search path, it follows that rank should be related to error rate. However, the predicted relationship between rank and number of errors is not linear, but is an exponential function of the form $P_s = 1 - P_c^R$, where P_s is the probability of a search error occurring, R is the rank position of the target word in the bin, and P_c is the probability, for each entry in the search path, of progressing to the correct subsequent entry. However, although this is clearly an exponential function, its form is close to linear if the value of P_e (the probability of any single "pointer error") is very small, as indeed it must be; otherwise, access would be a very unreliable process.

This basic pattern of results has been replicated in a separate group study,

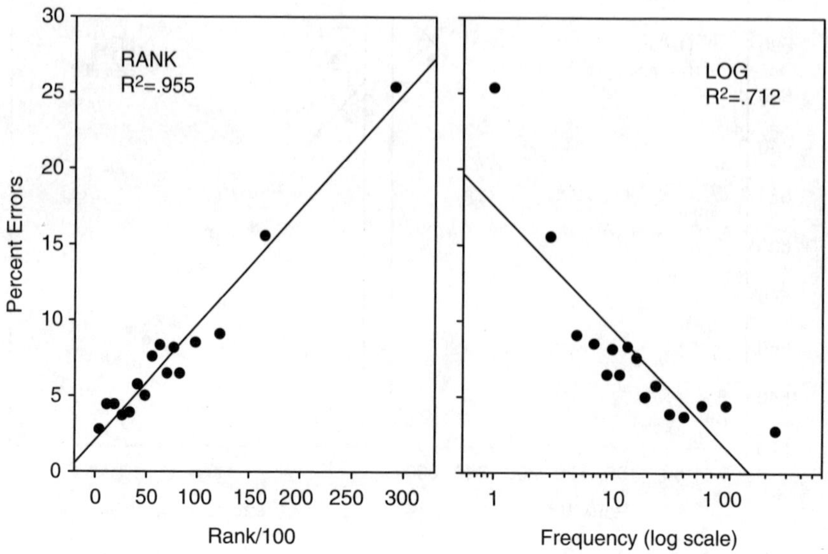

Figure 5.6 Mean error rates in lexical decision as a function of rank and log frequency. (Reprinted with permission from Murray & Forster, 2004.)

and in a study where the data were analyzed separately for individual subjects, and in a reanalysis of data reported by Balota and Spieler (1999). So it appears that there is something about the rank of a word in a frequency-ordered list that is very closely related to lexical decision times. However, it should be pointed out that a power function fits the data just as well as the rank function, and hence it cannot be claimed that the rank function provides the best fit to the data. But there are two points to consider if the power function is preferred. First, power functions have an extra parameter compared with linear functions, and this gives the power function a considerable data-fitting advantage. Second, what is it about the model that demands a power function, rather than, say, a log function? For example, in an IA-type model, why should the resting levels of word units be related to frequency by a power law? In an attractor model, why should the effect of frequency on the depth of the attractor basin be a power function? If compelling answers to these questions can be found, we will have a rival theory. Until then, a search model is the only theory that offers an *explanatory* account of the form of the frequency effect.

Addendum: Challenges for a search model

In closing, it must be acknowledged that parallel activation models are not the only models that face challenges—search models also face numerous challenges. The most obvious, and oft-cited, problem concerns the "fact" that search is far too slow to account for the speed with which "No" decisions can be reached in a lexical decision experiment. This seems a reasonable objection if one assumes that the entire lexicon has to be exhaustively searched, but of course this is not the case. In the bin model, only the contents of a single bin have to be searched, and so far, there is no evidence at all to indicate how many entries that might involve. An additional point worth considering is whether we currently understand enough about neural functioning to put limits on how fast a search process could proceed.

A more challenging problem is provided by indications that semantic variables play a role in lexical access. In a table look-up model, the meaning of a word cannot be retrieved until a matching entry at the level of form has been found, and therefore it is hard to see how meaning could determine how long it took to find that entry. This would not be a problem if lexical entries were organized semantically, and context provided a cue as to the likely location of the correct entry. But in the complete absence of any context, there is no way to explain how meaning could be involved. Yet there are an increasing number of such demonstrations. For example, imageable words are named faster if they are also low-frequency, irregular words (Strain, Patterson, & Seidenberg, 1995). Lexical decision and naming times are both affected by animacy (Andrews & Heathcote, 2001), and are faster for polysemous words (Borowsky & Masson, 1996; Hino & Lupker, & Pexman, 2002), and concrete words (Kroll & Mervis, 1986), but are slower for words that possess synonyms (Hino, Lupker, & Pexman, 2002; Pecher, 2001). Moreover, *Balota and Yap* (this volume) present findings from multiple regression analyses showing that factors such as imageability, association strength, and semantic connectivity are reliably associated with lexical decision (less so with naming) after the effects of other variables, such as frequency and age of acquisition, have been removed.

These findings are not only difficult for a search model to explain, but they are also problematic for models such as DRC and MROM. Proposing that these effects could all be explained by variations in resting levels of activation is unlikely to provide a very satisfying solution. However, a triangle model with distributed representations and both feed-forward and feedback connections does have the potential to explain these effects. The time taken for such a network to settle into a stable configuration depends not only on feed-forward activation, but also on the consistency of feedback activation. The clearest example is the analysis of synonyms developed by Pecher (2001), who points out that if the input word has a synonym, the feedback is more likely to be inconsistent. So, for example, the pattern of semantic activation produced by the input *couch* may produce feedback to the orthographic units that is consistent with the word *sofa* rather than *couch*. This inconsistent feedback will increase settling time.

This is not the place to attempt to evaluate this evidence, but it is worth considering one or two possible lines of defence for a search model. First, are we really sure that these effects occur during the process of finding a matching entry, and not afterwards? That is, there may be some secondary process that is required to actually recover the properties of the word, and it is this process that is affected by semantic variables. On this view, finding a matching entry is just the first step in a longer journey.

Second, are we sure that there are no confounds? The most obvious possibility is that some of these variables are correlated with age of acquisition (concreteness is a prime example), and there are good reasons to expect that early-acquired words should be accessed faster in a frequency-ordered search model than late-acquired words (e.g. Murray & Forster, 2004). The evidence from multiple regression analyses is particularly relevant here (e.g. *Balota & Yap*, this volume), since this appears to be the only way to convincingly rule out confounds. If these alternative explanations of semantic effects can be ruled out, the architecture of a search model (and perhaps other models as well) will have to be radically revised.

Finally, a major gap in the bin model is the lack of detail in specifying how the correct bin is located. The assumption is that there exists a hash function that assigns a bin number to any letter sequence, so that a search for a matching entry can be restricted to a single bin. One way to tackle this problem might be to use the data from masked form priming, on the grounds that priming could occur only if both the prime and target are assigned the same bin number (otherwise, the search for the prime would never encounter the entry for the target). So, if *nature* primes *mature*, they must both be in the same bin, and if *manure* also primes *mature*, it must be located there also. However, recent research indicates that there must be a considerable degree of flexibility in the hash function, since substantial priming effects are obtained from primes that are distortions of the target word. Peressotti and Grainger (1999) obtained priming when several letters have been omitted, as in *blcn–BALCON*. The implication would have to be that the same hash code is assigned to *blcn* as to *BALCON*. Perea and Lupker (2003, 2004) have established that strong priming is obtained with a prime in which two letters of the target word have been transposed, as in *jugde–COURT*. Further, these letters need not be adjacent, as in *caniso-CASINO*, suggesting that the precise position of the letter within the word is not critical. Finally, Guerrera (2004) has shown amazingly strong priming for long target words when multiple letters are transposed in the prime, as in *isdewakl–SIDEWALK*, although there is no priming when all letters in the prime are transposed, as in *isedawkl*. Devising a hash code that assigns the correct bin number to *isdewakl*, but not to *isedawkl*, is an extremely daunting task—sufficiently so as to raise doubts about whether this is the correct approach.

Postscript

This last point leads us to a recent development. In the summer of 2005, Thomas Hannagan and I worked on developing a new computational model of lexical access that would combine the strong points of parallel and serial models, while avoiding the weaker aspects. This model is termed PSM (parallel search model). The basic assumption of the model is that there must be a limit on the number of word nodes that a letter node can reliably activate. We call this the connectivity constraint. In standard parallel models, there is no limit. If you have a lexicon of 150,000 words, each letter node must be able to activate all 150,000 word nodes simultaneously (some are facilitatory connections, but others are inhibitory). If we impose a limit of, say, 1000 word nodes, it is clear that some kind of sequential search will be involved. Essentially, in PSM, the lexical network is subdivided into a number of subnets, each containing 1000 word nodes. The members of each subnet are activated in parallel, but only one subnet is activated at any one time. In order to optimize the search, the highest-frequency words would be allocated to the first subnet to be activated, and the lowest-frequency words would be allocated to the last subnet to be activated, thereby producing a frequency effect. In order to speed up the search, each subnet is activated for only one cycle, and the parameters are set so that the activation in a matching word node is guaranteed to reach criterion within one cycle. This has interesting consequences, because there is no time for competition or top-down effects to operate.

Somewhat ironically, this model provides a satisfactory response to three of the challenges issued in the body of this paper. First, activation is not incremental. Activation in a word node goes from zero to its final state in a single cycle. Second, the frequency effect produced by PSM is clearly a rank effect. Third, the model allows for parallel processing of multiple inputs (i.e. multitasking). A search for the prime can be launched, and while that search is in progress, a search for the target can be launched as well. An additional feature of the model is the introduction of a secondary network that is involved in the process of verification. When the subnet that contains the correct word unit is activated, the corresponding word unit in the second network is activated. When this unit reaches threshold, the orthographic, phonological, and semantic properties of the word are generated, which can then be used for verification purposes. Thus, lexical decision time is determined by several factors: (1) the time required to activate the word unit in the first network (solely determined by frequency); (2) the time required for the corresponding unit in the second unit to reach threshold (possibly influenced by semantic factors); and (3) the time required to verify the candidate unit against the input (possibly determined by length, body frequency, etc.). The fact that this hybrid model allows for three completely independent contributions to access time gives it a greater degree of flexibility than many existing models, and this is what it may take to accommodate the steadily increasing panoply of variables related to access time.

References

Andrews, S. (1997). The effect of orthographic similarity on lexical retrieval: Resolving neighborhood conflicts. *Psychonomic Bulletin and Review*, *4*, 439–461.

Andrews, S., & Heathcote, A. (2001). Distinguishing common and task-specific processes in word identification: A matter of some moment? *Journal of Experimental Psychology: Learning, Memory, and Cognition*, *27*, 514–544.

Balota, D. A., & Chumbley, J. I. (1984). Are lexical decisions a good measure of lexical access? The role of word frequency in the neglected decision stage. *Journal of Experimental Psychology: Human Perception and Performance*, *10*, 340–357.

Balota, D. A., & Chumbley, J. I. (1990). Where are the effects of frequency in visual word recognition tasks? Right where we said they were: Comment on Monsell, Doyle, and Haggard (1989). *Journal of Experimental Psychology: General*, *119*, 231–237.

Balota, D. A., & Spieler, D. H. (1999). Word frequency, repetition, and lexicality effects in word recognition tasks: Beyond measures of central tendency. *Journal of Experimental Psychology: General*, *128*, 32–55.

Balota, D. A., Cortese, M. J., Sergent-Marshall, S. D., Spieler, D. H., & Yap, M. (2004). Visual word recognition of single-syllable words. *Journal of Experimental Psychology: General*, *133*, 283–316.

Borowsky, R., & Masson, M. E. J. (1996). Semantic ambiguity effects in word identification. *Journal of Experimental Psychology: Learning, Memory, and Cognition*, *22*, 63–85.

Carreiras, M., Perea, M., & Grainger, J. (1997). Effects of the orthographic neighborhood in visual word recognition: Cross-task comparisons. *Journal of Experimental Psychology: Learning, Memory, and Cognition*, *23*, 857–871.

Clark, V. P., Fan, S., & Hillyard, S. A. (1995). Identification of early visual evoked potential generators by retinotopic and topographic analyses. *Human Brain Mapping, 2*, 170–187.

Coltheart, M., Davelaar, E., Jonasson, J. T., & Besner, D. (1977). Access to the internal lexicon. In S. Dornic (Ed.), *Attention and performance VI* (pp. 535–555). London: Academic Press.

Coltheart, M., Rastle, K., Perry, C., Langdon, R., & Ziegler, J. (2001). DRC: A dual route cascaded model of visual word recognition and reading aloud. *Psychological Review, 108*, 204–256.

Damian, M. F. (2001). Congruity effects evoked by subliminally presented primes: Automaticity rather than semantic processing. *Journal of Experimental Psychology: Human Perception and Performance, 27*, 154–165.

Dijkstra, T., & Van Heuven, W. J. B. (2002). The architecture of the bilingual word recognition system: From identification to decision. *Bilingualism: Language and Cognition, 5*, 175–197.

Drieghe, D., & Brysbaert, M. (2002). Strategic effects in associative priming with words, homophones, and pseudohomophones. *Journal of Experimental Psychology: Learning, Memory, and Cognition, 28*, 951–961.

Forster, K. I. (1976). Accessing the mental lexicon. In R. J. Wales & E. Walker (Eds.), *Approaches to Language Mechanisms* (pp. 257–287). Amsterdam: North-Holland.

Forster, K. I. (1989). Basic issues in lexical processing. In W. Marslen-Wilson (Ed.), *Lexical representation and process* (pp. 75–107). Cambridge, MA: MIT Press.

Forster, K. I. (1999). The microgenesis of priming effects in lexical access. *Brain and Language Special Issue: Mental Lexicon, 68*, 5–15.

Forster, K. I. (2004). Category size effects revisited: Frequency and masked priming effects in semantic categorization. *Brain and Language, 90*, 276–286.

Forster, K., Booker, J., Schacter, D. L., & Davis, C. (1990). Masked repetition priming: Lexical activation or novel memory trace? *Bulletin of the Psychonomic Society, 28*, 341–345.

Forster, K. I., & Davis, C. (1984). Repetition priming and frequency attenuation in lexical access. *Journal of Experimental Psychology: Learning, Memory, and Cognition, 10*, 680–698.

Forster, K. I., & Hector, J. (2002). Cascaded versus noncascaded models of lexical and semantic processing: The *turple* effect. *Memory and Cognition, 30*, 1106–1116.

Forster, K. I., & Shen, D. (1996). No enemies in the neighborhood: Absence of inhibitory neighborhood effects in lexical decision and semantic categorization. *Journal of Experimental Psychology: Learning, Memory, and Cognition, 22*, 696–713.

Forster, K. I., & Taft, M. (1994). Bodies, antibodies, and neighborhood-density effects in masked form priming. *Journal of Experimental Psychology: Learning, Memory, and Cognition, 20*, 844–863.

Gollan, T. H., Forster, K. I., & Frost, R. (1997). Translation priming with different scripts: Masked priming with cognates and noncognates in Hebrew-English bilinguals. *Journal of Experimental Psychology: Learning, Memory, and Cognition, 23*, 1122–1139.

Grainger, J., & Frenck-Mestre, C. (1998). Masked priming by translation equivalents in proficient bilinguals. *Language and Cognitive Processes, 13*, 601–623.

Grainger, J., & Jacobs, A. M. (1996). Orthographic processing in visual word recognition: A multiple read-out model. *Psychological Review, 103*, 518–565.

Guerrera, C. (2004). *Flexibility and constraint in lexical access: Explorations in transposed-letter priming*. Unpublished dissertation, Department of Psychology, University of Arizona.

Hino, Y., Lupker, S. J., & Pexman, P. M. (2002). Ambiguity and synonymy effects in lexical decision, naming, and semantic categorization tasks: Interactions between orthography, phonology, and semantics. *Journal of Experimental Psychology: Learning, Memory, and Cognition*, *28*, 686–713.

Jacobs, A. M., Graf, R., & Kinder, A. (2003). Receiver operating characteristics in the lexical decision task: Evidence for a simple signal-detection process simulated by the multiple read-out model. *Journal of Experimental Psychology: Learning, Memory, and Cognition*, *29*, 481–488.

Jared, D., & Seidenberg, M. S. (1991). Does word identification proceed from spelling to sound to meaning? *Journal of Experimental Psychology: General*, *120*, 358–394.

Jiang, N., & Forster, K. I. (2001). Cross-language priming asymmetries in lexical decision and episodic recognition. *Journal of Memory and Language*, *44*, 32–51.

Kroll, J. F., & Merves, J. S. (1986). Lexical access for concrete and abstract words. *Journal of Experimental Psychology: Learning, Memory, and Cognition*, *12*, 92–107.

Kunde, W., Kiesel, A., & Hoffman, J. (2003). Conscious control over the content of unconscious cognition. *Cognition*, *88*, 223–242.

Landauer, T. K., & Freedman, J. L. (1968). Information retrieval from long-term memory: Category size and recognition time. *Journal of Verbal Learning and Verbal Behavior*, *7*, 291–295.

Lukatela, G., & Turvey, M. T. (1994). Visual lexical access is initially phonological. I. Evidence from associative priming by words, homophones, and pseudohomophones. *Journal of Experimental Psychology: General*, *123*, 107–128.

McClelland, J. L., & Rumelhart, D. E. (1981). An interactive activation model of context effects in letter perception. I. An account of basic findings. *Psychological Review*, *88*, 375–407.

Monsell, S., Doyle, M. C., & Haggard, P. N. (1989). Effects of frequency on visual word recognition tasks: Where are they? *Journal of Experimental Psychology: General*, *118*, 43–71.

Morton, J. (1970). A functional model of human memory. In D. A. Norman (Ed.), *Models of human memory*. New York: Academic Press.

Murray, W. S., & Forster, K. I. (2004). Serial mechanisms in lexical access: The Rank hypothesis. *Psychological Review*, *111*, 721–756.

Paap, K. R., Chun, E., & Vonnahme, P. (1999). Discrete threshold versus continuous strength models of perceptual recognition. *Canadian Journal of Experimental Psychology*, *53*, 277–293.

Pecher, D. (2001). Perception is a two-way junction: Feedback semantics in word recognition. *Psychonomic Bulletin and Review*, *8*, 545–551.

Perea, M., & Gotor, A. (1997). Associative and semantic priming effects occur at very short stimulus-onset asynchronies in lexical decision and naming. *Cognition*, *62*, 223–240.

Perea, M., & Lupker, S. J. (2003). Does jugde activate COURT? Transposed-letter similarity effects in masked associative priming. *Memory and Cognition*, *31*, 829–841.

Perea, M., & Lupker, S. J. (2004). Can CANISO activate CASINO! Transposed-letter similarity effects with nonadjacent letter positions. *Journal of Memory and Language*, *51*, 231–246.

Peressotti, F., & Grainger, J. (1999). The role of letter identity and letter position in orthographic priming. *Perception and Psychophysics*, *61*, 691–706.

Plaut, D. C. (1997). Structure and function in the lexical system: Insights from distributed models of word reading and lexical decision. *Language and Cognitive Processes*, *12*, 765–805.

Rayner, K., Balota, D. A., & Pollatsek, A. (1986). Against parafoveal semantic preprocessing during eye fixations in reading. *Canadian Journal of Psychology*, *40*, 473–483.

Rodd, J. M. (2004). When do leotards get their spots? Semantic activation of lexical neighbors in visual word recognition. *Psychonomic Bulletin and Review*, *11*, 434–439.

Rueckl, J. G. (2002). The dynamics of visual word recognition. *Ecological Psychology*, *14*, 5–19.

Seidenberg, M. S., & McClelland, J. L. (1989). A distributed, developmental model of word recognition and naming. *Psychological Review*, *96*, 523–568.

Selfridge, O. G. (1959). Pandemonium: A paradigm for learning. In *Proceedings of a symposium on the mechanization of thought processes*. London: HMSO.

Sereno, S. C., Rayner, K., & Posner, M. I. (1998). Establishing a time-line of word recognition: evidence from eye movements and event-related potentials. *Neuroreport*, *9*, 2195–2200.

Strain, E., Patterson, K., & Seidenberg, M. S. (1995). Semantic effects in single-word naming. *Journal of Experimental Psychology: Learning, Memory, and Cognition*, *21*, 1140–1154.

Taft, M., & Kougious, P. (2004). The processing of morpheme-like units in monomorphemic words. *Brain and Language*, *90*, 9–16.

Van Heuven, W. J. B., Dijkstra, T., Grainger, J., & Schriefers, H. (2001). Shared neighborhood effects in masked orthographic priming. *Psychonomic Bulletin and Review*, *8*, 96–101.

Yonelinas, A. P. (1994). Receiver-operating characteristics in recognition memory: Evidence for a dual-process model. *Journal of Experimental Psychology: Learning, Memory, and Cognition*, *20*, 1341–1354.

Notes

1 It might be argued that there should nevertheless be a bias to respond "No" on the grounds that if no matching entry has been found after the search has covered a large proportion of the search space, the input is more likely to be a nonword. However, strictly speaking, all this implies is that the input is unlikely to be a high-frequency word.

2 On this interpretation, above chance performance on nonwords would not be expected until performance on low-frequency words approached 100%.

3 This can be seen by taking a random sample of, say, 100 words, and then ranking them according to frequency of occurrence.

4 Presumably, a backup search would normally be launched, but it would be unlikely to be completed before the deadline for making a decision was reached.

6 Cognitive processes in reading: The E-Z Reader model of eye-movement control

Keith Rayner
University of Massachusetts, Amherst, USA

Erik D. Reichle
University of Pittsburgh, USA

Alexander Pollatsek
University of Massachusetts, Amherst, USA

In this chapter, we will review the development of the E-Z Reader model of eye-movement control in reading and also describe the basic characteristics of the model (Pollatsek, Reichle, & Rayner, 2006; Rayner, Ashby, Pollatsek, & Reichle, 2004; Reichle, Pollatsek, Fisher, & Rayner, 1998; Reichle, Rayner, & Pollatsek, 2003). The model is relevant to the other chapters in the present volume because we argue that word recognition and lexical processing play a central role in determining when the eyes move from word to word in reading. We will first review background information regarding the development of the model and then review some basic data from the literature on eye movements in reading that any model of eye-movement control in reading must account for. We will then describe the model and discuss predictions of the model. We will also briefly describe some recent tests of the model. Along the way, we will discuss the most controversial aspects of the model and provide justifications for the stances we have taken with respect to the evolving development of the model.

Background to the development of E-Z Reader

In 1958, Miles Tinker published the last in a series of review articles that he wrote for *Psychological Bulletin* and other review outlets. He concluded this review with the following statement:

> The future study of eye movements in reading does not appear to be too promising. The eye-movement approach to the study of the reading process has probably made its major contributions. What we now need is less activity by dilettantes who are inadequately prepared to see the fundamental problems and unable to design suitable experiments in the field. Undoubtedly there will be a few researchers thoroughly grounded in the

> field who will sense basic problems and organize sound experimental procedures of investigation. Such individuals will be the ones to contribute worthwhile new information concerning eye movements in reading. (Tinker, 1958, p. 229)

In essence, Tinker concluded that eye-movement research had made whatever advance it was going to make to the study of reading and that future use of the technique did not look promising. There is no doubt that a lot of valuable information about eye movements was learned during the period from about 1870 until 1958 (see Rayner, 1978, 1998, for discussion). However, Tinker (1958) could not have been more wrong with respect to the value of future eye-movement research. First, rapid development of technology made certain types of eye-movement experiments possible (particularly the gaze-contingent type of experiment described below) and also allowed much more ambitious studies to be run because software became available that made it much easier to score and analyze eye-movement data. Second, advancements within the field of linguistics have led to a much better description of language and thus allowed people to ask more focused questions about the reading process.

Apparently, Tinker's premonitions regarding the uselessness of further eye-movement data were accepted by the majority of the research community because there was very little work on eye movement and reading from 1958 until the mid-1970s. However, some now classic research by McConkie and Rayner (1975) and Rayner (1975) with high-speed computers interfaced with eye-tracking systems to implement gaze-contingent display changes in text to study the size of the perceptual span in reading helped to bring about a new era in eye-movement research in reading. Shortly thereafter, articles started appearing (see Rayner, 1978) in which inferences were made about mental processing during reading on the basis of eye-movement data. Between 1978 and 1998, a large number of new studies appeared using the gaze-contingent technique, as did many studies dealing with the cognitive processes involved in reading (see Rayner, 1998, for a review). Furthermore, a large number of studies in which eye movements were used to assess some aspect of reading (from word recognition through comprehension) have appeared in the seven-year interval since 1998 than between 1978 and 1998 (see Rayner, 1998).

Given that two of us (K.R. and A.P.) had spent over 25 years doing research on eye movements in reading by the late 1990s, it seemed to us that we ought to be able to develop a computer simulation that incorporated many of the findings that had accumulated. That is, we wanted a simulation that would effectively predict which words readers would fixate (or skip over) as they read and how long they would look at the words that they did fixate on. Thus, the three of us, along with another colleague (Don Fisher), began to meet regularly to discuss ways to build such a system. The initial modelling utilized order-of-processing (OP) diagrams and PERT networks[1] to spell out the underlying logic of the system we were building, and then the model was more formalized as a computer program that effectively read sentences. We called the model "E-Z Reader", after a character played by Morgan Freeman in the US children's PBS television programme "Electric Company".

Prior to the development of E-Z Reader, there were other models (though they were largely verbal models) that attempted to account for eye movements in reading. A description of such models is provided elsewhere (Reichle et al., 2003). However, the emergence of E-Z Reader resulted in the development of quite a few other models of eye-movement control (see Reichle et al., 2003, for a discussion of many of these models). Some of these models incorporate components of the E-Z Reader model, whereas others are entirely separate entities. As we will argue below, E-Z Reader does a remarkably good job of accounting for a large amount of eye-movement data with a few simple principles.

Characteristics of eye movements in reading

When we read, we have the impression that our eyes are gliding smoothly across the page. However, this impression is an illusion; in reality, the eyes are making a series of fixations (where the eyes are relatively still for about a quarter of a second) separated by rapid movements of the eyes called saccades (which typically last about 30 ms or so in reading). New information enters the processing system only during the fixations. Another illusion that we have is that we can see the entire page of text and the line we are reading, but, in reality, letter information is processed only from a restricted area around the fixation point, typically called the *perceptual span* or *region of effective vision*.

Although the average fixation duration is about 200–250 ms and the average saccade length is about 8–9 letter spaces, perhaps the most striking aspect of eye movements in reading is the variability associated with these values. Thus, fixation durations for a single reader can range from 50 to over 500 ms and saccade lengths can range from 1 to 20–25 letter spaces. Although most very long saccades result from either (1) cases in which the reader makes a regression (a movement backward in the text to look at previously fixated words) and then comes back to the place in text ahead of the point from which the regression was launched or (2) a return sweep to fixate the beginning of a new line of text, there is still considerable variability in saccade lengths when these sources are removed. As a result, any viable model of eye-movement control in reading needs to account for the variability in fixation durations and saccade lengths.

Before we discuss the factors that models of eye movements in reading need to account for, we will make a slight digression to discuss some measures of processing time that are typically used in eye-movement research. If readers always made one and only one fixation on a word, the fixation time on that word would clearly be the best estimate of the time to process that word in reading. But, in fact, (1) readers sometimes skip words (so that only about two-thirds of the words are typically fixated, with short words, like function words, and predictable words often being skipped) and (2) readers not infrequently make more than one fixation on a word before moving to another word. Thus, when the unit of analysis is a single word, researchers typically report a number of related measures such as *first-fixation duration* (the duration of the first fixation on a word independent of the number of fixations on the word), *single-fixation duration* (cases when only one fixation is made on a word), *gaze duration* (the sum of all fixations on a word prior to moving to another word), and *total fixation time* (the sum of all fixations on a word, including regressions). In addition, the probability of fixating on a word and the frequency of regressions out of (and into) the word are also reported.

We turn now to a list of findings that a model of eye-movement control in reading needs to account for. In the list, we will repeat the point we made above concerning variability in basic eye-movement measures. For all of the points on this list, a more complete discussion of the findings can be found in Rayner (1998). Here, we make five general points.

First, there is variability in the fixation durations and saccade lengths for any given reader. The distributions for both fixation duration and saccade length look approximately normal, but are somewhat positively skewed.

Second, the size of the perceptual span (or region of effective vision) for readers of English extends 3–4 letters to the left of fixation to 14–15 letters to the right.

Third, readers tend to fixate about halfway between the beginning and the middle of a word, but the pattern is modulated by how far the reader was from the beginning of the word on the prior fixation. If the prior fixation was far from the beginning of a target word, the initial fixation on the word is more likely to be near the beginning of the word, whereas if it was close to the beginning of the word, the initial fixation tends to land further into the target word. However, overall, there is again a more or less normal looking distribution that is positively skewed.

Fourth, readers obtain a benefit from having a preview of the word to the right of fixation. If they have a valid preview of the next word (*word n+1*), fixations on that word are 30–50 ms shorter than when they do not have a valid preview. We call this advantage *preview benefit*. This benefit has been most accurately measured by the *boundary paradigm* (Rayner, 1975), wherein random letters or a string of Xs occupy the location of a target word until the reader's eyes cross the space to the left of the word, causing the target word to be displayed.

Finally, the amount of time that readers look at a word is strongly influenced by factors such as word frequency (Inhoff & Rayner, 1986; Rayner & Duffy, 1986) and how predictable the word is from prior discourse (Ehrlich & Rayner, 1981; Rayner & Well, 1986). In addition, there is sometimes a *spill-over effect* (a longer fixation on the next word or region in the text) as a result of processing difficulty on the prior word.

There are other effects in the literature that it may well be important for a model to be able to account for, and we will discuss some of them later in this chapter. However, for now, we argue that the five points listed above are basic and need to be accommodated by any model of eye movements in reading. The E-Z Reader model is able to account for the various points we have listed above as well as other important findings (see Pollatsek et al., 2006, for a more complete discussion). At this point, however, we turn to a discussion of how the model works.

The E-Z Reader model

Perhaps the most important assumption of the E-Z Reader model is that attention is allocated serially: to only one word at a time. Furthermore, this attention is intrinsically linked to lexical processing. That is, the early visual processing that is involved in lexical processing is not sufficient to support word identification, and thus attention needs to be focused on the word that is being processed. If one grants that it is more difficult to identify words than it is to identify single letters, our assumption that attention must be allocated to each word so that it can be identified is not unreasonable. In E-Z Reader, lexical processing begins as soon as attention is focused on a word's visual features enabling the systems that are responsible for lexical processing to begin computing the word's orthographic, phonological, and semantic codes.

Another benefit that comes from allocating attention serially is that it provides a simple mechanism for encoding the order of the words that are being read. This is highly advantageous in languages like English because word order conveys a large amount of syntactic information (for example, consider the difference in meaning between "The run home was very exciting" and "The home run was very exciting"). Even in a highly inflected language like German, in which much of the syntactic information is explicitly represented through case markings, nuances in meaning are nonetheless often conveyed through word order. In Finnish, a highly inflected language, word order conveys information about discourse status. Similarly, word order in Hungarian and Turkish (also highly inflected languages) conveys information about topic focus and given-new status.

In E-Z Reader, a distinction is made between an early stage of pre-attentive visual processing and a subsequent stage of attention-based lexical processing. Information available from this early pre-attentive visual stage is used in decisions about where to move the eyes. This distinction was motivated by our appreciation of the fact that the information on the retina is not transmitted instantaneously to the brain, but instead lags behind by some amount of time. Current estimates, from studies using physiological methods, are that the duration of the "eye-to-brain" lag is approximately 50 ms (see Pollatsek et al., 2006; Reichle, Pollatsek, & Rayner, 2006, for further discussion of these data). We have recently tested whether a 50-ms value for the duration of this pre-attentive stage (the lag between when visual information hits the retina and when lexical processing can begin) also works in the E-Z Reader model. These modelling tests indicate that the assumed duration of the visual stage has little consequence in normal reading except in situations involving very large saccades (such as long regressions, which are outside the scope of the model), but that to predict the observed size of preview benefit, 50 ms was just about the right value. We further assume that whatever visual information is extracted from one viewing location and has been attended to continues to be used by the cognitive system until new information from the next viewing location becomes available. Our reasons for making this assumption are beyond the scope of the present chapter (but see Pollatsek et al., 2006; Reichle et al., 2006, for further discussion). One consequence of this is that lexical processing of preview information will be continuous through the saccade and the ensuing fixation, but that the higher-quality visual information that results when the word is fixated will only displace the prior information 50 ms into the fixation.

Because the early visual processing is not dependent upon attention, some information from the entire visual field is processed from each new fixation. This means that low-level visual information from the entire page can be processed in parallel (subject to limitations in visual acuity, of course), leading to our impression that we can indeed see the entire page of text clearly. This assumption is important because, even though visual acuity drops off quite rapidly from the fixation point, low-spatial frequency information that is available from nonfoveal vision provides information about word length and the boundaries between words and helps provide information for targeting saccades. In general, the visual information that is actually used in word and letter identification is within a relatively narrow spatial window: from 3–4 letters to the left of fixation to about 14–15 letters to the right of fixation on the line of text being read. In E-Z Reader, we assume that this information can be used by the oculomotor system to select saccade targets. (This is shown in Figure 6.1, which is a schematic diagram of the model.) The assumption that low-level featural information is processed in parallel also suggests an explanation for why unusual letter sequences at the beginning of a word can affect fixation durations on the prior word (Hyönä, 1995; Inhoff, Radach, Eiter, & Juhasz, 2003). That is, because these letter sequences are unusual, they may contain unusual visual features that *pop out* and are immediately noticed by the reader. By this account, such low-level, *parafoveal-on-foveal* effects are not damning to our assumption that attention is allocated in a strictly serial manner because such effects do not require attention—they are pre-attentive (see below for a fuller discussion of parafoveal-on-foveal effects).

As already stated, the E-Z Reader model assumes that lexical processing of a word begins as soon as attention is allocated to the visual features of that word. Lexical processing is completed in two stages—an early stage that we initially referred to as the *familiarity check* (Reichle et al., 1998, 1999) and

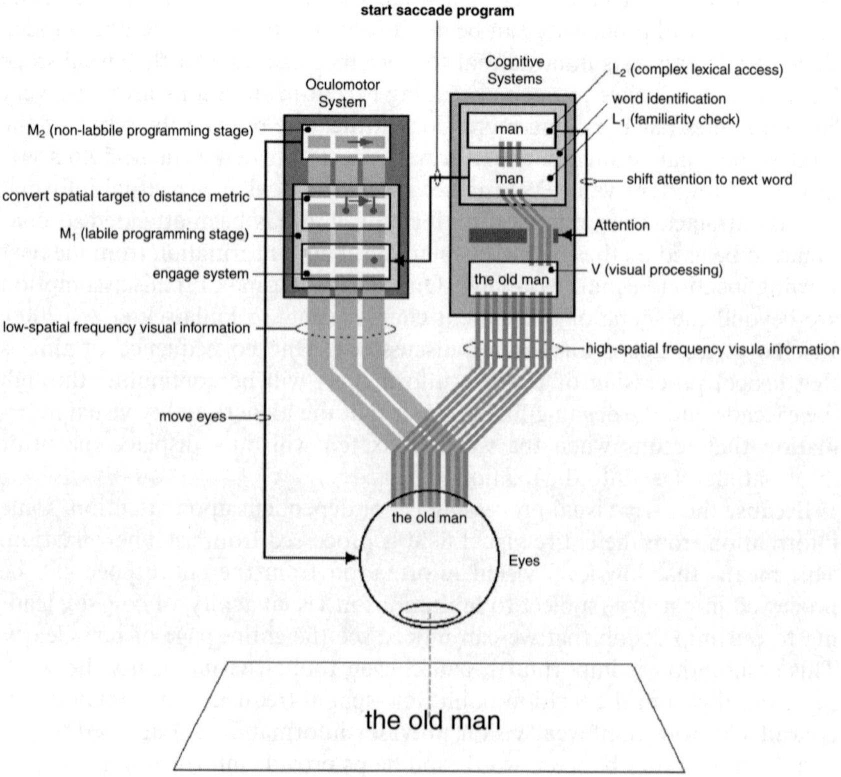

Figure 6.1 Schematic diagram of the E-Z Reader model of eye-movement control during reading.

a later stage called the *completion of lexical access*. In more recent work (Pollatsek et al., 2006; Reichle et al., 2003, 2006), we have referred to these two stages as L_1 and L_2, respectively, because we thought it was more agnostic with respect to the processes involved in the two stages of processing.

This distinction between L_1 and L_2 is the basis for the second core assumption of our model: saccadic programming is decoupled from shifts of attention. That is, the completion of L_1 for a given word causes the oculomotor system to begin programming a saccade to the next word, whereas the completion of L_2 for a given word causes attention to shift to the next word, so that lexical processing of that word can begin. The logic behind this assumption is that L_1 is a rapid assessment of whether or not the completion of lexical access is imminent. When the system "knows" that lexical access of word *n* is imminent, it can begin programming a saccade to word *n*+1 and thereby minimize the fixation duration on word *n* without moving the eyes too soon (which would result in word *n* being viewed from a more distant location and might necessitate a regressive saccade to move the eyes back to word *n*). In other words, L_2 can be viewed as a processing stage that needs to be reached before attention can be shifted to the next word, whereas L_1 is a more preliminary stage that allows one to cheat and begin programming an eye movement reasonably safely with a high probability. Without such a cheat, the reader would be condemned to spend the first 100–150 ms (the time it takes to program and execute an eye movement) of processing on each word with the upcoming word (i.e. the intended saccade target) in parafoveal vision.

The functional distinction between L_1 and L_2 can be conceptualized in at least three different ways (for further discussion of these alternative conceptualizations, see Rayner, Pollatsek, & Reichle, 2003). The first is based loosely on the idea that different types of lexical information about a word (e.g. its orthography, phonology, and meaning) become available at different points in time, and that a word's *familiarity* is based on information that is available early during its identification. For example, it may be that L_1 (the familiarity check) is based on word-form information (e.g. orthographic and/or phonological), whereas L_2 (the completion of lexical access) is based on meaning. A second interpretation of the L_1 versus L_2 distinction is consistent with the distinction in the memory literature between a rapidly available recognition process and a slower retrieval process (Yonelinas, 2002). Thus, L_1 would be based on the rapid recognition of the word, whereas L_2 would correspond to the point in time at which specific information about a word (such as its meaning) has actually been retrieved from memory (Reichle & Perfetti, 2003). A third, and final, interpretation of the L_1 versus L_2 distinction is that the former corresponds to lexical access (i.e. the point at which a word's meaning is available), while the latter corresponds to post-lexical integration (i.e. the point at which the word's meaning has been interpreted in the context of whatever sentence it occurs).

Of course, these three possible interpretations of the L_1 versus L_2 distinction that were just described are neither mutually exclusive nor exhaustive, and at this time we prefer to remain agnostic on the issue. However, it is important to note that, because the duration of the first fixation on a given word is largely a function of the time that is required to complete the familiarity check on that word, it may be possible to rule out certain interpretations of the familiarity check by showing which variables do and do not influence first fixation durations on a word.

Each time attention switches to a new word, there is some chance that the word will be *identified* entirely through the top-down constraints that are imposed by higher-level language processing. This assumption that words are sometimes guessed from the context is consistent with the fact that readers sometimes skip highly predictable words and do not regress to such words even under conditions where the word is visible only if it is directly fixated (as with a one-word *moving-window*, where all words other than the one being fixated are replaced with random letters or strings of Xs, Rayner, Well, Pollatsek, & Bertera, 1982). This suggests that the higher-level linguistic processing that is going on in parallel with the "bottom-up" lexical processing is, at least occasionally, rapid enough to "beat" lexical processing, making it unnecessary to identify some words. In E-Z Reader, we simply assumed that the probability of this happening for a given word is equal to the word's predictability (as determined through cloze-task norms). When a word is guessed in this manner, the completion of L_1 is not necessary, so that the duration of this process is effectively set equal to 0 ms. With this assumption, only a small proportion of words will be guessed (and most of these instances will involve function words like *the*). Instead, the majority of words will be identified, the time that is needed to do so being a function of the word's predictability and its frequency of occurrence. The relationship between these two variables and the mean time that is needed to complete L_1, $t(L_1)$, is specified by equation 1, where α_1 is an intercept parameter that represents the maximal amount of time that is needed to process a word, and $\alpha 2$ and $\alpha 3$ are free parameters that scale the degree to which the natural logarithm of the word's frequency and predictability decrement the maximal processing time. The actual time to complete L_1 for a given word during a simulation is a random deviate that is sampled from a gamma distribution with the mean given by equation 1 and a standard deviation equal to .22 of the mean. In our most recent simulation (Pollatsek et al., 2006), α_1 = 122 ms, $\alpha 2$ = 4 ms, and α_3 = 10 ms.

$$t(L_1) = \alpha_1 - \alpha_2 \ln(\text{frequency}) - \alpha_3 \text{ predictability} \qquad (1)$$

One other assumption regarding L_1 is that the rate at which this stage of lexical processing is completed is modulated by visual acuity. This assumption is based on the fact that the high visual acuity needed to extract the features of letters is limited to the *fovea*, or central 2° of the visual field, and that visual acuity decreases rapidly going from the centre of the fovea to the *parafovea* (which extends 5° out to either side of the centre of vision) and decreases further in peripheral vision. The drop-off in visual acuity explains why word recognition becomes slower and more prone to error as the angular disparity between the centre of the fovea and the centre of the word being processed increases (Lee, Legge, & Oritz, 2003; Rayner & Morrison, 1981).

To account for these facts, we adopted the assumption that the time that is needed to complete L_1 is modulated by visual acuity. This is specified by equation 2, where $t_{acuity}(x)$ is a function that increases the duration of $t(L_1)$ as visual acuity decreases. In equation 2, ε (=1.15) is a free parameter that modulates the effect of visual acuity, which is defined in terms of the mean absolute distance (i.e. number of character spaces) between the current fixation location and each of the letters in the word being processed (N is the number of letters in the word). The value of ε was selected so that the familiarity check would be slowed by factors of 1.15, 1.32, and 1.52 when the beginning letter of three-, five-, and seven-letters words, respectively, is fixated rather than the word centre. It thus takes more time to identify long words and words that are farther from the current fixation location. Both of these predicted outcomes are consistent with empirical results; as already mentioned, word identification is slower and less accurate in parafoveal vision (Lee et al., 2003; Rayner & Morrison, 1981), and longer words take longer to identify than shorter words (Just & Carpenter, 1980; Rayner & McConkie, 1976; Rayner, Sereno, & Raney, 1996).

$$t_{acuity}(t(L_1)) = t(L_1)\ \varepsilon^{\Sigma\,|\,distance\,|\,/\,N} \tag{2}$$

Our final assumption regarding word identification concerns L_2. As already mentioned, L_2 can be conceptualized in several different ways. In the current version of the E-Z Reader model, the extra time that is needed to complete L_2 is some fixed proportion of $t(L_1)$. This relationship is specified by equation 3, where $t(L_2)$ is the mean time that is needed to complete L_2, $t(L_1)$ is the mean time that is specified by equation 1 (prior to sampling from the gamma distribution), and Δ (= .5) is the free parameter that determines what proportion of $t(L_1)$ is required to complete L_2. Finally, the actual time that is required to complete L_2 for a given word during a given Monte Carlo simulation trial is also a random deviate that is sampled from a gamma distribution with a mean equal to $t(L_2)$ and a standard deviation equal to .22 of the mean.

$$t(L_2) = \Delta\ t(L_1) \tag{3}$$

A few points regarding L_2 warrant discussion. First, the completion of L_2, in contrast to L_1, is obligatory. In other words, unlike $t(L_1)$, which does not have to be completed if a word is predicted from its sentence context (and its value set equal to 0 ms), $t(L_2)$ is always equal to some fixed proportion of the time that would have been required to complete L_1 if the word had not been predicted (i.e. the nonzero value that is given by equation 1). This assumption that $t(L_2)$ always requires some minimal amount of time to complete reflects our conceptualization of L_2 as being involved with the processing of a word's meaning (either its access or its integration), so that, irrespective of how a word's meaning is obtained (that is, entirely through top-down constraints in the case of highly predictable words or through the more bottom-up route specified by equations 1 and 2), the process of accessing and/or integrating a word's meaning is necessary if the reader is to understand what is being read. Second, $t(L_2)$ is not modulated by visual acuity. This assumption also follows from our conceptualization of L_2 as being a later stage of lexical processing—one that is impervious to degradation in the quality of the visual information that comes from viewing a word in parafoveal vision. Finally, it is worth mentioning how long the model assumes word identification to take. If one includes the 50 ms that is necessary for visual processing time, then the E-Z Reader parameters specify the mean minimum (in cases where predictability < 1) and maximum times to identify words as being equal to 151 and 233 ms, respectively.[2]

This description of how visual processing, attention, and lexical processing interact in guiding the eye movements of skilled readers describes the front end of the model. Of course, a model of eye-movement control has to say something about oculomotor control. The remaining assumptions of our model thus concern the programming and execution of saccades. Figure 6.1 shows the oculomotor system, and how this system is related to the parts of the model that have already been described.

Our first assumption about saccadic programming is that saccades are programmed in two stages: a labile stage (M_1) that is subject to cancellation by the initiation of subsequent saccadic programs, and a nonlabile stage (M_2) that is not subject to cancellation. This assumption is consistent with the work of Becker and Jürgens (1979), McPeek, Skavenski, and Nakayama (2000), and Vergilino and Beauvillain (2000). In our simulations, the actual times that are required to complete M_1 and M_2 are random deviates that are sampled from a gamma distribution having means equal to 100 and 25 ms (for M_1 and M_2, respectively) and standard deviations equal to .22 of the means. With these parameter values, the mean *saccadic latency*, or minimal amount of time that is needed to detect a saccade target and then move the eyes to its location, is predicted to be approximately 175 ms (that is, the sum of the eye-to-mind lag and the mean durations of the two stages of saccadic programming). This estimate corresponds closely to empirical estimates of the saccadic latency (Becker & Jürgens, 1979; McPeek et al., 2000; Rayner, Slowiaczek, Clifton, & Bertera, 1983).

We also assume that the labile stage of programming consists of two substages, which, for the sake of simplicity, each take exactly half of the time that is required for $t(M_1)$ to complete. The first of these substages is devoted to general system preparation, during which the oculomotor system is engaged and made ready to begin programming a saccade. During the second substage, the coordinates of the spatial target (which in the model is the centre of the targeted word) are translated into the appropriate saccade distance or muscle force that is necessary to move the eyes to their target location.

Two important consequences emerge from the disparity between the time when a word is identified and the time when a saccade leaving it is executed that can best be explained by Figure 6.2. The *x*-axis of the graph in this figure shows one measure of word-processing difficulty (frequency of occurrence of the word in printed text), while the *y*-axis shows the mean times that are required to complete the two stages of word identification, $t(L_1)$ and $t(L_2)$, and the time needed to program a saccade, which is equal to $t(M_1) + t(M_2)$. An important point to remember is that attention will usually shift from word n to word n+1 before the program to move the eyes from word n to word n+1 has been completed. When this happens, lexical processing of word n+1 begins immediately, allowing the word to be processed from the parafovea. The mean amount of time spent engaged in this parafoveal processing is represented by the shaded area in the graph in Figure 6.2. Notice that the amount of parafoveal processing of word n+1 that can be accomplished varies as a function of how difficult word n is to process; difficult words afford

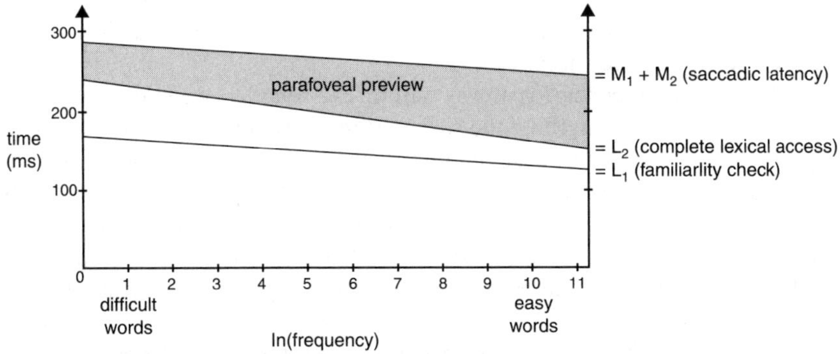

Figure 6.2 The time course of the two stages of word identification (L_1 and L_2) and saccadic programming. The grey (shaded) area shows how the amount of parafoveal preview varies as a function of the processing difficulty (e.g. frequency) of the fixated word.

less parafoveal processing than easy words. As Figure 6.2 shows, this stems from the fact that $t(L_2)$ increases as the difficulty of word processing increases, but the saccadic latency remains constant. The consequences of this are two-fold. First, any difficulty that is associated with processing word *n* will result in less parafoveal processing of word *n*+1, which will in turn cause some processing difficulty to *spillover* onto word *n*+1, inflating the durations of any subsequent fixations on that word. Second, any cost that is incurred on word *n*+1 that may come from preventing normal parafoveal preview of that word (Rayner, 1975) will be more pronounced if word *n* is easy to process, because such cases allow for more parafoveal processing. These consequences are consistent with the literature; spillover effects have been well documented (Rayner & Duffy, 1986; Rayner, Sereno, Morris, Schmauder, & Clifton, 1989), as have interactions between the difficulty of foveal processing and preview benefit (Henderson & Ferriera, 1990; Inhoff, Pollatsek, Posner, & Rayner, 1989; Kennison & Clifton, 1995; Rayner, 1986; White, Rayner, & Liversedge, 2005).

Our assumptions about where saccades are targeted and where they actually land are largely derived from the work of O'Regan, McConkie, and their colleagues, as well as our own work (McConkie, Kerr, Reddix, & Zola, 1988; McConkie, Zola, Grimes, Kerr, Bryant, & Wolff, 1991; Rayner, 1979; Rayner, Sereno, & Raney, 1996; Reichle et al., 1999). This work suggests that the eyes are targeted to land near the middle of words, but because of motor error often land short of that target. (However, when the intended saccade is short, there is a tendency to overshoot the target.) As a result, the distributions of fixation landing sites tend to resemble truncated Gaussians that are centred near the middle of the targeted words, with the missing tails reflecting those saccades where the eyes undershot or overshot their intended targets. The landing-site distributions also tend to shift toward the beginning of the target words and to become more variable as the saccade length increases, and as the fixation duration on the *launch-site* word (that is, the word from where the saccade originated) decreases.

To capture these general patterns within E-Z Reader, we started with the assumption that the length of the saccade (in character spaces) that is actually executed is the sum of three components: the actual intended saccade length, a *systematic error* component, and a *random error* component. The systematic error component is an amount by which the saccade will tend to undershoot or overshoot its intended target, and is a function of both how much the intended saccade length deviates from a preferred saccade length, and the fixation duration on the launch-site word. The systematic error tends to decrease as both the deviation between the intended and preferred saccade lengths decrease, and as the fixation duration on the launch-site word increases. These relationships are specified by equation 4, where Ψ is a parameter that represents the preferred saccade length (which in English is equal to seven character spaces), and Ω_1 (= 7.3) and Ω_2 (= 3) are free parameters that modulate the degree to which the launch-site fixation duration affects the systematic error.

$$\text{systematic error} = (\Psi - \text{intended length})\ [\Omega_1\ \ln(\text{fixation duration}) / \Omega_2] \tag{4}$$

The second source of saccadic error, the random error component, is meant to reflect true (random) motor error. As such, this error is a random deviate that is sampled from a Gaussian distribution having a mean equal to zero and a standard deviation that is a function of the intended saccade length, as given by equation 5. In this equation, η_1 (= .5) and η_2 (= .15) are free parameters that determine how much the variability of the random error increases with the intended saccade length.

$$\text{random error} = \eta_1 + \eta_2\ \text{intended length} \tag{5}$$

Our final assumption about saccades concerns refixations. As in the SWIFT model of eye-movement control (Engbert et al., 2005), we assume that, upon initially fixating a given word, a corrective refixation saccade can be programmed and executed to move the eyes to a better viewing location. The intuition here is that initial fixations landing on the beginnings or endings of words do not allow for efficient lexical processing because the processing of many letters in the word from such locations will be slow due to poor visual acuity (see equation 2). Thus, a rapid corrective saccade will (on average) move the eyes closer to the centre of the word (the optimal viewing position) to make lexical processing more efficient. As specified by equation 6, p, the probability of initiating a refixation saccade, is a function of the absolute distance (in character spaces) between the initial landing position on a word and the word's optimal viewing position, as scaled by the free parameter

λ (= .09). Note that longer words are also more likely to be the recipients of refixations than are shorter words, because the average absolute distance of the initial fixation from the centre of the word increases with word length, (Vergilino & Beauvillain, 2000). For it to be plausible that such an intelligent eye movement could be programmed, it was necessary to assume that the "decision" about whether or not to initiate a corrective refixation saccade could be made only after a delay that is greater than the time that is necessary to get the information about where the initial fixation is located from the eye to the brain. This delay was sampled from a gamma distribution with a mean equal to the free parameter R (= 117 ms); because feedback about the initial fixation location is based on visual information, the value of R was restricted so that $R > V$ (i.e. the duration of the eye-brain lag). Thus, upon fixating a word, a refixation saccade (obeying equations 4 and 5, just like interword saccades) is initiated: (1) if another labile saccade has not already been initiated; and (2) if a saccade has not already been initiated to move the eyes to the next word. These two restrictions are sufficient to prevent refixation saccades from cancelling saccades that would otherwise cause the eyes to move forward in the text.

$$p = \lambda \mid \text{optimal viewing position} - \text{initial landing position} \mid \tag{6}$$

This concludes our description of the E-Z Reader model. In the next section of this chapter, we will briefly describe the results of some recent experiments that have been motivated by the model. Elsewhere (see Pollatsek et al., 2006; Reichle et al., 2006), we have presented the simulation results of several benchmark phenomena that we think any viable model of eye-movement control should be able to explain.

Recent experiments and further modelling

In this section, we will briefly review some recent experiments that were intended to be tests of the model. Specifically, we will discuss some recent experiments we have carried out dealing with (1) the interaction of word frequency and word predictability, (2) disappearing text, and (3) the effects of degrading specific target words. We will also briefly touch on some recent modelling activities within the context of E-Z Reader.

Rayner, Ashby et al. (2004) reported a study in which readers read sentences containing target words that differed in frequency and predictability. Thus, a given target word could be (1) high frequency and highly predictable from the prior context (HF-HP), (2) high frequency and low predictable (HF-LP), (3) low frequency and highly predictable (LF-HP), or (4) low frequency and low predictable (LF-LP). The earliest versions of the model posited that the joint effects of word frequency and predictability were multiplicative; that is, we originally used a multiplicative version of equation 1 (Reichle et al., 1998, 2003). However, when confronted with the data of the Rayner, Ashby et al.

study (2004), we realized that the assumption was counterintuitive, as it predicted smaller predictability effects for frequent words. Table 6.1 shows the results of the Rayner, Ashby et al. (2004) study. The results are interesting in that for the fixation time measures the data are additive (or mildly interactive), while for the probability of fixation on a word the results are interactive (but not the type of interaction that a multiplicative model would have predicted).

The results of this study caused us to consider a number of alternatives to equation 1, but eventually we were able to fit the pattern of data within the model by assuming that word-encoding time is additively affected by frequency and predictability, and that difficulty with post-lexical processing of the target word causes a "double-take". The results of the study also led us to understand that the relationship between the duration of hypothetical word-encoding stages and observed fixation times is not likely to be fully transparent.

In the disappearing text studies (Liversedge, Rayner, White, Vergilino-Perez, Findlay, & Kentridge, 2004; Rayner, Liversedge, White, & Vergilino-Perez, 2003), the word that the reader is fixating disappears (or is masked) after 60 ms. Consistent with earlier work (Ishida & Ikeda, 1989; Rayner, Inhoff, Morrison, Slowiaczek, & Bertera, 1981), we found that reading proceeds quite smoothly when the fixated word disappears after 60 ms. Furthermore, we also found that the size of the word frequency effect (that is, that readers look longer at low-frequency words than high-frequency words) was the same when the fixated word disappeared as when the text was normal (see Table 6.2). However, more recently, we (Rayner, Liversedge, & White, 2006) have observed that if the word to the right of fixation disappears, reading is seriously disrupted. Although there is still a word frequency effect on these disappearing words, reading is slowed considerably when word n+1 disappears or is masked 60 ms after the fixation on word n begins.

Taken together, the results of the disappearing text studies fit quite nicely with the E-Z Reader model and with the assumption of attending to only one word at a time. These studies, however, indicated that there was a tacit

Table 6.1 Mean first-fixation durations (FFD), single-fixation durations (SFD), gaze durations (GD), and probability of a fixation (PrF) for the target words in Rayner et al. (2004)

Condition	*FFD*	*SFD*	*GD*	*PrF*
HF-HP	256	258	274	.77
HF-LP	263	268	290	.85
LF-HP	267	269	288	.86
LF-LP	282	287	310	.84

All durations are in milliseconds. HF = high-frequency target words, LF = low-frequency target words, HP = high-predictable target words, and LP = low-predictable target words.

Table 6.2 Mean first-fixation duration (FFD), single-fixation duration (SFD), and gaze duration (GD) as a function of text condition and word frequency in Rayner et al. (2003)

Condition	*FFD*	*SFD*	*GD*
Normal text			
HF	256	257	289
LF	288	298	328
FE	32	41	39
Disappearing text			
HF	276	277	291
LF	301	307	333
FE	25	30	42

All durations are in milliseconds. HF = high-frequency target words, LF = low-frequency target words, FE = frequency effect.

assumption that we had to make explicit (Pollatsek, et al., 2006). That is, these data are easily explainable if one assumes that visual information on a fixation is preserved for continued lexical processing only if it is attended to for a sufficient amount of time before it disappears. Because the fixated word is virtually always attended to when it is initially fixated (unless it has already been processed before that), a 60-ms exposure of the fixated word is long enough to ensure that lexical processing will continue on it even if it disappears or is masked after that. Moreover, the normal word frequency effects will be observed because lexical processing determines when the eyes move on. However, when the word to the right of fixation disappears after 60 ms, there is a reasonably high probability that attention has not yet moved to it, and thus, in those cases, there will be little or no visual information for lexical processes to operate on when attention does move from word n to word n+1. As a result, there will be considerable disruption to the reading process.[3]

The final experiment we discuss follows directly from an observation that Eyal Reingold made with respect to the E-Z Reader model. Specifically, he suggested that:

> searching for variables that influence the processing difficulty of word n without producing any processing effect on word n+1 is a critical test of the E-Z Reader framework. A closer examination of the L1 versus L2 distinction proposed by E-Z Reader 7 [the version of our model described in Reichle et al., 2003] suggests several potentially promising experimental manipulations. Essentially, the L1 versus L2 distinction assumes an early lexical processing stage corresponding to the extraction and identification of the orthographic form of a word and a late stage involving access to the phonological and semantic forms. Accordingly, a

> disruption early to the word identification system when visual features are encoded and abstract letter identities are computed should be expected to influence L1, but not L2. (Reingold, 2003, p. 501)

Reingold then went on to suggest that experiments in which word n was degraded should result in disruption to L_1, but not L_2, and the disruption should manifest itself in fixation time on word n, but not spillover to word n+1.

Reingold and Rayner (in press) conducted exactly this type of experiment. Basically, a fixated word could appear either in its normal fashion, or was made to be very faint, was made bold, or was presented in case alternation. Because the "faint" manipulation was the one that most plausibly affected only early processing (the bold manipulation had little effect on any dependent variable), we will focus on a comparison of the normal versus the faint condition. As can be seen in Table 6.3, the faint presentation of the target word made the word quite difficult to process and there was a very large effect on the gaze duration on the target word. However, consistent with the expectation that this manipulation would largely influence early stages of lexical processing (and thus L_1), there was virtually no spillover—no lengthening of fixation durations on word n+1. This is exactly what would be predicted by the E-Z Reader model if the manipulation of making the target word fainter affected only the duration of the L_1 stage.

The data from the three sets of studies that we have described in this section were consistent with the E-Z Reader model. However, we would be remiss to suggest that all recent studies that dealt with the model have provided confirmatory results. Indeed, recent papers by Kennedy and Pynte (2005) and Inhoff, Eiter, and Radach (2005) have claimed that their reported data are difficult to reconcile with the model. However, we are not convinced that these data are all that damaging to the model (see Pollatsek, Reichle, & Rayner, in press). The key test then becomes whether or not we can actually simulate the data via the model (though depending on the nature of the experimental manipulation, and how extreme it might be, it is not always possible even to attempt to simulate the data).

Table 6.3 Mean first-fixation duration (FFD), single-fixation duration (SFD), and gaze duration (GD) as a function of text condition in Reingold and Rayner (in press)

	Fixation on target word (Word n)			*Spillover fixation (Word n+1)*		
Condition	*FFD*	*SFD*	*GD*	*FFD*	*SFD*	*GD*
Normal	219	220	259	235	240	265
Faint	280	306	382	244	249	270

All durations are in milliseconds.

With respect to modelling advances, we (Pollatsek et al., 2006; Reichle et al., 2006) have recently reported further simulations that capture the essence of the disappearing text studies and some of the original preview benefit studies. Furthermore, we have also successfully simulated the so-called *inverted optimal viewing position effect* in which single fixations and the first of two fixations tend to be longer when the eyes actually land in the middle of a word than when they land on the end of the word. It had been claimed (Vitu, McConkie, Kerr, & O'Regan, 2001) that this finding was problematic for the E-Z Reader model, but our successful simulation indicates otherwise (see also Nuthmann, Engbert, & Kliegl, 2005).

In terms of the general points that we mentioned at the outset of this chapter that a model needed to account for, all of them are accounted for by E-Z Reader, either because the constraint is built into the architecture of the model (as with the size of the perceptual span and frequency/predictable effects) or because an effect follows naturally from the model. Indeed, in our opinion, the model accounts for an impressive array of data and findings. Furthermore, it is successful in the sense that it is motivating considerable amounts of research, and it has also inspired the development of other models, such as SWIFT (Engbert, Nuthmann, Richter, & Kliegl, 2005), Glenmore (Reilly & Radach, 2003, 2006), SERIF (MacDonald, Carpenter, & Shillcock, 2005), EMMA (Salvucci, 2001), SHARE (Feng, 2006), and others. We would be the first to admit that the model is not perfect, nor does it account for all of the important data regarding reading. For example, at the moment it does not really account for any higher-order effects (above lexical processing) on eye movements in reading, and such effects are clearly apparent (see Rayner, 1998, for a summary). Nor are we able to account for long-distance regressions (as the model reads sentences, not passages). However, with respect to the latter point, it is instructive that Sparrow, Miellet, and Coello (2003) were able to successfully run a version of E-Z Reader on passages of text, and they obtained quite reasonable fits to actual reading performance.

In essence, we would argue that E-Z Reader is an interesting case of an existence proof in that it shows how linguistic processing can guide eye movements during reading. Furthermore, E-Z Reader is a heuristic that can be used as a framework to examine theoretical assumptions about various reading phenomena.

Points of controversy regarding the model

We now turn to some major points of controversy concerning the model. Many of these points have been discussed elsewhere (see Rayner et al., 2003; Reichle et al., 2003), but we will provide further discussion in the present context. We focus on two points of controversy: (1) serial processing in the model, and (2) parafoveal-on-foveal effects.

We have already discussed the fact that the E-Z Reader model, in terms of word identification, posits strictly serial processing. It is important to realize that there are parallel components in the model (that is, saccades are programmed in parallel, and the pre-attentive scan of material to the right of fixation involved in deciding where to fixate next involves parallel processes), but in terms of how words are identified, it is in a left-to-right fashion. We offer two comments with respect to this assumption. First, as we noted earlier, we believe it is important for comprehension of textual material to get the word order straight. Second, we occasionally encounter the argument that reading has to involve more than serial word identification because of regressions. Indeed, regressions do disrupt the sequential nature of reading, but we would also maintain that readers still manage to keep the order of words that they are reading in mind when they regress. Otherwise, the input would be some type of "word salad" (Inhoff & Weger, 2005) in which comprehension would be compromised. We suspect that readers are so reluctant to make long-distance regressions in reading because they want to maintain the correct order of words as they read, and long-distance regressions may make it difficult to do this.

Parafoveal-on-foveal effects have been widely touted as causing difficulty for the E-Z Reader model (see the Commentary on the Reichle et al., 2003, article). A parafoveal-on-foveal effect occurs when some property of the word to the right of fixation (word n+1) influences the processing time on the currently fixated word (word n). These effects have also gained further credibility as a function of models like SWIFT (Engbert et al., 2002, 2005) which allow for parallel processing of words within a gradient of attention that can be distributed across as many as four words.

If, indeed, it could be convincingly demonstrated that the meaning of word n+1 influenced the duration of the fixation on word n, it would be problematic for the E-Z Reader model. However, the reality is that parafoveal-on-foveal effects are quite elusive and there are as many demonstrations of failures to find effects as there are reported effects (Hyönä & Bertram, 2004), and, unfortunately, when such effects are reported they are sometimes facilitative and sometimes inhibitory (Rayner & Juhasz, 2004). While there are clearly parafoveal-on-foveal effects due to unusual orthographic properties at the beginning of word n+1 (Hyönä, 1995; White & Liversedge, 2004), we are highly sceptical about claims related to lexical properties or meaning properties of the word to the right of fixation, and we suspect that most such reported effects are due to mislocalized fixations (see Rayner, Warren, Juhasz, & Liversedge, 2004, for a discussion).

Unsolved problems and future directions

One of the more unsatisfying aspects of our modelling is our vacillation about the nature of the L_1 and L_2 stages in the model. As noted earlier, in the earliest version of the model, we referred to L_1 as a familiarity check and L_2 as lexical access. We envisioned then, and still do, that the two stages serve a pragmatic function for the reader (as opposed to the modeller). That is, they facilitate the reading process (and perhaps many other visual tasks that require fairly "deep" processing of visual information) by having a preliminary stage that is less than full processing of the information. This allows eye movements to be programmed efficiently. Otherwise, if full processing of the foveal information were the stimulus for an eye-movement command, readers would be forced to spend the last 100 ms or more of each fixation (the time to execute the command) inefficiently processing parafoveal information. In contrast, if a "cheat" such as L_1 is part of the system, this relative "down time" at the end of each fixation can be minimized, and if the cheat is relatively conservative, there should be few saccades that come before the lexical information on the prior fixation is fully processed.

The key questions, of course, are whether there really is a plausible signal from the lexical processing system that could serve as a signal to move the eyes to the next word, and, if so, what it would be. Originally, we thought it was plausible to view the ends of L_1 and L_2 as representing discrete stages of lexical processing, where L_1 represented the completion of the access of the "lower-level" orthographic and phonological codes and L_2 represented the completion of access of the meaning of the word (under some construal of what "meaning" might be). However, we are now reasonably convinced that this assumption is likely to be wrong. There are several phenomena that seem to argue against such a neat dichotomy, but given space limitations, we will focus on one: lexical ambiguity.

In the now classic experiments by Rayner and Duffy (1986) and Duffy, Morris, and Rayner (1988), there is a clear pattern of results that indicate that access to the meaning of the word is occurring relatively early. They examined two kinds of lexically ambiguous words: *biased* ambiguous words (e.g. *bank*), where one meaning is much higher frequency than the other; and *balanced* ambiguous words (e.g. *count*), where the two meanings of the word have roughly equal frequency in the language. We will focus on the results from the biased ambiguous words. But, let us just briefly mention the results from the balanced ambiguous words. When such words appear in neutral context, readers tend to look at them longer than an unambiguous control word matched in length and frequency. It thus appears that the competition between the two meanings causes the reader to pause a bit longer on such words. However, when such words appear in disambiguating contexts, readers do not look at them any longer than the control words. Apparently, the context provides sufficient information for them to instantiate the correct meaning.

Returning now to the case of biased ambiguous words, when such words are preceded by a neutral prior context (in which either meaning of the word fits), fixation times on the ambiguous word are the same as an unambiguous control word having the same length and frequency, but if the following context indicates the less frequent meaning was intended, then disruption of the reading process is observed at this point. This implies that, in these cases, readers virtually always take the ambiguous word to have the dominant meaning, and if that was not what was intended, they do a "double-take". In contrast, when these biased ambiguous words are preceded by a prior context that makes clear that the lower-frequency meaning was intended, fixation times are longer on the ambiguous word than on a control word of equal frequency—even first-fixation durations (Sereno, O'Donnell, & Rayner, 2006).

The latter result suggests that the lower-frequency meaning of the ambiguous word takes longer to process than the higher-frequency meaning. While that is intuitively reasonable, it is not simply explained by the E-Z Reader model, assuming the interpretation of L_1 that we originally proposed. That is, if the eye is sent on to the next word by completion of orthographic and phonological coding, then multiplicity of meanings should be irrelevant to homographic homophones such as *bank*. This is a problem because, even if one posited that L_2 is lengthened by lexical ambiguity, that would have little or no effect on fixation times on the ambiguous word—certainly no effect on first-fixation durations. There are several ways to attempt to solve the problem, although each has some difficulties. The more straightforward way, which is what we are leaning toward, is to abandon such a qualitative distinction of L_1 and L_2 and to posit that activation of meaning (among other things) is involved in determining the duration of both stages. For example, one could posit something like *semantagens* (analogous to Morton's, 1969, logogens) that are memory representations of word meaning and that L_1 is completed when an appropriate semantagen reaches a critical threshold. (Further, the time to activate a semantagen is a function of the frequency of that word meaning.) Thus, in the case of the biased ambiguous word with no prior disambiguating context, the prior text would exert no inhibition on the dominant meaning, and thus it would reach threshold essentially as rapidly as the matched unambiguous word. In contrast, when there is prior context that makes this meaning improbable, this semantagen is inhibited, and the (correct) lower-frequency semantagen activates more slowly, and thus L_1 is longer.

There is nothing inherently wrong with this account, but it raises several important questions. The first is whether it is plausible for prior context to operate quickly enough to influence a process as rapid as L_1. At first blush, this context effect might not seem to be very different from what we have already assumed about word predictability. However, there are two important differences. First, for predictability, one has to assume only that the word's orthographic or phonological form is involved; for the lexical ambiguity data, one has to assume that a deeper level is involved. Perhaps more importantly, however, is the following distinction. Predictability merely assumes that prior context, using some priming-like mechanism, activates a single memory representation. For lexical ambiguity, one has to come up with a plausible mechanism for how prior context can inhibit a meaning that does not fit in, and can do so in a time scale congruent with assumptions about L_1 duration. Moreover, a full explanation would have to indicate why this constraint operates rapidly enough to produce effects on first-fixation duration whereas phenomena that seem to tap "lower-level" lexical processes, such as neighbourhood effects, seem to have their effects later—largely affecting spillover (i.e., fixation durations on the next word in the text). We are not saying this cannot be done; however, it is clear that one needs a very good model of lexical processing to make it more than "hand waving".

One alternative to explicitly identifying semantic processing with L_1 is to posit, consistent with our original view of L_1 and L_2, that the lexical ambiguity effects are due to lengthening the duration of L_2, but then broaden the influence of L_2 in the reading process. That is, one would have to come up with a plausible conception of how maintaining attention on a word could influence eye movements. While it might seem intuitively appealing to posit that maintaining attention on word n for an inordinate amount of time after an eye movement has been programmed to word n+1 could send out a signal to cancel the eye movement to word n+1—and thus lengthen fixation times on word n—it is not clear that this could really work. This is essentially a deadline model (Henderson & Ferreira, 1990), and these run into several related problems. First, you cannot set the deadline to be too long; otherwise, it would have no chance of cancelling any saccades to word n+1. On the other hand, if it is too short, it will cancel too many saccades and also cause regressions if the cancellation signal comes after the eye movement program to fixate word n+1 has gone into the nonlabile stage.

The other class of alternatives is to posit a more active cancellation process that is not waiting for a period of time to elapse, but instead is a process that decides that "something does not compute" and signals for a cancellation of the saccade to word n+1. This seems like a more plausible mechanism than the clock mechanism in the prior paragraph. It also has an advantage over the reinterpretation of L_1, as this computation may not have to operate as quickly, because it can "hang back" a bit, as it is a correction to L_1. The major problem is that, without further elaboration, it seems close to a "Deus ex machina", and there is a danger that it can explain anything.

We expect to be spending a large amount of time in the next few years trying to explore phenomena such as lexical ambiguity. We would hope either that an expanded version of the E-Z Reader model will give a satisfactory account of such phenomena or that the reasons for its failures are sufficiently clear so that we can figure out what to replace it with and which key assumptions need alteration. More generally, we hope that the above discussion of this phenomenon makes several points. First, that many deep questions about lexical processing, such as the relationship between "bottom-up" lexical access and "top-down" influences from sentence context, have been explored with eye movements in reading, and these experiments have come up with quite lawful data. Furthermore, the nature of the eye-movement record—naturally indicating the time course of events—places severe constraints on theorizing. Second, quantitative modelling is really needed to explore such phenomena. That is, with verbal models, it is easy to convince yourself that you understand phenomena such as lexical ambiguity, but when you force yourself to account for such phenomena in real time with realistic estimates of how long processes can take, you realize that we still do not understand lexical processing all that well. Hopefully, the next five years or so of research on processing of words will give us a better understanding. Indeed, many of the chapters in the present volume should be quite relevant in such an endeavour.

Acknowledgements

Preparation of this chapter was supported by grants HD17246 and HD26765 from the US National Institutes of Health and by grants R305H030235 and R305G020006 from the Institute of Education Sciences (Department of Education).

References

Becker, W., & Jürgens, R. (1979). An analysis of the saccadic system by means of double step stimuli. *Vision Research, 19*, 967–983.

Duffy, S. A., Morris, R. K., & Rayner, K. (1988). Lexical ambiguity and fixation times in reading. *Journal of Memory and Language, 27*, 429–446.

Ehrlich, S. F., & Rayner, K. (1981). Contextual effects on word perception and eye movements during reading. *Journal of Verbal Learning and Verbal Behavior, 20*, 641–655.

Engbert, R., Longtin, A., & Kliegl, R. (2002). A dynamical model of saccade generation in reading based on spatially distributed lexical processing. *Vision Research, 42*, 621–636.

Engbert, R., Nuthmann, A., Richter, E., & Kliegl, R. (2005). SWIFT: A dynamical model of saccade generation during reading. *Psychological Review, 112*, 777–813.

Feng, G. (2006). Eye movements as time-series random variables: A stochastic model of eye movement control in reading. *Cognitive Systems Research, 7*, 70–95.

Fisher, D. L., & Goldstein, W. (1983). Stochastic PERT networks as models of cognition: Derivation of the mean, variance, and distribution of reaction using order-of-processing (OP) diagrams. *Journal of Mathematical Psychology, 27*, 121–151.

Henderson, J. M., & Ferreira, F. (1990). Effects of foveal processing difficulty on the perceptual span in reading: Implications for attention and eye movement control. *Journal of Experimental Psychology: Learning, Memory, and Cognition, 16*, 417–429.

Hyönä, J. (1995). Do irregular letter combinations attract readers' attention? Evidence from fixation locations in words. *Journal of Experimental Psychology: Human Perception and Performance, 21*, 68–81.

Hyönä, J., & Bertram, R. (2004). Do frequency characteristics of nonfixated words influence the processing of fixated words during reading? *European Journal of Cognitive Psychology, 16*, 104–127.

Inhoff, A. W., Eiter, B., & Radach, R. (2005). Time course of linguistic information extraction from consecutive words during eye fixations in reading. *Journal of Experimental Psychology: Human Perception and Performance, 31*, 979–996.

Inhoff, A. W., Pollatsek, A., Posner, M. I., & Rayner, K. (1989). Covert attention and eye movements during reading. *Quarterly Journal of Experimental Psychology, 41A*, 63–89.

Inhoff, A. W., Radach, R., Eiter, B. M., & Juhasz, B. (2003). Distinct subsystems for the parafoveal processing of spatial and linguistic information during eye fixations in reading. *Quarterly Journal of Experimental Psychology*, *56A*, 803–828.

Inhoff, A. W., & Rayner, K. (1986). Parafoveal word processing during eye fixations in reading: Effects of word frequency. *Perception and Psychophysics*, *40*, 431–439.

Inhoff, A. W., & Weger, U. W. (2005). Memory for word location during reading: Eye movements to previously read words are spatially selective but not precise. *Memory and Cognition*, *33*, 447–461.

Ishida, T., & Ikeda, M. (1989). Temporal properties of information extraction in reading studied by a text-mask replacement technique. *Journal of the Optical Society A: Optics and Image Science*, *6*, 1624–1632.

Just, M. A., & Carpenter, P. A. (1980). A theory of reading: From eye fixations to comprehension. *Psychological Review*, *87*, 329–354.

Kennedy, A., & Pynte, J. (2005). Parafoveal-on-foveal effects in normal reading. *Vision Research*, *45*, 153–68.

Kennison, S. M., & Clifton, C. (1995). Determinants of parafoveal preview benefit in high and low working memory capacity readers: Implications for eye movement control. *Journal of Experimental Psychology: Learning, Memory, and Cognition*, *21*, 68–81.

Lee, H.-W., Legge, G. E., & Ortiz, A. (2003). Is word recognition different in central and peripheral vision? *Vision Research*, *43*, 2837–2846.

Liversedge, S. P., Rayner, K., White, S. J., Vergilino-Perez, D., Findlay, J. M., & Kentridge, R. W. (2004). Eye movements when reading disappearing text: is there a gap effect in reading? *Vision Research*, *44*, 1013–1024.

McConkie, G. W., Kerr, P. W., Reddix, M. D., & Zola, D. (1988). Eye movement control during reading: I. The location of initial eye fixations in words. *Vision Research*, *28*, 1107–1118.

McConkie, G. W., & Rayner, K. (1975). The span of the effective stimulus during a fixation in reading. *Perception and Psychophysics*, *17*, 578–586.

McConkie, G. W., Zola, D., Grimes, J., Kerr, P. W., Bryant, N. R., & Wolff, P. M. (1991). Children's eye movements during reading. In. J. F. Stein (Ed.), *Vision and Visual Dyslexia 13*. London: Macmillan.

McDonald, S. A., Carpenter, R. H. S., & Shillcock, R. C. (2005). An anatomically-constrained, stochastic model of eye movement control in reading. *Psychological Review*, *112*, 814–840.

McPeek, R. M., Skavenski, A. A., & Nakayama, K. (2000). Concurrent processing of saccades in visual search. *Vision Research*, *40*, 2499–2516.

Morton, J. (1969). Interaction of information in word recognition. *Psychological Review*, *76*, 165–178.

Nuthmann, A., Engbert, R., & Kliegl, R. (2005). Mislocated fixations during reading and the inverted optimal viewing position effect. *Vision Research*, *45*, 2201–2217.

Pollatsek, A., Reichle, E. D., & Rayner, K. (2006). Tests of the E-Z Reader model: Exploring the interface between cognition and eye-movement control. *Cognitive Psychology*, *52*, 1–56.

Pollatsek, A., Reichle, E. D., & Rayner, K. (in press). Serial processing is consistent with the time course of linguistic information extraction from consecutive words during eye fixations in reading: A reply to Inhoff, Eiter, and Radach (2005). *Journal of Experimental Psychology: Human Perception and Performance*.

Rayner, K. (1975). The perceptual span and peripheral cues in reading. *Cognitive Psychology, 7*, 65–81.

Rayner, K. (1978). Eye movements in reading and information processing. *Psychological Bulletin, 85*, 618–660.

Rayner, K. (1979). Eye guidance in reading: Fixation locations within words. *Perception, 8*, 21–30.

Rayner, K. (1986). Eye movements and the perceptual span in beginning and skilled readers. *Journal of Experimental Child Psychology, 41*, 211–236.

Rayner, K. (1998). Eye movements in reading and information processing: 20 years of research. *Psychological Bulletin, 124*, 372–422.

Rayner, K., Ashby, J., Pollatsek, A., & Reichle, E. (2004a). The effects of frequency and predictability on eye fixations in reading: Implications for the E-Z Reader model. *Journal of Experimental Psychology: Human Perception and Performance, 30*, 720–732.

Rayner, K., & Bertera, J. H. (1979). Reading without a fovea. *Science, 206*, 468–469.

Rayner, K., & Duffy, S. A. (1986). Lexical complexity and fixation times in reading: Effects of word frequency, verb complexity, and lexical ambiguity. *Memory and Cognition, 14*, 191–201.

Rayner, K., Inhoff, A. W., Morrison, R., Slowiaczek, M. L., & Bertera, J. H. (1981). Masking of foveal and parafoveal vision during eye fixations in reading. *Journal of Experimental Psychology: Human Perception and Performance, 7*, 167–179.

Rayner, K., & Juhasz, B. J. (2004). Eye movements in reading: Old questions and new directions. *European Journal of Cognitive Psychology, 16*, 340–352.

Rayner, K., Liversedge, S. P., & White, S. J. (2006). Eye movements when reading disappearing text: The importance of the word to the right of fixation. *Vision Research, 46*, 310–323.

Rayner, K., Liversedge, S. P., White, S. J., & Vergilino-Perez, D. (2003). Reading disappearing text: Cognitive control of eye movements. *Psychological Science, 14*, 385–389.

Rayner, K., & McConkie, G. W. (1976). What guides a reader's eye movements. *Vision Research, 16*, 829–837.

Rayner, K., & Morrison, R. M. (1981). Eye movements and identifying words in parafoveal vision. *Bulletin of the Psychonomic Society, 17*, 135–138.

Rayner, K., Pollatsek, A., & Reichle, E. D. (2003). Eye movements in reading: Models and data. *Brain and Behavioral Sciences, 26*, 507–526.

Rayner, K., Sereno, S. C., Morris, R. K., Schmauder, A. R., & Clifton, C. (1989). Eye movements and on-line language comprehension processes. *Language and Cognitive Processes, 4* (Special issue), 21–49.

Rayner, K., Sereno, S. C., & Raney, G. E. (1996). Eye movement control in reading: A comparison of two types of models. *Journal of Experimental Psychology: Human Perception and Performance, 22*, 1188–1200.

Rayner, K., Slowiaczek, M. L., Clifton, C., & Bertera, J. H. (1983). Latency of sequential eye movements: Implications for reading. *Journal of Experimental Psychology: Human Perception and Performance, 9*, 912–922.

Rayner, K., Warren, T., Juhasz, B. J., & Liversedge, S. P. (2004b). Eye movements and plausibility effects in reading. *Journal of Experimental Psychology: Learning, Memory, and Cognition, 30*, 1290–1301.

Rayner, K., & Well, A. D. (1996). Effects of contextual constraint on eye movements in reading: A further examination. *Psychonomic Bulletin and Review, 3*, 504–509.

Rayner, K., Well, A. D., Pollatsek, A., & Bertera, J. H. (1982). The availability of useful information to the right of fixation in reading. *Perception and Psychophysics*, *31*, 537–550.

Reichle, E. D., & Perfetti, C. A. (2003). Morphology in word identification: A word experience model that accounts for morpheme frequency effects. *Scientific Studies of Reading*, *7*, 219–237.

Reichle, E. D., Pollatsek, A., Fisher, D. L., & Rayner, K. (1998). Towards a model of eye movement control in reading. *Psychological Review*, *105*, 125–157.

Reichle, E. D., Pollatsek, A., & Rayner, K. (2006). E-Z Reader: A cognitive-control, serial-attention model of eye-movement behavior during reading. *Cognitive Systems Research*, *7*, 4–22.

Reichle, E. D., Rayner, K., & Pollatsek, A. (1999). Eye movement control in reading: Accounting for initial fixation locations and refixations within the E-Z Reader model. *Vision Research*, *39*, 4403–4411.

Reichle, E. D., Rayner, K., & Pollatsek, A. (2003). The E-Z Reader model of eye movement control in reading: Comparison to other models. *Brain and Behavioral Sciences*, *26*, 445–476.

Reilly, R., & Radach, R. (2003). Foundations of an interactive activation model of eye movement control in reading. In J. Hyönä, R. Radach, & H. Deubel (Eds.), *The mind's eye: Cognitive and applied aspects of eye movement research* (pp. 429–455). Oxford: Elsevier.

Reilly, R., & Radach, R. (2006). Some empirical tests of an interactive activation model of eye movement control in reading. *Cognitive Systems Research*, *7*, 34–55.

Reingold, E. (2003). Eye-movement control in reading: Models and predictions. *Behavioral and Brain Sciences*, *26*, 500–501.

Reingold, E., & Rayner, K. (in press). Examining the word identification stages hypothesized by the E-Z Reader model. *Psychological Science*.

Salvucci, D. D. (2001). An integrated model of eye movements and visual encoding. *Cognitive Systems Research*, *1*, 201–220.

Schilling, H. E. H., Rayner, K., & Chumbley, J. I. (1998). Comparing naming, lexical decision, and eye fixation times: Word frequency effects and individual differences. *Memory and Cognition*, *26*, 1270–1281.

Sereno, S. C., O'Donnell, P. J., & Rayner, K. (2006). Eye movements and lexical ambiguity resolution: Investigating the subordinate-bias effect. *Journal of Experimental Psychology: Human Perception and Performance*, *32*, 335–350.

Sparrow, L., Miellet, S., & Coello, Y. (2003). The effects of frequency and predictability on eye fixations in reading: An evaluation of the E-Z Reader model. *Behavioral and Brain Sciences*, *26*, 503–505.

Tinker, M. A. (1958). Recent studies of eye movements in reading. *Psychological Bulletin*, *55*, 215–231.

Vergilino, D., & Beauvillain, C. (2000). The planning of refixation saccades in reading. *Vision Research*, *40*, 3527–3538.

Vitu, F., McConkie, G. W., Kerr, P., & O'Regan, J. K. (2001). Fixation location effects on fixation durations during reading: an inverted optimal viewing position effect. *Vision Research*, *41*, 3513–3533.

White, S. J., & Liversedge, S. P. (2004). Orthographic familiarity influences initial eye positions in reading. *European Journal of Cognitive Psychology*, *16*, 52–78.

White, S. J., Rayner, K., & Liversedge, S. P. (2005). Eye movements and the modulation of parafoveal processing by foveal processing difficulty: A re-examination. *Psychonomic Bulletin and Review*, *12*, 891–896.

Yonelinas, A. P. (2002). The nature of recollection and familiarity: A review of 30 years of research. *Journal of Memory and Language*, *46*, 441–517.

Notes

1 See Fisher and Goldstein (1983) for a discussion of OP (*order-of-processing*) diagrams and PERT networks.

2 These estimates ignore the effects of visual acuity, which would in most instances increase the estimated values.

3 It is difficult to simulate experiments of this type because much of what determines the readers' behaviour (such as the decision to ignore missing text and to continue reading) is simply outside the scope of our model.

Part II

Models, methods, and measures: Converging approaches to investigating lexical processing

7 How does orthographic learning happen?

Anne Castles
University of Melbourne, Australia
Kate Nation
University of Oxford, UK

Word recognition develops with such remarkable speed that, by the end of eighth grade, we expect children learning to read English to know and recognize over 80,000 words (Adams, 1990). At a basic level, beginning readers must establish a system of mappings or correspondences between the letters or graphemes of written words and the phonemes of spoken words (Ehri, 1992), and it is generally thought that this alphabetic decoding system is underpinned by phonological skills (Brady & Shankweiler, 1991; Byrne, 1998; Goswami & Bryant, 1990). To become accurate and efficient readers of the English language, however, children need to do more than assemble or decode pronunciations on the basis of spelling-sound mappings. They need to acquire a rapid and flexible word-recognition system that embodies knowledge of both the regularities and the irregularities of the English orthography.

While it is clear that the development of skilled word recognition requires more than the mastery of alphabetic decoding, we know very little about exactly what is required beyond this, and how this is achieved. An advanced stage of reading development beyond the alphabetic stage, often referred to as the *orthographic stage* (e.g. Frith, 1985), is typically represented in developmental theories of reading acquisition, but such a stage tends to be posited, rather than described in terms of exactly how it is reached. Andrews and Scarratt (1996, p. 141) sum up the issue nicely:

> The existing literature provides little insight into exactly what is required for development of an optimal expert strategy for word identification in reading. The *outcome* of making the transition to this stage of development is assumed to be an "autonomous lexicon" (Share, 1995) which allows "automatic word identification", but how does that happen? What changes in the representations or processes underlying reading behaviour to afford these outcomes?

In this chapter, we attempt to answer some of these questions. We label the process by which children move from decoding alphabetically to reading via the fluent recognition of individual words as *orthographic learning* and ask the following questions: What characterizes successful orthographic learning? What are the predictors of successful orthographic learning, and what can we learn about this process from children whose orthographic skills have failed to develop normally? Finally, and most importantly, what is the mechanism by which this orthographic learning occurs and how can it be modelled?

What characterizes successful orthographic learning?

An understanding of the process by which orthographic learning occurs would seem to require at the outset a clear characterization of the outcome of that learning process. What does the product of successful orthographic learning look like? Thanks to the extensive work of Perfetti, Share, and Ehri in this area, we can identify several key features of a skilled orthographic word-recognition system. First, according to Perfetti (1992), it involves having developed *fully specified*, rather than partially specified, internal representations. By full specification, Perfetti means that the input code is sufficient to uniquely identify the word to be read, without the necessity for discriminating between several competing partially activated candidates. Because, in these circumstances, the correct word is specified completely by the input code, context does not need to be used to assist in the identification of the word. This leads us to the second attribute of a skilled word-recognition system according to Perfetti, which is that there is *autonomy* in the word-recognition process. He argues that, although the reading system itself is a highly interactive architecture, and although earlier stages of reading development are characterized by strong effects of this interactivity and of contextual factors, skilled "lexical" retrieval is effectively modular, and is only very minimally influenced by factors other than the input code. Ehri (2005) builds on this notion by arguing that the orthographic or "sight word" recognition process is also *automatic*: it cannot be turned on and off, and is not subject to strategic control. Finally, she argues, this process operates largely *unconsciously*. Citing well-known demonstrations of the Stroop effect, she argues that highly skilled word recognition proceeds in a mandatory fashion without the requirement for conscious attention to the presented stimulus. The benefit of this automatic and unconscious recognition of words is that conscious attention can be directed fully, and without interruption, to the task of deriving meaning from the text.

The characteristics of a skilled orthographic word-recognition system are presented above as a stage of reading development that is reached by a child at some certain point in time. However, it is also possible, and perhaps likely, that this process proceeds in an *item-based* fashion (Share, 1995). That is, at any particular point in time, a child may be reading some words slowly, effortfully, and with heavy reliance on context and alphabetic decoding, while reading other words rapidly, automatically, and with minimal contextual influence. So it may be that we need to look for evidence of the existence of full specificity, autonomy, automaticity, and unconsciousness at the item or word level, rather than at the individual child level. The important question for the present purposes, however, is: What factors modulate the transition from one kind of processing to the other?

Predictors of successful orthographic learning

A first step toward understanding the process by which orthographic learning occurs would seem to be to identify the major predictors of this skill. What factors appear to be most strongly associated with skilled, word-level reading of the form described above? Obtaining such predictors has proven to be surprisingly difficult, and this may in part explain why progress in understanding the nature of the transition to skilled word recognition has been so slow. In the section below, we review some of the putative predictors of successful orthographic learning, elaborating on the strengths and limitations of the data in relation to each measure.

Alphabetic and phonological skills

As noted above, alphabetic decoding is known to account for a large amount of variance in children's word recognition (Adams, 1990; Wagner & Torgesen, 1987), with some estimates of the correlation between nonword reading and word reading being as high as .9 (Firth, 1972). This correlation is borne out in longitudinal studies, which indicate that early alphabetic skills are predictive of later reading progress (Jorm, Share, McLean, & Matthews, 1984). Moreover, children with dyslexia, who have demonstrably poor word-level reading skills, also very frequently show nonword reading impairments (Rack, Snowling, & Olson, 1992). Thus, alphabetic skill, in itself, must be viewed as a strong predictor of successful orthographic learning. Indeed, one of the dominant theories of the mechanism by which orthographic learning takes place—the self-teaching hypothesis—ascribes a central role to alphabetic decoding in this process (Share, 1995; this theory will be discussed in detail in a later section).

Alphabetic skills are themselves thought to have a basis in phonological language ability, or phonological awareness (Brady & Shankweiler, 1991; Byrne, 1998; Goswami & Bryant, 1990; for further discussion, see Castles & Coltheart, 2004), and so it may be that the level of awareness of the basic sounds of spoken language also predicts, if somewhat more indirectly, skilled orthographic word recognition. Consistent with this, performance on phonological awareness tasks correlates strongly, not just with nonword reading performance, but also with word-level reading ability (for reviews, see Adams, 1990; Goswami & Bryant, 1990; Wagner & Torgesen, 1987).

However, as several researchers have noted, substantial variance in word reading remains unaccounted for when both alphabetic and phonological awareness skills are controlled for (e.g. Juel, Griffith, & Gough, 1986; Nation

& Snowling, 2004). This has led to the view that these abilities may be necessary, but not uniquely sufficient, for the development of skilled word recognition. Moreover, alphabetic skills do not seem to be as closely related to the ability to read words that explicitly require word-specific orthographic knowledge in order to be read correctly as they are to the ability to read words that can be sounded out without word-specific information: the correlation between nonword reading and *irregular* word reading is consistently weaker than that between nonword reading and *regular* word reading (Baron, 1979; Baron & Treiman, 1980). Therefore, it would seem that the transition to skilled word reading, characterized by full specificity and autonomy, may be modulated, at least in part, by other factors.

Orthographic processing skills

Responding to the findings in relation to alphabetic and phonological skills, a number of authors have suggested that a skill broadly termed "orthographic processing" may be a second key predictor of individual differences in word reading (for review, see Berninger, 1994, 1995). Orthographic processing skills are typically measured with tasks such as orthographic choice (e.g. which is a word? *rain* or *rane*) or sensitivity to orthographic constraints (e.g. which is most like a word? *beff* or *ffeb*). Although these tasks are contaminated by alphabetic decoding skills, such skills alone are not sufficient to perform the tasks successfully: children must bring orthographic knowledge to bear if they are to answer correctly. Consistent with this, orthographic processing skills have been found to predict variance in word recognition, even once phonological and alphabetic skills are controlled (e.g. Barker, Torgesen, & Wagner, 1992; Cunningham & Stanovich, 1990).

In addition, orthographic processing has been reported to be a reasonably reliable and valid construct. Cunningham, Perry, and Stanovich (2001) administered six different tests of orthographic processing to second-grade children. Performance on the different tests showed modest intercorrelations, and all tests loaded on the same factor. Consistent with other findings, orthographic processing skills in second grade accounted for unique variance in word reading in third grade, even after phonological processing and decoding were controlled. This, they argue, suggests that orthographic processing is not entirely parasitic on phonological processing, and that, therefore, the two sets of skills may contribute separately to the development of skilled word recognition.

However, in our view, there are some difficulties with the construct of "orthographic processing" and its status as an independent predictor of skilled word recognition. First, as other researchers have also noted (e.g. Vellutino, Scanlon, & Chen, 1995; Wagner & Barker, 1994), there is a lack of clarity about exactly how orthographic processing skill is to be defined. Some researchers focus on the ability to store information about general patterns or properties of the orthography. For example, Vellutino, Scanlon, and Tanzman (1994) define orthographic coding as "the ability to represent the unique array of letters that defines a printed word, as well as general aspects of the writing system such as sequential dependencies, structural redundancies, letter position frequencies, and so forth" (p. 314). Other definitions seem to equate orthographic processing skill with access to specific word representations themselves. For example, Frith (1985) defines orthographic skill as the ability to perform "instant analysis of words into orthographic units without phonological conversion" (p. 306) and Szeszulski and Manis (1990) propose that it "allows direct access to a mental lexicon for familiar words based on their unique orthography" (p. 182). Indeed, the tasks used to measure orthographic processing seem also to reflect this tension. A task which asks a reader, "Which is most like a word? *ffeb* or *febb*", is measuring sensitivities to general orthographic properties of the language, while a task which asks, "Which is a word? *rain* or *rane*", would appear to be measuring the ability to access unique, word-specific representations. We have represented this distinction in Figure 7.1.

Even if a definition can be converged upon, there would seem to remain difficulties with interpreting the results of many studies of orthographic processing in the context of identifying independent predictors of skilled word recognition. As noted also by Vellutino, Scanlon, and Tanzman (1994), if we define orthographic processing as assessing word-specific orthographic skills and use a task such as the *rain/rane* task, it would seem that, rather than measuring a *predictor* of skilled word recognition, we are measuring skilled word recognition itself (the right-hand side of Figure 7.1). To successfully perform the task requires, at the very least, the characteristics of full specification and autonomy described above. Therefore, the use of such tasks would appear to be circular if the aim is to identify a predictor of skilled word

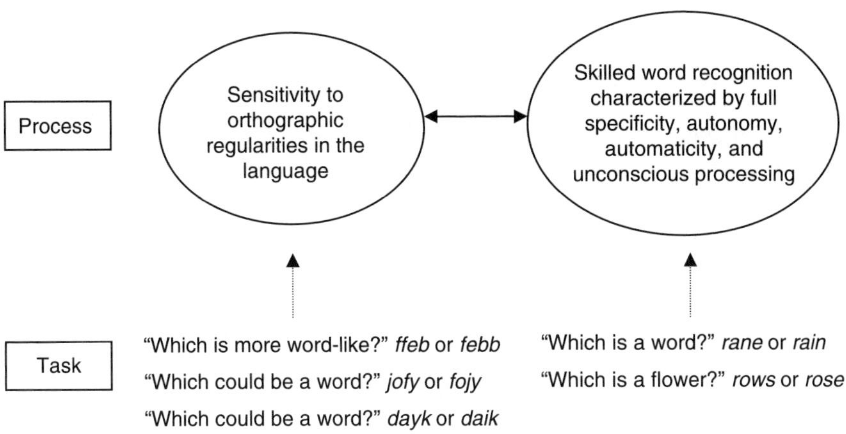

Figure 7.1 Orthographic processing tasks and their relationship to skilled word recognition.

recognition that is not the skill itself (we have no issue with the use of this task as a measure of skilled word-level reading per se).

Suppose we choose to define orthographic processing skills in terms of the awareness of general orthographic regularities, such as in the *ffeb/febb* task? The connection with skilled word recognition is less direct here, and the task thus represents a more promising predictor from that point of view. In terms of Figure 7.1, the task putatively measures a more distal skill that may predict the success of orthographic learning (the left-hand side of the figure) rather than measuring the result of that learning (the right-hand side of the figure). However, it would still seem to us possible that at least some of the knowledge required to perform these tasks emerges as a *product* of successful orthographic learning. Indeed, Cunningham et al.'s (2001) findings of significant correlations between performance on these kinds of tasks and word-specific orthographic choice tasks would seem to support this hypothesis. The difficulty in interpreting what is being measured in these kinds of orthographic processing tasks is compounded by the fact that longitudinal studies examining the predictive power of these measures have not controlled for the autoregressive effects of word-recognition ability itself. For example, in Cunningham et al.'s (2001) study, pre-existing word recognition skills in second grade were not controlled for before examining the relationship between orthographic processing in second grade and word reading in third grade. Therefore, it is difficult to know how much of the association found reflects the initial word-reading skills that the second-grade children brought to the tasks.

What would seem to be required to resolve this issue are studies that assess awareness of orthographic regularities or "orthographic sensitivity" in children very early in reading development, before they are likely to have developed skilled word-recognition processes. Fortunately, some studies of this kind have emerged. Cassar and Treiman (1997) report that, by 6 years of age, children are sensitive to the frequency and legality of different orthographic patterns, and even kindergarten children are able to decide that a written string such as *pess* is more likely to be a word than a string such as *ppes*. Similarly, Pacton, Perruchet, Fayol, and Cleeremans (2001) report a number of experiments demonstrating that, after as little as 4 months formal education, first-grade children learning to read French, like the children in Cassar and Treiman's studies of children learning to read English, are sensitive to which consonants can or cannot be doubled in French, and to the fact that consonants are doubled only in medial position, not in initial or final position.

These results suggest that gradually and after even quite limited exposure to written language, children become sensitive to orthographic constraints, based on the frequency of occurrence of letters in words that they have been exposed to. Just as young infants are sensitive to the features of spoken language and use this knowledge to learn about its phonological and phonotactic properties (e.g. Saffran, Aslin, & Newport, 1996), young children quickly become sensitive to the regularities of letter combinations that they see in orthography. It may be that this ability will prove to be a significant unique predictor of orthographic learning. However, as yet, we do not have a clear picture of the degree to which this skill is related to later reading outcomes. Does measured early sensitivity to orthographic regularities uniquely predict later skilled word-specific reading ability? To answer this question will require further longitudinal research that specifically examines orthographic sensitivity in prereaders and relates it to the children's subsequent success in orthographic learning.

Print exposure

As discussed above, there is a danger of circularity in proposing that children's ability to process the orthography of their language is a predictor of skilled word reading itself. In a series of studies, Cunningham and Stanovich have circumvented this problem in a novel way by measuring not children's orthographic processing skills per se, but their apparent exposure to, and experience of, written materials in their home and school environments (Cunningham & Stanovich, 1990, 1991, 1993, 1997). Broadly termed "print exposure", measures of this construct are typically in the form of checklists, which ask children to mark the titles of books, magazines, or other written materials that they are familiar with. Foils are included, in the form of titles of non-existent texts, to preclude guessing. This task has the advantage that it measures the differential reading experiences of children, without necessarily being confounded with the outcome of those experiences in terms of reading ability.

Print exposure does appear to make a modest, but significant, contribution to skilled word recognition above and beyond the contribution of alphabetic and phonological skills. For example, Cunningham and Stanovich (1993) gave 6–7-year-old children a battery of tasks that included measures of word recognition, measures of phonological and orthographic processing skill, and an index of exposure to print. Consistent with previous findings, phonological and orthographic processing abilities were found to account for independent components of variance in word recognition. Most interestingly for the present purposes, it was the variance in orthographic processing ability *not explained* by phonological abilities that was found to be associated with differences in print exposure. Phonological processing itself was not linked to the print-exposure measure. The authors therefore concluded that there are individual differences in word-recognition ability caused by variation in orthographic processing abilities, which are, at least in part, determined by print exposure differences.

Clearly, orthographic learning cannot occur without exposure to written words, and thus print exposure must, almost by definition, predict skilled word recognition to some degree. Measures of print exposure provide a valuable way of quantifying this required experience with written language.

However, as is extensively discussed by Cunningham and Stanovich themselves (e.g. Cunningham & Stanovich, 1998), it is very difficult to determine what the correlation between measures of print exposure and measures of reading ability tells us about the role of print exposure in orthographic learning. Does lots of exposure to print promote orthographic learning? Or is it that more skilled orthographic readers choose to expose themselves to more reading materials than less-skilled orthographic readers? Referring to the widely cited *Matthew effect* (Stanovich, 1986), Cunningham and Stanovich (1998) note that, very early in the reading acquisition process, poor readers begin to be exposed to much less text than their skilled peers (Allington, 1984). Exacerbating this problem, the text that these children *are* exposed to tends often to be too difficult for them (Allington, 1984). This is likely to result in their having unrewarding reading experiences and therefore choosing to expose themselves to even less print, in a "snowballing" fashion. Thus, there appears to be a complex reciprocal relationship between reading ability and print exposure. Although very important to untangle, this complexity, as with the findings for measures of orthographic processing, makes the status of print exposure as a *predictor* of the success of orthographic learning, as opposed to an *outcome* of the success of that learning, very difficult to ascertain.

Semantic knowledge

A number of studies have demonstrated that semantic variables influence word-recognition processes in skilled adults, and, as Lupker (2005) makes clear, "any successful model of word recognition will need to have a mechanism for explaining the impact of semantics, both the impact of the semantic context within which the word is processed and the impact of the semantic attributes of the word itself" (p. 40). Therefore, it is reasonable to ask whether semantic factors contribute to the development of orthographic learning. A clear demonstration of semantic variables influencing skilled word recognition was provided by Balota, Cortese, Sergent-Marshall, Spieler, and Yap (2004). Using a large-scale regression design, Balota et al. investigated the predictors of word naming and visual lexical decision across items for 2428 monosyllabic words. Most relevant here is the observation that semantic variables predicted naming speed and lexical decision speed and accuracy, even after substantial variance was accounted for by lexical factors such as frequency, neighbourhood size, consistency, and familiarity. This suggests that the input code activates meaning information very rapidly indeed, and, as Balota and colleagues conclude, their results are "consistent with a view in which meaning becomes activated very early on, in a cascadic manner, during lexical processing and contributes to the processes involved in reaching a sufficient level of information to drive a lexical decision or naming response" (p. 312).

If meaning information contributes to the lexical processing in skilled readers, it may be that sensitivity to semantic information is another source of information that can influence or contribute to orthographic learning. If so, one would expect there to be a relationship between children's semantic skills and word-level reading. Nation and Snowling (2004) addressed this issue by examining the relationship between verbal-semantic skills (vocabulary, semantic fluency and synonym judgement, and listening comprehension) and word recognition in 72 eight-year-old children. They found that all measures of verbal-semantic skill predicted word recognition, even after the powerful effects of decoding (nonword reading) and phonological skills were controlled. In addition, the relationship between verbal-semantic skills and word reading was maintained over time, with measures taken at 8 years predicting unique variance in word recognition some 4 years later when the children were 13 years old.

While these data provide evidence for a relationship between semantic factors and orthographic learning, the nature of this relationship—whether it is specific and direct or general and indirect—is not clear and many questions remain. An indirect relationship may emerge due to the fact that in a deep orthography, such as English, children need to deal with words that are inconsistent and irregular. One way they may do this is to utilize top-down knowledge from oral vocabulary, which, in combination with information gleaned from a partial decoding attempt, may help them decipher the appropriate pronunciation of words (Nation & Snowling, 1998a). Gradually, this leads to children with good vocabulary knowledge developing a better word-recognition system. This indirect and developmental account goes some way to accommodating findings that oral vocabulary may not play an important role early in reading development. For example, Muter, Hulme, Snowling, and Stevenson (2004) found that in 4–6-year-old children, phonological skills accounted for substantial amounts of unique variance in word reading, but oral vocabulary did not.

An alternative take on the relationship between semantic factors and word-level reading is to propose that meaning-based information has a direct influence in the word-recognition process itself, as has been shown to be the case in skilled readers (e.g. Balota et al., 2004). The finding that the rate at which written abbreviations of words could be learned by young children at the earliest stages of reading development depended on the word's imageability is consistent with this view (Laing & Hulme, 1999). Other evidence, however, is less consistent. For example, McKague, Pratt, and Johnston (2001) reasoned that if meaning-based information is implicated in word reading, pretraining the meaning of new words in the oral domain should influence the ease with which children subsequently learn the orthographic forms of those words. McKague et al. found that while previous exposure to the phonological forms of new words facilitated subsequent orthographic learning, pretraining in meaning-related information provided no additional boost. Arguably, however, McKague et al.'s attempt to pretrain vocabulary knowledge was rather artificial and therefore unlikely to mimic the effect of activation of a familiar word within a network of semantic connections in children's natural reading experiences (cf. Laing & Hulme, 1999).

Individual differences in success in orthographic learning

Another approach to identifying the underpinnings of orthographic learning has been to capitalize on individual differences in the acquisition of this skill. There are certain classes of poor reader who appear to have had particular difficulty in achieving skilled orthographic learning, while acquiring other reading skills at a normal or near-normal rate. The question from the point of view of understanding orthographic learning has been: How can these children's reading processes and, possibly, their more general cognitive profiles, be differentiated from those of normal readers and other kinds of poor readers? If such distinguishing characteristics can be found, they may provide some clues as to what is required for successful orthographic learning.

Developmental surface dyslexia

There are several case reports in the literature of children with the dyslexia profile usually referred to as *surface dyslexia*, who appear to have developed normal alphabetic decoding skills, but who, for some reason, have had difficulty in acquiring skilled orthographic word-recognition processes. For example, Castles and Coltheart (1996) report the case of M.I., a 10-year-old boy of very high general intelligence, normal educational and medical background, and supportive family environment, who had presented with difficulties in reading. On two separate testing occasions, 3 months apart, M.I. performed well within the average range for his age on nonword reading, but more than two standard deviations below average for his age on irregular word reading. The errors that he made in reading irregular words were consistent with the use of alphabetic decoding rules (for example, he read *break* as "breek" and *shoe* as "show"). He also had difficulty in performing homophone judgement tasks that required access to word-specific information (as in, "Which of these is a vegetable?": *been; bean*). His pattern of reading was thus consistent with a specific failure to acquire skilled word-specific reading skills, a pattern which has also been reported in several other cases (Coltheart, Masterson, Byng, Prior, & Riddoch, 1983; Goulandris & Snowling, 1991; Hanley, Hastie, & Kay, 1992; Samuelsson, 2000).

What kinds of deficits, then, are associated with this particular type of reading impairment? Once again, a definitive answer to this question has proven elusive. In fact, it has been difficult to distinguish consistently and reliably children with surface dyslexia from other readers on *any* measures other than the word-specific reading tasks used to identify them in the first place. Looking at the predictors of orthographic learning described above, children with surface dyslexia are clearly not impaired on alphabetic skills, as they are typically identified on the basis of their normal performance here. Phonological awareness skills are also generally unimpaired (Manis, Seidenberg, Doi, McBride-Chang, & Petersen, 1996). A more likely locus of deficits might be expected to be in the domain of print exposure. However, there is little evidence that this is the case. Although Castles, Datta, Gayan, and Olson (1999) found that a group of surface dyslexics performed more poorly than other kinds of dyslexics on some print-exposure measures in their large twin sample, the effect size was very small. Others, with smaller samples, have found no significant differences between groups on these measures (Manis et al., 1996). There is also no consistent evidence for semantic or vocabulary impairments in surface dyslexia (Castles & Coltheart, 1993, 1996). Finally, although there are some reports of impaired visual memory in these kinds of poor readers (Goulandris & Snowling, 1991), other surface dyslexic cases have not shown impairments here (Castles & Coltheart, 1996), and, as a group, surface dyslexics do not appear to display basic visual-perceptual deficits (Cestnick & Coltheart, 1999; Williams, Stuart, Castles, & McAnally, 2003).

How, then, can we learn more about orthographic acquisition by studying the surface dyslexic reading pattern? We would argue that it may be more fruitful, not to study the cognitive correlates of surface dyslexia per se, but instead to track more carefully the process by which surface dyslexics try to learn new words and to pinpoint precisely the locus of their difficulties. In this vein, Castles and Holmes (1996) investigated the performance of two different types of developmental dyslexics on an orthographic acquisition task, in which the children were required to learn the pronunciations of a set of "irregular" nonsense words over a series of training sessions (e.g. *macht* pronounced "mot"). The results indicated that surface dyslexics showed selective deficits on this task, compared to other poor readers, in their ability both to recognize and to read aloud the novel items. Bailey, Manis, Pederson, and Seidenberg (2004) have since reported a similar result. Thus, having identified a learning task that reliably distinguishes between the acquisition processes of poor orthographic readers and those of other kinds of poor readers, we may be in a better position to specify more precisely the mechanism of that acquisition process, and the ways in which it can fail.

Poor comprehenders

Poor comprehenders are not dyslexic; nevertheless, one study has argued that their orthographic learning may be compromised, relative to typically developing children. "Poor comprehender" is the term used to describe children who have difficulty understanding what they read, despite their reading accuracy and fluency being essentially age-appropriate. It is perhaps not surprising to find that poor comprehenders tend to have a variety of oral language weaknesses, including difficulty in listening comprehension, and in inferences and understanding figurative language, as well as (in some studies) weaknesses in vocabulary knowledge and semantic processing. Unlike children with dyslexia, however, poor comprehenders do not show phonological processing deficits (see Nation, 2005, for review). Drawing on the view that strengths and weaknesses in the oral language domain may influence the development of visual word recognition (Plaut, McClelland, Seidenberg, & Patterson, 1996), Nation and Snowling (1998b) reasoned that word recognition may be compromised in poor comprehenders due to lack of support from oral language. Poor comprehenders were matched to a group of control children for alphabetic decoding (nonword reading) and nonverbal ability. Although both groups showed word-level reading skills (as measured by a standardized test) in the normal range, the poor comprehenders achieved lower scores, despite the groups not differing in nonword reading accuracy or speed. To investigate this further, Nation and Snowing asked the children to read a set of words varying in frequency and regularity. Irregular words, especially if low in frequency, place considerable demands on the word-recognition system as they cannot be read correctly on the basis of alphabetic decoding alone and according to some theorists, top-down support plays an important role in reading these items (e.g. Plaut et al., 1996). In line with this view, poor comprehenders did not differ from controls when reading high-frequency regular words, but were slower and less accurate when reading low-frequency and irregular words.

These findings add to the body of evidence pointing to a relationship between verbal-semantic skills and word-level reading, and suggest that meaning-based factors may influence orthographic learning, although as noted earlier, the nature of this relationship and the mechanisms that underpin it are far from clear. Nevertheless, future experiments with poor comprehenders may inform our understanding of this issue. Unlike many children with dyslexia, difficulties with basic alphabetic decoding do not contaminate the word-recognition process in this group, thus allowing a relatively clear examination of other aspects of word recognition. It would also be interesting to investigate poor comprehenders' orthographic learning more directly, a clear prediction being that relative weaknesses should be revealed on a task such as Castles and Holmes' (1996) test of orthographic acquisition.

Mechanisms for orthographic learning

So far, our review has established that there is more to word reading than alphabetic decoding, and has provided a characterization of the nature of this skilled orthographic reading process. However, our analysis of the research into the predictors of orthographic reading skills has revealed that there is much still to be learned: predictors that have the strongest unique relationship to orthographic reading tend to be either (a) measures that are difficult to distinguish from tests of word recognition itself or (b) measures that may reflect the outcomes of successful orthographic learning rather than its antecedents. Similarly, examinations of the cognitive correlates of orthographic reading impairments in developmental dyslexia, and studies examining the influence of semantic factors in reading development, have produced only limited insights to date. In addition, none of the research reported so far addresses the question of *how* children acquire orthographic knowledge during the course of reading development. Very few studies have investigated this central issue, to which we will now turn.

The self-teaching hypothesis

One account that does provide some specification as to how orthographic learning develops is the self-teaching hypothesis, first described by Share (1995). The hypothesis comprises two basic principles. First, letter-sound knowledge and rudimentary decoding skills provide young children with a means of translating a printed word into its spoken form. In turn, this successful (but potentially fairly laborious) decoding experience provides an opportunity to acquire word-specific orthographic information of the nature needed to support fast and efficient word recognition. Central to this hypothesis is the view that phonological decoding provides the essential and fundamental basis for reading development—or, as Share describes it, phonological decoding is the sine qua non of reading acquisition. Share also proposes that the ability to use contextual information to determine exact word pronunciations on the basis of a partial decoding attempt plays an important role in self-teaching.

Direct evidence in support of the self-teaching hypothesis was provided by Share (1999). An overview of his methodology is presented in Table 7.1. Second-grade children (aged 8 years), learning to read Hebrew, read aloud short stories each containing a novel word, repeated either four or six times. They read independently, with no guidance or feedback from the experimenter. Three days later, Share tested whether orthographic learning had taken place. First, he asked whether children were able to recognize the correct spelling of the target words in an orthographic choice task. Each target word was presented alongside a homophone foil (as an English example, the target word *yait* would be presented alongside the homophone *yate*) and two nonhomophonic foils that shared letters with the target item. Children chose the target on 70% of occasions, five times more often than they chose the homophonic foil. Consistent with this, children named target items faster than homophone foils, and they were more likely to use the target spelling pattern, rather than the homophonic spelling pattern, when asked to spell the target words. Thus, across three different measures (orthographic choice, naming, and spelling), there was clear evidence of orthographic learning. There was no difference in learning after either four or six exposures, leading Share to conclude that 8-year-old children show substantial orthographic learning after as few as four exposures to a novel word.

Central to the self-learning account is that orthographic learning is parasitic upon initial phonological decoding. To test this aspect of the hypothesis, Share (1999; experiments 2–4) looked for evidence for orthographic learning

Table 7.1 Measuring orthographic learning via self-teaching (after Share, 1999)

Phase I: Exposure and phonological decoding	*Phase II: Test of orthographic learning*	*Evidence for orthographic learning*
Child reads aloud story about "the coldest place in the world", as follows: North Greenland is a place they say is the coldest in the world. The name of the city is Yait. In Yait, there is snow and ice all year round. The temperature is always around 0°, and it is dark most of the day. There is always a cold wind blowing in from the North. But there are also some good things to do in Yait. You don't have to hurry to put your food in the refrigerator to keep it cold. And there's always lots of ice for your drinks. In summer there is sunlight all day and all night, so you can go skiing and skating any time you want, even at night. In Yait you don't have to put on sunscreen when you go outside, because the sun is never too hot. And there are no flies in Yait to worry about. There is also a lake that is always frozen, so you can't ever fall in. But most of all, people are very nice and friendly.	1. *Homophone choice* Child asked, "Remember the coldest place in the world—was it *Yait, Yate, Yoit*, or *Yiat*?" 2. *Naming RT* Time taken to read aloud Yait versus Yate 3. *Spelling* Child told, "Write down 'yait', the coldest place in the world".	1. *Homophone choice* (*Yait*) chosen more often than homophone foil (*Yate*) 2. *Naming RT* *Yait* read faster than *Yate* 3. *Spelling* Spelling Y-A-I-T produced more often than Y-A-T-E

RT: response time.

under conditions when opportunities for initial phonological decoding were minimized (for example, by reducing initial exposure time to 300 ms, and by asking children to engage in concurrent vocalization during exposure). Under these conditions, no orthographic learning was observed, suggesting that initial phonological decoding is indeed essential, as stated by the self-teaching hypothesis.

Since Share provided initial direct evidence for the self-teaching hypothesis, two sets of studies (Cunningham, Perry, Stanovich, & Share, 2002; Share, 2004) have extended our knowledge of the role of self-teaching in orthographic learning. Share (2004; experiment 1) addressed two issues: how many exposures to a word do children need in order to support orthographic learning and how long does learning last? Using the same paradigm described above, grade 3 children (reading Hebrew) read stories containing one, two, or four repetitions of a target novel word. Orthographic learning was then assessed after intervals of 3, 7, and 30 days. Replicating Share (1999), clear evidence of orthographic learning was found across three tasks (orthographic choice, naming, and spelling). Remarkably, orthographic learning remained constant, regardless of whether the children had previously seen and decoded each word once, twice, or four times. It seems that a single decoding opportunity is enough to foster robust and long-lasting orthographic learning. This observation suggests that orthographic learning may be similar to fast mapping—the term used to describe rapid oral vocabulary acquisition after only a few incidental exposures to a new word (e.g. Markson & Bloom, 1997).

Hebrew is a highly regular orthography in which children learn to decode very quickly. In Share's studies described above, second- and third-grade children decoded target items very accurately (typically, decoding levels in excess of 90% are reported), and this high level of phonological decoding was considered to provide a strong basis for self-teaching and orthographic learning. Potentially, self-teaching may operate differently in children learning to read a less transparent orthography such as English, where levels of phonological decoding are considerably lower. Cunningham et al. (2002) examined this issue in second-grade children learning to read English, using Share's paradigm. Each target novel word appeared six times in a story. Consistent with the difficulty of phonological decoding in English, decoding accuracy was lower than in Share's Hebrew experiments (74% versus upward of 90%). Nevertheless, orthographic learning occurred. Three days after exposure, children were quicker and more accurate at naming, producing, and identifying target words, relative to homophonic control words. Cunningham et al. also found a relationship between initial target decoding accuracy and orthographic learning. Consistent with the self-teaching hypothesis, phonological decoding correlated with orthographic learning. However, it is important to note that although the correlation was reliable, it was relatively modest (.52), suggesting that there is considerable variance associated with orthographic learning that is not captured by initial phonological decoding.

Share's (1995) original instantiation of the self-teaching hypothesis stated that self-teaching was present and active from the very early stages of reading development. Yet, the majority of studies cited in support of the hypothesis are of children in the second or third grade. By this age, children have already established fairly substantial word-reading abilities. Indeed, Cunningham et al. (2002) found that existing orthographic knowledge was a reliable predictor of orthographic learning, even after phonological decoding was partialed out. Only one study has examined self-teaching in children younger than second grade. Share (2004; experiments 2 and 3) asked first-grade children (aged 7 years) learning Hebrew to read short stories containing target novel words. Although the children were able to read these words very accurately (> 90%), there was no evidence to suggest that orthographic learning had taken place. The children were just as likely to choose a homophonic foil as they were the target, and when asked to spell the target word, they were as likely to use a homophonic spelling pattern as the one contained in the target.

These findings are intriguing as they run counter to the predictions of the self-teaching hypothesis: Given the almost perfect decoding opportunity provided by the highly transparent Hebrew orthography, significant orthographic learning should have been observed. To accommodate these surprising data, Share (2004) suggested that orthographic learning via self-teaching is delayed in children learning to read Hebrew, relative to languages with a deeper orthography such as English or Dutch. On this view, a transparent orthography encourages a pattern of reading behaviour reminiscent of surface dyslexia, in which children rely on mappings between orthography and phonology when reading. Only after sufficient exposure to a significant number of words do children begin to develop orthographic sensitivity. In contrast to this, Share proposed that children learning to read a deep orthography such as English are sensitive to orthographic information from the outset, and, consequently, they show orthographic learning via self-teaching from a younger age than children learning to read Hebrew. He referred to this as the *orthographic depth* hypothesis.

Is there any evidence to support this view? We would argue not. Although Share (2004) described studies demonstrating orthographic learning in children at the early stages of learning to read English and Dutch (e.g. Manis, 1985; Reitsma, 1983), it is important to note that, in these studies, children were taught orthographic patterns over a number of testing sessions. While these data are consistent with the self-teaching hypothesis, they do not provide direct support for self-teaching: As noted by Share (1999), spelling patterns were taught explicitly, rather than discovered via a process of self-teaching stemming from successful decoding. Only one study has made a direct examination of self-teaching in children learning to read English, and in that study (Cunningham et al., 2002), only second-grade children were tested. Much like second-grade children learning to read Hebrew, these children showed orthographic learning. Until orthographic learning via self-teaching is demonstrated in children beginning to read a deep orthography, Share's (2004) orthographic depth hypothesis remains speculative.

To summarize, self-teaching is the most well-developed account of orthographic learning. As an item-based theory, it differs radically from traditional stage models, which see a child moving from one mode of processing to another. Share's experiments demonstrate orthographic learning in children as young as second grade, and, remarkably, by third grade, a single exposure to an orthographic form is enough to induce orthographic learning of that item. Clearly, however, by third grade, children have amassed a considerable amount of orthographic knowledge. The extent to which self-teaching operates from the beginning of reading remains largely unexplored. Another unexplored issue is the extent to which sensitivity to contextual information plays a role in self-teaching. According to Share, top-down knowledge helps children determine the exact pronunciation of a word on the basis of a partial decoding attempt. However, the role of top knowledge is impossible to ascertain, as, in Share's experiments, novel words were *always* presented in a meaningful context. It may be that the context is not obligatory and that similar (or even higher) levels of orthographic learning would ensue if novel words were presented without a context (cf. Stuart, Masterson, & Dixon, 2000). Alternatively, the process of instantiating a meaning or sense to novel words may be crucial to self-teaching. Another possibility is that context and meaning are not crucial, but top-down support facilitates or boosts self-teaching. If future experiments reveal that context does have a role in orthographic learning via self-teaching, this may help us understand the relationship between the development of word recognition and semantic factors discussed earlier.

Implicit learning of orthographic regularities

Pacton et al. (2001) take a somewhat different approach to the mechanism of orthographic learning by proposing that an associative learning mechanism may be able to account for the development of orthographic knowledge. They use a novel approach to support their claim, adopting methodology from the implicit learning and artificial grammar learning literature (e.g. Dienes & Altmann, 1997; Redington & Chater, 1998). As noted earlier, Pacton et al. first provided various demonstrations of the presence of orthographic knowledge in young, French-speaking children. For example, they constructed an orthographic constraints test comprising items containing a double vowel (e.g. *tuuke*) or a double consonant (e.g. *tukke*). Although *k* is never doubled in French, other consonants are, but there are no instances of doubled vowels. Even first-grade children considered items like *tukke* to be more word-like than items like *tuuke*, despite the fact that they had never seen words containing either *uu* or *kk*.

Pacton et al. then went on to address the question of how that knowledge was acquired. One possibility is that children may extract an abstract rule, such that they learn "words do not end with a consonant double". If so, they should use that rule to transfer their knowledge to novel situations. To some extent, this behaviour was observed: From first grade, children were less likely to accept an item as word-like if it ended with two consonants. Thus, a nonword such as *bukkox* was preferred over a nonword such as *bukoxx*, despite the fact that neither *kk* nor *xx* appear in the French language. However, there was a clear *transfer decrement*, in that performance in the novel situation was never as good as when items contained consonants that are doubled in the language: Performance was consistently higher for items such as *golirr* versus *gollir* (where both *l* and *r* are frequently doubled in French, but only in medial position), even in children in fifth grade. Pacton et al. (2001) argued that this observation is not consistent with the children having extracted an abstract rule: If they had, then application of that abstract rule (that consonants are never doubled in final position) should have been equal in both novel (i.e. never doubled consonants) and old (i.e. consonants that are doubled) situations.

Based on these results, Pacton et al. (2001) argued that children are very sensitive to distributional information embodied as regularities and patterns in the orthography to which they are exposed. They speculated that this sensitivity to statistical regularities in the written language domain is subtended by general learning mechanisms, akin to those used for other forms of statistical learning (e.g. Bates & Elman, 1996). In line with this view, they were able to model their behavioural data with a simple recurrent network (SRN). A SRN is not hard-wired with abstract rules such as "never double a consonant in final position". Instead, sensitivity to sequential dependencies in the input develops gradually after exposure to the input. Pacton et al. (2001) presented a network with one letter at a time. Its task was to predict the next input state, that is, the next letter. A learning algorithm then calculated the difference between the actual output state computed by the network and the correct output state. This was then used to adjust the weights on connections such that the network became more accurate at predicting the subsequent state. After training, the network quickly developed sensitivity to orthographic constraints such as which consonants are likely to be doubled and in which position.

Clearly, Pacton et al.'s (2001) SRN simulation is a long way from providing a full account of orthographic learning. Children do not receive thousands and thousands of exposures during initial training, nor does orthographic learning operate in isolation, without interaction from phonological, semantic, or morphosyntactic influences. Nevertheless, it successfully mirrored the patterns of sensitivity to orthographic and sequential dependencies seen in behavioural studies of children learning to read French. This indicates that orthographic knowledge of some form can emerge simply from the processing of input, without the need for any in-built representational constraint. It also demonstrates the utility of modelling orthographic development—a topic to which we now turn.

Computational models and orthographic learning

Many computational models of reading are models of skilled performance that say nothing about how the ability to read is acquired (e.g. the DRC model of Coltheart and colleagues; Coltheart, Rastle, Perry, Langdon, & Ziegler, 2001; see Jackson & Coltheart, 2000, for possible developmental implications). Furthermore, those models that have sought to explicitly model learning processes have usually focused on the development of mappings between orthography and phonology, that is, reading aloud, rather than recognizing and comprehending the meaning of words (e.g. Plaut et al., 1996; Seidenberg & McClelland, 1989; Zorzi, Houghton, & Butterworth, 1998). As computational models of reading aloud have been reviewed and critiqued at length elsewhere (e.g. Coltheart, 2005; Lupker, 2005; Plaut, 2005), we focus here on two computational approaches that have modelled aspects of orthographic development in very different ways.

PDP "triangle" models

The triangle framework was introduced by Seidenberg and McClelland (1989), based on the assumption that word recognition involves three types of mental representation: orthographic, phonological, and semantic. The 1989 simulations focused on the processes of orthography-phonology mapping and reading aloud; the semantic component of the triangle model was not implemented. Building on Seidenberg and McClelland, and further work by Plaut et al. (1996), Harm and Seidenberg (2004) described a full implementation of a triangle model.

At the heart of the triangle approach is the view that information is represented in sets of distributed, subsymbolic codes representing the attributes (semantic, phonological, and orthographic) of words that we know. The word-recognition process is considered to be the process of activating the appropriate sets of codes from visual input. During learning, connections between sets of units need to be learned. The first set of connections learned are those between phonology and semantics. Once the model is able to recognize and produce words, orthography is introduced. This approximates the fact that when children come to the task of learning to read, they have in place well-developed knowledge of the sound and meaning of many words. When presented with a word, units at all levels are activated. The resulting pattern of activation is then compared with the correct pattern of activation. Connection weights between units are then adjusted to reduce error, so that the next time the word is encountered, processing is more accurate. Gradually, patterns of activation across one set of units (e.g. phonology) produce corresponding patterns of activation across other sets of units in another domain (e.g. orthography). Harm and Seidenberg (2004) describe two pathways to activating meaning from print: a direct pathway from orthography to semantics (O→S) and a phonologically mediated pathway from orthography to phonology to semantics (O→P→S). It is important to note that meanings are not accessed in any sense. Instead, patterns of activation develop over the semantic units continuously, based on input from all sources and from both pathways. Thus, meanings are computed from print by both pathways working simultaneously and in parallel.

A feature that emerged from Harm and Seidenberg's simulations was that over development, the relative importance of the two pathways to the computation of word meaning changed. Early in development, the network relied heavily on phonological mediation (i.e. the O→P→S pathway). With reading experience, however, the network gradually shifted toward increased reliance on direct mapping (i.e. the O→S pathway), although, even at the end of training, both pathways continued to make a contribution to performance. The reason for this developmental change is that O→P connections are easier to form than O→S connections because the relationship between O and P (in an alphabetic language) is more systematic than O→S mappings. However, there is pressure for the system to form direct O→S connections, as (a) mappings of O→P are inherently ambiguous due to the many homophones in the language and (b) direct mappings are faster, as they do not require the intermediate computation from orthography to phonology en route to semantic activation.

This change in the division of labour between the two pathways over training fits well with what we know about children's reading development. Early on, children devote considerable attention to the task of decoding words but with experience, word recognition becomes faster and more automatic. Harm and Seidenberg's simulations suggest that the shift from decoding to automatic word recognition is not a consequence of a qualitative change from one distinct stage to another. Instead, experience with orthography and increased familiarity with the attributes of words leads to more efficient word recognition. While a model with just O→P connections can be trained to activate semantics, the additional presence of O→S connections does the job better. This fits with behavioural data showing that while alphabetic decoding accounts for large portions of variance in word recognition, considerable variance is unaccounted for, especially as children get older (e.g. Nation & Snowling, 2004).

Clearly, Harm and Seidenberg's model learns, but if it is to inform our understanding of orthographic learning, we need to reflect on its developmental plausibility. Two issues seem to us to be particularly problematic at the present time, although, as Harm and Seidenberg point out, both are issues that can be addressed in future modelling attempts. The first concerns the nature of training and the training set of words the network is exposed to. Learning is achieved by a variant of a back-propagation algorithm. This means that learning is *supervised*, in the sense that the output of the network is monitored by an external "teacher", and differences between the actual output and the correct output trigger changes in the network's connections. Although children learn through explicit instruction, they rarely receive feedback on each decoding attempt. Instead, training is much more variable, sometimes comprising direct modelling of appropriate response, sometimes explicit training in phonological awareness or letter-sound knowledge, and often no feedback at all. Harm and Seidenberg (2004) suggest that this rich and varied learning environment may be more advantageous than providing correct feedback on each trial, as it "may discourage the development of overly word-specific representations in favour of representations that capture structure that is shared across words, improving generalisation" (p. 673). This is an interesting issue for future research but, at present, we note that the nature of feedback provided to a network differs substantially from the experiences of children learning to read. A related issue concerning the learning algorithm used by Harm and Seidenberg is that very slow learning rates were employed so as to prevent the network's weights from oscillating wildly. The consequence of this is that many trials were required to learn each word: In Harm and Seidenberg (2004), the training set was presented thousands of times. This contrasts sharply with observations from children's learning: As described earlier, very few exposures may be sufficient for a child to learn a new word (e.g. Share, 1999).

A second problematic issue concerns the nature of orthographic representation employed by Harm and Seidenberg (2004). The model was not pretrained on orthography, unlike semantics and phonology, which were both trained heavily before the onset of reading. Given the importance of letter knowledge during the early stages of word learning (e.g. Muter, Hulme, Snowling, & Taylor, 1998), an elementary introduction to letters early in training is important if psychologically valid orthographic representations are to develop. In addition, the orthographic representations used by Harm and Seidenberg do not fully capture the sequential properties of written language; therefore, they do not embody expert knowledge of orthographic structure and its constraints—knowledge that is already evident in kindergarten-aged children (Pacton et al., 2001). More generally, it is surprising that we know so little about the nature of orthographic coding, given that this provides the entry point into the word-recognition system. One model that has attempted to provide a detailed account of orthographic coding and its development is discussed next.

The SOLAR model

The self-organizing lexical acquisition and recognition (SOLAR) model introduced by Davis (1999) in his doctoral thesis is, as far as we are aware, the only computational model of visual word recognition to date that has attempted to explain the *way* in which an orthographic lexicon develops. This model differs from parallel distributed processing (PDP) models in several ways, including in its assumptions about the input to learning, the nature of the learning process, and the outcome of that learning.

In relation to the nature of the input, the SOLAR model employs a novel means of coding letter order called *spatial coding*. In this scheme, all letter codes are position independent, and the order of the letters in a string is coded by a monotonically decreasing sequence of activities. Thus, the words *salt, slat*, and *last* are coded by different patterns of activity over the same set of letter nodes. An important advantage of spatial coding is that its position invariance enables familiar patterns to be recognized in novel contexts, enabling the SOLAR model to perform on-line segmentation of novel complex stimuli (e.g. reading CATHOLE as CAT + HOLE; Andrews & Davis, 1999). Spatial coding is also superior to other input coding schemes in its capacity to explain orthographic similarity effects (see *Davis*, this volume).

Turning to the nature of the learning process, in contrast to the type of learning that has been employed in PDP models, learning in the SOLAR model is rapid, stable, and unsupervised. The SOLAR model posits a competitive learning process that enables a neural network to learn new lexical representations when it encounters novel inputs (cf. Carpenter & Grossberg, 1987). Familiar inputs, on the other hand, drive a separate adaptive process that allows the network to update its internal representations without destabilizing learning. When presented with a letter string, the model attempts to match it against a previously learnt representation. If successful, the relative "strength" of this representation (its excitability) is slightly increased. This aspect of learning gives rise to word-frequency effects and long-term priming effects. If the input letter string does not match any of the words represented in the model's lexicon, a different form of learning is triggered, in which previously uncommitted nodes compete to learn the new input. A few learning trials are usually sufficient for a new word to be "unitized" at the word level. This leads to a change in the uncommitted node: Its links to the network's abstract letter units become fixed, ensuring the stability of the learned representation. Finally, connections between corresponding orthographic and phonological units are strengthened by Hebbian learning.

The SOLAR model has been able to explain some features of orthographic learning that have proven difficult for PDP accounts. The first concerns lexical substitution errors. Prior to the development of alphabetic reading, beginning readers confronted with a visually unfamiliar word are likely to respond in one of two ways. Either they will refuse to name the word at all, or, if they do respond, they are likely to produce a word that is orthographically similar to the word they are trying to read (e.g. Ehri, 1995; Seymour & Elder, 1986). For example, the word *horse* might elicit the response "house". An additional constraint is that these lexical substitutions tend to be of words that are in the reading vocabulary: beginning readers are typically reluctant to guess the identity of words that they have not *read* before, even if these words would be familiar in speech.

The SOLAR model, which implements an orthographic matching mechanism, correctly predicts the observed phenomenon: Novel words are either misidentified as orthographically similar words or else fail to activate any word nodes above threshold. In the latter case, learning will take place, enabling the novel orthographic form to be unitized after a small number of presentations. PDP models have difficulty in explaining why lexical substitutions should be words from the reading vocabulary, and not words that have been encountered in speech, but not in print.

A second characteristic of early reading is that beginning readers find it more difficult to learn lists of orthographically similar words than lists of orthographically dissimilar words (e.g. Byrne, 1992; Gough & Hillinger, 1980). This result has been obtained in simulations of the SOLAR model (Davis, 1999); for example, in a simulation in which a set of 60 words were learned, it took the model longer to learn items (e.g. *hi*) that were orthographically similar to words that had recently been unitized (e.g. *his*). PDP models appear to make an opposite prediction: Seidenberg and McClelland (1989) noted that, in a model with distributed representations, there is a facilitatory effect of similarity on learning, because similar words are coded by partially overlapping sets of connections.

Like the PDP models, the SOLAR model still has a long way to go before it can capture the full complexity of orthographic learning. At present, the SOLAR model is entirely "lexical"; there is no sublexical alphabetic mechanism for the conversion of letters into sounds. Yet, we know it is highly likely that such skills have an important role to play in the process of orthographic learning. It also contains no semantic representations, so if further work confirms that semantic involvement is important for orthographic learning, this aspect of the model will also require some modification. The important point from our perspective, however, is that we now have two very different computational models, which make different assumptions about the process of orthographic learning. Pitting these models against each other, and against data from behavioural studies of children's reading acquisition, has the potential to provide us with some very important insights.

Conclusions

What, then, is the best way forward for furthering our understanding of the process of orthographic learning? In our view, correlational approaches to the problem, which involve looking for factors that account for significant, unique variance in measures of word recognition, may be of limited further value. Although, as we have seen, a number of predictors of skilled word recognition have been identified in this manner, it has proven difficult to determine precisely what role these factors play, and whether they represent aspects of the mechanism for orthographic learning, or outcomes of the success of such learning. Similarly, simply comparing the cognitive profiles of different kinds of poor readers may be of limited utility. Instead, we feel that a focus is required at this point on carefully designed experimental studies that attempt to dissect the orthographic learning process itself. These may take the form of training studies with developing readers and different kinds of reading-impaired populations (following Bailey et al., 2004, Castles & Holmes, 1996), but may also involve looking at new learning processes in skilled readers—so-called lexical experts (Andrews & Scarratt, 1996). The key point is that we need to uncover the role played by different factors, *as individuals progress from alphabetic decoding to skilled recognition of new words*, perhaps at an item-based level, rather than examining their influence after such a transition has occurred.

Share's self-teaching experiments have provided a very important first step in this process. And they certainly demonstrate the centrality of alphabetic decoding in orthographic learning. However, we feel it would be a mistake to underestimate the role of other factors in orthographic learning by focusing too heavily on decoding skills. Share's experiments themselves show that there is considerable variance in orthographic learning *not* explained by decoding ability. In particular, we feel that there is much work to be done in specifying the precise role that vocabulary and semantic factors play in the transition from alphabetic reading to skilled word recognition. Although Share's experiments provide a semantic context for the learning process, they do not manipulate this factor per se, so its importance for orthographic learning cannot be determined from these experiments. Surprisingly, little other work that we are aware of has closely explored this apparently central issue.

A further focus for experimental studies would be to attempt to isolate the early and automatic components of skilled word recognition—the hallmarks of successful orthographic learning—and to explore these components independently of other, slower and more strategic influences on reading. This would involve capitalizing on techniques such as masked priming or perceptual identification, to explore the factors that appear to modulate rapid automatic word recognition and the way in which these factors may change as reading expertise develops. Studies of this kind have begun to be reported with developing reader populations, providing a valuable window into the brief and elusive initial moments of word recognition (Booth, Perfetti, & MacWhinney, 1999; Castles, Davis, & Letcher, 1999; Davis, Castles, & Iakovidis, 1998).

Finally, data from these carefully targeted experimental studies will need to be fed into the computational models of orthographic learning that have been described, and to be used to assist in elaborating and discriminating between them. At present, we have two, very different, computational implementations of the way in which orthographic representations may be formed. Both are, of course, incomplete at present, but we feel that the clarity of the key issues that is provided by the contrast in their approaches has the potential to take us a long way further in solving the complex problem of orthographic learning.

Acknowledgements

We are grateful to Judy Bowey and Colin Davis for extremely helpful comments on an earlier version of this chapter.

References

Adams, M. J. (1990). *Beginning to read: Thinking and learning about print*. Cambridge, MA: MIT Press.

Allington, R. L. (1984). Content coverage and contextual reading in reading groups. *Journal of Reading Behaviour*, *16*, 85–96.

Andrews, S., & Davis, C. J. (1999). Interactive activation accounts of morphological decomposition: Finding the trap in mousetrap? *Brain and Language*, *68*, 355–361.

Andrews, S., & Scarratt, D. R. (1996). What comes after phonological awareness? Using lexical experts to investigate orthographic processes in reading. *Australian Journal of Psychology*, *48*, 141–148.

Bailey, C. E., Manis, F. R., Pedersen, W. C., & Seidenberg, M. S. (2004). Variation among developmental dyslexics: Evidence from a printed-word-learning task. *Journal of Experimental Child Psychology*, *87*, 125–154.

Balota, D. A., Cortese, M. J., Sergent-Marshall, S., Spieler, D. H., & Yap, M. J. (2004). Visual word recognition of single-syllable words. *Journal of Experimental Psychology: General*, *133*, 283–316.

Barker, T. A., Torgesen, J. K., & Wagner, R. K. (1992). The role of orthographic processing skills on five different reading tasks. *Reading Research Quarterlyr*, *27*, 334–345.

Baron, J. (1979). Orthographic and word-specific mechanisms in children's reading of words. *Child Development*, *50*, 60–72.

Baron, J., & Treiman, R. (1980). Use of orthography in reading and learning to read. In J. F. Kavanagh & R. L. Venezky (Eds.), *Orthography, reading and dyslexia* (pp. 171–189). Baltimore, MD: University Park Press.

Bates, E., & Elman, J. (1996). Learning rediscovered: A perspective on Saffran, Aslin, and Newport. *Science*, *274*, 1849–1850.

Berninger, V. W. (Ed.). (1994). *The varieties of orthographic knowledge. I: Theoretical and developmental issues*. Dordrecht, The Netherlands: Kluwer.

Berninger, V. W. (Ed.). (1995). *The varieties of orthographic knowledge. II: Relationships to phonology, reading and writing*. Dordrecht, The Netherlands: Kluwer.

Booth, J. R., Perfetti, C. A., & MacWhinney, B. (1999). Quick, automatic, and general activation of orthographic and phonological representations in young readers. *Developmental Psychology*, *35*, 3–19.

Brady, S., & Shankweiler, D. P. (Eds.). (1991). *Phonological processes in literacy*. Hillsdale, NJ: Lawrence Erlbaum Associates, Inc.

Byrne, B. (1992). Studies in the acquisition procedure for reading: Rationale, hypotheses, and data. In P. Gough, L. C. Ehri, & R. Treiman (Eds.), *Reading acquisition* (pp. 1–34). Hillsdale, NJ: Lawrence Erlbaum Associates, Inc.

Byrne, B. (1998). *The foundation of literacy: The child's acquisition of the alphabetic principle*. Hove, UK: Psychology Press.

Carpenter, G. A., & Grossberg, S. (1987). A massively parallel architecture for a self-organizing neural pattern recognition machine. *Computer Vision, Graphics, and Image Processing*, *37*, 54–115.

Cassar, M., & Treiman, R. (1997). The beginnings of orthographic knowledge: Children's knowledge of double letters in words. *Journal of Educational Psychology*, *89*, 631–644.

Castles, A., & Coltheart, M. (1993). Varieties of developmental dyslexia. *Cognition*, *47*, 149–180.

Castles, A. & Coltheart, M. (1996). Cognitive correlates of developmental surface dyslexia: A single case study. *Cognitive Neuropsychology*, *13*, 25–50.

Castles, A., & Coltheart, M. (2004). Is there a causal link from phonological awareness to success in learning to read? *Cognition*, *91*, 77–111.

Castles, A., Datta, H., Gayan, J., & Olson, R. K. (1999). Varieties of developmental reading disorder: Genetic and environmental influences. *Journal of Experimental Child Psychology*, *72*, 73–94.

Castles, A., Davis, C., & Letcher, T. (1999). Neighbourhood effects on masked form-priming in developing readers. *Language and Cognitive Processes*, *14*, 201–224.

Castles, A. & Holmes, V. M. (1996). Subtypes of developmental dyslexia and lexical acquisition. *Australian Journal of Psychology*, *48*, 130–135.

Cestnick, L., & Coltheart, M. (1999). The relationship between language-processing and visual-processing deficits in developmental dyslexia. *Cognition*, *71*, 231–255.

Coltheart, M. (2005). Modelling reading: The dual route approach. In M. Snowling & C. Hulme (Eds.), *The science of reading: A handbook* (pp. 6–23). Oxford: Blackwell.

Coltheart, M., Masterson, J., Byng, S., Prior, M., & Riddoch, J. (1983). Surface dyslexia. *Quarterly Journal of Experimental Psychology*, *37A*, 469–495.

Coltheart, M., Rastle, K., Perry, C., Langdon, R., & Ziegler, J. (2001). DRC: A dual route cascaded model of visual word recognition and reading aloud. *Psychological Review*, *108*, 204–256.

Cunningham, A. E., Perry, K. E., & Stanovich, K. E. (2001). Converging evidence for the concept of orthographic processing. *Reading and Writing: An Interdisciplinary Journal*, *14*, 549–568.

Cunningham, A. E., Perry, K., Stanovich, K. E., & Share, D. L. (2002). Orthographic learning during reading: Examining the role of self-teaching. *Journal of Experimental Child Psychology*, *82*, 185–199.

Cunningham, A. E., & Stanovich, K. E. (1990). Assessing print exposure and orthographic processing skill in children: A quick measure of reading experience. *Journal of Educational Psychology*, *82*, 733–740.

Cunningham, A. E., & Stanovich, K. E. (1991). Tracking the unique effects of print exposure in children: Associations with vocabulary, general knowledge, and spelling. *Journal of Educational Psychology*, *83*, 264–274.

Cunningham, A. E., & Stanovich, K. E. (1993). Children's literacy environments and early word recognition skills. *Reading and Writing: An Interdisciplinary Journal*, *5*, 193–204.

Cunningham, A. E., & Stanovich, K. E. (1997). Early reading acquisition and its relation to reading experience and ability ten years later. *Developmental Psychology*, *33*, 934–945.

Cunningham, A. E., & Stanovich, K. E. (1998). The impact of print exposure on word recognition. In J. Metsala & L. Ehri (Eds.), *Word recognition in beginning literacy* (pp. 235–262). Mahwah, NJ: Lawrence Erlbaum Associates, Inc.

Davis, C., Castles, A., & Iakovidis, E. (1998). Masked homophone and pseudohomophone priming in children and adults. *Language and Cognitive Processes*, *13*, 625–651.

Davis, C. J. (1999). *The self-organising lexical acquisition and recognition (SOLAR) model of visual word recognition*. Unpublished doctoral dissertation, University of New South Wales, Australia.

Dienes, Z., & Altmann, G. (1997). Transfer of implicit knowledge across domains: How implicit and how abstract? In D. Berry (Ed.), *How implicit is implicit learning?* (pp. 107–123). Oxford: Oxford University Press.

Ehri, L. C. (1992). Reconceptualising the development of sight word reading and its relationship to decoding. In P. B. Gough, L. C. Ehri, & R. Treiman (Eds.), *Reading acquisition* (pp. 107–143). Hillsdale NJ: Lawrence Erlbaum Associates, Inc.

Ehri, L. C. (1995). Phases of development in learning to read words by sight. *Journal of Research in Reading*, *18*, 116–125.

Ehri, L. C. (2005). Learning to read words: Theory, findings and issues. *Scientific Studies of Reading*, *9*, 167–188.

Firth, I. (1972). *Components of reading disability*. Unpublished doctoral dissertation, University of New South Wales, Australia.

Frith, U. (1985). Beneath the surface of developmental dyslexia. In K. Patterson, J. Marshall, & M. Coltheart (Eds.), *Surface dyslexia* (pp. 301–330). Hove, UK: Lawrence Erlbaum Associates Ltd.

Goswami, U., & Bryant, P. (1990). *Phonological skills and learning to read*. Hove, UK: Lawrence Erlbaum Associates Ltd.

Gough, P. B., & Hillinger, M. L. (1980). Learning to read: An unnatural act. *Bulletin of the Orton Society*, *30*, 179–196.

Goulandris, N. K., & Snowling, M. (1991). Visual memory deficits: A plausible cause of developmental dyslexia? Evidence from a single case study. *Cognitive Neuropsychology*, *8*, 127–154.

Hanley, R., Hastie, K., & Kay, J. (1992). Developmental surface dyslexia and dysgraphia: An orthographic processing impairment. *Quarterly Journal of Experimental Psychology*, *44*, 285–319.

Harm, M., & Seidenberg, M. S. (2004). Computing the meanings of words in reading: Cooperative division of labor between visual and phonological processes. *Psychological Review*, *111*, 662–720.

Jackson, N., & Coltheart, M. (2001). *Routes to reading success and failure*. Hove, UK: Psychology Press.

Jorm, A. F., Share, D. L., Maclean, R., & Matthews, R. G. (1984). Phonological recoding skills and learning to read: A longitudinal study. *Applied Psycholinguistics*, *5*, 201–207.

Juel, C., Griffith, P. L., & Gough, P. B. (1986). Acquisition of literacy: A longitudinal study of children in first and second grade. *Journal of Educational Psychology*, *78*, 243–255.

Laing, E., & Hulme, C. (1999). Phonological and semantic processes influencing beginning readers' ability to learn to read words. *Journal of Experimental Child Psychology*, *73*, 183–207.

Lupker, S. J. (2005). Visual word recognition: Theories and findings. In M. Snowling & C. Hulme (Eds.), *The science of reading: A handbook* (pp. 39–60). Oxford: Blackwell.

Manis, F. R. (1985). Acquisition of word identification skills in normal and disabled readers. *Journal of Educational Psychology*, *77*, 78–90.

Manis, F. R., Seidenberg, M. S., Doi, L. M., McBride-Chang, C., & Petersen, A. (1996). On the bases of two subtypes of developmental dyslexia. *Cognition*, *58*, 157–195.

Markson, L., & Bloom, P. (1997). Evidence against a dedicated system for word learning in children. *Nature*, *385*, 813–815.

McKague, M., Pratt, C., & Johnston, M. B. (2001). The effect of oral vocabulary on reading visually novel words. *Cognition*, *80*, 231–262.

Muter, V., Hulme, C., Snowling, M., & Taylor, S. (1998). Segmentation, not rhyming, predicts early progress in learning to read. *Journal of Experimental Child Psychology*, *71*, 3–27.

Muter, V., Hulme, C., Snowling, M. J., & Stevenson, J. (2004). Phonemes, rimes, vocabulary, and grammatical skills as foundations of early reading development: Evidence from a longitudinal study. *Developmental Psychology*, *40*, 665–681.

Nation, K. (2005). Children's reading comprehension difficulties. In M. Snowling & C. Hulme (Eds.), *The science of reading: A handbook* (pp. 248–265). Oxford: Blackwell.

Nation, K., & Snowling, M. J. (1988a). Individual differences in contextual facilitation: Evidence from dyslexia and poor reading comprehension. *Child Development*, *69*, 996–1011.

Nation, K., & Snowling, M. J. (1998b). Semantic processing and the development of word recognition skills: Evidence from children with reading comprehension difficulties. *Journal of Memory and Language*, *39*, 85–101.

Nation, K., & Snowling, M. J. (2004). Beyond phonological skills: Broader language skills contribute to the development of reading. *Journal of Research in Reading*, *27*, 342–356.

Pacton, S., Perruchet, P., Fayol, M., & Cleeremans, A. (2001). Implicit learning in real world context: The case of orthographic regularities. *Journal of Experimental Psychology: General, 130*, 401–426.

Perfetti, C. A. (1992). The representation problem in reading acquisition. In P. Gough, L. Ehri, & R. Treiman (Eds.), *Reading acquisition* (pp. 145–174). Hillsdale, NJ: Lawrence Erlbaum Associates, Inc.

Plaut, D. C. (2005). Connectionist approaches to reading. In M. Snowling & C. Hulme (Eds.), *The science of reading: A handbook* (pp. 24–38). Oxford: Blackwell.

Plaut, D. C., McClelland, J. L., Seidenberg, M. S., & Patterson, K. (1996). Understanding normal and impaired word reading: Computational principles in quasi-regular domains. *Psychological Review, 103*, 56–115.

Rack, J. P., Snowling, M. J., & Olson, R. K. (1992). The nonword reading deficit in developmental dyslexia: A review. *Reading Research Quarterly, 27*, 28–53.

Redington, M., & Chater, N. (1998). Connectionist and statistical approaches to language acquisition: A distributional perspective. *Language and Cognitive Processes, 13*, 129–191.

Reitsma, P. (1983). Printed word learning in beginning readers. *Journal of Experimental Child Psychology, 75*, 321–339.

Saffran, J. R., Aslin, R. N., & Newport, E. L. (1996). Statistical learning by 8-month-old infants. *Science, 274*, 1926–1928.

Samuelsson, S. (2000). Converging evidence for the role of occipital regions in orthographic processing: A case of developmental dyslexia. *Neuropsychologia, 4*, 351–362.

Seidenberg, M. S., & McClelland, J. L. (1989). A distributed developmental model of word recognition and naming. *Psychological Review, 96*, 523–568.

Seymour, P. H. K., & Elder, L. (1986). Beginning reading without phonology. *Cognitive Neuropsychology, 3*, 1–36.

Share, D. L. (1995). Phonological recoding and self-teaching: Sine qua non of reading acquisition. *Cognition, 55*, 151–218.

Share, D. L. (1999). Phonological recoding and orthographic learning: A direct test of the self-teaching hypothesis. *Journal of Experimental Child Psychology, 72*, 95–129.

Share, D. L. (2004). Orthographic learning at a glance: On the time course and developmental onset of self-teaching. *Journal of Experimental Child Psychology, 87*, 267–298.

Stanovich, K. E. (1986). Matthew effects in reading: Some consequences of individual differences in the acquisition of literacy. *Reading Research Quarterly, 21*, 360–407.

Stuart, M., Masterson, J., & Dixon, M. (2000). Spongelike acquisition of sight vocabulary in beginning readers? *Journal of Research in Reading, 23*, 12–27.

Szeszulski, P. A., & Manis, F. R. (1990). An examination of familial resemblance among subgroups of dyslexics. *Annals of Dyslexia, 40*, 180–191.

Vellutino, F. R., Scanlon, D. M., & Chen, R. S. (1995). The increasingly inextricable relationship between orthographic and phonological coding in learning to read: Some reservations about current methods of operationalizing orthographic coding. In V. W. Berninger (Ed.), *The varieties of orthographic knowledge. II: Relationships to phonology, reading and writing* (pp. 47–111). Dordrecht, The Netherlands: Kluwer.

Vellutino, F. R., Scanlon, D. M., & Tanzman, M. S. (1994). Components of reading ability: Issues and problems in operationalizing word identification, phonological coding and orthographic coding. In G. R. Lyon (Ed.), *Frames of reference for the assessment of learning disabilities: New views on measurement issues* (pp. 279–329). Baltimore, MD: Brookes.

Wagner, R. K., & Barker, T. A. (1994). The development of orthographic processing ability. In V. W. Berninger (Ed.), *The varieties of orthographic knowledge. I: Theoretical and developmental issues* (pp. 243–276). Dordrecht, The Netherlands: Kluwer.

Wagner, R. K., & Torgesen, J. K. (1987). The nature of phonological processing and its causal role in the acquisition of reading skills. *Psychological Bulletin, 101*, 192–212.

Williams, M. J., Stuart, G. W., Castles, A., & McAnally, K. (2003). Contrast sensitivity in subgroups of developmental dyslexia. *Vision Research, 43*, 467–477.

Zorzi, M., Houghton, G., & Butterworth, B. (1998). The development of spelling–sound relationships in a model of phonological reading. *Language and Cognitive Processes, 13*, 337–371.

8 Orthographic input coding: A review of behavioural evidence and current models

Colin J. Davis
University of Bristol, UK

Successful identification of a printed word requires the reader to construct an orthographic input code—a representation that encodes both the identity and the order of the letters in the input stimulus. There is now a very considerable body of evidence relating to orthographic input coding. In this chapter, I review and synthesize this evidence in order to establish a set of behavioural criteria that a successful model of orthographic input coding must satisfy. I then assess the ability of existing models to satisfy these criteria. None of these models succeed in satisfying all of the criteria, and I will argue that this is due to fundamental problems with the way in which letter order is coded in these models. In the final part of the chapter, I very briefly review an alternative approach to orthographic input coding, which may offer a more promising approach (Davis, submitted, 1999).

Orthographic input codes

Until fairly recently, relatively little empirical work had been directed at assessing the relative merits of different orthographic input coding schemes. In part, this may have been because the choice of input coding scheme was viewed as an assumption of little theoretical interest. In reality, though, the choice of coding scheme plays a central role in the performance of computational models of reading, because it determines the similarity relationships between letter strings. These similarity relationships are central to lexical matching and help to determine which word representations will tend to be activated in response to given letter string; this in turn is critical for explaining interactions among lexical competitors. The limitations of the coding schemes used in previous models have played a major role in failure of these models to successfully simulate data from human readers (e.g. Andrews, 1996). The choice of input and output coding schemes is also critically important in models that attempt to simulate learning, because the relationship between inputs and outputs greatly influences the difficulty of the learning process. A good illustration of this is provided by the development of parallel distributed processing (PDP) models of reading. The Seidenberg and McClelland (1989) model used a form of coding scheme that made learning of orthography-to-phonology correspondences difficult and hindered generalization. Subsequent PDP models introduced revised input/output coding schemes that enabled better generalization (Harm & Seidenberg, 1999; Plaut, Seidenberg, McClelland, & Patterson, 1996). However, these revised schemes introduced other problems, which were in some cases even more serious, as we shall see. Theoretical problems of this sort can only be solved by choosing an appropriate input coding scheme.

One aspect of orthographic input coding about which there is widespread agreement is that the elementary orthographic input units are abstract letter identities. These letter units are "abstract" in the sense that they do not code for case, font, size, colour, or other aspects of printed letters that are independent of letter identity. For example, the same letter unit at the orthographic input level is assumed to activate in response to the sensory inputs *A*, *a*, and a. This assumption is supported by evidence from a variety of sources, including studies of eye movements during reading (McConkie & Zola, 1979; Rayner, Well, & Pollatsek, 1980), neuropsychological case studies (e.g. Bowers, Bub, & Arguin, 1996; Coltheart, 1981), and experiments with normal readers (e.g. Bowers, 2000; McClelland, 1976; Pelli, Farell, & Moore, 2003; Rastle & Coltheart, 1998).

How is letter position coded?

In addition to coding letter identities, the orthographic input level needs to code the relative position of the letters in the stimulus (otherwise, readers would be unable to distinguish anagrams like *stop* and *post*). A key problems for models of visual word identification is specifying how readers do this; that is, how they simultaneously code both the identity of the letters in the input stimulus and their relative order.

Two distinct approaches to coding letter position can be distinguished from very early on in the work on modelling perception of language (e.g. Johnston, 1978; McClelland, 1976; McClelland & Rumelhart, 1981; Rumelhart, 1970; Wickelgren, 1969). In the first of these, a letter's position is coded with respect to its specific serial position. For example, the *A* in *cat* occurs in the second position, and hence it would be coded by a unit that specifically represents *A* in position 2 (A_2). The second approach codes a letter's position with respect to its local context. For example, the *A* in *cat* can be coded by noting that it has a *C* to its left and a *T* to its right. In both types of approach, the problem of coding letter order is handled by assuming elementary orthographic input units that convey information about letter position or order. Within both of these broad categories, there are several variants, which are described more fully below.

Position-specific coding

Position-specific coding is presently the most common method for coding letter position in computational models of visual word recognition. A survey of implemented computational models of visual word identification reveals at least six distinct variants of position-specific coding. The simplest variant was used by McClelland and Rumelhart (1981) in their IA model. In this scheme, there are four separate sets of letter units, one for each of the serial positions in a four-letter stimulus. For example, the word *stop* is coded by activating the *S* in the first slot, the *T* in the second slot, the *O* in the third slot, and the *P* in the fourth slot. The division of the letter units into separate slots has led this type of scheme to be commonly referred to as "slot-coding". Note that the letter *S* in position 1 has no connection with the letter *S* in other positions—*S* in position 1 is no more similar to *S* in position 2 than it is to *X* in position 2 (or any other letter node).

Related schemes have been employed by Grainger and Jacobs (1996); Coltheart et al. (2001); and Jacobs, Rey, Ziegler, and Grainger (1998). In their simulations of the IA model, Grainger and Jacobs (1996) overcame the length restrictions of the original model by introducing a separate set of position-specific letter units for each stimulus length. For example, not only do separate units code the letter *A* in positions 1 and 2 of a four-letter word, but there are also distinct units that code the letter *A* in positions 1 and 2 of a five-letter word. Thus, to code all four- and five-letter words requires nine distinct units that code the letter *A*.

The input coding scheme in Coltheart et al.'s (2001) DRC model is similar to McClelland and Rumelhart's, but assumes eight slots of letter units (enough to code any monosyllabic word in English). For strings that contain fewer than eight letters, the absence of a letter in a particular letter slot is coded explicitly by activating a space character in that slot. This scheme provides an alternative approach to dealing with the length restrictions of the original IA model, and one that is more parsimonious than assuming separate sets of slots for each length.

The variant of slot-coding proposed by Jacobs et al. (1998) codes the first half of the word according to absolute letter position and the second half relative to the final letter. For example, given the stimulus *stop*, the outer letters are assigned to slots for the initial and final letters (i.e. S_I and P_F, where the subscripts *I* and *F* denote initial and final letters respectively) and the internal letters are assigned to slots relative to these boundaries (i.e. T_{I+1} and O_{F-1}). This ensures that the first letter is always coded by the first slot and the last letter is coded by the final slot.

Other variants of slot coding code letters relative to the vowel component. Because the existence of a (single) vowel grapheme is a defining feature of syllables in English, this type of scheme can be used to code any monosyllable. One such coding scheme was suggested by Zorzi et al. (1998). This scheme contains eight letter slots, where the first vowel of a word is always coded by slot 4, and letters are assigned to other slots by their position relative to the vowel (note that the maximum number of consonants that can occur prior to a vowel in a legal English monosyllable is three; e.g. *str*). Consonants prior to the vowel are left-aligned; for example, the word *stop* would be coded by the letter units S_1, T_2, O_4, and P_5. A very similar coding scheme was used by Harm and Seidenberg (1999), except that in their scheme the consonants prior to the vowel are right-aligned (for example the word *stop* would be coded by the letter units S_2, T_3, O_4, and P_5).

Context-specific coding

The major alternative to position-specific coding schemes in the literature to date has been some form of context-specific coding (Grainger & Van Heuven, 2003; Mozer, 1983, 1991; Rumelhart & McClelland, 1986; Schoonbaert & Grainger, 2004; Seidenberg & McClelland, 1989; Whitney, 2001; Whitney & Berndt, 1999; Wickelgren, 1969). The idea of using local context to avoid explicit coding of serial position was suggested by Wickelgren (1969), as a means of coding phonology. A variant of this approach—called "Wickelcoding"—was employed by Rumelhart and McClelland (1986), in their model of past-tense learning, and subsequently by Seidenberg and McClelland (1989), in their model of visual word recognition. Other variants of local context coding (Grainger & Van Heuven, 2003; Mozer, 1983, 1991; Whitney, 2001) are discussed later in this chapter. For another variant, which combines aspects of both position-specific and context-specific coding, see *Kello* (this volume).

In Wickelcoding, a letter is coded with respect to the immediately preceding letter and the immediately following letter, and thus the units of representation are contiguous letter triples ("Wickelfeatures") like *sto*. Combining a set of these units enables the identity of a word to be represented (although not unambiguously, as Pinker & Prince, 1988, noted). For example, *stop* can be coded by the following set of Wickelfeatures: *#st*, *sto*, *top*, and *op#* (where # indicates a word boundary).[1] A completely general implementation of Wickelcoding requires 18,954 Wickelfeatures. However, a smaller number is sufficient if orthotactic constraints are taken into consideration. Thus, Seidenberg and McClelland's (1989) implementation of Wickelcoding included a set of 400 input units, each of which could be used to form part of the code for 1000 different Wickelfeatures.

Perceptual correspondence and seven criteria for a satisfactory theory of orthographic input coding

A key means of evaluating the adequacy of models of orthographic input coding is to assess their *perceptual correspondence* (Davis, 1999). This refers to the extent to which letter strings that are perceptually similar are represented by similar input codes in the model. A satisfactory theory of orthographic input coding should be able to explain why some pairs of orthographic stimuli are more similar (and more susceptible to confusion) than others. In the following, I adopt this approach in order to describe a set of seven *perceptual correspondence criteria* that can be used to evaluate the descriptive adequacy of models of orthographic input coding. These criteria offer a means of assessing the perceptual correspondence of a model—the degree to which the "similarity space" of the model corresponds to the perceptual "similarity space" of readers. Each criterion is based on experimental data, often derived from multiple studies, by different researchers using different methodologies. These seven criteria are summarized in Table 8.1. The failure of a model to satisfy any of these criteria can be considered as indicative of an underlying problem in the way that model codes orthographic inputs.

Criterion 1. Transposition neighbours are more similar than substitution neighbours

The type of orthographic similarity relationship that has been studied most intensively is the similarity between letter strings that are identical save for the substitution of a single letter at a single position (e.g. *trail–train*). Pairs like this are often referred to simply as orthographic neighbours (or sometimes as "Coltheart neighbours", to mark the first experimental investigation of neighbourhood effects in the lexical decision task, which was conducted by Coltheart, Davelaar, Jonasson, & Besner, 1977). However, I shall use the more specific term "substitution neighbours" (SNs) to describe this type of similarity. Many studies have addressed the impact of the number of substitution neighbours of a letter string (for a review, see Andrews, 1997). Furthermore, many studies have demonstrated that even a single substitution neighbour can influence lexical processing in a wide variety of experimental paradigms (e.g. Bowers, Davis, & Hanley, 2005b; Carreiras, Perea, & Grainger, 1997; Forster & Hector, 2003; Forster & Shen, 1996; Grainger,

Table 8.1 Summary of the capacity of different models to satisfy the seven perceptual correspondence criteria

		Model				
	Criterion	*PSC*	*WC*	*BLIRNET*	*OBC*	*SPATIAL*
1	TN > SN	No	No	?	Yes	Yes
2	NATN > DSN	No	No	?	Yes	Yes
3	SN > NATN	Yes	Yes	?	No	Yes
4	REV ANAG	Yes	Yes	Yes?	Yes	Yes
5	N1R > DSN	No	No	Yes?	Yes	Yes
6	SN > N1R	Yes	Yes	Yes?	No	Yes
7	AN/DN similarity	No	Yes	Yes?	Yes	Yes

SN = substitution neighbour (e.g. *stop–shop*), DSN = double-substitution neighbour (e.g. *stop–ship*), TN = transposition neighbour (e.g. *slat–salt*), NATN = nonadjacent transposition neighbour (e.g. *stop–spot*), N1R = neighbour once-removed (e.g. *stop–soap*), AN = addition neighbour (e.g. *stop–stomp*), DN = deletion neighbour (e.g. *stop–top*), REV ANAG = reversal anagram (e.g. *stop–pots*).
PSC = position-specific coding, WC = Wickelcoding, OBC = open-bigram coding, SPATIAL = spatial coding scheme used in the SOLAR model.

1990; Grainger, O'Regan, Jacobs, & Segui, 1989; Grainger & Segui, 1990; Perea & Pollatsek, 1998; Rodd, 2004).

There are also many experiments that have demonstrated the perceptual similarity of letter strings that differ only with respect to the transposition of adjacent letters (e.g. Andrews, 1996; Chambers, 1979; Forster et al., 1987; Johnson, Rayner, & Perea, submitted, 2005; O'Connor & Forster, 1981; Perea & Lupker, 2003a, 2003b; Perea, Rosa, & Gómez, 2005; Schoonbaert & Grainger, 2004; Taft & van Graan, 1998). Word pairs that have this property (e.g. *trial–trail*, *calm–clam*) are often referred to as TL words, but I will use the general term *transposition neighbour* (TN) to refer to a letter string (which may be a word or a nonword) involving an adjacent-letter transposition.

Several studies have explicitly compared transposition neighbours and substitution neighbours (e.g. Chambers, 1979; Forster et al., 1987; Perea & Lupker, 2003a, 2003b; Perea, Rosa, & Gómez, 2005). Chambers (1979, experiment 2) found that lexical decisions to nonwords that had transposition neighbours were slower than to control nonwords without transposition neighbours (e.g. it took longer to classify *wodner* as a nonword than *lodnet*). By contrast, the interference effect for nonwords with substitution neighbours (e.g. *narive*, which is a substitution neighbour of *native*, versus *navint*, which has no neighbours) was much weaker, and attained significance over subjects, but not items.

A lexical decision experiment reported by Forster et al. (1987) used the masked form priming paradigm to directly compare the similarity of transposition and substitution neighbours. In their experiment, target words were preceded by either (a) an identity prime, e.g. *answer–ANSWER*; (b) a transposition neighbour, e.g. *anwser–ANSWER*; (c) a substitution neighbour, e.g. *ansmer–ANSWER*; or (d) an orthographically unrelated word, e.g. *orclid–ANSWER*. They found that the facilitatory effect of transposition neighbour primes (63 ms) was just as great as that for identity primes (64 ms), and greater than that for substitution neighbours (50 ms) (exactly the same pattern was observed in the accuracy data).[2]

In another set of masked priming experiments, Perea and Lupker (2003b) found that transposition neighbour primes produced associative priming effects (e.g. *jugde–COURT*) that were virtually as strong as those for untransposed associates (e.g. *judge–COURT*). By contrast, much weaker associative priming was observed for primes that were substitution neighbours of an associate (e.g. *judpe–COURT*; the priming effects in this condition were not statistically significant). The presence of associative priming effects for transposition neighbour primes indicates that transposition neighbours can activate the semantic representation of the untransposed word and its associates. This argues against an account in which masked priming effects are entirely mediated by activity in sublexical representations (e.g. Masson & Bodner, 2003). Thus, there is now substantial evidence showing that pairs of transposition neighbours are more similar to each other than pairs of substitution neighbours. This provides an important constraint on theories of orthographic input coding.

Criterion 2. Nonadjacent transposition neighbours are more similar than double-substitution neighbours

Most of the experiments that have examined letter transposition effects have focused on the case in which the transposed letters are immediately adjacent (e.g. *trial–trail*). However, several recent masked priming experiments have shown that facilitatory form priming is also observed for nonadjacent transposition neighbours like *caniso–CASINO* (Perea & Lupker, 2004). Perea and Lupker observed that lexical decision responses to the target *CASINO* were significantly faster when preceded by *caniso* relative to a prime that was a *double-substitution neighbour* (DSN) of the target (e.g. *caviro–CASINO*). This result, which was obtained with Spanish-language stimuli, has been replicated in English (Davis & Bowers, 2005; Lupker, Perea, & Davis, in preparation, 2006). Perea and Lupker (2004) also reported an unprimed lexical decision experiment in which they found that "No" responses to nonwords like *caniso* were significantly slower than responses to nonwords like *caviro*. This reinforces the conclusions of the priming experiments and implies that transposition neighbours separated by one intervening letter position are more similar than double-substitution neighbours. This provides a further constraint on theories of orthographic input coding.

Criterion 3. Nonadjacent transposition neighbours are less similar than substitution neighbours

A further observation regarding nonadjacent transposition neighbours concerns their relative similarity to substitution neighbours. Perea and Lupker (2004) reported three separate lexical decision experiments that included both a nonadjacent transposition neighbour prime condition and a substitution neighbour prime condition. In all three cases, the difference between these conditions was statistically significant: substitution neighbour primes (e.g. *casiro–CASINO*) resulted in greater priming than nonadjacent transposition neighbour primes (e.g. *caniso–CASINO*). This finding (which has been replicated by Davis & Bowers, 2005), implies that transposition neighbours separated by one intervening letter position are less similar than substitution neighbours. When combined with the first and second criteria, this result places rather strict constraints on theories of input coding, because it provides a yardstick by which to measure the differential impact of replacing a letter versus altering the position of that letter. For example, a satisfactory model needs to capture the fact that *slate* and *stale* are more similar to each other than *slate* and *space*, but *less* similar to each other than *slate* and *slave*. The first inequality indicates that the presence of two additional matching letters (that is, five versus three matching letter identities) outweighs the fact that the additional letters are misordered. The second inequality indicates that the presence of only one additional matching letter (that is, five versus four matching letter identities) is insufficient to outweigh this misordering of letters; however, when the misordering is less severe, as in the case of adjacent transpositions, a single additional letter does outweigh the misordering of two letters (criterion 1). As will be seen, current models have great difficulty in explaining this set of inequalities.

Criterion 4. Reversal anagrams are relatively dissimilar to their base words

The above findings with transposition neighbours (both adjacent and nonadjacent) point to the perceptual similarity of letter strings that share the same letters in a different order (i.e. anagrams). However, this does not imply that all anagrams are perceptually similar. Although *judge* and *jugde* are very similar, intuitively, it would seem that *judge* and *egduj* are not. Very few studies have investigated the similarity of *reversal anagrams* like *judge* and *egduj* and *wolf* and *flow*. The few that have, though, have found no evidence of perceptual similarity between anagrams of this sort. Huntsman (1998) reported a set of repetition priming experiments which showed that identity primes resulted in strong facilitation (for example, lexical decision latencies to *dog* were considerably faster on its second occurrence), but that reversed word primes did not significantly facilitate lexical decisions (for example, responses to *dog* were not facilitated by prior presentation of *god*). Likewise, Andreas and Deutsch (1965) found no tendency for participants to recognize reversed words in a recognition memory experiment. A related finding has recently been observed by Guerrera (2004), who found no priming at all (in a masked form priming lexical decision experiment) from primes like *edisklaw–SIDEWALK*, in which the prime reverses the letters in both the first and second halves of the target (see also *Forster*, this volume). Another relevant finding, described by *Davis and Kim* (this volume), comes from a task in which participants are asked to determine whether a letter string is a word when its letter order is reversed (thus, the correct response to the target *ECAF* is "Yes", because *face* is a word). Masked primes like *ecaf* do not facilitate the judgement that the target *ECAF* is a reversed word (whereas the prime *face* does facilitate this judgement; that is, activating the lexical representation for the word *face* is helpful in this task, but the reversed prime *ecaf* is insufficient to prime this representation). Thus, a satisfactory theory of orthographic input coding must be able to explain why some anagrams are perceptually similar, but others—notably, reversal anagrams—are not.

Criterion 5. Neighbours once-removed are more similar than double-substitution neighbours

Davis and Bowers (2004) coined the term "neighbours once-removed" (N1R) to refer to pairs of letter strings that would count as substitution neighbours were it not for the fact that one of the common letters was shifted by one position. An example is *stop* and *soup*: these share three out of four letters, but one of the common letters (the letter *O*) occurs in position 2 of *soup* and position 3 of *stop*. In effect, N1R pairs consist of a letter transposition followed by a substitution of one of the transposed letters. Given that transposition neighbours are more similar than substitution neighbours (criterion 1), it seems reasonable to expect that letter strings that involve a transposition and a single substitution should be more similar than double-substitution neighbours.

The relative similarity of N1R pairs and DSN pairs has been tested in several experiments using the illusory word (or "letter migration") paradigm. In this paradigm, two letter strings are presented briefly and simultaneously at different locations. When readers attempt to attend to both strings, they occasionally perceive an illusory word that combines letters from the two strings (e.g. Davis & Bowers, 2006; Davis & Coltheart, 2002; McClelland & Mozer, 1986; Mozer, 1983; Shallice & McGill, 1978). For example, if subjects are given the word pair *step–shop*, and subsequently asked to report the word on the left, they will occasionally report that this word was *stop*. This illusory word phenomenon seems to require that both letter strings in the display (that is, both the target string, which subjects are asked to report, and the context stimulus) resemble the illusory word, although it does not require that both strings are words (e.g. Davis & Bowers, 2004; Mozer, 1983). Davis and Bowers (2004) reported two experiments showing that illusory word reports occur significantly more often when the context stimulus is a word that is a neighbour once-removed of the illusory word (e.g. *soup*) than when it is a double-substitution neighbour of the illusory word (e.g. *slap*). Davis and Bowers (2006) observed a similar result for context stimuli that were nonwords. For example, the illusory word *stop* was reported more often when the target *step* was paired with the nonword *smop* than when it was paired with the nonword *somp*. This suggests that the perceptual similarity of *smop* and *stop* is greater than that of *somp* and *stop*; that is, that N1R pairs are more similar than DSN pairs.

Additional support for the conclusion that N1R pairs are more similar than DSN pairs comes from an unpublished lexical decision experiment by Davis and Bowers, using the masked form priming technique. The results showed significant facilitatory priming for N1R primes (e.g. *derm–DRUM*) relative to an unrelated baseline (e.g. *gleb–DRUM*), but no priming for DSN primes (e.g. *delm–DRUM*).

Criterion 6. Substitution neighbours are more similar than neighbours once-removed

A more subtle difference concerns that between (single) substitution neighbours (SN pairs) and neighbours once-removed. It seems reasonable to expect some difference in the similarity of SN pairs like *stop* and *step* and N1R pairs like *stop* and *soup*, given that the former involve only a single substitution, whereas the latter involve both a substitution and a transposition. To date, few experiments have investigated this difference. Davis and Bowers (2004) reported two experiments using the illusory word paradigm, which included both SN and N1R conditions, but these experiments were not designed specifically to perform this comparison: the target, context, and illusory words differed across the SN and N1R conditions. However, in a subsequent experiment that was designed specifically to examine this difference, Davis and Bowers (2006) compared SN and N1R conditions in which the target and illusory words were exactly the same. For example, the target word *step* was paired with the nonword context *smop* (an SN of *stop*) for half of the subjects and with the nonword context *somp* (a neighbour once-removed of *stop*) for the other half. The results of the experiment showed that there were significantly more illusory words for the SN context condition than for the N1R context condition.

Davis and Bowers (2006) also reported two masked form priming lexical decision task (LDT) experiments in which SN primes (e.g. *azkle–ANKLE*) resulted in significantly greater facilitatory priming than N1R primes (e.g. *akzle–ANKLE*). In summary, then, there is good evidence to support the claim that SN pairs are more similar than N1R pairs.

Criterion 7. Words are perceptually similar to their addition and deletion neighbours

I shall define an *addition neighbour* of a word to be a letter string that involves the addition of a single letter (in any position) to that word; for example, the words *plane*, *widow*, and *lower* have the addition neighbours *planet*, *window*, and *flower*, respectively. Likewise, a *deletion neighbour* of a word is a letter string that differs from that word by the deletion of a single letter; for example, the word *paint* has the deletion neighbours *pain*, *pant*, *pint*, and (possibly) *aint*. Until fairly recently, there has been a paucity of evidence regarding these forms of orthographic similarity. However, several recent findings provide evidence for the perceptual similarity of addition and deletion neighbours (Bowers, Davis, & Hanley, 2005a; Davis & Perea, submitted, 2005; Davis & Taft, 2005; De Moor & Brysbaert, 2000; Drews & Zwitserlood, 1995; Schoonbaert & Grainger, 2004).

Schoonbaert and Grainger (2004) reported a lexical decision experiment in which they found that nonwords like *cultre* (which has the addition neighbour *culture*) took longer to classify than matched control nonwords. Davis and Taft (2005) reported a lexical decision experiment in which nonwords like *preal* and *gleaf* (which have the deletion neighbours *real* and *leaf*) showed significantly slower decision latencies than nonwords like *gleal* and *preaf* (which have no deletion neighbours). A recent pair of lexical decision experiments conducted by Davis and Perea (submitted, 2005), using Spanish stimuli, obtained similar interference effects for nonwords with deletion or addition neighbours. These results suggest that the lexical representations of addition and deletion neighbours are automatically activated, causing them to interfere with the production of a "No" response.

The automatic activation of deletion and addition neighbours also interferes with "Yes" responses in lexical decision. Davis and Taft (2005) compared lexical decisions for low-frequency words that have high-frequency deletion neighbours (e.g. *plank*, *swarm*, and *truce*, which have the deletion neighbours *plan*, *warm*, and *true*, respectively) with latencies for matched control words without deletion neighbours. Latencies were significantly slower for words with deletion neighbours than for control words, suggesting that activation in the representations of the deletion neighbours interfered with identification of the target word. This finding has recently been replicated with Spanish stimuli by Davis and Perea (submitted, 2005), who found a similar effect for low-frequency words with higher-frequency addition neighbours.

Masked form priming experiments have also provided evidence of the perceptual similarity of addition and deletion neighbours. In one experiment, Schoonbaert and Grainger found that deletion neighbour nonwords were effective form primes for their addition neighbours. For example, a facilitatory priming effect of 38 ms was observed for prime-target trials like *balnce–BALANCE*, relative to the same targets preceded by an unrelated prime. The effect of form priming is rather different when the prime is itself a word, because prior presentation of a word's neighbour enhances the usual competition between these two words. Consequently, although a nonword neighbour prime results in facilitation of a target word (For example, responses to *axue–AXLE* are faster than to *doir–AXLE*), a word neighbour prime typically results in inhibition of the same target, relative to targets that are preceded by orthographically dissimilar words (Davis & Lupker, 2006; Segui & Grainger, 1990). The majority of experiments investigating inhibitory masked priming have used conventional substitution neighbours, but a couple of experiments with addition/deletion neighbours have reported corresponding inhibitory effects (De Moor & Brysbaert, 2000; Drews & Zwitserlood, 1995). For example, De Moor and Brysbaert (2000) found that participants took longer to classify *rover* (Dutch for "robber") as a word when it was preceded by the deletion neighbour *over* than when it was preceded by an unrelated word prime. This is consistent with the idea that a target word ordinarily competes with its addition and deletion neighbours; prior presentation of one of these neighbours enhances this competition, resulting in an inhibitory effect on target recognition, relative to targets that are preceded by orthographically dissimilar words.

A different approach to demonstrating the automatic activation of addition and deletion neighbours was reported by Bowers et al. (2005a), using a semantic competition paradigm. For example, subjects took longer (and were less accurate) to respond "No" when asked to decide whether the word *rabbi* (which has the addition neighbour *rabbit*) refers to a type of animal than to decide whether *rabbi* refers to a type of clothing. In a separate experiment, subjects took longer (and were less accurate) to respond "No" when asked to decide whether the word *apex* (which has the deletion neighbour *ape*) refers to a type of animal than to decide whether *apex* refers to a type of vehicle. This suggests that addition neighbours were processed to the level of meaning and impaired performance when they required a different response than the presented word.

A related issue concerns the effect of the position of overlap between a word and its deletion neighbour. There seems to be some indication that similarity effects are strongest for pairs involving outer overlap (e.g. *trace–trance*) and weakest for those involving final overlap (e.g. *eagle–beagle*; Davis & Perea, submitted, 2005; Davis & Taft, 2005). However, effects of addition/deletion neighbour similarity have been observed for pairs involving initial overlap (e.g. *rabbi–RABBIT*; Bowers et al., 2005a; Davis & Perea, submitted, 2005; Drews & Zwitserlood, 1995), outer overlap (e.g. Bowers et al., 2005a; Davis & Perea, submitted, 2005; Schoonbaert & Grainger, 2004), and final overlap (e.g. Bowers et al., 2005a; Davis & Taft, 2005; De Moor & Brysbaert, 2000).

In summary, evidence for the perceptual similarity of addition and deletion neighbour pairs has been amassed in several different paradigms (facilitatory masked form priming, inhibitory masked form priming, unprimed lexical decision with word and nonword stimuli, and semantic competition) using many different languages (English, French, German, Spanish, and Dutch) and across all overlap positions (initial, final, and outer). Thus, a satisfactory coding scheme needs to be able to explain the similarity between a letter string and its addition and deletion neighbours.

Problems for position-specific and Wickelcoding schemes

Having specified the above set of perceptual correspondence criteria, I will now review the ability of current models to satisfy these criteria. As we shall see, each of the models faces problems in satisfying the criteria. In the case of position-specific coding models, there is the general difficulty of accounting for similarity effects that involve changes in a letter's position. In the case of context-specific coding models, there is the general problem of accounting for similarity effects that involve changes in a letter's context. In particular, these problems result in an inability to explain the similarity of transposition neighbours and neighbours once-removed, and hence to satisfy criteria 1, 2, and 5.

Position-specific coding and Wickelcoding cannot explain the perceptual similarity of transposition neighbours

Position-specific coding schemes encounter a fundamental problem in attempting to explain the perceptual similarity of transposition neighbours, because these schemes are not sensitive to the overlap of common letters in different positions. For example, according to the slot-coding scheme used in the IA model, *slat* and *salt* share only two letter units (S_1 and T_4), and hence pairs like this are less similar than substitution neighbours (e.g. *slat* and *slot*). Exactly the same concerns apply to the other variants of slot coding. The same problem applies to explaining the greater perceptual similarity of non-adjacent transposition neighbours relative to double-substitution neighbours. For example, according to the slot-coding scheme used in the DRC model, *casino* and *caniso* share four letter units (C_1, A_2, I_4 and O_6), and hence pairs like this are no more similar than double-substitution neighbours like *casino* and *caviro*.

A similar problem in explaining the similarity of transposition neighbours is encountered by Wickelcoding, because letter transpositions disrupt the local context of both the transposed letters and the immediately adjacent letters. For example, the transposition neighbours *trail* and *trial* share only one Wickelfeature (*#tr*). By contrast, the substitution neighbours *trail* and *trawl* share two Wickelfeatures (*#tr*, *tra*); that is, Wickelcoding incorrectly predicts that transposition neighbours are less similar than substitution neighbours. It also incorrectly predicts that nonadjacent transposition neighbours like *stale* and *slate* are no more similar than double-substitution neighbours like *stale* and *space* (there are no overlapping Wickelcodes in these pairs). Thus, both position-specific coding schemes and Wickelcoding fail to satisfy criteria 1 and 2.

Position-specific coding and Wickelcoding cannot explain the perceptual similarity of neighbours once-removed

In neighbours once-removed, like *stop* and *soup*, one of the common letters occurs in a different letter position and local context, and hence this type of similarity also produces problems for position-specific coding and Wickelcoding. For example, according to the slot-coding scheme used in the IA model, *stop* and *soup* share only two common letter units (S_1 and P_4), and so are no more similar than a pair of double-substitution neighbours (e.g. *stop* and *snap*). Exactly the same concerns apply to the other variants of slot coding: none of the position-specific coding schemes used in current models can explain the findings reported by Davis and Bowers (2006). Likewise, neighbours once-removed, like *stop* and *soup*, do not share any Wickelcodes. Thus, both position-specific and Wickelcoding schemes fail to satisfy criterion 5.

Position-specific coding schemes do not explain the perceptual similarity of addition and deletion neighbours

The perceptual similarity of addition and deletion neighbours poses a further problem for position-specific coding schemes, because letter additions or deletions lead to misalignment of common letters.[3] As noted above, it is possible to distinguish between three different positions of overlap among addition and deletion neighbours: initial overlap (e.g. *drawl–draw*), final overlap (e.g. *beach–each*), and outer overlap (e.g. *width–with*). None of the position-specific coding schemes can predict similarity across all three types of overlap. For example, DRC's scheme explains the similarity between *drawl* and *draw* (which share the letter codes D_1, R_2, A_3, and W_4), but cannot explain the similarity between *beach* and *each* (which do not share any common letter units), or between *width* and *with* (which share only two out of five letter units, and hence are no more similar than *width* and *wing*). Jacobs et al.'s (1998) scheme captures the similarity of outer-overlap pairs (e.g. *width* and *with* share four out of five letter units), but not of pairs with word-initial or word-final overlap (for example, *drawl* and *draw* share only two out of five letter units, as do *beach* and *each*, and hence the match is no greater than that between *drawl* and *drink* or *beach* and *witch*). Finally, vowel-centred schemes capture the similarity of initial overlap and final overlap pairs, but not of outer overlap pairs. For example, *width* and *with* share only the vowel and the initial consonant (the post-vocalic consonants are misaligned), implying that this pair is no more similar than *width* and *wing*. Likewise, *fright* and *freight* share only three out of six common units (the consonants are aligned, but the vowel graphemes are misaligned). Given that effects of all three types of overlap between addition and deletion neighbours have been observed in published experiments, it must be concluded that position-specific coding schemes are unable to satisfy criterion 7.

Wickelcoding does a better job at explaining the similarity of addition and deletion neighbours, because it is a position-invariant method of letter coding. Thus, *plane* shares all but one of its Wickelcodes (*ne#*) with its addition neighbour *planet*, and *lower* shares all but one of its Wickelcodes (#lo) with its addition neighbour *flower*; in both cases, four out of five Wickelcodes match. Addition neighbours that involve word-outer overlap are slightly less similar (for example, *widow* shares three out of five of its Wickelcodes with its addition neighbour *window*). The predictions for deletion neighbours are similar, except that Wickelcoding predicts slighter weaker similarity in this case; that is, a target letter string is more similar to its addition neighbours than to its deletion neighbours. For example, *planet* shares four out of six of its Wickelcodes with its deletion neighbour *plane*, *flower* shares four out of six of its Wickelcodes with its deletion neighbour *lower*, and *window* shares three out of six of its Wickelcodes with its deletion neighbour *widow*. The prediction of poorer matches for deletion neighbours that involve word-outer overlap is in the opposite direction to the trend observed by Davis and Taft (2005) and Davis and Perea (submitted, 2005), who observed greater interference for pairs involving word-outer overlap than for those involving word-initial or word-final overlap. Thus, Wickelcoding explains the perceptual similarity of addition/deletion neighbours, but not the pattern of overlap effects.

In summary, position-specific coding schemes fail to satisfy four of the seven perceptual correspondence criteria (criteria 1, 2, 5, and 7). Evidence from a broad variety of experimental methods therefore suggests that the fundamental principle underlying position-specific coding is incorrect. Wickelcoding does not fare much better, failing to satisfy at least three of the seven criteria (its capacity to satisfy the remaining criteria merely stems from the fact that it predicts no similarity between anagrams of any kind, and little or no similarity between neighbours once-removed). It can be concluded that these schemes are unsatisfactory as models of letter position coding.

Can the problems with existing schemes be solved through the addition of position uncertainty?

Many of the problems encountered by position-specific and context-specific coding schemes relate to the "brittleness" of the letter position coding; for example, the way in which a letter A in position 2 has no bearing on words which contain an A in position 3. One way to try to overcome this brittleness is to introduce the assumption that there is some uncertainty in the coding of letter position. This assumption is not implausible: Indeed, there is considerable experimental evidence that letter position is coded in a relatively "sloppy" way, especially during the early stages of processing a visually presented letter string. For example, tasks in which participants are asked to report the letters in briefly presented, random letter strings reveal frequent location errors, but relatively few errors in which participants report a letter that is not present in the stimulus array (e.g. Estes, Allmeyer, & Reder, 1976; Mewhort, Campbell, Marchetti, & Campbell, 1981). It is therefore appropriate to consider whether the incorporation of position uncertainty can solve the problems faced by existing position-specific and context-specific coding schemes.

"Sloppy" slot coding

A possible variant of position-specific coding is a "sloppy" slot-coding scheme in which each letter of the input stimulus is coded by activity across several letter units representing adjacent serial positions (e.g. Perea, Gómez, & Ratcliff, 2003). For example, a letter *O* in the second position may result in a gradient of activity over slots, so that the *O* node in the second position is most strongly activated, but the *O* nodes in the first and third positions are also somewhat activated, as is, to a lesser extent, the *O* node in the fourth slot. This blurring of position information will increase the overlap between neighbours once-removed and transposition neighbours (for example, both *stop* and *soap* will activate the *O* nodes in positions 2 and 3).

However, the addition of position uncertainty to slot coding leads to a separate problem. If a (nonword) stimulus like *balnce* is coded by activity in not only the A_2 letter unit, but also, to a lesser extent, in the A_4 letter unit, it follows that the latter activity should boost the activation of the *balance* word node; in a sense, the stimulus could be said to contain all seven letters of its addition neighbour (or, at any rate, six and a half). By contrast, the stimulus *balace* contains only six of the letters of its addition neighbour, and position uncertainty cannot compensate for the absence of the letter *N*. This suggests that *balnce* should lead to slower lexical decision latencies than *balace*; if anything, Schoonbaert and Grainger (2004) observed a trend in the opposite direction: nonwords like *balace* took 22 ms longer to reject than nonwords like *balnce* in an unprimed LDT (furthermore, a separate masked priming experiment found no difference in the effectiveness of primes like *balace* and *balnce* for the target *balance*).

Another problem faced by sloppy position-specific coding is the evidence for position-insensitive form priming effects (e.g. Grainger et al., in press; Jordan, 1986; Peressotti & Grainger, 1999). For example, Peressotti and Grainger (1999) investigated masked form priming for six-letter target words. They found that relative-position primes (e.g. *flcn–FALCON*) produced significant priming compared to unrelated primes (e.g. *brsd–FALCON*). The magnitude of facilitatory priming was not increased by inserting filler letters or characters (e.g. *fxlcdn*, *f-lc-n*) to provide absolute position information. Similarly, Grainger et al. (in press) found comparable priming effects for primes sharing initial letters with seven- and nine-letter targets (e.g. *magni*–MAGNITUDE) and primes sharing final letters (*itude–MAGNITUDE*). Sloppy position-specific coding cannot explain these findings, because the addition of "sloppiness" does not overcome the basic dependence on position-specific codes.

In summary, the addition of position uncertainty may help to ameliorate some of the problems associated with position-specific coding (although it may also introduce other problems), but there is no avoiding the basic failing of these schemes, which is their inability to accommodate the positional flexibility that is apparent in skilled readers' capacity to identify familiar words. It must be concluded that letter position is coded in a relatively flexible way that does not involve position-specific letter units.

Adding position uncertainty to Wickelcodes: BLIRNET coding

A more sophisticated version of Wickelcoding, which includes the assumption of position uncertainty, was developed by Mozer (1991) in his BLIRNET model. In addition to the letter triples of conventional Wickelcoding, Mozer's scheme includes codes for just the initial letter or final letter (e.g. ——S or P——). Mozer's scheme also allows for Wickelcodes that code three letters in four consecutive positions, including wild-card characters. For example, the code *S*OP* would be used to code both *stop* and *shop* (and any other letter string where some letter is preceded by the letter *S* and followed by *OP*). The addition of these extra units results in a considerable increase in the number of codes that are required: all told, a full implementation requires 56,966 possible letter-cluster units, although 24,419 letter clusters is sufficient for the model to code all of the words in the Kucera and Francis (1967) corpus, and 6000 letter clusters is sufficient to code most of the letter clusters of the majority of English words (Mozer, 1991). Even this imposes a huge computational burden, however (due to the number of connections required in the network), and so Mozer used only 540 letter clusters in his simulations (this still necessitated over 600,000 connections in the model). This restriction in the available letter clusters enabled 909 words to be found, for which at least 70% of their letter clusters were represented in the model.

BLIRNET's coding scheme is similar to Wickelcoding (with many extra letter clusters), and so it faces the same challenges with regard to the seven perceptual correspondence criteria. For example, of the 18 letter clusters required to code the word *carve*, only five are shared with its transposition neighbour *crave*. This is no more than a double-substitution neighbour like *chive*, and considerably fewer than the nine clusters shared by a substitution neighbour. Similar considerations suggest that, in the absence of position uncertainty, the model would have difficulty satisfying criteria relating to transposition neighbours and neighbours once-removed.

However, the implemented BLIRNET model incorporates a somewhat noisy representation at the letter-cluster level, resulting in uncertainty regarding both letter identity and position. As a consequence, spurious letter clusters will sometimes be activated (for example, the word *carve* may give rise to weak activity in the *——*CR* cluster). Although this clearly affects the similarity of different sorts of orthographic neighbours, it is very difficult to evaluate the consequences of position uncertainty in this model. Mozer's (1991) simulations focused on demonstrating the ability of the model to encode letter strings veridically, rather than on attempting to model orthographic similarity effects in tasks like lexical decision.

The BLIRNET model also faces a problem in explaining the results of Schoonbaert and Grainger (2004) concerning the effects of deleting repeated versus nonrepeated letters. Mozer's simulations of the model led to the prediction that "errors involving the insertion or deletion of repeated letters in a word should be particularly difficult to detect . . . [for example] DIMINSHED and DIMINISHED yield quite similar patterns of activity, certainly more so than DIMINISED and DIMINISHED" (Mozer, 1991, p. 133). However, Schoonbaert and Grainger (2004) found that deletions of repeated letters are no different than deletions of nonrepeated letters.

In summary, the BLIRNET model may offer a better account of lexical matching than Wickelcoding. However, a series of highly computationally intensive simulations would be required to properly evaluate the predictions of the model regarding the relative similarity of different forms of orthographic neighbours (e.g. transposition versus substitution neighbours), and hence to assess the model's capacity to satisfy the correspondence criteria. In the absence of such simulations, this remains an open question (though one that is worthy of investigation).

An alternative form of local context coding: Open-bigram (OB) coding

As has been seen, the type of local context coding embodied in Wickelcoding is problematic because manipulations such as letter transpositions (which give rise to perceptually similar letter strings) result in a very different set of Wickelcodes. One way to overcome this problem is to relax the contiguity constraint that underlies local context coding schemes like Wickelcoding. This is the key idea underlying open-bigram (OB) coding schemes. In these schemes, a letter string is coded in terms of all of the ordered letter pairs that it contains (Grainger & Van Heuven, 2003; Schoonbaert & Grainger, 2004; Whitney, 2001; Whitney & Berndt, 1999). For example, the word *clam* would be coded by the set {*cl*, *ca*, *cm*, *la*, *lm*, *am*}, while its transposition neighbour *calm* would be coded by the set {*ca*, *cl*, *cm*, *al*, *am*, *lm*}. It can be noted that these two sets are very similar, sharing five out of six OBs; the only bigram that differs is that which codes for the (contiguous) transposed letters. This high degree of overlap suggests that this type of scheme will be successful in explaining the perceptual similarity of transposition neighbours.

Two slightly different versions of OB coding have been proposed. In the version of OB coding that is used in the SERIOL model (Whitney, 2001; Whitney & Berndt, 1999), bigram units are associated with continuous activities, and these activities code information about both letter position and letter contiguity. In the version of OB coding proposed by Grainger and Van Heuven (2003) (see also Schoonbaert & Grainger, 2004), OB units are associated with binary patterns of activation. Thus, in the case of *clam*, the units *cl*, *ca*, *cm*, *la*, *lm*, and *am* would each have activities of 1, while all other bigram units would be coded by activities of 0. In this version, OB units are activated only for letter pairs that are contiguous or separated by one or two letters (for example, the unit *cm* is activated by the word *clam*, but not by the word *claim*). As we shall see below, the two versions of OB coding make some slightly different empirical predictions.

Does OB coding satisfy the seven correspondence criteria?

OB coding is reasonably successful at explaining anagram similarity. It correctly predicts the dissimilarity of reversed word pairs like *wolf* and *flow*, because such pairs do not share any OBs (which are defined as left-to-right ordered letter pairs). It also correctly predicts that transposition neighbours are more similar than substitution neighbours. As already noted, the transposition neighbours *clam* and *calm* share five out of six OBs; by contrast, the substitution neighbours *clam* and *cram* share only three out of six OBs (*ca*, *cm*, and *am*). OB coding also correctly predicts that nonadjacent transposition neighbours are more similar than double substitution neighbours (for example, *stale* and *slate* share six out of nine OBs, whereas *stale* and *space* share only two out of nine).

Furthermore, OB coding correctly predicts that neighbours once-removed are more similar than double substitution neighbours, thereby satisfying criterion 5. For example, *stop* and *soup* share three out of six of their bigrams (i.e. *so*, *sp*, and *op*), whereas double-substitution neighbours like *stop* and *snap* share only a single OB (*sp*).

OB coding can also explain the similarity of addition and deletion neighbours. For example, *plane* shares all nine of its OB codes with its addition neighbour *planet*, and likewise *lower* shares all nine of its OB codes with its addition neighbour *flower*. Interestingly, though, OB coding (like Wickelcoding) predicts smaller match values for pairs that involve outer overlap. For example, *plane* shares only five out of nine of its OB codes with its deletion neighbour *pane*. As noted already, the (limited) data available show a trend in the opposite direction, such that word pairs involving outer overlap are the most similar perceptually (Davis & Perea, submitted, 2005; Davis & Taft, 2005). A further problem concerns the effect of deleting repeated versus unrepeated letters: OB coding predicts that deleting a repeated letter (such as one of the *A*s in *balance*) should result in a closer match to the original letter string than deleting a unique letter (such as the *N* in *balance*). Schoonbaert and Grainger (2004) showed that this prediction is incorrect (see Davis, submitted, for further details).

Some problems for OB coding

The above considerations demonstrate that OB coding can successfully satisfy criteria 1, 2, 4, 5, and possibly 7 (notwithstanding problems relating to the pattern of position of overlap effects and of unique versus repeated letter deletions). However, consideration of the remaining criteria reveals some problems for this type of coding scheme. In particular, OB coding fails to satisfy criterion 3, as it incorrectly predicts that nonadjacent transposition neighbours, like *slate* and *stale*, are *more* similar than substitution neighbours like *slate* and *slave*. This prediction contradicts the pattern observed by both Davis and Bowers (2005) and Perea and Lupker (2004). The reason for this prediction is that a single letter substitution is relatively disruptive to an OB code (for example, changing an internal letter of a seven-letter word changes five OBs), whereas reversal of nonadjacent letters is rather less disruptive. It is unclear how this prediction could be altered by any straightforward modification to OB coding.

OB coding also has a problem in satisfying criterion 6, according to which substitution neighbours should result in greater match values than neighbours once-removed. The problem is that substitution neighbours like *stop* and *shop* share the same three (out of six) bigrams as neighbours once-removed like *stop* and *soup* (i.e. *so*, *sp*, and *op*). The reason for this is that the *so* OB is activated by both *stop* and *soup*. The specific predictions made by the two forms of OB coding differ: the coding scheme proposed by Grainger and colleagues predicts that substitution neighbours and neighbours once-removed are equally similar, whereas the scheme proposed by Whitney (2001) predicts that neighbours once-removed like *stop* and *soup* are more similar than substitution neighbours like *stop* and *shop* (the reasons for this prediction are discussed by Davis & Bowers, 2006). However, both predictions are violated by experimental evidence suggesting that SN pairs are more similar than N1R pairs (Davis & Bowers, 2006). Once again, the reason for the incorrect prediction reflects a fundamental aspect of OB coding, namely, its claim that letter contiguity is not a critical factor in the determination of perceptual similarity. It remains to be seen whether a modified version of OB coding can address criterion 6 more successfully.

In summary, OB coding satisfies five of the seven perceptual correspondence criteria. This is better than position-specific coding schemes or Wickelcoding. However, its failure to account for the greater similarity of substitution neighbours relative to neighbours once-removed indicates a basic problem related to this scheme's insensitivity to letter contiguity. Furthermore, its prediction regarding the relative similarity of substitution neighbours and nonadjacent transposition neighbours (which is in the opposite direction to the observed effect) points to another problem regarding the model's ability to predict the relative effect of letter substitutions and transpositions.

Letter units are position- and context-independent

The conclusions to be drawn from the above review of the problems with existing coding schemes can be stated quite simply. The first conclusion is that letter units are position-independent. For example, the visual word-recognition system does not rely on a unit that codes the letter *A* in position 2 in order to code words like *cat* and *man*. The second conclusion is that letter units are context-independent. For example, the visual word-recognition system does not rely on a unit that represents "A after C" to code *cat* and a distinct unit that represents "A after M" to code *man*. One interpretation of the conclusion that letter units are both position- and context-independent could be that the basic units of orthographic input coding are mental *symbols* of the form posited by Fodor's (1975) representational theory of mind.

It is interesting to note that a similar conclusion regarding the importance of context-independent representations has been drawn in other domains (e.g. Bowers, 2002). Context-independent categories are critical for rule-based systems. In Hummel and Holyoak's (1997) model of analogical access, for example, the use of context-independent representations is critical to allowing successful analogies (for example, the concept TAIL is coded by the same unit whether in the context of a cat or a dog, enabling the model to encode the similarity of the concepts CAT and DOG, and facilitating the ability to make analogies and draw logical inferences). Bowers (2002) also notes that the assumption of context-specific representations leads to implausible empirical predictions; for example, that "it should be possible to find a person with a semantic disorder who has difficulty in conceiving of a DOG in some contexts (e.g. The DOG liked the CAT), but not others (e.g. the CAT liked the DOG)" (p. 434).

Spatial coding: An alternative form of orthographic input coding

The conclusion that letter nodes are position- and context-independent raises a fundamental question concerning how to encode information about the order of the letters in a string across such units. A solution to this problem is offered by the SOLAR (self-organizing lexical acquisition and recognition) (Davis, 1999) model, which uses an alternative type of orthographic input coding scheme, called spatial coding. This scheme assumes an orthographic input level comprising position-independent letter units. Activity at this level codes information about relative (rather than absolute) letter position. The relative order of the letters in a string is coded by the relative activity of the letter nodes (Figure 8.1). This approach has its origins in Grossberg's (1978)

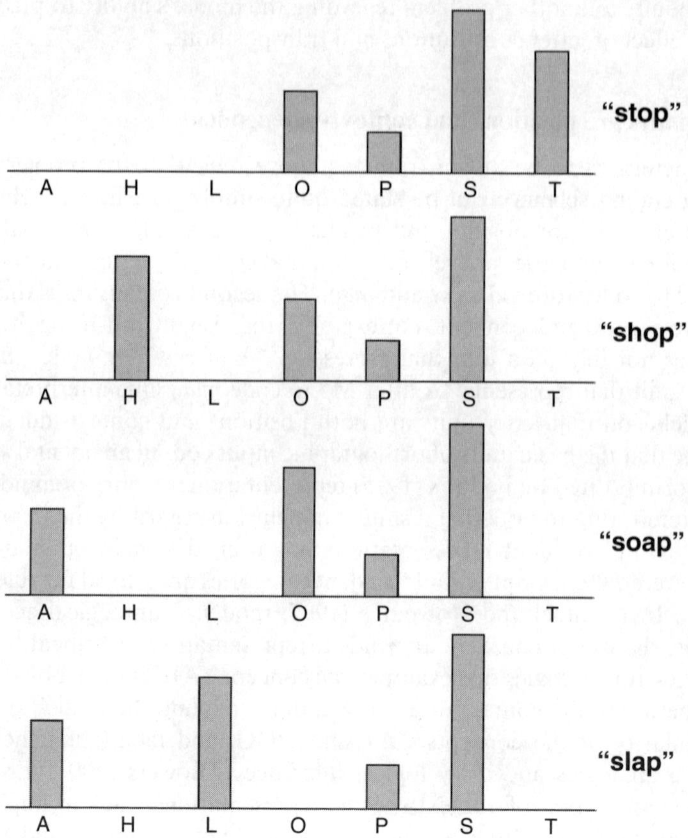

Figure 8.1 Examples of spatial coding for the words STOP, SHOP, SOAP, and SLAP.

use of spatial patterns to encode temporal input sequences; more recently, similar coding schemes have been employed by Page (1994) in a model of melody perception and by Page and Norris (1998) in their primacy model of serial recall. This type of coding implies that each possible letter string is coded by a unique spatial activity pattern. However, letter strings that share common letters are coded by relatively similar spatial codes, even if the common letters are found in different serial positions. In the SOLAR model, each word detector computes its input by calculating the match between two spatial codes: (1) the spatial code corresponding to the word represented by this detector, and (2) the spatial orthographic code corresponding to the input stimulus. A match score is calculated by evaluating the degree of pattern overlap among these two spatial codes. It should be noted that the calculation does not rely on a standard dot-product; that is, it is not the case that later letters (which are coded by smaller values) play a less important role in the match calculation. Furthermore, a letter that is common to the two codes contributes to the match calculation even if it occurs in different serial positions in the input stimulus and the word coded by the word detector. A program for computing these match values (as well as the match values for the other schemes described in this chapter) can be downloaded from the following website: www.maccs.mq.edu.au/~colin/

Some advantages of spatial coding are illustrated by the examples shown in Figure 8.1. As can be seen, the codes for the substitution neighbours *stop* and *shop* are quite similar: There is perfect overlap in the codes for the letters *S*, *O*, and *P*. The codes for the neighbours once-removed *stop* and *soap* are also quite similar: Again, there is overlap in the codes for the letters *S*, *O*, and *P*, although the overlap is not perfect this time, because the magnitude of activity in the *O* unit differs slightly in the two codes. However, the codes for double-substitution neighbours *stop* and *slap* are less similar, because they overlap for only two letters. Thus, the spatial codes for N1R pairs like *stop* and *soap* are *more* similar than the codes for N2R pairs like *stop* and *slap*, but *less* similar than the codes for SN pairs like *stop* and *shop*, which is consistent with criteria 5 and 6. A more detailed account is beyond the scope of the present review chapter, but the reader is referred to Davis (submitted) for a quantitative analysis of these predictions, including a detailed description of the way in which match calculations can be performed with spatial codes. That paper also demonstrates that spatial coding, when combined with an appropriate method for computing matches, satisfies all seven of the perceptual correspondence criteria discussed here.

In conclusion, the present review of experimental evidence pertaining to orthographic input coding indicates that readers utilize a code in which letters are not tied to specific positions or contexts. This code is sensitive to both the relative position of letters and to the contiguity of letters. This poses a challenge to the input coding schemes that are used in current computational models of word identification. The spatial coding scheme, which explains how letter order can be encoded across a set of position- and context-independent letter units, offers a promising alternative (Davis, submitted, 1999). This scheme also suggests a number of novel predictions concerning orthographic similarity effects. To offer just a single example, the model predicts that anagrams which preserve letter contiguity are more similar to their base word than anagrams which do not (for example, that *ichr* is closer to *rich* than is *ihrc*; by contrast, OB coding schemes predict that *ichr* and *ihcr* are equally similar to *rich*). Future research testing such predictions should help to elucidate the exact nature of the orthographic input code used by skilled readers.

References

Andreas, B. G., & Deutsch, E. (1965). Processes of verbal memorization revealed in correct and erroneous recall of words and paralogs. *Psychonomic Science, 2*, 381–382.

Andrews, S. (1996). Lexical retrieval and selection processes: Effects of transposed-letter confusability. *Journal of Memory and Language, 35*, 775–800.

Andrews, S. (1997). The effect of orthographic similarity on lexical retrieval: Resolving neighborhood conflicts. *Psychonomic Bulletin and Review, 4*, 439–461.

Bowers, J. S. (2000). In defense of abstractionist theories of repetition priming and word identification. *Psychonomic Bulletin and Review, 7*, 83–99.

Bowers, J. S. (2002). Challenging the widespread assumption that connectionism and distributed representations go hand-in-hand. *Cognitive Psychology, 45*, 413–445.

Bowers, J. S., Bub, D. N., & Arguin, M. (1996). A characterization of the word superiority effect in a case of letter-by-letter surface alexia. *Cognitive Neuropsychology, 13*, 415–442.

Bowers, J. S., Davis, C. J., & Hanley, D. A. (2005a). Automatic semantic activation of embedded words: Is there a "hat" in "that"? *Journal of Memory and Language, 52*, 131–143.

Bowers, J. S., Davis, C. J., & Hanley, D. A. (2005b). Interfering neighbours: The impact of novel word learning on the identification of visually similar words. *Cognition, 97*, 45–54.

Carreiras, M., Perea, M., & Grainger, J. (1997). Effects of the orthographic neighborhood in visual word recognition: Cross-task comparisons. *Journal of Experimental Psychology: Learning, Memory, and Cognition, 23*, 857–871.

Chambers, S. M. (1979). Letter and order information in lexical access. *Journal of Verbal Learning and Verbal Behavior, 18*, 225–241.

Coltheart, M. (1981). Disorders of reading and their implications for models of normal reading. *Visible Language, 15*, 245–286.

Coltheart, M., Davelaar, E., Jonasson, J. T., & Besner, D. (1977). Access to the internal lexicon. In S. Dornic (Ed.), *Attention and performance VI* (pp. 535–555). New York: Academic Press.

Coltheart, M., Rastle, K., Perry, C., Langdon, R., & Ziegler, J. (2001). DRC: A dual route cascaded model of visual word recognition and reading aloud. *Psychological Review, 108*, 204–256.

Davis, C. J. (1999). *The self-organising lexical acquisition and recognition (SOLAR) model of visual word recognition* (doctoral dissertation, University of New South Wales, 1999). *Dissertation Abstracts International, 62(1-B)*, 594 (www.maccs.mq.edu.au/~colin).

Davis, C. J. (submitted). *A Model of Orthographic Input Coding and Lexical Matching*. Manuscript submitted for publication.

Davis, C. J., & Bowers, J. S. (2004). What do letter migration errors reveal about letter position coding in visual word recognition? *Journal of Experimental Psychology: Human Perception and Performance*, *30*, 923–941.

Davis, C. J., & Bowers, J. S. (2005). *How is letter position coded?: Further evidence for a spatial coding model*. Paper presented at the XIVth meeting of the European Society for Cognitive Psychology, Leiden, 31 August–4 September.

Davis, C. J., & Bowers, J. S. (2006). Contrasting five theories of letter position coding. *Journal of Experimental Psychology: Human Perception & Performance*, *32*, 535–557.

Davis, C. J., & Coltheart, M. (2002). Paying attention to reading errors in acquired dyslexia. *Trends in Cognitive Sciences*, *6*, 359–361.

Davis, C. J., & Lupker, S. J. (2006). Masked inhibitory priming in English: Evidence for lexical inhibition. *Journal of Experimental Psychology: Human Perception & Performance*, *32*, 668–687.

Davis, C. J., & Perea, M. (2005, submitted). *Re(de)fining the orthographic neighbourhood: Evidence for the similarity of addition and deletion neighbours in Spanish*.

Davis, C. J., & Taft, M. (2005). More words in the neighborhood: Interference in lexical decision due to deletion neighbors. *Psychonomic Bulletin and Review*, *12*, 904–910.

De Moor, W., & Brysbaert, M. (2000). Neighborhood-frequency effects when primes and targets are of different lengths. *Psychological Research*, *63*, 159–162.

Drews, E., & Zwitserlood, P. (1995). Morphological and orthographic similarity in visual word recognition. *Journal of Experimental Psychology: Human Perception and Performance*, *21*, 1098–1116.

Estes, W. K., Allmeyer, D. H., & Reder, S. M. (1976). Serial position functions for letter identification at brief and extended exposure durations. *Perception and Psychophysics*, *19*, 1–15.

Fodor, J. A. (1975). *The language of thought*. New York: Thomas Y. Crowell.

Forster, K. I., Davis, C., Schoknecht, C., & Carter, R. (1987). Masked priming with graphemically related forms: Repetition or partial activation? *Quarterly Journal of Experimental Psychology*, *39A*, 211–251.

Forster, K. I., & Hector, J. (2002). Cascaded versus noncascaded models of lexical and semantic processing: The *turple* effect. *Memory and Cognition*, *30*, 1106–1116.

Forster, K. I., & Shen, D. (1996). No enemies in the neighborhood: Absence of inhibitory neighborhood effects in lexical decision and semantic categorization. *Journal of Experimental Psychology: Learning, Memory, and Cognition*, *22*, 696–713.

Grainger, J. (1990). Word frequency and neighborhood frequency effects in lexical decision and naming. *Journal of Memory and Language*, *29*, 228–244.

Grainger, J., & Jacobs, A. M. (1996). Orthographic processing in visual word recognition: A multiple read-out model. *Psychological Review*, *103*, 518–565.

Grainger, J., O'Regan, J. K., Jacobs, A. M., & Segui, J. (1989). On the role of competing word units in visual word recognition: The neighborhood frequency effect. *Perception and Psychophysics*, *45*, 189–195.

Grainger, J., & Segui, J. (1990). Neighborhood frequency effects in visual word recognition: A comparison of lexical decision and masked identification latencies. *Perception and Psychophysics*, *47*, 191–198.

Grainger, J., & Van Heuven, W. J. B. (2003). Modeling letter position coding in printed word perception. In P. Bonin (Ed.), *The mental lexicon*. New York: Nova Science.

Grainger, J., Granier, J. P., Farioli, F., Van Assche, E., & van Heuven, W. (in press). Letter position information and printed word perception: The relative-position priming constraint. *Journal of Experimental Psychology: Human Perception and Performance*.

Guerrera, C. (2004). *Flexibility and constraint in lexical access: Explorations in transposed-letter priming*. Unpublished dissertation, Department of Psychology, University of Arizona.

Harm, M. W., & Seidenberg, M. S. (1999). Phonology, reading acquisition, and dyslexia: Insights from connectionist models. *Psychological Review*, *106*, 491–528.

Hummel, J. E., & Holyoak, K. J. (1997). Distributed representations of structure: a theory of analogical access and mapping. *Psychological Review*, *104*, 427–466.

Huntsman, L. A. (1998). Testing the direct-access model: GOD does not prime DOG. *Perception and Psychophysics*, *60*, 1128–1140.

Jacobs, A. M., Rey, A., Ziegler, J. C., & Grainger, J. (1998). MROM-p: An interactive activation, multiple readout model of orthographic and phonological processes in visual word recognition. In J. Grainger & A. M. Jacobs (Eds.), *Localist connectionist approaches to human cognition* (pp. 147–188). Mahwah, NJ: Lawrence Erlbaum Associates, Inc.

Johnson, R. L., Rayner, K., & Perea, M. (2005, submitted). *Transposed-letter effects in reading*.

Johnston, J. C. (1978). A test of the sophisticated guessing theory of word recognition. *Cognitive Psychology*, *10*, 123–153.

Jordan, M. I. (1986). *Serial order: A parallel distributed processing approach*. No. 8604, ICS Technical Report. University of California at San Diego, La Jolla, CA.

Kucera, H., & Francis, W. N. (1967). *Computational analysis of present day American English*. Providence, RI: Brown University Press.

Lupker, S. J., Perea, M. & Davis, C. J. (in preparation, 2006). *Letter position encoding of consonants and vowels*.

Masson, M. J., & Bodner, G. E. (2003). A retrospective view of masked priming: Toward a unified account of masked and long-term repetition priming. In S. Kinoshita & S. J. Lupker (Eds.), *Masked priming: The state of the art* (pp. 57–94), Hove, UK: Psychology Press.

McClelland, J. L. (1976). Preliminary letter identification in the perception of words and nonwords. *Journal of Experimental Psychology: Human Perception and Performance*, *2*, 80–91.

McClelland, J. L., & Mozer, M. C. (1986). Perceptual interactions in two-word displays: Familiarity and similarity effects. *Journal of Experimental Psychology: Human Perception and Performance*, *12*, 18–35.

McClelland, J. L., & Rumelhart, D. E. (1981). An interactive activation model of context effects in letter perception. I. An account of basic findings. *Psychological Review*, *88*, 375–407.

McConkie, G. W., & Zola, D. (1979). Is visual information integrated across successive fixations in reading? *Perception and Psychophysics*, *25*, 221–224.

Mewhort, D. J., Campbell, A. J., Marchetti, F. M. & Campbell, J. L. (1981). Identification, localization and "iconic memory". *Memory and Cognition*, *9*, 50–67.

Mozer, M. C. (1983). Letter migration in word perception. *Journal of Experimental Psychology: Human Perception and Performance*, *9*, 531–546.

Mozer, M. C. (1991). *The perception of multiple objects: a connectionist approach*. Cambridge, MA: MIT Press.

O'Connor, R. E., & Forster, K. I. (1981). Criterion bias and search sequence bias in word recognition. *Memory and Cognition*, *9*, 78–92.

Page, M. P. A. (1994). Modelling the perception of musical sequences with self-organizing neural networks. *Connection Science: Journal of Neural Computing, Artificial Intelligence and Cognitive Research*, *6*, 223–246.

Page, M. P. A., & Norris, D. (1998). The primacy model: A new model of immediate serial recall. *Psychological Review*, *105*, 761–781.

Pelli, D. G., Farell, B., & Moore, D. C. (2003). The remarkable inefficiency of word recognition. *Nature*, *413*, 752–756.

Perea, M., & Pollatsek, A. (1998). The effects of neighborhood frequency in reading and lexical decision. *Journal of Experimental Psychology: Human Perception and Performance*, *24*, 767–777.

Perea, M., & Lupker, S. J. (2003a). Transposed-letter confusability effects in masked form priming. In S. Kinoshita & S. J. Lupker (Eds.), *Masked priming: The state of the art*. Hove, UK: Psychology Press.

Perea, M., & Lupker, S. J. (2003b). Does jugde activate COURT? Transposed-letter confusability effects in masked associative priming. *Memory and Cognition*, *31*, 829–841.

Perea, M., & Lupker, S. J. (2004). Can CANISO activate CASINO? Transposed-letter similarity effects with nonadjacent letter positions. *Journal of Memory and Language*, *51*, 231–246.

Perea, M., Gómez, P., & Ratcliff, R. (2003). *A model of encoding letter positions: The overlap model*. Paper presented at the 12th congress of the European Society for Cognitive Psychology, September, Granada, Spain.

Perea, M., Rosa, E., & Gómez, C. (2005). The frequency effect for pseudowords in the lexical decision task. *Perception and Psychophysics*, *67*, 301–314.

Peressotti, F., & Grainger, J. (1999). The role of letter identity and letter position in orthographic priming. *Perception and Psychophysics*, *61*, 691–706.

Pinker, S., & Prince, A. (1988). On language and connectionism: Analysis of a PDP model of language acquisition. *Cognition*, *28*, 73–193.

Plaut, D. C., McClelland, J. L., Seidenberg, M. S., & Patterson, K. (1996). Understanding normal and impaired word reading: Computational principles in quasi-regular domains. *Psychological Review*, *103*, 56–115.

Rastle, K., & Coltheart, M. (1998). Whammies and double whammies: The effect of length on nonword reading. *Psychonomic Bulletin and Review*, *5*, 277–282.

Rayner, K., Well, A. D., & Pollatsek, A. (1980). Asymmetry of the effective visual field in reading. *Perception and Psychophysics*, *27*, 537–544.

Rodd, J. (2004). When do leotards get their spots? Semantic activation of lexical neighbours in visual word recognition. *Psychonomic Bulletin and Review*, *11*, 434–439.

Rumelhart, D. E. (1970). A multicomponent theory of the perception of briefly exposed visual displays. *Journal of Mathematical Psychology*, *7*, 191–218.

Rumelhart, D. E., & McClelland, J. L. (1982). An interactive activation model of context effects in letter perception. II. The contextual enhancement effect and some tests and extensions of the model. *Psychological Review*, *89*, 60–94.

Rumelhart, D. E., & McClelland, J. L. (1986). On learning the past tenses of English verbs. In D. E. Rumelhart & J. L. McClelland (Eds.), *Parallel distributed processing, Vol. 2: Explorations in the microstructure of cognition* (pp. 216–271). Cambridge, MA: MIT Press.

Schoonbaert, S., & Grainger, J. (2004). Letter position coding in printed word perception: Effects of repeated and transposed letters. *Language and Cognitive Processes, 19*, 333–367.

Segui, J., & Grainger, J. (1990). Priming word recognition with orthographic neighbors: Effects of relative prime-target frequency. *Journal of Experimental Psychology: Human Perception and Performance, 16*, 65–76.

Seidenberg, M. S., & McClelland, J. L. (1989). A distributed, developmental model of word recognition and naming. *Psychological Review, 96*, 523–568.

Shallice, T., & McGill, J. (1978). The origins of mixed errors. In J. Requin (Ed.), *Attention and performance VII* (pp. 193–208). Hillsdale, NJ: Lawrence Erlbaum Associates, Inc.

Taft, M., & van Graan, F. (1998). Lack of phonological mediation in a semantic categorization task. *Journal of Memory and Language, 38*, 203–224.

Whitney, C. (2001). How the brain encodes the order of letters in a printed word: The SERIOL model and selective literature review. *Psychonomic Bulletin and Review, 8*, 221–243.

Whitney, C., & Berndt, R. S. (1999). A new model of letter string encoding: simulating right neglect dyslexia. *Progress in Brain Research, 121*, 143–163.

Wickelgren, W. A. (1969). Auditory or articulatory coding in verbal short-term memory. *Psychological Review, 76*, 232–235.

Zorzi, M., Houghton, G., & Butterworth, B. (1998). Two routes or one in reading aloud? A connectionist dual-process model. *Journal of Experimental Psychology: Human Perception and Performance, 24*, 1131–1161.

Notes

1 Note that the order in which these features are listed is arbitrary; for example, {*top*, *op#*, *#st*, *sto*} is an equivalent set.

2 Although this experiment did not find a difference between transposition neighbour primes and identity primes, this does not imply that transposition neighbours are as similar as identical pairs (clearly, it is possible to distinguish transposition neighbours, even if it may be relatively difficult sometimes). One finding that is relevant here is Andrews' (1996) observation of inhibitory (rather than facilitatory) effects of lexical transposition neighbour primes in a speeded naming task (for example, the prime *calm* inhibited responses to the target *CLAM*). Furthermore, Johnson et al. (submitted, 2005) have recently reported that parafoveal preview of a transposition neighbour of the next word in a sentence resulted in longer fixation durations than preview of the word itself.

3 The worst-case scenario is the coding scheme employed by Grainger and Jacobs (1996), in which the assumption of both position- and length-specificity implies that an entirely different set of letter units is used to encode addition and deletion neighbours (for example, *draw* and *drawl* do not share any common letter units in this scheme).

9 Changing circumstance: How flexible is lexical access?

Chris Davis
Department of Psychology, University of Melbourne, Australia

Jeesun Kim
Graduate School of Education, Sejong University, Seoul, South Korea

We can do a lot with words. Reading a word can trigger a poignant recollection of things past. A word can fascinate us because of the way it sounds or even looks. A word can delight us because of the way it fits a context so perfectly. It is clear that we can be extremely flexible in the way that we process words. In this chapter, we pose the question of whether this processing flexibility extends to all aspects of word processing. Specifically, we focus on the basic process of word recognition and review evidence and arguments about the extent to which factors such as context, task requirements, and participant expectancies play a role. Below we describe how even for the highly specified domain of word recognition the issue of the interaction of cognition, memory and perception is important. We consider two approaches:

(1) A traditional view, in which word recognition is based upon stable, abstract representations and involves inflexible processes that are set off automatically.
(2) A view in which word recognition and general memory phenomena are based upon common underlying mechanisms.

This latter view has been developed with reference to the straightforward notion that recognition "depends not only on our learning experiences with similar things in the past but also on the context in which the recognition attempt is being made" (Bodner & Masson, 2001, p. 616). We conclude that the initial stage of word recognition appears remarkably stable (a property that fits more with the traditional view) but point out that there is a need for models of the whole word identification process to take account of context, task, and decision effects (here we direct the reader to the chapter by *Balota & Yap*, this volume).

Studying a complex system

Although skilled reading can be minimally described in terms of simply decoding print into meaning, the process of achieving this surely involves the operation and marshalling of a wide and complex range of processes and strategies. How, then, to study this complex, potentially interactive, system? "Special purpose computation: All is not one", the title of Forster's commentary on Fodor (1985), provides a pithy summary of one approach. In his article, Forster proposed that language processing can be usefully conceived of in terms of separate levels of processing that are characterized by different types of operations across the various stages of processing. These various stages were presumed to involve different domains of knowledge and different processing procedures. Given that these processes are separate, it is simply up to researchers to show ingenuity in devising suitable measurement techniques to tap the domain of interest.

A modular lexicon

The notion of domain-specific processing is a core concept in cognitive science. This idea has had a strong influence on reading research, as typically the achievement of an automatic, autonomous word-recognition process is taken to be the end point of reading development (see *Castles & Nation*, this volume). Although there are differences in opinion as to what properties might best capture the essence of modularity (see Coltheart, 1999), most word-recognition models distinguish between processes relating to word recognition per se (driven by the input) and decision/task processing. Indeed, even when modelling lexical processing where context makes a radical difference (as for bilinguals processing different languages), the assumption of a distinction between an encapsulated word-identification system and a task/decision system is standard (e.g. Dijkstra & van Heuven, 2002).

The notion that the initial stage of word recognition is modular is almost axiomatic. However, as *Forster* (this volume) has pointed out, it is sometimes useful to question dominant assumptions so that new ideas about information processing might emerge. Recently, Masson and Bodner (2003) have proposed a general account of information retrieval that attempts to explain memory and perception within a common framework (Jacoby, 1983; Jacoby & Dallas, 1981). As this proposal blurs the distinction between perception and memory, Masson and Bodner have noted that their view might appear radical or even absurd; it could be pointed out, however, that such an impression is likely to be generated by any position that presents an alternative view to an established orthodoxy.

The view that Masson and Bodner have presented is that memory and perception are jointly determined by the cues that the stimulus provides at the time of test and those provided by memories of prior episodes (something argued to be seldom consciously recalled). This view is radically different from that in which word recognition is based upon processing of a stable memory representation. For under the former view, processing reflects a conglomeration of memories of all similar episodes recruited by the current stimulus configuration. It is suggested that memory and perception are grounded upon numerous memories for prior episodes. In order to sharpen the contrast between these approaches, we begin by presenting a brief background to these different conceptions about how words might be stored and processed.

As mentioned above, the traditional approach to word recognition views the process in terms of a mapping problem (from a printed form to an abstract memory representation, e.g. Forster, 1989). A corollary of this view is that the process of mapping is handled by a specialized process. The notion that the storage and processing of words might be functionally separate from other types of information processing dates at least as far back as Wernicke (1874). Some 100 years later, the idea of a specialized processor and a separate store of encoded word forms (a lexicon) had become an entrenched approach to word recognition (and linguistic theory; e.g. Collins & Loftus, 1975; Forster, 1976; Kintsch, 1980). This approach attempted to understand complex information processes (be they in the service of speaking, listening, reading, or spelling) through a descriptive, componential analysis of the functional requirements of an information-processing system. This approach suggests a theory of perception that develops and utilizes abstract canonical lexical representations (see Goldinger, 1998, for a discussion of this view).

Why modular?

A basic rationale for assuming that word recognition is carried out by a dedicated modular process has often been made in terms of the benefits that accrue from such an architecture (see Fodor, 1983). The first benefit is that perceptual devices are protected from highly developed inferential systems (central systems) and so can be kept tuned to the environment. The second is that modular construction allows for speed and efficiency, since the range of confirmatory facts needed to verify a perceptual belief is kept to a minimum. One way that processing might be encapsulated is to place constraints on the type of input a system deals with (see Carruthers, 2003). A system can be informationally encapsulated by virtue of a restriction on what it processes. For instance, the classic processing/storage distinction that Tulving (1972) made between semantic and episodic memory has often been appealed to as a basis for a modular word-recognition system. That is, if the word-recognition system is part of a store of factual knowledge (semantic memory) that is separate from the memory of events (episodic memory), then, after a period of initial learning, it could be encapsulated, since it would only need to process ahistoric abstract data. Under this conception, research on word recognition could be conducted independently of that concerned with other aspects of memory (e.g. Lachman & Lachman, 1979).

A feature of this traditional view is a system division that minimized any impact of recent episodes on perceptually driven processes and likewise the extent to which processing could adjust to take advantage of particular environments. When this idea was specifically applied to word recognition, the notion of what it means to be modular has been sharpened to one dealing more with process encapsulation. This view essentially boiled down to a processing module having access only to a database of a particular type (Sperber, 2002). That is, the only stored information that a module can use is information stored in the module itself; it cannot draw on any external information, so the memory systems used to support the processing of the module must be built into the module. A related idea is that processing within a module might be inflexible (that is, a well-formed input triggers processing in the manner of a cognitive reflex). Of course, the process would need to be adaptable enough to encode new representations.

Remembering to be flexible

With this background in hand, let us now consider a challenge to the traditional view of word recognition that has come from models that incorporate episodic information. Goldinger (1998) points out that episodic (or exemplar) theories of memory extend back at least to Semon (1909), who proposed that each experience of a stimulus creates a unique memory trace and the presentation of a new stimulus activates all stored traces to an extent to which each is similar to the presented stimulus. In such models, there is no division between data types, so one might wonder how the issue of efficient information retrieval is handled. Retrieval efficiency would be compromised by mixing episodic and semantic processing only if there was no constraint on how the various aspects of episodic information were accessed and if it were necessary that all information about a word needed to be processed before a decision could be made.

However, it is clear that the storage of specific instances does not necessarily lead to lack of structure. Indeed, through a process of generalization over episodes, episodic information may take on the characteristics of abstract representations (Hintzman, 1986; Tenpenny, 1995). Further, this aspect of storage suggests a principle for how the retrieval of this information might be organized. For example, Hintzman has developed a model in which an input stimulus activates an accumulation of memory traces comprising a weighted average of multiple traces. This weighting, combined with the notion of the decay of individual features over time, has the effect of consolidating information corresponding to central properties because the impact of idiosyncratic information tends to be washed out whereas common information is strengthened. An outcome of this is that frequent information will be most strongly represented. Given that the activation and response of the combined memory trace to an input stimulus takes time, it seems reasonable that the more robust/frequent aspects of a memory trace should be available more rapidly. Such a time course in the retrieval of information would mean that abstract codes will dominate the initial contact of sensory input with memory representations (see Luce, McLennan, & Charles-Luce, 2003; McLennan & Luce, 2005).

The above discussion of the possibility that episodic information might play a role in word recognition sets the scene for a more radical conception of lexical processing which forms the major focus of this review. This proposal is not only that lexical representations store episodic instances, but also that the process of word recognition is malleable and can adapt to processing environments. That is, what is radical about the memory recruitment view developed by Bodner, Masson, and colleagues (and different from strictly instance-based memory accounts) is the proposal that basic word recognition processes can be influenced by the previous context under which the recruitment of processing operations had occurred and that this influence can occur very rapidly. The clearest evidence for this memory-recruitment view comes from the results of masked repetition-priming experiments. Before describing these, we will first briefly describe the logic of repetition priming and the motivation for masked priming.

A measure of processing: The logic of priming

The logic behind the repetition paradigm is straightforward. When a word is repeated in a word-recognition task, its processing is typically facilitated (as measured by accuracy, processing time, or both relative to an all-letter different control). Effects of this kind have been used to make inferences about the properties of the information-processing systems underlying word-recognition performance. The particular interest of the following review of data centres on Masked repetition priming and the variables influencing its occurrence and magnitude. There are a number of versions of masked priming; in this chapter, we will review only experiments that have used a version similar to that employed by Forster and Davis (1984). In this particular technique, a sequence of visual stimuli is presented in rapid succession, each stimulus being superimposed on the previous one. The initial stimulus is a series of hash marks (e.g. ########) whose only purpose is to act as a forward mask. The second stimulus is a lower-case prime, and the third is an upper-case target, which also acts as a backward mask. The initial forward mask and the target (backward mask) are clearly visible, and are typically displayed for a period of approximately 500 ms, whereas the prime is displayed for typically only 50 ms. One of the critical differences between this and other version of masked priming is that in this version the target is clearly displayed.

Forster and Davis (1984) introduced the masked priming paradigm partly in response to the finding by long-term repetition priming (where a response is made to both the prime and the target, and the lag between them might be several seconds) that the standard word frequency effect is attenuated. This frequency-attenuation effect suggested that processes of word recognition could be changed by a single encounter, and this challenged the idea of a stable lexicon. Forster and Davis suggested that the frequency-attenuation effect might be a by-product of episodic influences on long-term repetition priming and so masked the prime and radically restricted prime processing time by presenting the target immediately after. Forster and Davis found that masked priming effects were short-lived, that there was no masked priming for nonwords, and that high- and low-frequency words produced equal-sized priming. These results are consistent with the assumption that the influence of masked primes is mediated through the automatic access of stable lexical information. These results and interpretation have become the focus of several studies that have produced divergent results (see Masson & Bodner, 2003, for review).

Given that the motivation for the development of masked priming was to minimize any episodic influence of the prime on the target, the use of masked priming by Bodner and Masson to support their memory-recruitment account is striking. Based on the results of masked priming, Bodner and Masson have proposed that word recognition is not achieved via the activation of a dedicated word-recognition mechanism but that word recognition and general memory phenomena are based upon common underlying mechanisms (e.g. Bodner & Masson, 2001, 2004). Bodner and Masson propose that the processes underlying word recognition (even in masked conditions) cannot be separated from other information-processing operations, that is, memory processes. They point out that a memory-recruitment account allows for flexibility in the basic process that produces priming.

The result used to support this account is that the masked repetition-priming effect is bigger for items in a block that include a larger proportion (.8) of repetition trials than for items in a block containing a low proportion (.2) of repetition trials. This "prime validity effect", as Bodner and Masson call it, has been found in the lexical decision and naming tasks (Bodner & Masson, 1997, 2004). These results suggest that the process of word recognition, even at a basic level, is flexible and, as Bodner and Masson (2004) point out, has "significant consequences for theories of visual word recognition". In what follows, we present a selective review of a number of unpublished masked priming experiments which we suspect might help specify the boundaries of the memory recruitment view.

The basis of masked priming: The relationship between the prime, the target, and the task

The first (unpublished) experiments that we review were selected because they provide an understanding of the basis of masked priming, which is the tool we will be using to probe the character of the word-recognition system. The following two experiments make a simple point about masked priming: Priming relies on there being a connection between the information conveyed by the prime and the task that is carried out on the target.

These simple demonstrations of masked priming consist of two parallel masked priming experiments that differed only in the task instructions given to participants. The stimulus materials in both experiments were exactly the same: Each item consisted of the standard masked priming sequence: a forward mask (a set of hash marks, displayed for 570 ms), a lower-case prime word or nonword (displayed for 50 ms) that was followed immediately by an upper-case target word or nonword (displayed for 570 ms). Half of the targets also had very small squares placed at random above or below them (Figure 9.1). Half of the primes were repetition primes (lower-case versions of the target words or nonwords) and half were control primes (all-letter different words or nonwords). The tiny squares appeared only with the target items, not the primes. Two versions of the item lists were prepared, so that across the versions all targets appeared with either a repeated or a control prime. One experiment was a standard masked priming experiment in which participants were asked to classify targets as words or nonwords, a lexical decision task (LDT) (no mention was made of the tiny squares that were sometimes presented). In the other experiment, the task was whether the target (word or nonword) contained a square or not. Fourteen participants were run in each task.

This set of experiments was designed to demonstrate that masked priming will occur only when the target task draws on information that has been previously processed by the prime. That is, repetition priming should occur in the LDT, and not the square task, because in the square task the critical task-related information has not been presented in the prime. The results are shown in Table 9.1.

For the LDT, there was a masked repetition priming effect for the word targets (36-ms priming), $F_1(1,13) = 30.92$, $p < .05$. For the nonword target in the LDT, there was an 8-ms effect in the priming direction, but this was not significant, $F_1(1,13) = 1.42$, $p > .05$. For the square detection task, there was no priming; $F_1 < 1$ for both the words and nonword targets. The LDT shows the standard results for this type of experiment, a robust priming effect for the word targets, and no significant priming for the nonword targets

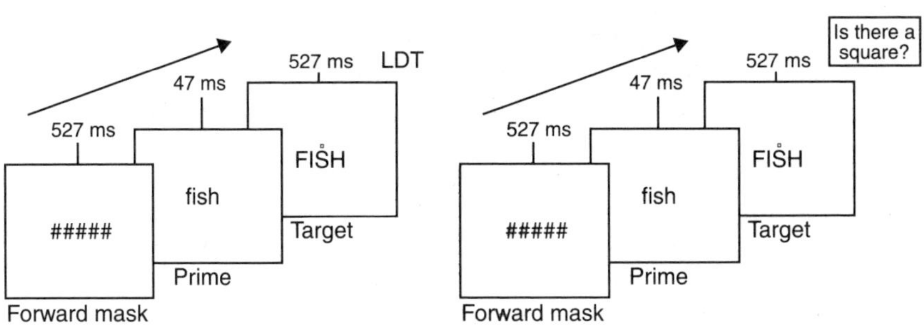

Figure 9.1 The setup of the standard lexical decision task (LDT) and square detection task.

Table 9.1 Mean response latencies (ms) for the lexical decision and square detection tasks for word and nonword targets

Lexical decision task		*Square detection task*	
Target and prime type	*RT (ms)*	*Target and prime type*	*RT (ms)*
Word repeated	544	Word repeated	458
Word control	580	Word control	458
Amount of priming	36	Amount of priming	0
Nonword repeated	610	Nonword repeated	455
Nonword control	618	Nonword control	450
Amount of priming	8	Amount of priming	–5

RT: response time.

(although see Masson & Bodner, 2003, for a review of nonword priming results).

The explanation for the lack of priming when the task is square detection is straightforward. There is no priming simply because the prime does not provide the participants with any information that is relevant to detecting the square. This shows that the mere repetition of some element in a display (the word and nonword primes and targets) does not produce a bias to respond faster overall; the critical ingredient is whether work done of the prime is RELEVANT to the target decision.

Given this analysis, why, then, was there no priming for repeated nonwords in lexical decision (because, at the letter level, the information from primes and targets was repeated)? Following the logic outlined above, it would appear that letter-level information is not relevant to making a LDT. This interpretation in terms of task relevance is given support by the finding that, after altering the target task from lexical decision to one of detecting a letter in the target (that is, is there an "s" in the target "FISH"), masked letter priming does occur whether the target is a word or a nonword (Davis, 1990). This analysis of the lack of masked nonword repetition priming fits in with the idea that the processing of different types of information (letters, strings of letters, etc.) is functionally independent (if letter processing blended with that involved in making a lexical decision, nonwords should show masked priming).

There is of course an alternative explanation for the lack of nonword priming in the LDT, and we will return to reasons for the lack of such priming after the discussion of the following experiments. For the moment, however, we wish to follow up on the priming effect that was found for the word stimuli (in the LDT). In trying to get a grip on the nature of masked priming, it seems useful to consider whether producing a masked priming effect is a general property of all words, or whether different vocabulary types produce different size effects. The experiments that we will consider below examined masked repetition priming contrasting words of high and low concreteness and open- and closed-class words. One reason for examining the variable of word type is that factors such as concreteness and the specification of referent have been found to have a strong influence in explicit memory tasks (see Paivio, 1971). Finding that different types of words showed different-sized masked priming effects would raise significant issues for the view that the initial stage of word recognition is largely driven by the input and indifferent to the particulars of information content.

Davis (1990) conducted an experiment that was designed to determine whether abstract and concrete words produce different-sized masked priming effects. This manipulation is interesting in terms of the notion of the prime providing a processing resource for the retrieval of the target. This is because the concreteness effect in LDT, that is, slower lexical decisions to low- than to high-concrete words, has also been interpreted in terms of context availability (Schwanenflugel, Harnishfeger, & Stowe, 1988). That is, Schwanenflugel et al. presumed that high- and low-concrete words differ in terms of information content and that contextual information is less readily available for words of low concreteness, and so these words are classified as words more slowly because additional information needs to be extracted from the lexical representation. If a masked prime can act as a processing resource to help retrieve the target, then low-concrete words would be expected to benefit more than high-concrete ones; that is, concreteness and priming should interact.

The experiment used the masked priming method described above and contrasted 30 high-concrete word targets (Toglia & Battig, 1978) (semantic norm M = 6.7) and 30 low-concrete targets (semantic norm M = 2.9). Sixteen participants were tested, eight in each of two counterbalanced versions. The results are shown in Table 9.2. First, there was a main effect of concreteness, with the high-concrete words more accurately classified as words than the low, $\min F'(1,60) = 7.60$, $p < .005$. The high-concrete word targets attracted a 40-ms priming effect compared to a 31-ms effect for the low-concrete words. The interaction between priming and word type was not significant, $F < 1$. The pattern of data for the errors differed slightly from that for the latencies, the priming effect apparently only occurring for low-concrete words. However, there was no significant interaction between concreteness and prime type, $F_1(1,14) = 2.18$, $p > .05$; $F_2(1,56) = 1.94$, $p > .05$.

Davis (1990) also contrasted a more striking difference in word type; that is, the distinction between elements of the major lexical categories (noun, verb, and adjective) and elements of the minor lexical categories (auxiliary, such as *have* and *were*; determiner, such as *the*; preposition, such as *to* and *by*; quantifier, such as *most*). Following Bradley and Garrett (1983), these subsets will be referred to as the open and closed classes, respectively. If the priming effect is related in some way to the meaning of primes and targets, it might be expected that the open and closed classes would produce

Table 9.2 Mean lexical decision times (ms) and percentage of error (E) rates for word and nonword targets as a function of concreteness and prime type

Item type	*Example*	*RT*	*%E*
High-concrete word			
Identity	rice/RICE	511	4.2
All-letter-different	spin/RICE	551	4.2
Priming		40	0
Low-concrete word			
Identity	wish/WISH	562	11.7
All-letter-different	sand/WISH	593	17.0
Priming		31	5.3
Nonwords			
Identity	deat/DEAT	607	7.1
All-letter-different	lume/DEAT	614	9.2
Priming		7	2.1

RT: response time.

different-sized priming effects, since these item types differ so radically in meaning (not only are there differences with respect to the specification of referents between the classes but also open-class forms are likely to be ambiguous in their grammatical category, whereas for the closed-class forms this is less common).

The details of the experiment were similar to those described above; 16 participants and 30 stimuli of each class were tested. The results are presented in Table 9.3. The pattern of the data was very similar to the previous experiment; that is, a variable (form class), which affected lexical decision latencies, min$F'(1,56) = 4.23$, $p < .05$, and did not interact with the priming effect, which was itself significant; min$F'(1,45) = 23.19$, $p < .001$. Patterns in the error data roughly followed that of the latency data. There were, on average, 3.5% fewer errors made on the open-class words than on the closed class; however, this failed to be significant in the item analysis, $F_1(1,14) = 5.16$, $p < .05$; $F_2(1,56) = 3.51$, $p > .05$. Fewer errors were made on identity-primed words than on control-primed words, min$F'(1,53) = 3.10$, $p < .10$. However, the interpretation of this main effect is complicated by the presence of an interaction, with the closed-class words showing a larger error reduction when primed than the open-class words, min$F'(1,67) = 2.90$, $p < .10$. One reason for this interaction is that there was a floor effect; that is, so few errors were made on the high-frequency open-class words (in the all-letter-different control condition) that there just was not room for improvement in the identity condition.

Once again there was no masked priming effect shown by the nonword

Table 9.3 Mean lexical decision times (ms) and percentage of error (E) rates for word and nonword targets as a function of form class and prime type

Item type	*Example*	*RT*	*%E*
Open-class word			
Identity	work/WORK	455	3.3
All-letter-different	snow/WORK	495	4.2
Priming		40	0.9
Closed-class word			
Identity	such/SUCH	473	3.8
All-letter-different	hear/SUCH	514	10.8
Priming		41	7.0
Nonwords			
Identity	nool/NOOL	544	7.9
All-letter-different	desh/NOOL	550	5.0
Priming		6	–2.9

RT: response time.

targets. In summary, the results (at least for latencies) have shown that the masked priming effect is unaffected by vocabulary type even for a cut as dramatic as that between the open- and closed-class vocabularies.

It was suggested above that the lack of nonword masked repetition priming (shown in all of the experiments described above) could be explained in terms of the sources over which the target recruits information for use in coming to a decision. That is, the relevant level of information over which to make a lexical decision is at the level of the lexical entry, not at the letter level. However, there is another explanation of the failure to observe masked nonword repetition priming. Bodner and Masson (1997) and Bowers and Kouider (2003) have argued that the apparent lack of nonword priming in the LDT might be because participants take the processing fluency induced by a masked repetition prime as evidence in favour of a WORD response. In this case, generating a correct response to masked repetition-primed nonword targets would require additional time to overcome the tendency to misclassify such targets and hence wash out the (perceptual fluency-based) priming effect. In the next (unpublished) experiment that we review, the issue of nonword priming and decision conflict is addressed. This experiment also investigates the type of information that is able to support priming.

The following experiment examined the circumstances in which repeated primes and targets (words and nonwords) produce masked priming. The experiment used the standard masked priming procedure but employed a task in which participants were asked to decide on the number of syllables in a target item (which were either monosyllable or disyllabic). This particular, rather artificial, task was employed to address a specific issue: Whether masked priming would occur for judgements that might not be automatically triggered by the input (the masked prime) but required additional processing in order to arrive at an answer. Consider the nonword "pook": The fact that it is monosyllabic is not immediately apparent but seems to require some reflection. Given this, would "pook" prime "POOK" in the syllable number task? We outlined above a simple idea, that priming would not occur unless the information processed by the prime was used in the target decision. According to this idea, repeated nonwords (such as pook/POOK) should only prime if the presentation of the masked prime (pook) was able to trigger processing that led to the determination of whether it had one or two syllables. In describing their view of masked priming, Bodner and Masson (2004) state that "[t]his view begins with the assumption that any processing operations applied to a prime, whether the prime is masked or not, are encoded into a new memory resource" (p. 3), and this might be taken to suggest that a priming effect should be expected for words in the syllable number task (presumably, it would also be expected for nonword targets that were repetition primed as well). This task also should overcome the proposed use of perceptual fluency (due to prime-target repetition) as a guide to how to respond, since an item's familiarity in no way relates to whether it is mono- or disyllabic.

The results of the experiment are presented in Table 9.4. There was a repetition priming effect for the words, $F(1,21) = 5.5$, $p < 0.05$, but not for nonword targets, $F(1,21) = 1.2$, $p > 0.05$. This is interesting because the lexical status of the target was not relevant to the decision. However, response times for correct classified word targets were faster than those for the nonwords, $F(1,21) = 12.55$, $p < 0.05$.

This evidence of lexical support in making the decision is consistent with the idea that participants develop a pronunciation of the target in order to carry out the task. Retrieving the lexical entry presumably assists in doing this. Given that this lexical recruitment assists in making the decision, a repetition effect should be observed. Of course, in the case of nonwords, that lexical support never comes, so the decision rests wholly upon an analysis of

Table 9.4 Mean response times (RT) (ms) and percentage of error (E) rates for the syllable number task as a function of prime type (collapsed over monosyllabic and disyllabic responses)

Target and prime type	*RT*	*E (%)*
Word repeated	592	10
Word control	614	14.5
Amount of priming	22	4.5
Nonword repeated	633	10.1
Nonword control	640	10.4
Amount of priming	7	0.3

the structural properties of the item. However, in this case, the appropriate analysis generated on the basis of the prime does not appear to be transferred to the making of the decision on the nonword target. In the syllable number task, it seems unlikely that the lack of a priming for nonwords was due to participants having a bias that counteracts the improved perceptual processing of the nonwords. It appears, then, that masking the prime limits the degree to which a prime can be processed. In the case of a word, this does not impose a necessary limitation because information about the word has been previously stored. In the case of a nonword, this limitation might restrict the opportunity for the prime to have already processed information that is relevant to making a decision on the target.

We close this section with a brief summary. The data of experiments reviewed above lend support to the view that priming depends upon the existence of a lexical entry, rather than upon the type of information represented within the entry. Priming was vocabulary-general in that all types of words, despite substantial variations in content and form class, showed priming; but it was also vocabulary-specific, in the sense that it occurred only for words in the vocabulary, and not for nonwords. The results of the final experiment suggested that the lack of nonword priming might be due to nonword primes not being able to contact previously stored information that could then assist in nonword target processing.

The prime–target relationship and task

Recent cross-language priming experiments by Kim and Davis (2003) suggest that the size of masked priming can be modulated by more than simply whether a lexical entry exists or not. Masson and Bodner (2003) have suggested that demonstrations that masked priming is contextually sensitive are consistent with the notion that masked priming is based on recruitment of a form of memory for a briefly presented prime event. In the following section, we outline what Kim and Davis found and what this might indicate about the early stages of word recognition.

Kim and Davis used masked cross-language priming and three different target-processing tasks, LDT, naming, and semantic classification. The primes were all presented in Hangul (the Korean alphabetic script), and the targets were presented in English. All of the participants were Korean university students who had learned English in secondary school. As well as the three different tasks, three different prime–target relationships were tested: repeated phonology and semantics ("cognate" translation equivalents); repeated phonology but different semantics (interlingual homophones), and finally repeated semantics but different phonology ("non-cognate" translation equivalents).

The results showed that there was an across-task dissociation in the semantic and phonological priming effects (that is, there was noncognate translation priming in all but the naming task, and interlingual homophone

Table 9.5 Summary of the cross-language masked priming results of Kim and Davis (2003); Yes indicates significant cross-language priming; No indicates no effect. It is clear that the pattern of priming varies as a function of task

Prime–target relationship	*Naming task*	*Lexical decision task*	*Semantic categorization task*
Semantic + phonological + (cognate)	Yes	Yes	Yes
Semantic + phonological – (noncognate	No	Yes	Yes
Semantic – phonological + (interlingual homophone)	Yes	No	No

Primes and targets that had a (+) semantic relationship were translation equivalents. Primes and targets that had a (+) phonological relationship were selected to sound approximately the same. In all conditions, primes were in Korean (Hangul) and targets were in English.

priming only in the naming task (see Table 9.5 for a summary). This change in the size of priming effects as a function of prime–target relationship and task does fit with a memory-recruitment interpretation. That is, in the naming task, only masked primes that provided an appropriate phonological resource (cognates and interlingual homographs) were recruited for the task of naming the target. In semantic classification, the relevant resource was the semantic overlap between the prime and the target, and so on. Describing the outcome with a memory-recruitment framework is straightforward. Indeed, it appears to be almost a prediction of this approach, as Bodner and Masson (2001) have proposed that recruitment of masked prime episodes will be more likely to occur when prime and target processing overlap in some task-relevant fashion.

How might this "context" sensitivity in masked priming be explained in a framework in which priming occurs due to automatic prime processing? In explaining why the size of masked homophone priming was modulated by the type of nonword targets included in their experiment, Ferrand and Grainger (1996) proposed that such contextual effects can be accounted for in terms of how automatically computed prime information is used in making a decision on the target. A similar point was made by Forster (1998), who noted that the effect of context can be due to altered task conditions whereby information from an automatically processed prime is ignored because of changes in the way the target decision is made.

This account takes us back to the argument on why there was no priming in the square detection task. However, now the situation is slightly more complicated. It was obvious that the task of detecting the square had nothing to do with whether the prime was processed or not. To explain the lack of semantic priming in the naming task (Kim & Davis, 2003, experiment 2), we must presume that the common prime and target meaning had nothing to do with naming the target. The same goes for the semantic classification task, where it was found that the same sounding primes and targets had no effect on performance. To explain these results, then, an initially automatic word-recognition system would need to interface with a more flexible task/decision system in which the major readout codes selected for the semantic categorization task were semantic and in the naming task were phonological (necessary for articulation). This framework fits with the general approach of *Balota and Yap* (this volume). Indeed, when considering Ferrand and Grainger's proposal (above), Bodner and Masson (2001) have pointed out that the inclusion of such a decision system would be "consistent with the more general idea that the influence of a masked prime may be variable and dependent on processing operations that occur after the prime event has transpired" (p. 64). Thus, it might be that such an approach offers a way that different views of word recognition can begin to be reconciled.

The convergence of prime and target processing

Having considered the manner in which masked priming is generated and having discussed what this suggests about the information base that is used to support task decisions, we now move on to consider the degree to which masked priming might be influenced by the manner in which primes and targets are related and the predictability of the prime–target context. In describing why there was no repeated masked priming effect for nonwords in the syllable number task (above), we suggested that masking the prime limited the degree to which a prime could be processed and that for nonword primes the requisite information relevant to deciding upon syllable number could not be reliably extracted. For words, however, we suggested that all that was necessary for the relevant information to be available was for a prime to be able to contact its appropriate entry. The following experiment (Davis & Kim, under revision) was motivated by an attempt to investigate further the circumstances in which repeated primes and targets might not be expected to lead to a priming effect. As just mentioned, one circumstance might be when the prime and target do not have pre-existing representations (i.e. nonwords). However, more interestingly, a word prime might not prime a repeated target if it was not processed rapidly enough (or automatically), so that its representation was not accessed in time to affect the response to the target.

The way Davis and Kim implemented this for word primes and targets was to alter the stimulus presentation of both so that a nonautomatic process was required before the word could be identified. That is, both prime and target words were presented written in reversed order (starting from the right and proceeding left; for example, the word "FACE" was written as "ECAF"). Since both the prime and target were reversed, participants first needed to read the target from right to left and then perform a LDT on what resulted. If, as assumed above, masking limits the operations that can be performed on the prime, no priming effect would be predicted. It is not clear what the memory recruitment view might predict. In setting out this view, Bodner and

Masson have often pointed to what they called the "mere exposure effect", in which they suggest that episodes can be formed for very briefly presented stimuli (Boder & Masson, 2001; Masson & Bodner, 2003). Given this, one might imagine that any sort of record of the prime could prove useful in dealing with a repeated target.

As it turned out, there was no priming for either the repeated word items (ecaf/ECAF) or nonword items (emap/EMAP). There was, however, substantial priming from word primes that were presented in the standard fashion (face/ECAF), but once again, there was no priming from nonword primes that provided the solution to the initial reversing operation (pame/EMAP). What is interesting in these results is that even though primes should be useful in making a target decision, priming was robust only when the prime was a word presented in its usual format. This finding fits nicely with the view that the initial stages of the word-recognition system are automatic yet rather inflexible. If one adopts a memory recruitment view, the null finding for repeated primes and targets suggests interesting limits to the type of processing that can be done on a masked prime when forming a processing resource.

Masked priming and context

Can short-term learning have a prolonged influence on the initial word recognition process? Once again we collected evidence with the masked priming paradigm (this experiment was carried out by Sylvia Thalmeier from our laboratory). This experiment consisted of a learning phase in which participants were required to learn a specific rule (for example, every time you see the * symbol, replace it with the letter "a"). Participants were instructed to read aloud words and nonwords and replace the asterisk symbol with the letter "a" (e.g. W*TCH, D*RK, FL*F, G*TCH). There were 34 words and 34 nonwords for the learning phase. Each word or nonword was shown one at a time. Participants who had gone through the list once were then presented with each item again (in random order). On the first trial, participants correctly named the words in an average of 670 ms and made 5.3% errors. The nonwords were named slightly slower, 791 ms, but attracted about the same percentage of errors (5.1%). On the second trial, the words were named 90 ms faster and with 2.1% fewer errors. The nonwords were also named faster (by 109 ms and with 1.9% fewer errors).

Following this learning phase, participants (109 first-year students) made lexical decisions to targets preceded by different masked primes. These targets were mask primed by stimuli that should lead to differential priming effects if the learning of the rule influenced priming. That is, learning the "* = a" rule, should have led to more priming for b*ll/BALL primes and targets than in a group of participants who did not receive this training (for example, a third of the participants learnt another rule and the other third no rule at all). It was found that even though participants could explicitly use the learned rule (in training and after the experiment), this had no effect on priming.

Another method of examining whether the basic processes of word recognition (as indexed by masked priming) can be influenced by context is to directly manipulate the extent to which the prime information is informative about the target decision. This is one of the major research strategies that Bodner and Masson have used to argue for the flexibility of lexical processing. As outlined above, they have presented evidence that the size of masked repetition priming can be modulated by the proportion of repeated trials in an experiment (more priming when there are a higher proportion of repeated items in the experiment). We were interested in charting the limits of this effect, and so the following experiment (run by Mairead Dundas from our laboratory) was designed to gauge the sensitivity of masked priming to large changes in the proportion of repeated primes and targets in an experimental list.

Unlike the design of Bodner and Masson, this experiment was set up in order to be able to contrast exactly the same item set under two different list environments. To do this, we contrasted two masked priming experiments. These experiments consisted of what we will call the filler items, exactly the same 78 words and 78 nonword targets. In the first experiment, the primes for these filler items consisted of half repeated and half nonrepeated items (0.50 related). In the second experiment, there were no repeated primes and targets (0.0 related). In both experiments, after the filler items, there was the same set of 48 items (12 repeated and 12 unrelated control word primes; 12 repeated and 12 unrelated control nonword primes). These identical final item sets provided the crucial measure of priming because these remained constant across the two experiments. We will refer to this final set of items as the *critical set*, for it is this set that is used to compare priming effects across the different experiments. Within each experiment, two versions of the list were created so that each target was preceded by each prime type (repeated or control) without repeating a target within a list.

The results of the experiment are shown in Table 9.6. For response latencies,

Table 9.6 Response latencies (ms) and percentage of errors (E) to word targets as a function of prime type for the two repetition-priming context groups

Item type	*RT*	*%E*
No previous repetition		
Repeated	485	5.4
Control	515	12.9
Priming	30	6.5
50% previous repetition		
Repeated	477	7.2
Control	513	9.2
Priming	36	2.0

RT: response time.

there was an overall priming effect, $F_1(1,46) = 46.35$, $p < .05$. In the 50% related condition, the priming effect for the critical words was 36 ms and in the 0% related condition, the priming effect for the critical words was 30 ms. There was no interaction between the size of these priming effects ($F_s < 1$). What is interesting about this experiment is that it shows that the relationship between the primes and targets of the filler items (the previous context) had very little impact (statistically none) on the amount of priming shown by the critical items, although in the no-relationship list the fillers contained no repeated items at all.

The reason for not finding a prime validity effect is unclear. Bodner and Masson (2001) have also reported failures to find an effect of prime validity. They suggested that a null effect might be generated due to variations in item-processing difficulty. Specifically, it was suggested that in cases where there was marked variability in target processing, as between processing high-frequency words and pronounceable nonwords, the processing system may rely on the recruitment of prime resources for all trials. The current experiment did use relatively high-frequency word targets (the frequency of occurrence was 50–150 occurrences per million, M = 78; Kucera & Francis, 1967), and the nonwords were pronounceable. However, a system which relied on prime recruitment when processing 156 consecutive targets in which none of the primes were related (in the unrelated filler experiment) does not appear to be particularly adaptive. This highlights a problem with the Bodner and Masson position; not only does it need to explain why there was no differential sensitivity to the proportion of repeated primes and targets in an experiment (prime validity), but it also needs to explain why there was any reliance on masked primes at all (why there was priming).

Recently, Kinoshita, Forster, and Mozer (2005) have proposed an account of the prime validity effect that explains the effect in terms of sensitivity of speeded responses to the difficulty of recent trials (what they call an adaptation to the statistics of the environment (ASE) account). In essence, they propose, on the one hand, that repeated primes speed up in easy processing environments (such as those containing a large number of repeated primes) because the criterion of when to respond adapts to the environment. On the other hand, they show that the response to targets preceded by control primes does not adapt. This difference between repeated and control primes targets in sensitivity to task difficulty appears as an increase in priming under easy processing conditions. This account applies to the decision-making processes, and so, like the explanations by Ferrand and Grainger (1996) and Forster (1998) described above, it does not bring into question the presumed automaticity and/or inflexibility of the initial process of word recognition. That is, the proposal is entirely independent of assumptions about what generates masked priming. As such, the same general mechanism is not required to account for both priming and prime validity effects. For instance, the ASE account could describe the lack of an effect of different proportions of masked primes in terms of the processing environment required to promote more rapid responding to the primed targets, but this explanation does not have to simultaneously account for the priming effect in the 0% repetition filler list.

Conclusion

We began by considering two quite different conceptions of the lexicon and lexical processing: The traditional view, in which word recognition is subserved by stable, abstract word representations that are triggered automatically by appropriately configured input stimuli, and the view in which word recognition and general memory phenomena are based upon common underlying mechanisms.

It is clear that at some point in perceptual-cognitive analysis the perceptual input representing a word can be interpreted with enormous subtlety and flexibility by reference to past experience. What is surprising is that the view that Bodner and Masson have developed was based on data (from masked priming) that most likely have more to do with the initial stages of the word-recognition process. To this end, the current view sought to revisit some basic phenomena of masked priming and to see whether these hint at an adaptable and flexible process.

Taken as a whole, our review suggests that the initial stage of word recognition as indexed by masked priming is remarkably stable. For instance, the same-sized masked priming effects occurred across dramatic cuts in vocabulary type, and the recognition system did not adapt to produce priming from primes that had the potential to enable target processing to get a head start (for example, repeated nonwords and the repeated primes in the right-to-left LDT experiment). Likewise, masked repetition priming was the same magnitude whether no previous repeated primes and targets had been encountered or whether many had been. In sum, masked priming appears to tap a system whose main function is to identify perceptual inputs. For the highly developed skill of word recognition, this process (at least initially) seems largely driven by the input and the contact that this makes with previously stored, functionally abstract information.

The challenge for the view that memory and perception are highly interactive at all levels is to explain how perceptual stability within the word-recognition system is maintained. In essence, this issue touches on a key problem for nonstationary models of pattern recognition: How to allow the process of recognition to learn new information yet also remain stable in response to irrelevant information. Grossberg (1987) argues that coping with these divergent properties requires that a recognition system learns prototypes that represent invariants within the set of experienced input patterns. Such prototypes might develop from agglomerations of episodic instances, yet the trick is that, once formed, these need to be stable. In a recent investigation of spoken word recognition, McLennan and Luce (2005) have demonstrated that abstract codes appear to predominate when processing is fast. This finding is consistent with the view that the initial processes of mapping an input to a memory representation are rapid because they have been repeatedly established over nonidiosyncratic properties (a property that fits with a modular process). It should not be forgotten, however, that ultimately the recognition-decision process in its entirety needs to be adaptable; thus, the characterization of how context, task, and decision systems interact with more basic systems is essential. This is where more large-scale overviews (such as that suggested by *Balota & Yap*, this volume) will be useful.

References

Andrews, S. (1989). Frequency and neighborhood effects on lexical access: Activation or search? *Journal of Experimental Psychology: Learning, Memory, and Cognition, 15*, 802–814.

Bodner, G. E., & Masson, M. E. J. (1997). Masked repetition priming of words and nonwords: Evidence for a nonlexical basis for priming. *Journal of Memory and Language, 37*, 268–293.

Bodner, G. E., & Masson, M. E. J. (2001). Prime validity affects masked repetition priming: Evidence for an episodic resource account of priming. *Journal of Memory and Language, 45*, 616–647.

Bodner, G. E., & Masson, M. E. J. (2004). Beyond binary judgments: Prime validity modulates masked repetition priming in the naming task. *Memory and Cognition, 32*, 1–11.

Bowers, J. S., & Kouider, S. (2003). Developing theories of priming with an eye on function. In J. S. Bowers & C. S. Marsolek (Eds.), *Rethinking implicit memory* (pp. 41–64). New York: Oxford University Press.

Bradley, D. C., & Garrett, M. F. (1983) Hemisphere differences in the recognition of closed and open class words. *Neuropsychologia, 21*, 155–159.

Carruthers, P. (2003). On Fodor's problem. *Mind and Language, 18*, 502–523.

Collins, A. M., & Loftus, E. F. (1975). A spreading-activation theory of semantic processing. *Psychological Review, 82*, 407–428.

Coltheart, M. (1999). Modularity and cognition. *Trends in Cognitive Sciences, 3*, 115–120.

Davis, C. (1990). *Masked priming in word recognition*. Unpublished PhD thesis, Monash University.

Davis, C., & Kim, J. (under revision). The basis of masked priming in word judgment tasks.

Dijkstra, A., & Van Heuven, W. J. B. (2002). The architecture of the bilingual word recognition system: From identification to decision. *Bilingualism: Language and Cognition, 5*, 175–197.

Ferrand, L., & Grainger, J. (1996). List context effects on masked phonological priming in the lexical decision task. *Psychonomic Bulletin and Review, 3*, 515–519.

Fodor, J. A. (1983). *The modularity of the mind*. Cambridge, MA: MIT Press.

Fodor, J. A. (1985). Precis of the modularity of mind. *Behavioral and Brain Sciences, 8*, 1–46.

Forster, K. I. (1976). Accessing the mental lexicon. In R. J. Wales & E. Walker (Eds.), *New approaches to language mechanisms* (pp. 257–287). Amsterdam: North-Holland.

Forster, K. I. (1985). Special purpose computation: All is not one. *Behavioral and Brain Sciences*, *8*, 9–11.

Forster, K. I. (1989). Basic issues in lexical processing. In W. Marslen-Wilson (Ed.), *Lexical representation and process* (pp. 75–107). Cambridge, MA: MIT Press.

Forster, K. I. (1998). The pros and cons of masked priming. *Journal of Psycholinguistic Research*, *27*, 203–233.

Forster, K. I., & Davis, C. (1984). Repetition priming and frequency attenuation in lexical access. *Journal of Experimental Psychology: Learning, Memory, and Cognition*, *10*, 680–698.

Goldinger, D. (1998). Echoes of echoes? An episodic theory of lexical access. *Psychological Review*, *105*, 251–279.

Grossberg, S. (1987). Competitive learning: From interactive activation to adaptive resonance. *Cognitive Science*, *11*, 23–63.

Hintzman, D. L. (1986). "Schema abstraction" in a multiple-trace memory model. *Psychological Review*, *93*, 411–428.

Jacoby, L. (1983). Perceptual enhancement: Persistent effects of an experience. *Journal of Experimental Psychology: Learning, Memory, and Cognition*, *9*, 21–38.

Jacoby, L., & Dallas, M. (1981). On the relationship between autobiographical memory and perceptual learning. *Journal of Experimental Psychology: General*, *110*, 306–340.

Just, M. A., & Carpenter, P. A. (1987). *The psychology of reading and language comprehension*. Boston, MA: Allyn and Bacon.

Kim, J., & Davis, C. (2003). Task effects in masked cross-script translation and phonological priming. *Journal of Memory and Language*, *49*, 484–499.

Kinoshita, S., Forster, K., & Mozer, M. C. (2005). *Prime validity effects reflect adaptation to the statistics of the environment*. Paper presented at the 32nd Australasian Experimental Psychology Conference, University of Melbourne, Australia, April 2005.

Kintsch, W. (1980). Learning from text, levels of comprehension, or: Why anyone would read a story anyway. *Poetics*, *9*, 87–98.

Kucera, H., & Francis, W. N. (1967). *Computational analysis of present day American English*. Providence, RI: Brown University Press.

LaBerge, D., & Samuels, S. J. (1974). Toward a theory of automatic information processing in reading. *Cognitive Psychology*, *6*, 293–323.

Lachman, J., & Lachman, R. (1979). Theories of memory organization and human evolution. In C. R. Puff (Ed.), *Memory organization and structure* (pp. 134–190). New York: Academic Press.

Luce, P. A., McLennan, C., & Charles-Luce, J. (2003). Abstractness and specificity in spoken word recognition: Indexical and allophonic variability in long-term repetition priming. In J. S. Bowers & C. S. Marsolek (Eds.), *Rethinking implicit memory* (pp. 197–214). New York: Oxford University Press.

Masson, M. E. J., & Bodner, G. E. (2003). A retrospective view of masked priming: Toward a unified account of masked and long-term repetition priming. In S. Kinoshita & S. J. Lupker (Eds.), *Masked priming: The state of the art* (pp. 57–94). New York: Psychology Press.

McLennan, C., & Luce, P. A. (2005). Examining the time-course of indexical specificity effects in spoken word recognition. *Journal of Experimental Psychology: Learning, Memory, and Cognition*, *31*, 306–321.

Paivio, A. (1971). *Imagery and verbal processes*. New York: Holt, Rinehart and Winston.

Perfetti, C. A. (1992). The representation problem in reading acquisition. In P. B. Gough, L. C. Ehri, & R. Treiman (Eds.), *Reading acquisition* (pp. 145–174). Hillsdale, NJ: Lawrence Erlbaum Associates, Inc.

Rayner, K., & Sereno, S. C. (1994). Eye movements in reading: Psycholinguistic studies. In M. A. Gernsbacher (Ed.), *Handbook of Psycholinguistics* (pp. 57–81). San Diego, CA: Academic Press.

Schwanenflugel, P. J., Harnishfeger, K. K., & Stowe, R. W. (1988). Context availability and lexical decisions for abstract and concrete words. *Journal of Memory and Language*, *27*, 499–520.

Semon, R. (Original work published 1909/1923). *Mnemic psychology* (B. Duffy, Trans.). Concord, MA: George Allen & Unwin.

Sperber, D. (2002). In defense of massive modularity. In E. Dupoux (Ed.), *Language, brain and cognitive development: Essays in honor of Jacques Mehler* (pp. 47–57). Cambridge, MA: MIT Press.

Tenpenny, P. L. (1995). Abstractionist versus episodic theories of repetition priming and word identification. *Psychonomic Bulletin and Review*, *2*, 339–363.

Toglia, M. P., & Battig, W. F. (1978). *Handbook of semantic word norms*. Hillsdale, NJ: Lawrence Erlbaum Associates, Inc.

Tulving, E. (1972). Episodic and semantic memory. In E. Tulving & W. Donaldson (Eds.), *Organization and memory* (pp. 381–403). New York: Academic Press.

Wernicke, K. (1874). *Der aphasiche Symptomencomplex*. Breslau, Germany: Cohn & Weingart.

Whaley, C. P. (1978). Word-nonword classification time. *Journal of Verbal Learning and Verbal Behavior*, *17*, 143–154.

10 Attentional control and the flexible lexical processor: Explorations of the magic moment of word recognition

David A. Balota and Melvin J. Yap
Department of Psychology, Washington University, USA

In studying any behaviour, an initial critical step is to operationalize the targeted behaviour. In the present case, the targeted behaviour is performance on simple word-recognition tasks such as lexical decision and speeded word naming. At one level, this behaviour is deceptively simple to understand. Adult readers have intimate knowledge of this acquired skill. However, as shown in this volume, the processes involved in visual word-recognition tasks are remarkably complex. This should not be surprising because experimental psychologists have been working on this topic for well over 100 years (Cattell, 1890). We believe that at least some of the complexities and controversies in this area are due to a lack of agreement in the theoretical assumptions regarding the targeted behaviour, the specific tasks used to study the behaviour, and the analytic methods used to measure the processes underlying this behaviour. In this chapter, our mission is to attempt to elucidate some of these theoretical assumptions and the methodological approaches to studying word recognition. We will use the influence of meaning on standard word-recognition tasks to guide our discussion, because the theoretical and methodological assumptions are nicely unearthed by considering the influence of this variable.

Measuring the magic moment in word-recognition tasks

A reasonable, yet often implicit, assumption underlying models of visual word-recognition tasks is that there is a *magic moment* in word processing (Balota, 1990), a discrete instant when a reader recognizes a word, but does not yet know its meaning. At first glance, this seems quite reasonable and inherent in most models of pattern recognition; that is, how could one interpret a stimulus unless one has first recognized what that something is? In more technical terms, the magic moment is that instant when *lexical identification* takes place; that is, a lexical representation is sufficiently activated for a response to be executed (Balota, Ferraro, & Connor, 1991). This event unlocks access to meaning. For example, in activation-class models

(Coltheart, Rastle, Perry, Langdon, & Ziegler, 2001; McClelland & Rumelhart, 1981; Morton, 1969), the magic moment is when the activation level for a word detector exceeds some threshold, and lexical identification takes place. In search-class models (Becker, 1980; Forster, 1976; Paap, Newsome, McDonald, & Schvaneveldt, 1982), the magic moment is when there is sufficient overlap between a word's sensory representation and its internal orthographic representation, resulting in successful search/lexical identification.

Assuming there *is* such a magic moment, it is critical that one can measure the processes leading up to this point. Although there are many measures of the magic moment (such as on-line reading measures and perceptual identification), this construct is most typically defined via two major tasks: *lexical decision* and *speeded naming*. In lexical decision, participants are presented with either a real word or a nonword, and the time it takes to make word/nonword binary responses is measured. In speeded naming, participants are presented with words, and the time it takes participants to initiate a vocal response is measured. For both tasks, response latencies are often assumed to reflect word-recognition processes that presumably are decoupled from meaning access, and appear to be relatively immune to attentional control mechanisms (see Coltheart et al., 2001; Murray & Forster, 2004).

However, the notion that lexical decision and naming latencies tap *presemantic* aspects of the presumed word-recognition point is inconsistent with the empirical observation that semantic effects *have* been reliably observed in isolated lexical decision, and to a lesser degree, naming. To the extent that these two tasks are windows into the magic moment of word recognition (if such a moment exists), such a disjunction is indeed puzzling. However, it is increasingly clear that neither lexical decision nor speeded naming reflect a magic moment. There is a basic problem with both paradigms; they measure both word-identification processes and operations that are specific to each task.

Task-appropriate processing and the flexible lexical processor

We believe that it is critical to consider word recognition within a task-appropriate processing framework. This perspective has considerable similarity to the transfer-appropriate processing approach (Morris, Bransford, & Franks, 1977; Roediger, 1990), which has been particularly useful for understanding the effects of variables in the memory domain. Memory researchers have recognized that the influence of a variable strongly depends on the tasks used to tap that variable. For example, although pictures are better remembered than words in a free-recall task, words show greater repetition priming than pictures in a word-fragment completion task (Weldon & Roediger, 1987). Blaxton (1989) demonstrated that, compared to perceptually driven retrieval tasks (e.g. word-fragment completion and graphemic cued recall), conceptually driven retrieval tasks (e.g. free recall, semantic cued recall, and a general knowledge test) produced better memory performance when encoding operations emphasized meaning-based analyses than surface-based analyses, whereas the opposite pattern was obtained for perceptually driven retrieval tasks. The assumption underlying the transfer-appropriate processing perspective is that different memory tasks require different retrieval operations and therefore benefit from different types of processing during encoding. To the extent that there is a match between encoding and retrieval operations, performance is facilitated.

Of course, in language processing, there is a rich tradition of considering modular/dedicated systems that are immune to top-down control systems (Fodor, 1983). We believe that this curse of automaticity has produced the conception of a relatively inflexible lexical processor that emphasizes pre-existing structures and processes. Here we argue that word-recognition tasks, like memory tasks, are modulated via attentional control systems and the processes that are relevant to accomplishing the goals of the task. Just as Jacoby (1991) has argued there are no process-pure measures of memory, we would argue there are no process-pure measures of word recognition. Hence, lexical decisions will be modulated more by variables that aid in discriminating familiar words from unfamiliar nonwords, whereas naming performance benefits from manipulations that emphasize the pathways necessary for mapping orthographic codes onto the phonology used in speech production. Armed with the task-appropriate processing perspective and the notion of a flexible lexical processor, we shall now turn to the search for a magic moment in word-recognition tasks.

Beyond measures of central tendency in measuring the magic moment in word-recognition tasks

Thus far, we have discussed how task-specific characteristics may stymie efforts to measure a simple magic moment. Of course, current mental chronometric methods also make assumptions about factors that may diminish the rate of knowledge accumulation about the underlying processes involved in measuring the magic moment. Consider, for example, the standard experimental paradigm wherein participants are presented with a set of type A words and a set of type B words, such as high- and low-frequency words. If we obtain an effect of frequency on some estimate of central tendency (most typically means) in one of the windows (lexical decision or naming) of the magic moment, then we may assume that we have captured an effect of a variable on the processes leading up to the word-identification processes. Of course, using estimates of central tendency to isolate the influence of processes extends far beyond visual word-recognition tasks and persists across virtually all domains of cognitive psychology.

However, there are at least two aspects of these chronometric assumptions that one may question. First, there is the notion that estimates of central tendency are the best way to measure the influence of a variable on performance in a task. By using the mean as an estimate of the central tendency, one is making the implicit assumption that a variable is shifting the underlying response latency distribution; that is, the distribution of low-frequency words is simply slower by some constant compared to the distribution of high-frequency words. However, the mean of a response time distribution can be influenced by shifting the distribution and/or skewing the distribution. Interestingly, there is even some evidence of trade-offs between the two components, in which case there would be no effect in the means. For example, the congruent condition in the standard Stroop colour-naming task, relative to a neutral baseline condition, simultaneously decreases the modal portion of the response time distribution and increases the slow tail of the distribution. This finding was initially reported by Heathcote, Popiel, and Mewhort (1991), and has since been replicated by Spieler, Balota, and Faust (1996). In this case, there are two distinct effects in the data that are being masked when one uses only measures of central tendency because of opposing influences on the means.

There is a rich literature on measuring the influence of a variable on the shape of underlying response time distributions (see, for example, Luce, 1986). One procedure is to fit an empirical response latency distribution to a theoretical distribution such as the Weibull or ex-Gaussian distribution. With such procedures, one can measure whether a variable is shifting the distribution (as typically assumed) and/or changing the shape of the distribution (e.g. Andrews & Heathcote, 2001; Balota & Spieler, 1999; Spieler, Balota, & Faust, 2000).

An alternative procedure for measuring the locus of an effect is to simply plot the data as a function of Vincentiles (Andrews & Heathcote, 2001; Vincent, 1912). In this procedure, for each participant, one rank orders the response latencies, and then produces a mean for each bin of a given size, such as every 10% of the data. One can then examine the locus of an effect of a variable; that is, is the effect of the variable constant across all Vincentiles or is the effect more localized at the early or late Vincentiles?

For illustrative purposes, we present the data from a recent study collected in our laboratory, which examines the interactive effects of semantic relatedness and visual degradation in a lexical decision task. In this study, visual degradation (clear versus degraded) and semantic relatedness were factorially manipulated to create four conditions, with 75 observations in each condition. As one typically finds in such studies (e.g. Becker & Killion, 1977), the semantic priming effect was larger for degraded items (related = 630 ms; unrelated = 696 ms) than for clear items (related = 545 ms; unrelated = 578 ms). More interestingly, Figure 10.1 plots the semantic priming effect across each of the Vincentiles for the clear and degraded conditions.

As shown in this figure, the effect of semantic priming in the clear condition is constant across the Vincentiles (which is consistent with the notion that priming simply shifts the response time distribution), whereas the interaction between relatedness and degradation primarily occurs at the later

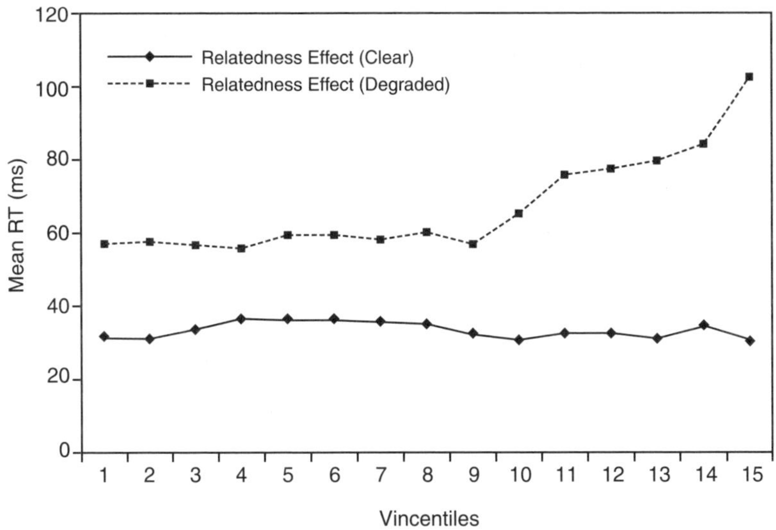

Figure 10.1 Vincentile means of the participant's lexical decision response times (RT) as a function of semantic relatedness and visual degradation.

Vincentiles (suggesting that the interaction is due to a disproportionate skewing of the unrelated degraded distributions). This was also reflected in parameters from the ex-Gaussian analyses, wherein the interaction between degradation and relatedness was mediated more by the Tau parameter (reflecting distributional skewing) than by the Mu parameter (reflecting distributional shifting). Models such as the multiple read-out model (Grainger & Jacob, 1996) and Ratcliff, Gomez, and McKoon's (2004) recent model of lexical decision performance are ideally suited for testing the influence of variables on characteristics of the underlying response latency distributions. It will also be particularly illuminating to test other models, such as the PDP model of lexical decision (Plaut, 1997) and the dual-route cascaded model of word naming (Coltheart et al., 2001), at the level of response time distributions. The important point here is that with the increasing sophistication of the extant models, it is time to increase the sophistication of the analytic tools used to test the models.

Another assumption that most models of mental chronometry make is that the influence of most variables ends at a decision point wherein participants initiate a relatively dumb ballistic response (see Logan & Cowan, 1984, for a discussion of the point of no return). This latter ballistic response is simply an additive constant above and beyond the interesting processes that ended at the decision point. Hence, one can use the triggering of an electronic microswitch as an accurate terminal marker of the processes leading to the initiation of the response, that is, the magic moment. However, even this assumption has qualifications. Although the triggering of a microswitch measures important temporal requirements of targeted processes, such measures tap only a *single* point in the information-processing stream (Balota & Abrams, 1995), and do not capture mental operations that may extend beyond response onset. For example, there is evidence that some lexical influences persist *after* response initiation (Abrams & Balota, 1991; Balota & Abrams, 1995). In these studies, participants made lexical decisions by moving a joystick handle rapidly to the right for words and to the left for nonwords. Hence, one can measure both the initiation of the response and the dynamics (e.g. acceleration, peak force, duration) of the response after the response has been initiated. One would argue that the initiation of the response is related to the magic moment, as typically conceived, and hence variables that influence the processes tied to recognition processes should terminate at the onset of the response. However, the results from these studies indicated that word frequency influenced the force of the response after response initiation. Hence, frequency effects extend beyond the assumed decision point in lexical decision, and so the magic moment is not so clearly discernible. Similarly, in speeded naming, word frequency has been shown to influence both the onset and the production duration of pronunciation responses (see Balota & Abrams, 1995). Clearly, the kinematic aspects of responses *after* the response has been initiated can be influenced by a lexical-level variable like word frequency. Classic models of word recognition assume that variables (e.g. word frequency) influence word-identification processes up to the point when a response is initiated (i.e. the magic moment); this assumption is simply inconsistent with the post-initiation effects observed.

It is also interesting to consider how binary decision processes such as lexical decision may be realized in the neural hardware. Are decisions that produce overt behaviour driven by relatively localized neural tissue or a large ensemble of interconnected networks? Is there a common neural decision system for lexical decision and semantic classification, or do different binary tasks engage different neural ensembles for each type of binary decision? Answers to such questions could provide some insight into the appropriate model. Interestingly, in a recent review that examined the neural correlates of decision making, Schall (2003) found support for at least two neural processes that drive simple decision processes. Neurons in sensorimotor structures accumulate evidence via a diffusion process (Smith & Ratcliff, 2004), while other neurons prepare and initiate overt movements. Importantly, these two processes can be dissociated, supporting the view that evidence accumulation and response production are formally dissociable at the neuro-anatomical level. Coupled with the preceding discussion on post-initiation frequency effects, this suggests that variables such as word frequency could actually be influencing both the decision-making stage and the response stage at the neural level. While it is as yet unclear how one might implement such effects, models of word identification will ultimately need to consider how the brain engages such decision processes and ultimately how the same system enables the overt responses.

The observations reviewed in this section highlight how some of the methodological assumptions regarding the locus of an effect of a variable on response latencies appear to be limited. These assumptions do not simply constrain the inferences drawn from studies of processes involved in word recognition, but also apply to chronometric studies in other domains of psychology. The results reviewed in this section question the basic assumption of chronometric studies; that there is a point in time when a lexical representation's threshold is reached, at which point a response is executed. In fact, there may not be any discrete moment when word identification takes place. Rather, lexical processing may reflect a more continuous, cascadic flow of information, where experimental variables can influence early identification, decision, and late post-decision processes (McClelland, 1979), depending upon the goals of the task (i.e. the task-appropriate processes).

Meaning-level influences in isolated word-recognition tasks: Some of the initial evidence, and possible concerns

Armed with the above considerations and the potential limitations in any measure of lexical identification, we shall now turn to the literature concerning meaning-level influences on lexical identification processes. Again, the critical question here is whether meaning provides a top-down influence during word-recognition tasks (Coltheart et al., 2001; Harm & Seidenberg, 2004), or whether the processes up to the presumed magic moment mandatorily precede access to meaning (Becker, 1980; Morton, 1969). Of course, it is again important to remember that "word recognition" is operationalized here by the influence of meaning on isolated word naming or lexical decision tasks, the primary tasks used to constrain the available models of word recognition. Hence, one must keep in mind the caveats presented earlier about the task constraints. Meaning-level characteristics are operationalized by variables such as *concreteness* (the degree to which a word refers to an object, material or person), *imageability* (the degree to which a word generates mental imagery; Cortese & Fugett, 2004), and *meaningfulness* (the degree to which a word evokes associates and other words; Toglia & Battig, 1978). However, as described later, more recent notions of semantic memory have indicated that additional measures, such as network *connectivity* (how interconnected a word is to other words; Steyvers & Tenenbaum, 2005), may also be useful to consider.

Although there has been considerable interest in this topic, the empirical evidence for meaning-level influences in isolated word-recognition tasks remains relatively sparse and controversial, particularly for speeded naming. For example, Strain, Patterson, and Seidenberg (1995) observed a three-way interaction between word frequency, spelling-to-sound consistency, and imageability in speeded naming performance. Specifically, imageability effects in speeded naming were strongest for low-frequency, inconsistent items, that is, items that have relatively inconsistent mappings between orthography and phonology. They interpreted this finding as consistent with a triangle model of word recognition, wherein semantic information provides more support for items that have relatively weak spelling-to-sound mapping (Strain, Patterson, & Seidenberg, 2002). Monaghan and Ellis (2002) disputed this finding, and demonstrated that the critical interaction was not significant once age of acquisition (AoA), a confounding variable, was controlled for (but see Strain et al., 2002, for a reply). Of course, Gernsbacher (1984) pointed out over 20 years ago that many word-recognition studies investigating meaning-level variables have not adequately controlled for stimulus familiarity, a variable that is correlated with many semantic variables.

One possible reason for these controversies is that studies usually manipulate variables using a relatively small set of items (typically fewer than 20 items per condition). Factorial experiments, while valuable, may also produce some problems. First, Forster (2000) found that word-recognition researchers were quite good at predicting which of two words would produce faster response latencies in a lexical decision task, even though obvious variables such as frequency and length were equated. Hence, not surprisingly, word-recognition researchers appear to have implicit knowledge concerning the effects of lexical variables, and this could contaminate item-selection processes. Specifically, researchers could consciously or unconsciously select items for categorical manipulations that support their hypotheses (Rosenthal, 1995), a phenomenon we have informally referred to as "Forster fibbing". Second, lists contexts (i.e. characteristics of words in a list) vary across studies, and the varying list environments may modulate the effect of interest (Andrews, 1997; Glanzer & Ehrenreich, 1979; Zevin & Balota, 2000). For example, Glanzer and Ehrenreich (1979) found large modulations of the word-frequency effect depending on the frequency of filler words. Third, standard factorial designs categorize continuous variables, reducing power and reliability (Cohen, 1983). For example, studies that dichotomize imageability, a continuous variable, are less likely to find significant imageability effects. Finally, given the large number of variables known to influence word-recognition tasks, it is becoming virtually impossible to control for all potentially extraneous and confounding variables (Cutler, 1981). The presence of putatively contaminating factors makes it particularly vexing for the field to establish the reliability (or the lack thereof) of factors (consider the debate between Ellis & Monaghan, 2002, and Strain et al., 2002, noted earlier).

Further explorations of semantic effects in visual word-recognition tasks: Results from multiple-regression analyses of large-scale databases

An approach that minimizes list-selection and list-context effects is to examine lexical decision and naming performance for a large corpus of stimuli. There have been a number of attempts to explore the utility of this approach in the literature (e.g. Seidenberg & Plaut, 1998; Spieler & Balota, 1997;

Treiman, Mullennix, Bijeljac-Babic, & Richmond-Welty, 1995). In fact, *Kello* (this volume) has used such a database to develop and test his powerful juncture model of word naming. Recently, we (Balota et al., 2004) reported the results from a megastudy of lexical decision latencies (n=30) and naming latencies (n=31) for virtually all the monosyllabic words in the Kuĉera and Francis (1967) norms. In this way, the language is defining the stimulus set, instead of laborious selection processes engaged by the researchers. Through the use of multiple regression, we were able to estimate the unique variance accounted for by targeted semantic variables, after potential confounding variables have been partialed out in earlier steps.

In the three-step hierarchical regression analysis we carried out, phonological onset variables (voicing, location, and manner of articulation of word-initial phonemes) were entered in step 1, and lexical variables (length, orthographic neighbourhood density, objective and subjective frequency, and feed-forward and feedback consistency) were entered in step 2. As expected, the phonological onset variables predicted significantly more variance in naming ($R^2 = .35$) than in lexical decision ($R^2 = .01$), an outcome consistent with the idea that naming performance is influenced by word-initial phonemes (Kawamoto & Kello, 1999). By entering the lexical variables in step 2, and then the semantic variables in step 3, we were able to determine whether semantic variables exert unique effects in word-recognition tasks after other potentially confounding variables are controlled for (cf. Gernsbacher, 1984). Here we will focus on the semantic effects in step 3, but we will return to the results from step 2 in a later section.

Two parallel analyses of semantic variables were conducted. In the first analysis, we examined how well imageability predicts lexical decision and naming latencies, using a new set of imageability norms for all monosyllabic words (Cortese & Fugett, 2004). Imageability was reliably facilitatory in both tasks, with stronger effects in lexical decision ($\beta = -.27$, $p < .001$) than in speeded naming ($\beta = -.04$, $p < .05$). Motivated by the work of Strain and colleagues (1995), we also explored interactions among imageability, word frequency, and consistency. None of the interactions were reliable ($p > .2$), suggesting that the interaction between meaning-level variables and other variables is relatively modest when all single-syllable words are considered.

In the second analysis, we explored the influence of two semantic variables, using Steyvers and Tenenbaum's (2005) work on semantic network structures. These researchers were motivated by recent evidence suggesting that naturally occurring networks (such as the neural system of *C. elegans*) and man-made networks (such as the power grid of the western USA and the World Wide Web) exhibit intriguing characteristics consistent with what they call *small-world structure* (Watts & Strogatz, 1998). Specifically, such networks are sparsely connected, show strong local clustering, and possess short average path lengths between nodes. Steyvers and Tenenbaum (2005) were interested in whether naturally occurring semantic networks conform to small-world structural principles. Hence, they examined the degree of connectivity in three large-scale databases, *Roget's Thesaurus of English Words and Phrases* (Roget, 1911), *The University of Florida Word Association Norms* (Nelson, McEvoy, & Schreiber, 1998), and *WordNet* (Miller, 1990), and computed connectivity measures that reflect how densely a particular word is connected to other words. Networks were then created from these norms. For example, using the Nelson et al. norms, Steyvers and Tenenbaum connected two words in an undirected manner if one of the words was generated as a free associate to the other word. Once the networks are formed, it is possible to compute a set of metrics that capture the organization of the network, such as the number of nodes, the number of connections, clustering coefficients, and the average path length between nodes. Using these metrics, Steyvers and Tenenbaum determined that semantic networks indeed exhibit a small-world structure—most words are sparsely interconnected, the average path length between words is short, and there is a high degree of local clustering. Interestingly, a few nodes are highly interconnected (*hubs*), and these hubs afford relatively short path lengths within the network. An example of the hubs and connections described by Steyvers and Tenenbaum (2005) is shown in Figure 10.2.

For the semantic connectivity analysis, we entered two connectivity measures based on Nelson et al.'s (1998) word association norms and Miller's (1990) WordNet in step 3 of the regression analysis. Both connectivity

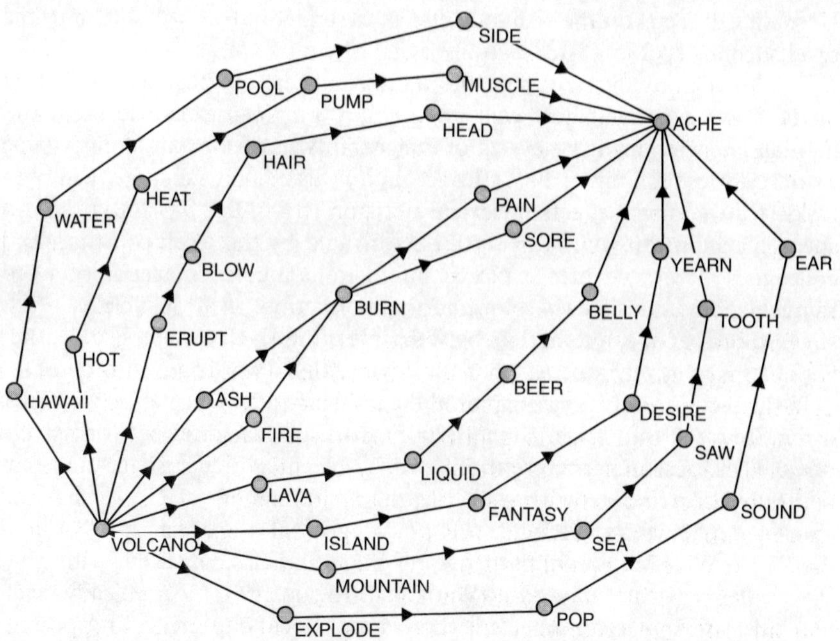

Figure 10.2 Partial semantic network derived from free association (reprinted with permission from Steyvers & Tenenbaum, 2005). Each directed edge reflects an association between a cue and response.

measures yielded reliable facilitatory effects in lexical decision ($\beta_{\text{word association}} = -.21, p < .001$; $\beta_{\text{WordNet}} = -.07, p < .01$). In naming, the influence of WordNet connectivity was weakly facilitatory ($\beta_{\text{WordNet}} = -.04, p < .10$). It is interesting that two quite different definitions of meaning, imageability and connectivity, yielded such convergent results. The significant effects of connectivity also suggest that readers' semantic networks may be characterized by a small-world structure. It is important to note that Steyvers and Tenenbaum (2005) also reported the predictive power of these measures in naming and lexical decision performance; however, there were fewer predictors included in their paper.

In order to assess the reliability and generalizability of the findings discussed above, we replicated our analyses with items selected from the English Lexicon Project (ELP) database (http://elexicon.wustl.edu), a repository of lexical decision and naming data for over 40,000 words and 1242 participants (Balota et al., 2002). The ELP represents a collaboration among six universities to provide the lexical and behavioural characteristics of the majority of words that are recognized by a typical college undergraduate. Despite the methodological diversity underlying the data set (heterogeneity of participant populations and testing environments), the ELP replication was clearly consistent with the megastudy's findings, yielding standardized regression coefficients that were remarkably comparable in magnitude (Table 10.1). In both datasets, semantic effects were reliably facilitatory even when confounding variables were controlled for, and were stronger in lexical decision than in naming.

It is important to remember that these effects were significant *after* other variables were partialed out in the first two steps of the regression analyses. The stronger semantic effects observed in lexical decision compared to naming are not surprising, since the constraints of the lexical-decision task (discriminating meaningful words from relatively meaningless nonwords) are likely to place a premium on semantics as a dimension for carrying out word/nonword decisions. More interestingly, one also observes reliable semantic

Table 10.1 Standardized regression coefficients of semantic measures in lexical decision task (LDT) and naming performance, across the megastudy and the English Lexicon Project (ELP)

LDT	**Megastudy**	**ELP**
Imageability	−.27*	−.27*
Word association	−.21*	−.22*
WordNet	−.07*	−.08*
Naming		
Imageability	−.04*	−.09*
Word association	−.04	−.06*
WordNet	−.04#	−.08*

# $p < .10$; * $p < .05$.

effects in speeded naming, a task that does *not* require meaningful words to be discriminated from non-meaningful nonwords. Taken together, the results support the notion that meaning is activated very early in the word-recognition tasks process via cascadic mechanisms, and interactively contributes to the processes culminating in a lexical-decision or naming response. Furthermore, it is apparent that there are large *task-specific* effects for semantic variables, with stronger effects for lexical decision than naming. Again, to borrow terminology from the memory literature, this is consistent with the argument there are no *process-pure* measures (Jacoby, 1991), but rather different tasks place different emphases on aspects of the lexical processing system to achieve the task goals.

The flexible lexical processor

As the preceding discussion makes clear, semantic effects are stronger in lexical decision than naming. The notion of *task-appropriate processing* and the flexible lexical processor is a useful heuristic for accommodating these results. Balota, Paul, and Spieler (1999) developed the framework displayed in Figure 10.3, which schematically captures how attention-control systems might influence the contribution of different aspects of the lexical processing system to maximize performance in a given task. Of course, this is merely used for illustrative purposes and is not intended to be portrayed as a model of lexical processing.

In this framework, a number of distinct processing pathways subserve the computations involved in orthography, phonology, meaning, syntax, and high-level discourse integration (Balota et al., 1999), with the specific goals of the task directing attention to the appropriate processing dimensions. Of course, these different processing pathways clearly are available to people

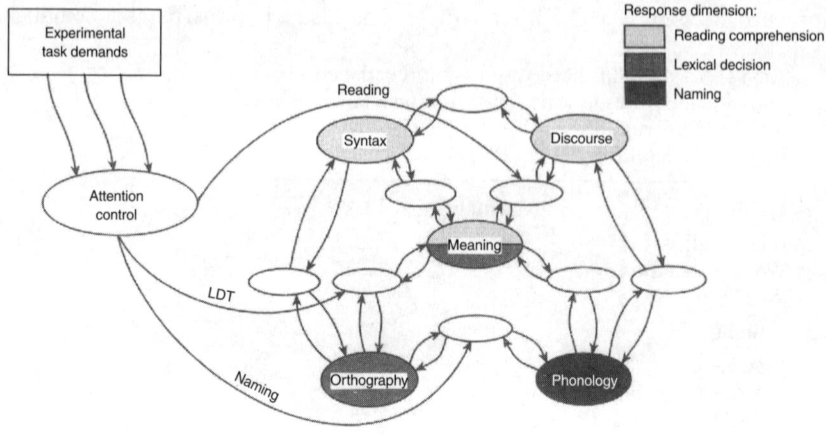

Figure 10.3 The flexible lexical processor.

(along with many more such as size, colour, grammatical class, and spatial location). The influence of these pathways is modulated by attentional control systems that are engaged by the experimental task demands. For example, speeded naming, which requires spelling-to-sound conversion, is primarily driven by the connections between the orthography and phonology modules. In contrast, in lexical decision, participants discriminate between meaningful words and relatively meaningless nonwords (Balota & Chumbley, 1984), and hence are more likely to emphasize the computations between the orthography and meaning. This is consistent with the larger semantic effects in lexical decision than in naming.

Of course, bringing on-line different processing components of performance in anticipation of task demands is a two-way street. Not only should one obtain stronger semantic effects in lexical decision, but one should also expect stronger phonological (e.g. spelling-to-sound consistency) effects in naming. Figure 10.4, taken from Balota et al. (2004), reports the mean regression coefficients from the second and third steps of the large-scale regression analyses from both the megastudy and the same items from the ELP presented above.

There are two things to note about these results. First, there is considerable consistency across the two data sets. Hence, if one is concerned about the reliability of the results from large-scale databases, it appears that these concerns are unwarranted. The current pattern is particularly intriguing in that the items in the megastudy were only single-syllable words, whereas the items from the ELP were the same single-syllable words embedded among multisyllabic words, proper names, and even contractions. Second, there is relatively little consistency in the size of the regression coefficients across lexical decision and naming performance. Specifically, lexical decision is driven primarily by familiarity and meaning, whereas naming is primarily driven by length, orthographic neighbourhood size, and spelling/sound consistency measures. At this level, it appears that participants are bringing on-line a very different set of processes depending upon the task demands.

Just how flexible is the flexible lexical processor?

An important question that one must ask is how much control there actually is in the system. For example, can one produce more subtle effects of attentional control? Control ultimately depends on the strength of the pathway that needs to be controlled. For example, researchers originally argued that the priming effects from short stimulus onset asynchrony (SOA) semantic priming studies (e.g. Neely, 1977) and the interference of the word dimension in Stroop performance were outside the influence of control within a typical experimental setting, because these pathways were so well practised. Such findings were used to support the automatic/modular aspect of the lexical processing system. However, subsequent research has indicated that even short SOA priming effects (e.g. Balota, Black, & Cheney, 1992) and the interference

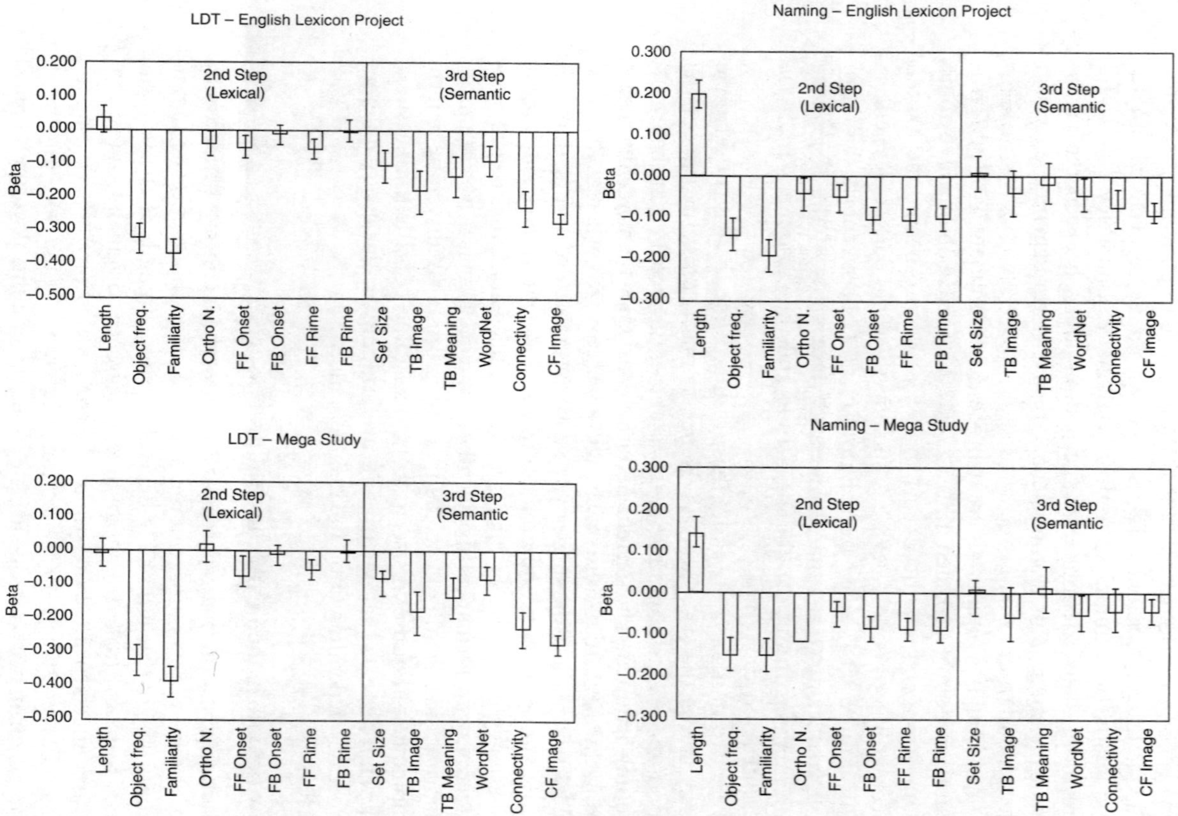

Figure 10.4 Replication of lexical decision task (LDT) and naming results from the English Lexicon Project (ELP). Error bars represent 95% confidence intervals (taken from Balota et al., 2004). CF Image = the Cortese & Fugett (2003) imageability measure; TB Meaning = the Toglia & Battig (1978) meaningfulness measure; TB Image = the Toglia & Battig imageability measure; FB Rime = feedback rime consistency; FF Rime = feed-forward rime consistency; FB Onset = feedback onset consistency; FF Onset = feed-forward onset consistency; Ortho. N. = orthographic neighbourhood; Object. Freq. = objective frequency.

effects in Stroop (e.g. Besner, 2001) are sensitive to control manipulations. Interestingly, there is even evidence that masked repetition priming effects can be modulated by context manipulations (Bodner & Masson, 2004; however, see also *Davis & Kim*, this volume, for an alternative perspective). Hence, the classic evidence for uncontrollable pathways, that is, modular automatic systems, has clearly been called into question.

One area where there has been considerable interest in control systems in word recognition is the extent to which subjects can exert control over lexical and sublexical pathways in naming performance. (Although the notion of lexical and sublexical pathways would appear most consistent with a dual-route model, such as Coltheart et al.'s 2001 model, we are using this term only descriptively here, and such effects could also be accommodated by a division of labour perspective, as reflected by the Harm & Seidenberg, 2004, model.) For example, Balota, Law, and Zevin (2000) directly attempted to exert control of the lexical pathway in their *regularization* condition. In this condition, participants were required to name a set of words and nonwords according to the spelling to sound principles in the language (that is, pronounce PINT such that it rhymes with HINT). In a second condition, participants were given normal naming instructions. As one might suspect, participants had some difficulty in naming exception words under the regularization instructions (mean accuracy was .65 and correct response latencies were on the order of 1 s). More interesting, however, was performance on a set of regular words, which were named in an identical fashion in both the regularization and normal naming blocks of trials. These items produced a typical word-frequency effect (23 ms) in the normal naming conditions, but actually produced a reversal of the word-frequency effect (–43 ms) in the regularization conditions. Balota et al. also included nonwords in both the regularization and normal naming blocks. Interestingly, there was no hint of a lexicality effect (words faster than nonwords) in the regularization condition (1 ms), but there was a large effect of lexical status (76 ms) in the normal naming conditions. These results suggest that one can access a sublexical spelling-to-sound route when directly instructed, albeit at a cost to accuracy and response times. The elimination of the lexicality effect suggests that readers can modulate the reliance on lexical information. However, since word frequency still exerted an influence on performance, albeit reversed compared to normal naming, these results suggest that subjects cannot totally control the influence of lexical information within this paradigm. This could be viewed as consistent with a Stroop type effect, wherein one finds *greater* interference from the prepotent lexical pathway (that is, in this case, high-frequency words compared to low-frequency words). Further research would be useful in addressing the following two issues: First, can one can modulate the size of the reversed frequency effect by increasing practice on the sublexical route? Second, can meaning-level variables be modulated by such regularization instructions?

Let us now turn to a more subtle level of control. Consider, for example, the possibility that participants may exert control over the relative contributions of a pathway that computes spelling-to-sound correspondences and a pathway that computes lexical-level information in a *normal* speeded naming task. Indeed, preliminary evidence for strategic control in word recognition was provided by a speeded naming study that manipulated list composition (Monsell, Patterson, Graham, Hughes, & Milroy, 1992). Monsell et al. examined naming performance for high-frequency *exception* words (words that violate English spelling-sound rules, such as PINT) when embedded within a list of other exception words, compared to when these items were embedded in a list of *nonwords* (such as FLIRP). When only exception words were presented, naming latencies were shorter and *regularization* errors (that is, pronouncing PINT so that it rhymed with HINT) were less likely, compared to when only nonwords were presented. This finding suggests that participants were able to strategically inhibit or control sublexical orthography-to-phonology computations when they were anticipating *only* exception words, since sublexical processes will, by definition, generate incorrect pronunciations for exception words.

This issue has been further investigated by Zevin and Balota (2000), using a variation of a task developed by Midgley-West (1979). Midgley-West had participants read aloud a single list of 24 monosyllabic nonwords followed by an exception word (WOLF). Seven of 18 participants regularized WOLF (so that it rhymed with GOLF), suggesting that lexical knowledge may have been suppressed by the predominantly nonword context. In Zevin and Balota's modified priming procedure, each trial consisted of six items that participants had to name. The first five items were primes (either low-frequency exception words like BISCUIT or nonwords like FLIRP) and the sixth, final word was the target, which could vary on some targeted dimension. The basic prediction was that low-frequency exception word primes should increase emphasis on lexical processing, while nonword primes should increase emphasis on sublexical processing. In fact, Zevin and Balota observed pathway influences on *lexicality*, *frequency*, *regularity*, and *imageability* effects. When the lexical pathway was primed, there were larger lexicality effects (words named faster than nonwords), frequency effects (high-frequency words named faster than low-frequency words), and imageability effects (high-imageable words named faster than low-imageable words) than when the sublexical pathway was primed. In contrast, priming the sublexical pathway produced larger regularity effects (regular words, which conform to spelling-sound rules, named faster than exception words).

It is important to point out that there are competing explanations for the phenomena observed by Monsell et al. (1992) and Zevin and Balota (2000). Instead of viewing list composition/context effects as evidence for strategic pathway control, some researchers have argued that these results are more compatible with a *flexible time-criterion* hypothesis (Kinoshita & Lupker, 2003; Lupker, Brown, & Colombo, 1997). In this account, when readers are presented with a word, they do not initiate articulation as soon as they are able to, that is, as reflected by the magic moment hypothesis. Rather, a flexible time criterion is adopted so that articulation begins either *before* or *after* the articulatory program is fully compiled (Kinoshita & Lupker, 2003). The time criterion for articulation onset is mainly determined by the difficulty of items in a trial block; "difficult" blocks consist mainly of slow (that is, long response latencies) items, while "easy" blocks consist mainly of fast (that is, short response latencies) items. This implies that the same items will be responded to faster when embedded in an "easy" block than when embedded in a "difficult" block. Kinoshita and Lupker used a different context manipulation than Zevin and Balota, and investigated the same variables that Zevin and Balota investigated in their first three experiments. Kinoshita and Lupker found that target processing was influenced only by the relative difficulty of contextual primes, not by the different routes presumably engaged by the primes per se. Kinoshita and Lupker did not address the finding that imageability effects can be modulated by pathway manipulations. It should also be noted that Kinoshita, Lupker, and Rastle (2004) have recently provided evidence that one can indeed modulate the lexicality (but not the regularity) effect via list context manipulations. In addition, Reynolds and Besner (2005) have recently demonstrated within a task switching paradigm that one can find lexical and sublexical pathway switching above and beyond any response latency criterion effects. Hence, there does appear to be converging evidence from other paradigms of some level of pathway control.

If Kinoshita et al. (2004) were correct, and the Zevin and Balota results were due to the difficulty of the items in the priming conditions, as reflected by the latencies for the priming items, then one should be able to eliminate the effects in the Zevin and Balota (2000) study by statistically controlling for this possibility. That is, by covarying out the response latencies on the prime trials, one can determine whether there is still an effect of condition. In fact, we recently conducted this analysis, and route priming continued to reliably modulate lexicality, regularity, and imageability effects even *after* prime response times were controlled for. Hence, it appears that setting one's criterion by the speed of context items is an insufficient explanation of the Zevin and Balota results.

The current status of the route-priming results suggests that one needs relatively strong manipulations to modulate the lexical and sublexical contributions to naming performance via context manipulations. As Zevin and Balota (2000) argued, such effects are likely to depend on the strength of the manipulations. In fact, because of inconsistencies in the past literature, Zevin and Balota developed the within-trial priming procedure to increase the strength of the manipulation. Although the debate between pathway control and time-criterion is clearly important, it is perhaps misleading to view the two hypotheses as mutually exclusive. We believe that it is likely that both mechanisms work in tandem, and as pointed out earlier, one way to empirically test this is to determine whether pathway selection effects are reliable after the difficulty of the list context has been controlled for. More importantly, both variables reflect the influence of a control mechanism that influences performance due to the local context. In the pathway-priming experiments, this produces a bias in the type of information used to drive a response, while in the time-criterion studies this biases when a response should be emitted. Ultimately, the degree of both types of control is likely to depend on factors such as: (1) the ability of contextual factors to engage an appropriate task set, (2) the ability to maintain a representation of this task set over time, and (3) the prepotent strength of the pre-existing pathways. Indeed, some processes may even be impenetrable by attentional mechanisms (see, for example, discussion by *Davis & Kim*, this volume, regarding context effects in masked repetition priming). Such processes are of particular interest because they appear to be inconsistent with the accumulating evidence from cognitive neuroscience indicating that neural areas that were initially presumed to be dedicated to very early modular visual field processing, also appear to be susceptible to attentional variables (see Luck & Vecera, 2002; Vogel, Woodman, & Luck, 2005).

Meaning versus control: Evidence from dementia of the Alzheimer's type and semantic dementia

Examining different types of language breakdowns across distinct clinical populations may afford another converging line of evidence concerning how control mechanisms may interact with structural systems. For example, there is currently some debate regarding the nature of the language breakdowns that occur in early-stage dementia of the Alzheimer's type (DAT). Individuals with early-stage DAT produce large deficits in tasks such as picture naming and category fluency. Some researchers (e.g. Salmon, Butters, & Chan, 1999) have suggested that this reflects a breakdown in the integrity of the semantic network, but others (e.g. Balota, Watson, Duchek, & Ferraro, 1999; Nebes, 1989; Ober, 1995) have argued from intact semantic priming effects that such breakdowns are more likely to be due to changes in the control systems used to access the semantic network. The distinction between these two positions is not only theoretically important but also has implications when considering the types of tasks one wishes to employ to identify individuals with early-stage DAT.

One way to adjudicate between these accounts is to compare individuals who have a clear semantic deficit with those who have DAT. Recently, we have been exploring a group of individuals who have a variant of frontotemporal lobe dementia referred to as semantic dementia (SD) (see Hodges, Garrard, & Patterson, 1998, for a review of this literature). Figure 10.5 (reproduced from Cortese, Balota, Sergent-Marshall, & Buckner, 2003) displays performance on a group of healthy control, DAT, and SD individuals on a set of semantic (Animal Fluency, Boston Naming, and American Version of the Adult Reading Test) and nonsemantic tasks (Benton Copy, Digit Span Forward, Digit Span Backward, WAIS Block Design, and WAIS Digit-Symbol

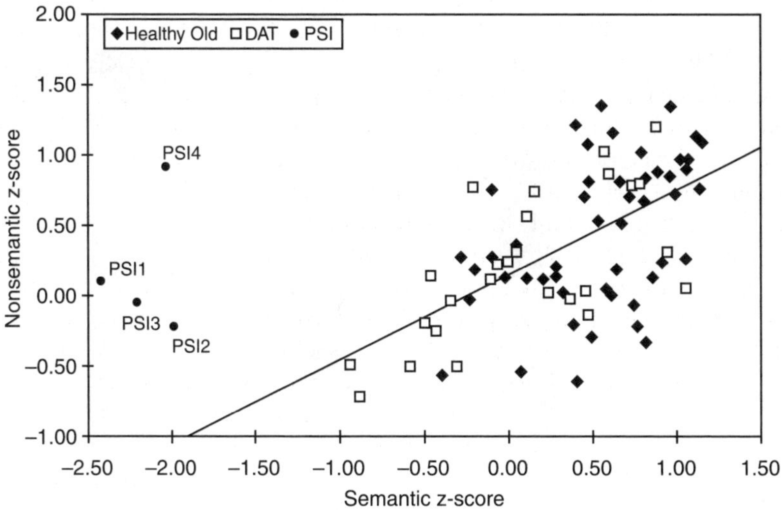

Figure 10.5 Scatter plot of semantic and nonsemantic z-scores of 83 participants who participated in the Cortese et al. (2003) study. The line represents the best fit to the data with the four primary semantic impairment (PSI) participants excluded (r = 0.58).

Test). As one can see, in general, performance for most participants on semantic and nonsemantic tasks is positively correlated. However, this figure also shows that there are a few participants who showed disproportionate breakdowns in semantic tasks. We have since classified three of the four participants as having SD.

Gold et al. (2005) explored speeded naming performance in individuals with SD and those who have early-stage DAT. Gold et al. argued that if there was a deficit in the lexical/semantic system, one should find disproportionate length effects in these individuals. Such effects would be indicative of a greater reliance on a more serial spelling-to-sound computation. Indeed, Weekes (1997) has provided evidence that nonwords (items that are semantically barren) produce large length effects, whereas words produce relatively little length effect when other extraneous variables are controlled. Hence, one might expect individuals with SD to treat words as nonwords, and hence produce large length effects. Likewise, if individuals with DAT also have such a breakdown in the semantic/lexical route, they should at least produce larger length effects than healthy age-matched control individuals. The results from the speeded naming task are displayed in Figure 10.6.

As shown here, individuals with SD produce exaggerated length effects, compared to both healthy control individuals and those with early-stage DAT, with no difference between the latter two groups. Because the DAT individuals produced similar length effects to the healthy controls, and individuals with a clear semantic deficit produce exaggerated effects of length,

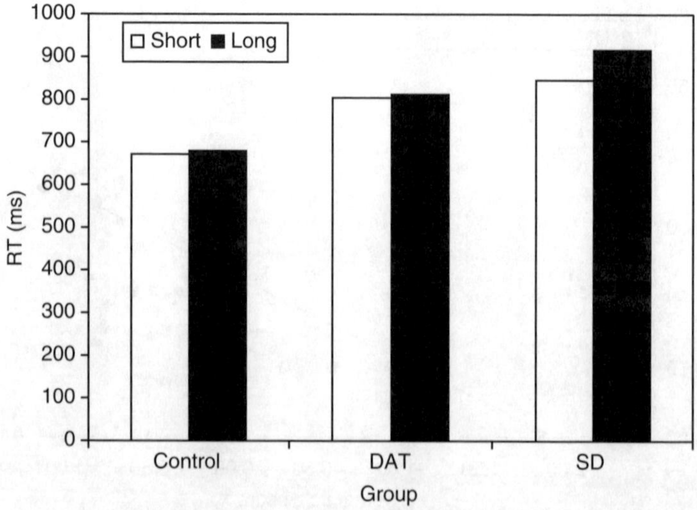

Figure 10.6 Mean group word-naming latencies as a function of letter length. RT: response time; DAT: dementia of Alzheimer's type; SD: semantic dementia.

one can argue that the breakdown is not in the lexical/semantic structure, at least in early-stage DAT.

A similar conclusion was made by Cortese et al. (2003) from a homophone spelling task. Cortese et al. compared spelling performance on a set of items in which both the sound-to-spelling dominance and the meaning dominance of auditorily presented words converged on the same spelling (for example, /weist/ should be spelled WASTE according to both sound-to-spelling consistency and meaning dominance). Alternatively, there was a set of items in which the sound-to-spelling consistency diverged from the meaning dominance (for example, /plein/ should be spelled PLAIN according to sound-to-spelling consistency and PLANE according to meaning dominance). Although there was little difference in spelling the items that converged on meaning and spelling dominance across the participants, there was a clear difference in performance on the items that diverged on meaning and spelling dominance. In particular, as shown in Figure 10.7, the DAT individuals and healthy controls were equally likely to rely on meaning dominance in spelling the homophones (that is, spelling /plein/ like PLANE), whereas the individuals with SD were much more likely to rely on the spelling-dominant pathway (that is, spelling /plein/ as PLAIN). It is important to note here that both spelling patterns are acceptable in this situation, and so there is no need to exert control over one of the spelling patterns.

Cortese et al. (2003) also compared spelling performance on a set of words that had consistent sound-to-spelling correspondence (e.g. SLICK), and a set of words that had inconsistent sound-to-spelling correspondence (e.g.

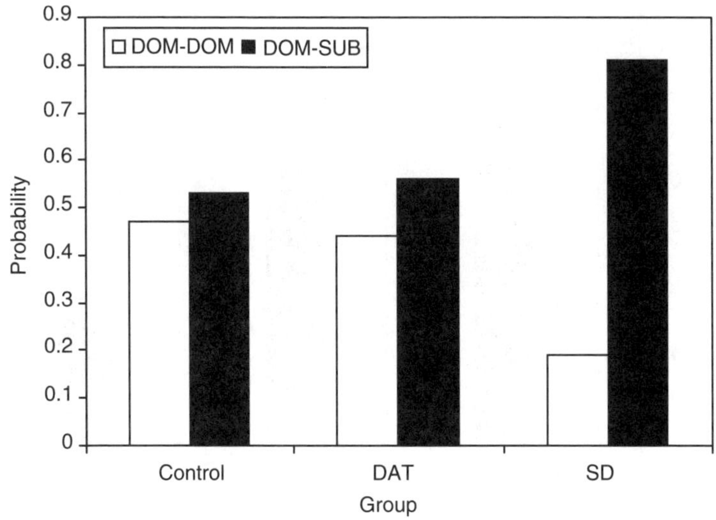

Figure 10.7 The probability of producing the spelling of the homophone with the dominant meaning/subordinate spelling (DOM–DOM) and the homophone with the subordinate meaning/dominant spelling (DOM–SUB) given that a correct spelling was produced (taken from Cortese et al., 2003). DAT: dementia of Alzheimer's type; SD: semantic dementia.

PLAID). For inconsistent words, there is a conflict between the correct spelling (lexical pathway) and the regularized spelling (sublexical pathway), and the system needs to exert control, that is, suppress the sublexical sound-to-spelling route to output a correct spelling. Interestingly, as shown in Figure 10.8, the individuals with DAT produced a reliable impairment in spelling the inconsistent words, compared to the healthy age-matched controls.

It is noteworthy that a similar pattern is found in speeded naming performance, wherein DAT individuals are more likely to regularize irregular words than healthy, age-matched control individuals (see Balota & Ferraro, 1993; Patterson, Graham, & Hodges, 1994). Instead of considering this pattern as a reflection of semantic memory degradation, we believe that this pattern, coupled with the length effects in naming and the homophone spelling data reviewed above, is more consistent with a breakdown in controlling the output from a sublexical pathway, which needs to be suppressed in this context to produce a correct spelling.

The results reviewed in this section indicate that it is useful to again consider the task constraints when making inferences about the locus of observed semantic deficits. In particular, the breakdowns that DAT individuals exhibit in supposed semantic tasks, such as picture naming and category fluency, could be signalling deterioration in task-specific control systems rather than the integrity of the semantic network. Comparing groups of individuals who have clear semantic memory loss (individuals with SD)

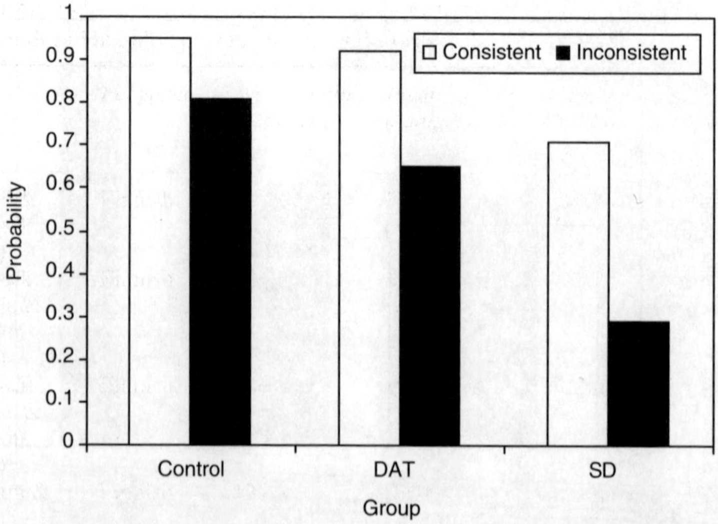

Figure 10.8 Mean correct spelling performance for consistent and inconsistent words across groups. DAT: dementia of Alzheimer's type; SD: semantic dementia.

with healthy older adults and individuals with early-stage DAT provides leverage in understanding the nature of such deficits.

Task set and neuroimaging

The present chapter has emphasized the argument that one needs to consider task-appropriate processing to understand the manner in which a variable influences performance in a lexical task. We end with a few observations from the neuroimaging domain regarding attempts to provide leverage on such task signals. Of course, the field of cognitive neuroimaging has developed considerably since the seminal work of Petersen, Fox, Posner, Mintun, and Raichle (1989), who were the first to observe remarkably distinct regions of the brain activated as a function of task set. In particular, positron-emission tomography (PET) scans of participants while processing single words indicated that, compared to baseline fixation performance, occipital areas were engaged for passive viewing of words, temporal areas were engaged for reading words aloud, and frontal regions were involved when participants generated verbs to nouns. Since this classic work, there have been many further developments. For example, researchers began tracking manipulations within the same task. In this vein, Fiez, Balota, Raichle, and Petersen (1999) used PET imaging to examine responses as participants read lists that varied as a function of frequency, consistency, and lexicality. The results indicated clearly that there is a region in the left medial inferior frontal area (near BA 45) that is particularly sensitive to low-frequency inconsistent words, whereas there is bilateral activation of the primary motor cortex that is sensitive only to consistency. This later effect may suggest that consistency effects in part reflect an influence in motoric aspects of response initiation or articulation. Such an effect would be difficult to uncover in a standard behavioural naming study.

More recently, Palmer, Brown, Petersen, and Schlaggar (2004) have provided an updated review of imaging work pertaining to the functional neuroanatomy of single-word reading. Activations in different brain regions are reliably associated with different language functions. For example, orthographic processing is associated with the temporal lobe (Petersen et al., 1989), spelling-to-sound conversion is associated with the left inferior frontal region (Fiez et al., 1999), phonological decomposition is associated with the left posterior temporal lobe (Simos, Breier, Fletcher, Foorman, Castillo, & Papanicolaou 2002), and semantic processing is associated with both the temporal lobe (between the superior and middle temporal gyrus) and the inferior frontal regions (Petersen et al., 1989; Price, Moore, Humphreys, & Wise, 1997).

One important limitation that applies to both PET studies and early functional magnetic resonance imaging (fMRI) studies is that *blocked designs* are mandatory. As a result, neural activity may reflect either item-specific processing, or task-related strategic states that are sustained across the trials of a task; item and state effects are completely confounded in blocked designs. Of course, one of the main points of the current chapter is that it is critical to decompose these two components of performance. This problem has been partly remedied with the advent of *event-related fMRI designs* (Dale & Buckner, 1997). Using event-related fMRI, one can now extract the BOLD (blood oxygen level-dependent) response for specific trials. Although this was an important advance, event-related fMRI is still insensitive to task-related effects that may be sustained across trials. Fortunately, there has also been progress in developing fMRI designs that are a hybrid of block and event-related designs. In the *mixed block/event-related design* (Donaldson, 2004), one can separately extract signals that are sustained across task trials (*state effects*), and transient signals that are associated with specific trial events (*item effects*). State effects, which are potentially related to task-level control signals (Visscher et al., 2003), may afford important leverage in understanding task-related attentional modulations within the lexical processing system.

Although mixed designs are relatively new, there is compelling evidence for their efficacy. For example, Otten, Henson, and Rugg (2002) conducted a mixed fMRI study where participants made semantic or phonological decisions about visually presented words. After statistically controlling for item-related activity, they found that the semantic encoding condition was associated with sustained activity in the inferior medial parietal and left prefrontal cortex, whereas the phonological encoding condition was associated with sustained activity in the medial parietal cortex. Interestingly, the magnitude of sustained brain activity predicted subsequent memory performance. These results are consistent with the notion that the different encoding instructions induced different "encoding modes" in participants; these modes are evinced by sustained activity in brain regions that support memory encoding (Donaldson, 2004). Other studies have successfully used the mixed design to clarify the neuroanatomical bases of cognition in domains as diverse as memory encoding (Reynolds, Donaldson, Wagner, & Braver, 2004), memory retrieval (Velanova, Jacoby, Wheeler, McAvoy, Petersen, & Buckner, 2003), and task switching (Braver, Reynolds, & Donaldson, 2003).

There has not yet been much systematic work examining state and item effects in visual word recognition (but see Palmer, 2003). However, the mixed design is potentially a powerful tool for elucidating, at the neuroanatomical level, the task-related effects we have been discussing in this chapter. For example, the task-appropriate processing framework predicts that one should be able to identify item effects that generalize across different reading tasks but are modulated by the relevance to the task demands, and state effects that are specific to the reading task being employed. In this way, one may be able to clarify how the brain flexibly implements operations to accomplish a given task goals.

Conclusions

The present chapter has had three interrelated goals. First, at a theoretical level, we have attempted to elucidate the consequences of particular stances taken regarding the influence of meaning on lexical processing tasks. In this light, we have provided evidence that meaning-level variables do indeed play a role in both lexical decision and word naming, with smaller effects in the latter task. Hence, we question the utility of the assumption that there is a measurable point in time where a lexical representation has been accessed but meaning has not become available. Second, we have reviewed a series of methodological considerations that may afford some progress in understanding how processes evolve across time to influence response time distribution and the actual implementation of the response. We have also attempted to show how large-scale databases can provide particularly important converging evidence concerning the influence of lexical variables on word-recognition tasks. Finally, we have emphasized the importance of task-specific operations and a flexible lexical processor, and have discussed the potential utility of exploring differences in process and structure across different populations and via recent neuroimaging techniques. We believe that ultimately any model of word processing will need to incorporate both structural mechanisms and attentional mechanisms that bring to the fore a configuration that is ideally tuned to accomplish the goals of a given word-recognition task.

Acknowledgements

This work was supported by grants from the US National Institute on Aging (NIA AGO3991) and the National Science Foundation (BCS 0001801). We thank Chris Davis and Sally Andrews for their helpful comments on a previous version of this chapter. Correspondence regarding this chapter should be sent to David Balota at dbalota@artsci.wustl.edu

References

Abrams, R. A., & Balota, D. A. (1991). Mental chronometry: Beyond reaction time. *Psychological Science*, *2*, 153–157.

Andrews, S. (1997). The effect of orthographic similarity on lexical retrieval: Resolving neighborhood conflicts. *Psychonomic Bulletin and Review*, *4*, 439–461.

Andrews, S., & Heathcote, A. (2001). Distinguishing common and task-specific processes in word identification: A matter of some moment. *Journal of Experimental Psychology: Learning, Memory, and Cognition*, *27*, 514–544.

Balota, D. A. (1990). The role of meaning in word recognition. In D. A. Balota, G. B. Flores d'Arcais, & K. Rayner (Eds.), *Comprehension processes in reading* (pp. 9–32). Hillsdale, NJ: Lawrence Erlbaum Associates, Inc.

Balota, D. A., & Abrams, R. A. (1995). Mental chronometry: Beyond onset latencies in the lexical decision task. *Journal of Experimental Psychology: Learning, Memory, and Cognition*, *21*, 1289–1302.

Balota, D. A., Black, S. R., & Cheney, M. (1992). Automatic and attentional priming in young and older adults: Reevaluation of the two-process model. *Journal of Experimental Psychology: Human Perception and Performance*, *18*, 485–502.

Balota, D. A., & Chumbley, J. I. (1984). Are lexical decisions a good measure of lexical access? The role of word frequency in the neglected decision stage. *Journal of Experimental Psychology: Human Perception and Performance*, *10*, 340–357.

Balota, D. A., Cortese, M. J., Hutchison, K. A., Neely, J. H., Nelson, D., Simpson, G. B. et al. (2002). *The English Lexicon Project: A web-based repository of descriptive and behavioral measures for 40,481 English words and nonwords*. Accessed 30 January 2004, on the Washington University Web site: http://elexicon.wustl.edu

Balota, D. A., Cortese, M. J., & Pilotti, M. (1999). Item-level analyses of lexical decision performance: Results from a mega-study. In *Abstracts of the 40th Annual Meeting of the Psychonomic Society* (p. 44). Los Angeles: Psychonomic Society.

Balota, D. A., Cortese, M. J., Sergent-Marshall, S. D., Spieler, D. H., & Yap, M. J. (2004). Visual word recognition of single-syllable words. *Journal of Experimental Psychology: General*, *133*, 283–316.

Balota, D. A., & Ferraro, F. R. (1993). A dissociation of frequency and regularity effects in pronunciation performance across young adults, older adults, and individuals with senile dementia of the Alzheimer's type. *Journal of Memory and Language*, *32*, 573–592.

Balota, D. A., Ferraro, F. R., & Connor, L. T. (1991). On the early influence of meaning in word recognition: A review of the literature. In P. J. Schwanenflugel (Ed.), *The Psychology of Word Meanings* (pp. 187–222). Hillsdale, NJ: Lawrence Erlbaum Associates, Inc.

Balota, D. A., Law, M. B., & Zevin, J. D. (2000). The attentional control of lexical processing pathways: Reversing the word-frequency effect. *Memory and Cognition*, *28*, 1081–1089.

Balota, D. A., & Spieler, D. H. (1999). Word frequency, repetition, and lexicality effects in word recognition tasks: Beyond measures of central tendency. *Journal of Experimental Psychology: General*, *128*, 32–55.

Balota, D. A., Paul, S., & Spieler, D. H. (1999). Attentional control of lexical processing pathways during word recognition and reading. In S. Garrod & M. Pickering (Eds.), *Language processing* (pp. 15–57). Hove, UK: Psychology Press.

Balota, D. A., Watson, J. M., Duchek, J. M., & Ferraro, F. R. (1999). Cross-modal semantic and homograph priming in healthy young, healthy old, and in Alzheimer's disease individuals. *Journal of International Neuropsychological Society*, *5*, 626–640.

Becker, C. A. (1980). Semantic context effects in visual word recognition: An analysis of semantic strategies. *Memory and Cognition*, *8*, 493–512.

Becker, C. A., & Killion, T. H. (1977). Interaction of visual and cognitive effects in word recognition. *Journal of Experimental Psychology: Human Perception and Performance*, *3*, 389–401.

Besner, D. (2001). The myth of ballistic processing: Evidence from Stroop's paradigm. *Psychonomic Bulletin and Review*, *8*, 324–330.

Blaxton, T. A. (1989). Investigating dissociations among memory measures: Support for a transfer appropriate processing framework. *Journal of Experimental Psychology: Learning, Memory, and Cognition*, *15*, 657–668.

Bodner, G. E., & Masson, M. E. J. (2004). Beyond binary judgments: Prime validity modulates masked repetition priming in the naming task. *Memory and Cognition*, *32*, 1–11.

Braver, T. S., Reynolds, J. R., & Donaldson, D. I. (2003). Neural mechanisms of transient and sustained cognitive control during task switching. *Neuron*, *39*, 713–726.

Cattell, J. M. (1890). Mental tests and measurements. *Mind*, *15*, 373–381.

Cohen, J. (1983). The cost of dichotomization. *Applied Psychological Measurement*, *7*, 249–253.

Coltheart, M., Rastle, K., Perry, C., Langdon, R., & Ziegler, J. (2001). DRC: A dual route cascaded model of visual word recognition and reading aloud. *Psychological Review*, *108*, 204–256.

Cortese, M. J, & Fugett, A. (2004). Imageability ratings for 3,000 monosyllabic words. *Behavior Research Methods, Instruments and Computers*, *36*, 384–387.

Cortese, M. J., Balota, D. A., Sergent-Marshall, S. D., & Buckner, R. L. (2003). Sublexical, lexical, and semantic influences in spelling: Exploring the effects of age, Alzheimer's disease and primary semantic impairment. *Neuropsychologia*, *41*, 952–967.

Cutler, A. (1981). Making up materials is a confounded nuisance, or: Will we be able to run any psycholinguistic experiments at all in 1990? *Cognition*, *10*, 65–70.

Dale, A. M., & Buckner, R. L. (1997). Selective averaging of rapidly presented individual trials using fMRI. *Human Brain Mapping*, *5*, 329–340.

Donaldson, A. M. (2004). Parsing brain activity with fMRI and mixed designs: what kind of a state is neuroimaging in? *Trends in Neuroscience*, *27*, 442–444.

Ellis, A. W., & Monaghan, J. (2002). Reply to Strain, Patterson, and Seidenberg. *Journal of Experimental Psychology: Learning, Memory, and Cognition*, *28*, 215–220.

Fiez, J. A., Balota, D. A., Raichle, M. E., & Petersen, S. E. (1999). Effects of lexicality, frequency, and spelling-to-sound consistency on the functional anatomy of reading. *Neuron*, *24*, 205–218.

Fodor, J. (1983). *The modularity of mind*. Cambridge, MA: MIT Press.

Forster, K. I. (1976). Accessing the mental lexicon. In R. J. Wales & E. C. T. Walker (Eds.), *New approaches to language mechanisms* (pp. 257–287). Amsterdam: North Holland.

Forster, K. I. (2000). The potential for experimenter bias effects in word recognition experiments. *Memory and Cognition, 28*, 1109–1115.

Gernsbacher, M. A. (1984). Resolving 20 years of inconsistent interactions between lexical familiarity and orthography, concreteness, and polysemy. *Journal of Experimental Psychology: General, 113*, 256–281.

Glanzer, M., & Ehrenreich, S. L. (1979). Structure and search of the internal lexicon. *Journal of Verbal Learning and Verbal Behavior, 18*, 381–398.

Gold, B. T., Balota, D. A., Cortese, M. J., Sergent-Marshall, S. D., Snyder, A. Z., Salat, D. H. et al. (2005). Differing neuropsychological and neuroanatomical correlates of abnormal reading in early-stage semantic dementia and dementia of the Alzheimer type. *Neuropsychologia, 43*, 833–846.

Grainger, J., & Jacobs, A. M. (1996). Orthographic processing in visual word recognition: A multiple read-out model. *Psychological Review, 103*, 518–565.

Harm, M. W., & Seidenberg, M. S. (2004). Computing the meanings of words in reading: Cooperative division of labor between visual and phonological processes. *Psychological Review, 111*, 662–720.

Heathcote, A., Popiel, S. J., & Mewhort, D. J. K. (1991). Analysis of response time distributions: An example using the Stroop task. *Psychological Bulletin, 109*, 340–347.

Hodges, J. R., Garrard, P., & Patterson, K. (1998). Semantic dementia. In A. Kertesz & D. G. Munoz (Eds.), *Pick's disease and Pick complex* (pp. 83–104). New York: Wiley-Liss.

Jacoby, L. L. (1991). A process dissociation framework: Separating automatic from intentional uses of memory. *Journal of Memory and Language, 30*, 513–541.

Kawamoto, A. H., & Kello, C. T. (1999). Effect of onset cluster complexity in speeding naming: A test of rule-based approaches. *Journal of Experimental Psychology: Human Perception and Performance, 25*, 361–375.

Kinoshita, S., & Lupker, S. J. (2003). Priming and attentional control of lexical and sublexical pathways in naming: A reevaluation. *Journal of Experimental Psychology: Learning, Memory, and Cognition, 29*, 405–415.

Kinoshita, S., Lupker, S. J., & Rastle, K. (2004). Modulation of regularity and lexicality effects in reading aloud. *Memory and Cognition, 32*, 1255–1264.

Kučera, H., & Francis, W. N. (1967). *Computational analysis of present day American English*. Providence, RI: Brown University Press.

Logan, G. D., & Cowan, W. B. (1984). On the ability to inhibit thought and action: A theory of an act of control. *Psychological Review, 91*, 295–327.

Luce, R. D. (1986). *Response times: Their role in inferring elementary mental organization*. New York: Oxford University Press.

Luck, S. J., & Vecera, S. P. (2002). Attention. In H. Pashler (Series Ed.) & S. Yantis (Volume Ed.), *Stevens' Handbook of experimental psychology: Vol. 1. Sensation and perception* (3rd ed., pp. 235–286). New York: Wiley.

Lupker, S. J., Brown, P., & Colombo, L. (1997). Strategic control in a naming task: Changing routes or changing deadlines? *Journal of Experimental Psychology: Learning, Memory, and Cognition, 23*, 570–590.

McClelland, J. L. (1979). On the time relations of mental processes: An examination of systems of processes in cascade. *Psychological Review, 86*, 287–330.

McClelland, J. L., & Rumelhart, D. E. (1981). An interactive activation model of context effects in letter perception. P I. An account of basic findings. *Psychological Review, 88*, 375–407.

Midgley-West, L. (1979). *Strategies in reading*. Unpublished doctoral dissertation, Birkbeck College, London.

Miller, G. A. (1990). WordNet: An on-line lexical database. *International Journal of Lexicography*, *3*, 235–312.

Monsell, S., Patterson, K. E., Graham, A., Hughes, C. H., & Milroy, R. (1992). Lexical and sublexical translation of spelling to sound: Strategic anticipation of lexical status. *Journal of Experimental Psychology: Learning, Memory, and Cognition*, *18*, 452–467.

Morris, C. D., Bransford, J. D., & Franks, J. J. (1977). Levels of processing versus transfer appropriate processing. *Journal of Verbal Learning and Verbal Behavior*, *16*, 519–533.

Morton, J. (1969). The interaction of information in word recognition. *Psychological Review*, *76*, 165–178.

Murray, W. S., & Forster, K. I. (2004). Serial mechanisms in lexical access: The rank hypothesis. *Psychological Review*, *111*, 721–756.

Nebes, R. D. (1989). Semantic memory in Alzheimer's disease. *Psychological Bulletin*, *106*, 377–394.

Neely, J. H. (1977). Semantic priming and retrieval from lexical memory: Roles of inhibitionless spreading activation and limited-capacity attention. *Journal of Experimental Psychology: General*, *106*, 226–254.

Nelson, D. L., McEvoy, C. L., & Schreiber, T. A. (1998). *The University of South Florida word association, rhyme, and word fragment norms*. Retrieved 1 June 2000, from the University of South Florida Web site: http://www.usf.edu/FreeAssociation/

Ober, B. A., Shenaut, G. K., & Reed, B. R. (1995). Assessment of associative relations in Alzheimer's disease: Evidence for preservation of semantic memory. *Aging and Cognition*, *2*, 254–267.

Otten, L. J., Henson, R. N. A., & Rugg, M. D. (2002). State-related and item-related neural correlates of successful memory encoding. *Nature Neuroscience*, *5*, 1339–1344.

Paap, K. R., Newsome, S. L., McDonald, J. E., & Schvaneveldt, R. W. (1982). An activation-verification model for letter and word recognition: The word superiority effect. *Psychological Review*, *89*, 573–594.

Palmer, E. D. (2003). *Neural mechanisms underlying single word reading: An fMRI investigation*. Unpublished doctoral dissertation, Washington University in St Louis, St Louis, Missouri.

Palmer, E. D., Brown, T. T., Petersen, S. E., & Schlaggar, B. L. (2004). Investigation of the functional neuroanatomy of single word reading and its development. *Scientific Studies of Reading*, *8*, 203–223.

Patterson, K. E., Graham, N., & Hodges, J. R. (1994). Reading in dementia of the Alzheimer's type: A preserved ability? *Neuropsychology*, *8*, 395–412.

Petersen, S. E., Fox, P. T., Posner, M. I., Mintun, M., & Raichle, M. E. (1989). Positron emission tomographic studies of the processing of single words. *Journal of Cognitive Neuroscience*, *1*, 153–170.

Plaut, D. C. (1997). Structure and function in the lexical system: Insights from distributed models of word reading and lexical decision. *Language and Cognitive Processes*, *12*, 765–805.

Price, C. J., Moore, C. J., Humphreys, G. W., & Wise, R. J. S. (1997). Segregating semantic from phonological processes during reading. *Journal of Cognitive Neuroscience*, *9*, 727–733.

Ratcliff, R., Gomez, P., & McKoon, G. (2004). A diffusion model account of the lexical decision task. *Psychological Review*, *111*, 159–182.

Reynolds, M., & Besner, D. (2005). Contextual control over lexical and sublexical routines when reading English aloud. *Psychonomic Bulletin and Review*, *12*, 113–118.

Reynolds, J. R., Donaldson, D. I., Wagner, A. D., & Braver, T. S. (2004). Item- and task-level processes in the left inferior prefrontal cortex: positive and negative correlates of encoding. *NeuroImage*, *21*, 1472–1483.

Roediger, H. L. (1990). Implicit memory: Retention without remembering. *American Psychologist*, *45*, 1043–1056.

Roget, P. M. (1911). *Roget's thesaurus of English words and* phrases. Available from Project Gutenberg, Illinois Benedictine College, Lisle, IL.

Rosenthal, R. (1995). Critiquing Pygmalion: A 25-year perspective. *Current Directions in Psychological Science*, *4*, 171–172.

Salmon, D. P., Butters, N., & Chan, A. S. (1999). The deterioration of semantic memory in Alzheimer's disease. *Canadian Journal of Experimental Psychology*, *53*, 108–116.

Schall, J. D. (2003). Neural correlates of decision processes: Neural and mental chronometry. *Current Opinion in Neurobiology*, *13*, 182–186.

Seidenberg, M. S., & Plaut, D. C. (1998). Evaluating word-reading models at the item level: Matching the grain of theory and data. *Psychological Science*, *9*, 234–237.

Simos, P. G., Breier, J. I., Fletcher, J. M., Foorman, B. R., Castillo, E. M., & Papanicolaou, A. C. (2002). Brain mechanisms for reading words and pseudowords: An integrated approach. *Cerebral Cortex*, *12*, 297–305.

Smith, P. L., & Ratcliff, R. (2004). The psychology and neurobiology of simple decisions. *Trends in Neuroscience*, *27*, 161–168.

Spieler, D. H., & Balota, D. A. (1997). Bringing computational models of word naming down to the item level. *Psychological Science*, *8*, 411–416.

Spieler, D. H., Balota, D. A., & Faust, M. E. (1996). Stroop performance in normal older adults and individuals with senile dementia of the Alzheimer's type. *Journal of Experimental Psychology: Human Perception and Performance*, *22*, 461–479.

Spieler, D. H., Balota, D. A., & Faust, M. E. (2000). Levels of selective attention revealed through analyses of response time distributions. *Journal of Experimental Psychology: Human Perception and Performance*, *26*, 506–526.

Steyvers, M., & Tenenbaum, J. B. (2005). The large-scale structure of semantic networks: Statistical analyses and a model of semantic growth. *Cognitive Science*, *29*, 41–78.

Strain, E., Patterson, K., & Seidenberg, M. S. (1995). Semantic effects in single-word naming. *Journal of Experimental Psychology: Learning, Memory, and Cognition*, *21*, 1140–1154.

Strain, E., Patterson, K., & Seidenberg, M. S. (2002). Theories of word naming interact with spelling-sound consistency. *Journal of Experimental Psychology: Learning, Memory, and Cognition*, *28*, 207–214.

Toglia, M. P., & Battig, W. F. (1978). *Handbook of semantic word norms*. Hillsdale, NJ: Lawrence Erlbaum Associates, Inc.

Treiman, R., Mullennix, J., Bijeljac-Babic, R., & Richmond-Welty, E. D. (1995). The special role of rimes in the description, use, and acquisition of English orthography. *Journal of Experimental Psychology. General*, *124*, 107–136.

Velanova, K., Jacoby, L. L., Wheeler, M. E., McAvoy, M. P., Petersen, S. E., & Buckner, R. L. (2003). Functional-anatomic correlates of sustained and transient processing components engaged during controlled retrieval. *Journal of Neuroscience*, *23*, 8460–8470.

Vincent, S. B. (1912). The function of vibrissae in the behavior of the white rat. *Behavioral Monographs*, *1* (Whole No. 5).

Visscher, K. M., Miezin, F. M., Kelly, J. E., Buckner, R. L., Donaldson, D. I., McAvoy, M. P. et al. (2003). Mixed blocked/event-related designs separate transient and sustained activity in fMRI. *NeuroImage*, *19*, 1694–1708.

Vogel, E. K., Woodman, G. F., & Luck, S. J. (2005). Pushing around the locus of selection: Evidence for the flexible-selection hypothesis. *Journal of Cognitive Neuroscience*, *17*, 1907–1922.

Watts, D. J., & Strogatz, S. H. (1998). Collective dynamics of "small-world" networks. *Nature*, *393*, 440–442.

Weekes, B. S. (1997). Differential effects of number of letters on word and nonword naming latency. *Quarterly Journal of Experimental Psychology: Human Experimental Psychology*, *50A*, 439–456.

Weldon, M. S., & Roediger, H. L. (1987). Altering retrieval demands reverses the picture superiority effect. *Memory and Cognition*, *15*, 269–280.

Zevin, J. D., & Balota, D. A. (2000). Priming and attentional control of lexical and sublexical pathways during naming. *Journal of Experimental Psychology: Learning, Memory, and Cognition*, *26*, 121–135.

11 Reading complex morphological structures

Gary Libben
University of Alberta, Edmonton, Canada

The last three decades of research in lexical psycholinguistics has been characterized by an increasing concentration on words that contain more than one morpheme. This development has opened up new areas of discussion and new opportunities for theoretical and experimental advancement. The development has also played a role in bringing greater language diversity to a field in which canonical words tended to be viewed as morphologically simple units. In fact, however, simple words constitute the exceptional, rather than normal, word types in the majority of the world's languages.

Indeed, even English, which is often cited as a language with an impoverished morphological system, shows this pattern. Although monomorphemic words tend to have high token frequency, they comprise only a quarter of the word types in the language, as can be seen in Table 11.1. Interestingly, this is roughly equivalent to the proportion of monomorphemic words in German, a language which is often contrasted to English morphologically.

As can also be seen in Table 11.1, about a quarter of all the words in both English and German contain three or more morphemes. Yet, to date, the investigation of the representation and processing of such longer morphological sequences has been relatively rare in the psycholinguistic literature. The reason for this is undoubtedly that more complex morphological structures present additional challenges to the researcher, who must control and balance for an increasingly large number of stimulus characteristics in the design of experiments.

There may, however, be substantial advantages to the study of longer

Table 11.1 Percentage of monomorphemic, bimorphemic, trimorphemic, and longer words in English and German, calculated from the CELEX lemma database. Percentages are based on a sample size of 43,956 for English and 51,728 for German

Language	*Number of morphemes in a word*			
	One	Two	Three	More than three
English	26%	49%	20%	5%
German	25%	44%	21%	10%

morphological strings that outweigh the difficulties that they present for experimental design. Chief among these is the opportunity to investigate the processing consequences of a fundamental characteristic of morphologically complex strings—they are arrangements, rather than simple concatenations, of elements (Baker, 2001; Bauer, 1983). This characteristic, which is irrelevant to the processing of monomorphemic words and trivial for the processing of bimorphemic words (in which only one type of hierarchical organization is possible), is central to how longer words are interpreted by speakers of a language. However, there is very little that is presently known about the nature of morphological arrangement, its overall role in processing, and the stage of lexical processing at which this role might become relevant. My goal in this chapter is to address this gap in our understanding of how words are represented and processed in the mind through a proposal for how morphological arrangement is constructed in on-line word reading and by discussing the extent to which the proposal can provide an account of aspects of the available evidence on how multimorphemic strings are processed in visual word recognition.

The phenomena

Triconstituent compounds

The investigation of how morphemes are arranged within words requires that one consider structures that contain at least three constituents. We might begin, then, with the least complicated of such structures, triconstituent compounds. For these words, there is typically no controversy concerning whether their constituents constitute processing units in the mental lexicon. The word *football* seems clearly composed of *foot* and *ball*. Similarly, the compound *football field* is uncontroversially composed of *foot, ball*, and *field*. The question of whether and how the constituents of such triconstituent compounds are arranged seems also quite straightforward. The word *football field* has an interpretation that is consistent with the arrangement shown in Figure 11.1a. A compound such as *field football*, on the other hand, has an interpretation consistent with the arrangement shown in Figure 11.1b.

Two things are important to note at this point. The first is that, because we are beginning with a descriptive overview of the phenomenon, I am

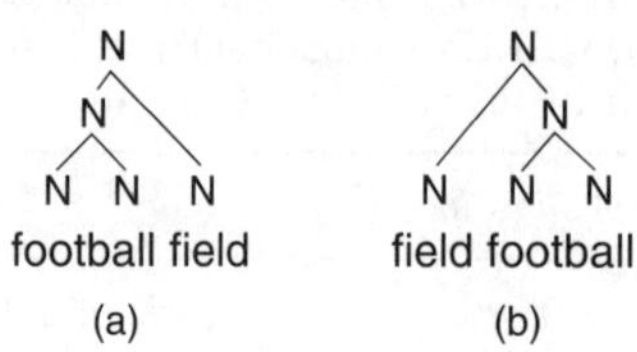

Figure 11.1 Two morphological arrangements of triconstituent compounds. All whole words and constituents and subcompounds are nouns (N).

employing the terms *arrangement* and *interpretation* rather than the more traditional term *morphological structure* (e.g. Lieber, 1980; Selkirk, 1983) to refer to the configurations in Figure 11.1. Whether such words are indeed morphologically structured in the mind is still an open question. That they are interpreted along the lines shown in Figure 11.1 seems relatively certain. Here I am referring to interpretation as the end point of the word-reading process.

The second point concerns the question of whether triconstituent compounds, which are not written as single words in English, can be properly considered to be words. I claim that they can. The orthographic convention for triconstituent compounds in English is that a space at the compound's major constituent boundary is obligatory, whereas a space may or may not be present at the minor constituent boundary. Thus, *football field* is spaced at the major constituent boundary, whereas *ice cream cone* is spaced at both (see de Jong et al., 2002; Juhasz, Inhoff, & Rayner, 2005, for recent discussion of processing differences between spaced and nonspaced compounds). The German compound corresponding to the English *football field* is written as *Fussballfeld*. Its interpretation is left-branching, just as it is for English.

Prefixed and suffixed roots

We might turn our attention now to a somewhat more complicated type of trimorphemic word. These are words such as *relockable* and *unthinkable* in English. As can be seen in Figure 11.2, these words can be described as having left-branching and right-branching arrangements that are comparable to those shown for the compounds in Figure 11.1. The affixed forms differ from the compounds, however, in some important respects. The psychological status of the affixes is not comparable to that of the compound roots, because these derivational affixes (*re-, un-, -able*) can be said to have word-formation functions rather than meanings of the types typically associated with word roots. More importantly, the motivation for positing the hierarchical arrangement of elements in Figure 11.2 differs from that of Figure 11.1. The word *unthinkable* is assigned a right-branching configuration primarily because the alternative left-branching structure would involve positing a subword *unthink*, which does not exist in English and is not easily interpretable, given the meaning of the word *think*. A third alternative, positing a flat

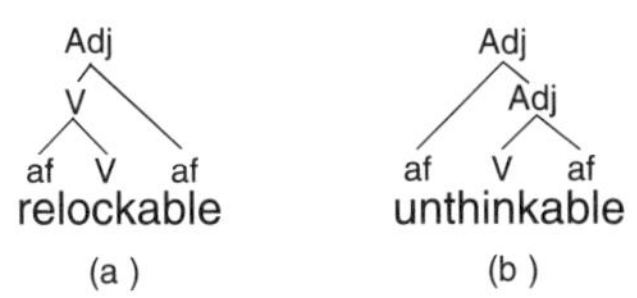

Figure 11.2 The arrangement of morphemes within prefixed and suffixed English words. Both words are adjectives. Item (a) has a verb (V) as its subunit, whereas item (b) has an adjective. af: affix.

nongrouped arrangement of the three morphemes, is disfavoured because of the general view that branching is binary in English morphology.

The arrangement of morphemes in the word *relockable* is dictated both by the general view that branching is binary and by the specific selectional restriction of the prefix *re-* in English. This prefix combines only with verbs. Almost any combination of *re-* plus a verb is interpretable in English, whereas any combination of, for example, *re-* plus an adjective is uninterpretable (e.g. **re-happy, *re-quick, *re-small*). Because of this restriction, the left-branching morphological analysis of *relockable* is "forced". The prefix *re-* cannot attach to adjectives, so an analysis such as *[re[lockable]]* is impossible.

It is important to note that, although the notion of selectional restrictions has played an important role in accounting for constraints on word-formation patterns (Aronoff & Sridhar, 1987; Kiparsky, 1983; Pesetsky, 1985; Sproat, 1988; Zwicky, 1988), it remains somewhat less clear whether they also constrain the manner in which words are processed in on-line reading. While there seems little doubt that the configurations shown in Figure 11.1 correspond to native speakers' interpretations, so that *football field* is understood as *football* plus *field*, it is far less clear that *relockable* must be interpreted as *relock* plus *able* because of the selectional restrictions of the prefix *re-*. We will return to this issue in greater depth below. In the meantime, however, one more phenomenon concerning the arrangement of morphemes within tri-morphemic words requires discussion.

All the cases that we have discussed so far involve the assumption that a single word has a single arrangement of morphemes. The examples in Figure 11.3 show that there are also words that can have two alternate arrangements that are each associated with a particular interpretation of the word. These words are thus structurally ambiguous in the way that multiword units such as *French history teacher* (either "a teacher of French history" or "a teacher of history who is French") and sentences such as *She photographed the man with the cell phone* are structurally ambiguous (assuming that she could be in possession of a cell phone that has photographic ability).

The configurations shown in Figure 11.3 are particularly interesting in that they allow us to separate the putative arrangement of morphemes within a word from the sequence of morphemes themselves. The ambiguity of these strings also raises an important question concerning the place that morphological arrangement might have in the overall modelling of complex word

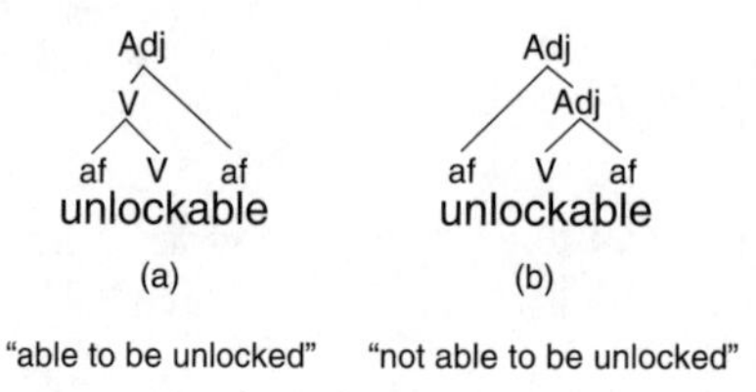

Figure 11.3 Two morphological arrangements for the word "unlockable". Each is associated with a distinct interpretation. af: affix; V: verb.

reading. If these words are in fact structurally ambiguous in the same sense that phrases and sentences are structurally ambiguous, we must consider that morphological arrangement might be a simply a linguistic shorthand for describing how the word is understood in on-line reading. In the case of the ambiguous sentence, *She photographed the man with the cell phone*, it would be extremely improbable that there were actually two pre-existing, structurally distinct sentences which correspond to (1) the interpretation "she used her cell phone to photograph the man" or (2) the interpretation "the man was holding a cell phone". Rather, it seems that structural ambiguity results from the on-line parsing procedure itself. Now, is it also the case that the arrangement of morphemes is constructed on-line during visual word processing? It seems to me that there is evidence that it is, and that the morphological parsing procedure is distinct from the subsequent interpretive processes which it feeds with multiple parsing alternatives (see Gibson, 1998, for a multiple parse account of sentence ambiguity). In the sections below, I sketch a hypothesis of the characteristics of morphological arrangement in on-line word reading and discuss the extent to which this hypothesis can account for the available evidence on the reading of triconstituent words.

Local morphological parsing

I argue that there is evidence that the arrangement of morphemes is in fact formed during on-line visual lexical processing, but that these arrangements are local. They result not from a system that seeks to assign a morphological analysis to a word as a whole, but rather from a parsing mechanism that isolates individual morphemes as episodic memory traces and constructs bimorphemic strings from activated adjacent elements. Thus, in the processing of the German triconstituent compound *Fussballfeld*, the parser isolates the substrings <*fuss, ball, fuss+ball, feld, ball+feld*>. For the English word *relockable*, it isolates <*re-, lock, re+lock, -able, lock+able*>. For the string *unthinkable*, it isolates <*un-, think, un+think, -able, think+able*>. Finally, for a novel trimorphemic string such as *reponkity*, it would isolate <*re, ponk, re+ponk, -ity, ponk+ity*>.

The sequencing of activated elements within the multimorphemic string (e.g. <*re-, lock, re+lock, -able, lock+able*>) highlights the assumption that there is a left-right asymmetry in the processing of English words (Andrews & Davis, 1999; Hudson & Buis, 1995). This asymmetry is in accord with findings that have been documented early in the morphological processing literature (Mandelis & Tharp, 1977; Taft & Forster, 1976). Thus, we might assume that morphological parsing, particularly of long words, is progressive (that is, it proceeds from beginning to end).

Libben (1994) and Libben, Derwing, and de Almeida (1999) claimed that morphological parsing is not an analysis of a string but, rather, a means by which a hungry language-processing system is fed with as many candidate lexical representations and combinations as possible. Under this view, morphological parsing stops short of constructing a full analysis of a word that might rule out other analyses. It makes hierarchical interpretation possible, but does not create hierarchical interpretation.

This approach could be most accurately labelled "naive parsing". The parser is simply scanning a string from beginning to end. If this scan results in a "hit" (that is, the activation of a morphemic memory trace along the way), two things happen: The parser binds the activated morpheme to the immediately preceding morpheme (if one exists) and then restarts the parsing procedure, now with the "hit" morpheme as the first morpheme of the parse. I claim that the hypothesis of naive morphological parsing has the key advantage of not trying to do too much. To perform its function of giving the language-processing system as much as possible to work with, the parser cannot rule out possible structures. Thus, for the input word *unthinkable*, it isolates *un+think* as well as *think+able*. That *un+think* is not an interpretable word of English is determined at a later stage of processing. This later stage would reassign weightings to the activated substrings so that the set <*un-, think, un+think, able, think+able*> would be weighted to favour *think+able* over *un+think*. Thus, using underscore to indicate stronger weighting, the substrings would be re-evaluated as <*un-, think, un+think, -able, think+able*>.

Finally, the feature of local binary binding requires additional comment. As we have seen in Table 11.1, the majority of English words are bimorphemic. Thus, the most common morphological activity that a native speaker would engage in would simply be to bind two morphemes together. As has also been discussed above, the fundamental word-formation process in English is binary, leading to the formal view that morphological structure can be described as having a binary branching structure. In my view, it is possible that this binary branching structure is not a "design" constraint on English morphology, but rather a processing effect that follows from the local nature of human morphological parsing.

Explaining evidence from trimorphemic reading

The morphological parsing hypothesis sketched above claims that morphological parsing is a rather small component of the overall word-reading process. Nevertheless, as discussed below, it provides us explanatory ability that can bring together what appear on the surface to be unrelated experimental results. In the sections below, I review a set of experiments that have been conducted in our laboratory on the visual processing of triconstituent words and point out the manner in which the local morphological processing hypothesis can aid in the interpretation of the results of these experiments.

Prefixed and suffixed nonsense roots

Our investigation of the role of hierarchical morphological structure began by asking whether on-line word lexical processing is indeed sensitive to the kinds of roots to which an affix can attach. Libben (1993) constructed both morphologically legal and illegal trimorphemic nonsense words by adding the prefix *re-* to consonant–vowel–consonant–consonant (CVCC) nonsense roots such as *ponk*. These strings were suffixed with either the suffix *-able* or the suffix *-ity* to create stimuli such as *re-ponkity* (composed of *re+ponk+ity*) and *re-ponkable* (composed of *re+ponk+able*). The critical difference between these stimuli is that *re-ponkity* does not allow the selectional restrictions of the affixes to be resolved because, as has been stated above, the prefix *re-* attaches to verbs in English. The suffix *-ity* attaches to adjectives to form nouns. Thus, *re-ponkity* can have neither a left-branching nor right-branching interpretation. In a naming latency experiment, Libben (1993) found that strings such as *re-ponkity* yielded greater response times than words such as *re-ponkable*. In one sense, these results are surprising, because, on the surface, these strings seem equally easy or difficult to read aloud, particularly considering that both begin with *re-* + *nonsense root* and that response latency is measured from visual stimulus presentation to response onset. On the other hand, the results might seem to be expected, given that no English words have the structure [re+root+ity]. One could claim therefore that the latency differences between the two types of strings are due to analogical processes. Taken strictly on the surface, however, there are a good number of words in English that begin with *re-* and end with *-ity* (172 occurrences, e.g. *reciprocity*, in the Wortschatz Leipzig database). Thus, it seems difficult to get around the necessity of morphological parsing.

The local morphological parsing hypothesis offers a straightforward account of these results. For a word such as *reponkable*, the parser yields <*re-, ponk, re+ponk, -able, ponk+able*>. For a words such as *reponkity*, the parser yields <*re-, ponk, re+ponk, -ity, ponk+ity*>. The difference between these two cases is that, in the case of *reponkity*, a single representation *ponk* cannot be given an interpretation that is consistent with both substrings *re+ponk* and *ponk+ity* that have been generated by the parser. I claim that the attempt to resolve this inconsistency results in the elevated response times found by Libben (1993).

Prefixed and suffixed words

The question of how prefixed and suffixed words with different putative morphological structures are processed in visual word recognition was investigated by Libben (2003). This study contrasted left-branching (e.g. *relockable*) and right-branching (e.g. *unthinkable*) stimuli, as shown in Figure 11.2, and compared these to the processing of ambiguous stimuli (e.g. *unlockable*), as shown in Figure 11.3. A lexical decision task with an artificial morpheme boundary paradigm was employed with real prefixed and suffixed words such as *relockable* and *unthinkable*, novel words such as *refloodable* and *unfloodable*, and words that contained nonsense roots (e.g. *reponkable, unponkable*). Participants saw stimuli in one of three conditions: In the first condition, trimorphemic stimuli were presented with three hyphens at the major constituent boundary as determined by formal morphological analysis (e.g. *relock---able, un---thinkable*). In the second condition, the break was at the minor constituent boundary (e.g. *re---lockable, unthink---able*). Finally, in a third control condition, words were presented in their normal orthographic forms. It was reasoned that if participants do indeed construct hierarchical representations for trimorphemic words along the lines suggested in Figures 11.2 and 11.3, then breaks at the major constituent boundary would disrupt processing less than breaks at the minor constituent boundary.

The results were not at all in support of the view that trimorphemic words have branching structures that correspond to their formal morphological analyses. Both the left-branching items and the right-branching items showed less disruption when hyphens were presented between the prefix and the root as compared to between the root and the prefix. Indeed, the patterns of response between the left-branching and right-branching stimuli were identical. It might be expected that, because of a general tendency for prefix stripping in English (Taft, 1981; Taft & Forster, 1976) and the (possibly related) English orthographic convention of placing a hyphen after the prefix rather than before the suffix, there would be a general tendency for a break in that condition to be less disruptive. Nevertheless, the postulation of a strict hierarchical structure for trimorphemic words would predict a difference between the two conditions against the general background of right-branching preference. Moreover, the considerations above would apply to all prefixed and suffixed words. As can be seen in Table 11.2, however, the ambiguous stimuli showed equal disruption in both conditions.

The data shown in Table 11.2 indicate that, contrary to the morphological arrangement shown in Figure 11.2, an analysis of a word such as *relockable* as *re+lockable* is not ruled out. The situation for ambiguous words, however, is different. As can be seen in Table 11.2, disruption of either the prefix+root combination or the root+suffix combination results in a relatively large processing cost. I interpret this finding to suggest that both bimorphemic outputs of the morphological parse of an ambiguous word such as *unfoldable* <*un-, un+fold, -able, fold+able*> are needed by subsequent interpretive

Table 11.2 Response times (in milliseconds) for the artificial morpheme boundary conditions in Libben (2003)

Category	*Control*	*Prefix–root (cost)*	*Root–suffix (cost)*	*Cost difference*
Left-branching	relockable 927	re---lockable 960 (33)	relock---able 1010 (83)	–50
Right-branching	unthinkable 985	un---thinkable 1014 (19)	unthink---able 1059 (74)	–55
Ambiguous	unfoldable 951	un---foldable 1014 (63)	unfold---able 1000 (49)	14

procedures. It also suggests that ambiguous words such as these do not have a default (e.g. right-branching) structure.

These lexical decision results are consistent with off-line segmentation data reported for the same stimulus types by Libben (2006). Here, participants were presented with stimuli in their unaltered form (e.g. *refillable*) and were asked to segment them by drawing a single line at the most appropriate location in the word. For words prefixed by *re-*, participants provided segmentation after the prefix (e.g. *re / lockable*) 46% of the time. For novel re-prefixed words, the preference for segmentation after the prefix was 76%. Ambiguous stimuli (e.g. *unlockable*) were segmented between the prefix and the root 56% of the time. This contrasts with the segmentation preferences for unambiguous words prefixed by *un-* (e.g. *unthinkable*), which show a preference for segmentation between the prefix and the root 93% of the time. Thus, segmentation preferences are not simply guided by the surface form of a word. What seems to be important is whether an isolated bimorphemic string within the word is itself a word. As shown in 1a, 1b, and 1c below (using the underscore convention for existing words), the local morphological parsing hypothesis generates sufficient information for this determination. It should also be noted that, in terms of the result of local morphological parsing, the results for 1a and the ambiguous structure in 1c are identical.

(1a) relockable <re-, lock, re+lock, -able, lock+able>
(1b) unthinkable <un-, think, un+think, -able, think+able>
(1c) unlockable <un-, lock, un+lock, -able, lock+able>

Structurally ambiguous words

The claim above that words such as *relockable* and *unlockable* have identical parses can also be represented as the claim that, as whole words, they have identical lexical network representations. Using the notation in Libben (2003), those representations would have the form shown in Figure 11.4.

It should be noted, that in a sense, both words in Figure 11.4 have a single representation, and that representation includes specifications of whole-word structure, both free and bound morphemes, and bimorphemic substrings (see *Pollatsek & Hyönä*, this volume, for further discussion of morphological constituency in word recognition, and *Taft*, this volume, for a discussion of

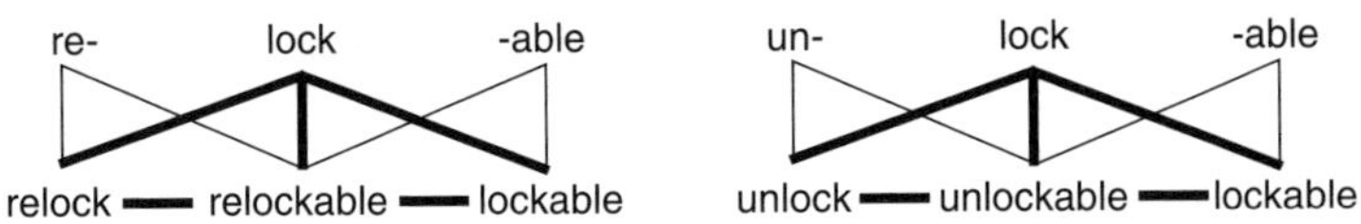

Figure 11.4 Lexical network configurations for *relockable* and *unlockable*. In both cases, the whole words are linked to two bimorphemic substrings and to their monomorphemic constituents. The difference between thick and thin lines of association reflects the claim that associations are stronger between free morphemes than between free and bound morphemes.

the representation of bound morphemes). Moreover, links between whole-word forms and monomorphemic and bimorphemic constituents enable differences in interpretation to be made when necessary, without the need to postulate separate lexical representations for each interpretation. In the case of a word such as *unlockable*, those interpretations can be paraphrased as "able to be unlocked" and "not able to be locked".

The available evidence (Popescu, 2004) suggests that native speakers are not consciously aware of the ambiguity of strings such as *unlockable*. This is consistent with the view that they do not have alternative parses, but rather a malleable morphological representation that enables two interpretations, as required. Experiments reported in de Almeida and Libben (2005) demonstrate this malleability.

In an initial experiment, de Almeida and Libben (2005) asked participants to rate the acceptability of sentences that contained ambiguous words such as *unlockable*. Sentences were constructed so that they biased interpretation toward either the meaning "able to be unlocked" or "not able to be locked", as in 2a and 2b below.

(2a) When the zookeeper tried to lock the birdcage, he noticed that the birdcage was unlockable.
(2b) When the zookeeper tried to unlock the birdcage, he noticed that the birdcage was unlockable.

They key biasing words in these sentences are those that occupy the sixth position (*lock* or *unlock*). Participants found both sentences to be semantically acceptable, suggesting that the final trimorphemic word of the sentence can be assigned one or another interpretation on demand. As a check on whether the contexts were indeed sufficiently biasing and whether ambiguous words are given the interpretations expected, an additional set of sentences were presented to participants for rating. These sentences were identical to those shown in (2a) and (2b), except that, for each sentence, the final ambiguous word was replaced by both its paraphrases, yielding the four sentences in (3a–d) below.

(3a) When the zookeeper tried to lock the birdcage, he noticed that the birdcage was not able to be locked.
(3b) When the zookeeper tried to unlock the birdcage, he noticed that the birdcage was able to be unlocked.
(3c) When the zookeeper tried to lock the birdcage, he noticed that the birdcage was able to be unlocked.
(3d) When the zookeeper tried to unlock the birdcage, he noticed that the birdcage was not able to be locked.

Participants in the experiment rated sentences (3a) and (3b) as acceptable and sentences (3c) and (3d) as unacceptable, indicating that the sentence contexts

Table 11.3 Semantic acceptability ratings on a scale of 1 to 5 for sentences presented in de Almeida and Libben (2005)

	Sentence type	*Rating (1 to 5)*
(2a)	lock . . . unlockable	3.9
(2b)	unlock . . . unlockable	3.8
(3a)	lock . . . able to be unlocked	4.1
(3b)	unlock . . . not able to be locked	3.8
(3c)	lock . . . able to be unlocked	2.4
(3d)	unlock . . . not able to be locked	2.3

were sufficiently biasing against the inappropriate interpretation of the ambiguous word. In fact, as can be seen in Table 11.3, the ratings for the ambiguous words and their correct paraphrases were almost identical.

These findings are consistent with the view that morphologically ambiguous words are assigned distinct interpretations in on-line sentence reading. However, the ability of participants to assign different interpretations to a word does not require that there be a distinct lexical representation associated with each reading. This raises the question of how we might be able to represent the fact that an ambiguous word is given one interpretation or the other. I claim that the answer to this question is not to be found in the morphological parsing procedure itself. That procedure simply yields the substrings <*un-, lock, un+lock, -able, lock+able*>. The resulting lexical network, however, can be seen as shiftable, so that when *unlockable* has the interpretation "not able to be locked", the focus of the network is shifted to the right, as shown in Figure 11.5.

This perspective provides a framework in which to understand the cross-modal priming effects reported in de Almeida and Libben (2005). In their second experiment, participants heard sentences such as 2a and 2b above and were presented at sentence offset with a visual target for lexical decision. In the critical conditions of the experiment, the visual target was the right substring of the ambiguous trimorphemic word (e.g. *lockable*). It was reasoned that when the sentence was biased toward the "not able to be locked" interpretation of the ambiguous word, responses to the target *lockable* would be faster. Indeed, lexical decision response times to *lockable* were faster when it was preceded by sentence 2a than when it was preceded by sentence 2b. However, the results showed that sentence context alone could not result

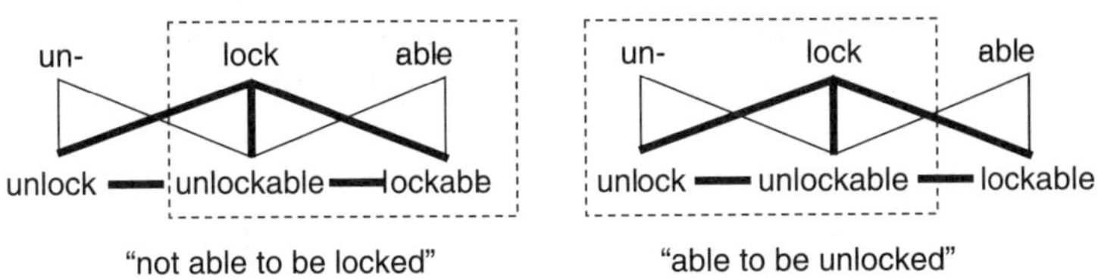

Figure 11.5 Shifting the focus of ambiguous prefixed and suffixed words.

in response latency differences, because when the ambiguous word was replaced with a neutral word such as *unapproachable*, the lexical decision latencies to the target *lockable* did not differ when preceded by the two sentence contexts.

Are triconstituent compounds parsed in the same manner as trimorphemic words? Thus far, our discussion of experimental results has concentrated on prefixed and affixed words. This concentration results from the fact that, as noted above, the structuring of triconstituent compounds is much more straightforward. Nevertheless, it is important to point out that the approach to morphological parsing outlined here seems to apply to compounds just as it applied to prefix and suffixed words. For a string such as *Fussballfeld*, the parser yields the set <*Fuss, Ball, Fussball, Feld, Ballfeld*>. The fact that all substrings except *Ballfeld* are existing words is sufficient to create the hierarchical interpretation. Again, the key point here is that the driving force in interpretation is not the assignment of a strict hierarchical structure over a set of morphemes, but rather the activation of substrings which have their own representations in the mental lexicon and which may themselves be morphologically complex (in this case, bimorphemic compounds).

There is one additional phenomenon associated with triconstituent compounds, however, that is important to a discussion of morphological parsing. That is, for the right-headed languages that have been thus far investigated, triconstituent compounds show a tendency to be left-branching. This was documented in Krott et al. (2004), who found 65% of the triconstituent compounds in both German and Dutch to be left-branching by a CELEX corpus analysis. A segmentation experiment that they conducted with triconstituent nonsense strings found that Dutch participants also showed a 65% preference for segmentation between the second and third constituents. This tendency is opposite to that observed by Libben (2006) for the segmentation of prefixed and suffixed words and to the finding of Popescu (2004) that, all other things being equal, participants prefer a right-branching parse of an ambiguous string.

The preference for right-branching compounds in Dutch reported by Krott et al. (2004) seems also to be evident in Chinese. Yin, Derwing, and Libben (2004) reported a series of experiments which show that native speakers of Chinese show a 65% preference for left-branching compounds in a variety of off-line segmentation tasks. The most striking of their results was that the preference for left-branching compounds was greatest in cases where the semantics of the compound plays no role. The critical cases for this observation were three-character compounds such as *mai-ke-feng*, which translates as *wheat-gram-wind*. These three characters are used to represent the phonology of the Chinese loanword from English *microphone*, to which *mai-ke-feng* is the closest sounding. Thus, it seems that the preference for left-branching compounds in Chinese (and in Dutch, based on the segmentation patterns for nonsense strings) is structural rather than semantic in nature.

This brings us to a potential paradox. If it is claimed that the same morphological parsing mechanism is employed for both affixed and compound words, why would that parsing mechanism yield a left-branching preference for compounds, but a right-branching preference for prefixed and suffixed words? I suggest that the reason for these opposing preferences is to be found in the fact that all the languages we have discussed are morphologically right-headed. Taking English as an example, right-headedness describes the fact that it is generally the rightmost element of the string that determines its lexical category. Thus, suffixes are typically category changing in English, but prefixes are not. In the case of compounds, right-headedness plays a significant role in how the compound can be understood. If a speaker of English encounters the string *orange juice* for the first time, that speaker will know that it is a type of juice, just as *juice orange* must be a type of orange. Of course, this is a significant heuristic in the interpretation of novel compounds, and is most effective when the head is morphologically simple, as it is for left-branching compounds. The interpretive advantage of head simplicity can perhaps be observed in the following example: The novel compounds *teddybear puppet* and *puppet teddybear* in English mean more or less the same things. Nevertheless, *teddybear puppet* seems more natural and easier to understand. If it is, the reason would lie in the fact that its head, *puppet*, as the semantic pivot of the string, is morphologically simple.

In the case of compounds, a left-branching structure ensures that the root morpheme, which is the morphological head of the construction, is isolated to the right of the major constituent boundary. For prefixed and suffixed words, however, such a left-branching structure places the word's single-root morpheme to the left of the majority constituent boundary, in the non-head position. While a great many English words are left-branching (e.g. *unhappiness, endearment*), it may be that these carry with them a processing cost, so that, when all things are in fact equal, native speakers prefer a right-branching analysis of prefixed and suffixed words. This "all other things being equal" clause seems also to account for why Chinese left-branching parses were greatest for loan words such as *mai-ke-feng*. These structures allow the greatest freedom of morphological arrangement.

Conclusions

The discussion above of the role of morphological head simplicity and position within the string is still incomplete. At present, we do not know whether the patterns of parsing preference generalize across languages and whether they would show reversal for languages that are morphologically left-headed. We also do not know at what stage of lexical processing morphological headedness is determined and interpreted. Yet, it is clear that the phenomenon itself could come under scrutiny only through a consideration of how words with three or more morphemes are processed. This consideration also allows us to explore the relation between formal analyses of language and on-line lexical processing in reading.

The exploration of this relation in this chapter has yielded a perspective in which formal and processing accounts are related, but not identical. I have proposed, for example, that bimorphemic subunits of the tree structures shown in Figures 11.1–11.3 are generated as part of on-line morphological parsing, but that the uppermost level is generated by interpretive processes, so that notions such as "major constituent boundary" represent part of a shorthand for how a word is interpreted, not how it is parsed. In addition, it has been argued that the configuration of this shorthand is probabilistic, so that a word such as *unlockable* may be interpreted as *un+lockable* or *unlock+able*, depending on the context in which it is encountered.

The local hypothesis of morphological parsing that I have outlined raises the following question: Why would morphological parsing simply scan a word from beginning to end, isolating morphemes and creating bimorphemic constituents, when the ecological goal of word recognition is to recognize the word as a whole? One answer to this question is that, as we have assumed throughout this discussion, morphological parsing is carried out in parallel with whole-word recognition, which would identify a trimorphemic word above the frequency threshold as an independent memory trace. This explanation, however, would not account for the majority of cases of trimorphemic word recognition, which are typically associated with productive compounding and affixation. Neither would it provide an explanation of why the morphological parser stops short. There is ample evidence of redundancy throughout human cognition, and having whole-word activation "checked" from two sources would most likely be advantageous.

I would argue that the reason that the morphological parser stops short of constructing a full parse of the word, or even multiple complete parses of the word, is that its function is to feed the language-processing system with as much as possible. The true ecological goal of lexical processing is, upon reflection, not word recognition but the creation of meaning. A local morphological parser allows for as much meaning creation as possible as quickly as possible. By parsing words from beginning to end, the parser allows lexical activation to begin immediately (a feature that might be critical in spoken-word recognition). By creating bimorphemic substrings from adjacent elements, the parser provides the interpretive processes with as much substructure as is needed, while not ruling out potential interpretations.

This last characteristic—not disallowing potential interpretations—constitutes perhaps the most important difference between morphological processing, as outlined in this parsing proposal, and morphological representation, as characterized in the first three figures of this chapter. A morphological representation specifies that a morphologically complex string has one structure, and therefore not another. In my view, if there is an overarching design characteristic in morphological processing, it is that this is exactly what it does not do. The most adaptive morphological parser is one that opens as many doors to meaning as possible and closes as few as possible.

Acknowledgement

This research was supported by a Major Collaborative Research Initiative Grant from SSHRC to Gary Libben (Director), Gonia Jarema, Eva Kehayia, Bruce Derwing, and Lori Buchanan.

References

Andrews, S., & Davis, C. (1999). Interactive activation accounts of morphological decomposition: Finding the trap in mousetrap. *Brain and Language*, *68*, 355–361.

Aronoff, M., & Sridhar, S. (1987). Morphological levels in English and Kannada. In E. Gussmann (Ed.), *Rules and the lexicon*. Lublin, Poland: Redakcja Wydawnictw Katolickiego Uniwersytetu Lubelskiego.

Baker, M. (2001). *The atoms of language*. New York: Basic Books.

Bauer, L. (1983). *English word formation*. New York: Cambridge University Press.

de Almeida, R. G., & Libben, G. (2005). Changing morphological structures: The effect of sentence context on the interpretation of structurally ambiguous English trimorphemic words. *Language and Cognitive Processes*, *20*, 373–398.

de Jong, N. H., Feldman, L., Schreuder, R., Pastizzo, M., & Baayen, R. H. (2002). The processing and representation of Dutch and English compounds: Peripheral morphological and central orthographic effects. *Brain and Language*, *81*, 555–567.

Gibson, E. (1998). Linguistic complexity: Locality of syntactic dependencies. *Cognition*, *78*, 1–76.

Hudson, P. T. W., & Buis, D. (1995). Left-to-right processing of derivational morphology. In L. B. Feldman (Ed.), *Morphological aspects of language processing* (pp. 386–396). Hillsdale, NJ: Lawrence Erlbaum Associates, Inc.

Juhasz, B. J., Inhoff, A. W., & Rayner, K. (2005). The role of interword spaces in the processing of English compound words. *Language and Cognitive Processes*, *20*, 291–316.

Kiparsky, P. (1983). Word formation and the lexicon. In F. Ingemann (Ed.), *Proceedings of the 1982 Mid-America Linguistics Conference*. University of Kansas.

Krott, A., Libben, G., Jarema, G., Dressler, W., Schreuder, R., & Baayen, H. (2004). Probability in the grammar of German and Dutch: Interfixation in triconstituent compounds. *Language and Speech*, *47*, 83–106.

Libben, G. (1993). Are morphological structures computed during word recognition? *Journal of Psycholinguistic Research*, *22*, 535–544.

Libben, G. (1994). How is morphological decomposition achieved? *Language and Cognitive Processes*, *9*, 369–391.

Libben, G. (2003). Morphological parsing and morphological structure. In A. Egbert & D. Sandra (Eds.), *Reading complex words* (pp. 221–239). Amsterdam: Kluwer.

Libben, G. (2006). Getting at psychological reality: On- and off-line tasks in the investigation of hierarchical morphological structure. In G. Wiebe, G. Libben, T. Priestly, R. Smyth, & S. Wang (Eds.), *Phonology, morphology and the empirical imperative: Papers in honour of Bruce Derwing* (pp. 349–370). Taipei: Crane.

Libben, G., Derwing, B. L., & de Almeida, R. G. (1999). Ambiguous novel compounds and models of morphological parsing. *Brain and Language*, *68*, 378–386.

Lieber, R. (1980). *The organization of the lexicon*. Doctoral dissertation, MIT. (Distributed by Indiana University Linguistics Club 1981a).

Mandelis, L., & Tharp, D. A. (1977). The processing of affixed words. *Memory and Cognition*, *5*, 690–695.

Pesetsky, D. (1985). Morphology and logical form. *Linguistic Inquiry*, *16*, 193–246.

Popescu, A. (2004). *Structural ambiguity in trimorphemic English words: Morphological processing and lexical access in structurally ambiguous words presented in isolation*. Unpublished MSc thesis. University of Alberta, Edmonton, Canada.

Selkirk, E. O. (1982). *The syntax of words*. Linguistic Inquiry Monograph I. Cambridge, MA: MIT Press.

Sproat, R. (1988). Bracketing paradoxes, cliticization and other topics: The mapping between syntax and phonological structure. In M. Everaert, A. Evers, R. Huybregts, & M. Trommelen (Eds.), *Morphology and modularity* (pp. 339–360). Dordrecht, The Netherlands: Foris.

Taft, M. (1981). Prefix stripping revisited. *Journal of Verbal Learning and Verbal Behavior*, *20*, 289–297.

Taft, M., & Forster, K. I. (1975). Lexical storage and the retrieval of prefixed words. *Journal of Verbal Learning and Verbal Behavior*, *14*, 630–647.

Taft, M., & Forster, K. I. (1976). Lexical storage and retrieval of polymorphemic and polysyllabic words. *Journal of Verbal Learning and Verbal Behavior*, *15*, 607–620.

Yin, H., Derwing, B. L., & Libben, G. (2004). *Branching preferences for large lexical structures in Chinese*. Poster presented at the Fourth International Conference on the Mental Lexicon, Windsor, Canada, June 2004.

Zwicky, A. (1988). Morphological rules, operations and operation types. *Proceedings of the Fourth Annual Meeting of the East States Society for Computational Linguistics* (pp. 318–334).

12 Processing of morphemically complex words in context: What can be learned from eye movements

Alexander Pollatsek
University of Massachusetts, USA
Jukka Hyönä
University of Turku, Finland

Until recently, a large majority of the research on the processing of visual words has ignored whether morphemes are involved in the recognition or the understanding of words. This research either has been conducted with morphemically simple words or, if not, has largely ignored whether the words are morphemically complex or not. Among other things, this seems to have shaped views of how words are processed; processing is often discussed in terms of *lexical entries*, and identification and/or access to a word's meaning are often seen as occurring when the excitation of a single lexical entry either rises above some threshold or is sufficiently greater than the excitation of any competitor. That is, identifying words is seen as a memory-retrieval process that is quite distinct from the obviously productive processes involved in computing syntax and putting together the meanings of words to understand the meaning of discourse. Parallel distributed models have a somewhat more complex view of how identification of words and access to their meaning occur, but these networks usually have only letters, letter clusters, and words as the meaningful units which enter into the processing of visual words, and if morphemes are used, they are likely to have no special status beyond syllables or other sequences of letters that may co-occur frequently in words.

The fact that morphemes have largely been ignored in the word-identification literature (at least up until fairly recently) may partially be due to the fact that a large majority of word-identification studies have been done in English, which is relatively impoverished inflectionally. As a result, it may be easier to forget that multimorphemic words are quite common. (In fact, at least a third of the words in the first sentence of this paragraph are multimorphemic, and this is not atypical of written English.) It also may be due to the fact that multimorphemic words are likely to be harder to study, both because they tend to be long, and because it becomes clear that there are many added variables one should control for. However, it also may be due to a tacit belief that morphemes are largely irrelevant in processing visual words and that morphemically complex words are processed no differently than morphemically simple words (that is, they are accessed through their lexical entries or by the same parallel distributed process that morphemically simple words are—depending on one's theoretical preferences). If so, what may underlie this belief is that word identification is so rapid that we do not have time to do a morphemic analysis and that morphemic analysis may be needed only for novel words or those very low-frequency words that are essentially novel for some readers (Caramazza, Laudanna, & Romani, 1988).

We thought it would be of some value to present some analysis and discussion, prior to discussing the reading data, of what the likely costs and benefits are to a system that involves morphemic analysis in the identification of words relative to a system that merely has a direct identification process and eschews any such analysis process. For simplicity, we will couch this discussion in terms of models that assume lexical entries instead of parallel-distributed types of models; however, we think that many of the points are relevant to these models as well.

Benefits and costs of morphemic analysis as a component of word identification

Naively, it seems that the chief cost of inserting morphemic analysis into the identification of words is that it introduces an extra step. However, it may be that two (or more) quick steps are faster than one really slow one. Perhaps a reasonable place to start is thinking about how one identifies *antidisestablishmentarianism*, which is often trotted out to US schoolchildren as the longest word in the English language. Given that research has shown that the window for viewing letters in reading is about 12 letters, this word extends way beyond the window and thus one is unlikely to process it in a single eye fixation (that is, process it without moving the eyes to bring other parts of the word into sharp foveal vision). One might counter this example by positing that one does not have to process all the letters of a long word such as this in order to identify it because knowing the first few letters allows an unambiguous identification. However, that is questionable even in this case, as it could be *antidisestablishmentarian* or *antidisestablishment* and it could be singular or plural. Moreover, if we get past English, there are many long words (e.g. compound words) in other languages, such as German and Finnish, for which the first few letters do not come close to unambiguously identifying the word. Moreover, if we define *word* linguistically rather than "the thing between the spaces", then there are quite a few long compounds in English as well, such as *Washington cherry blossom festival*.[1]

The need to process a word on more than one fixation, of course, does not necessarily mean that one has to process a long word segmentally. That is, one can register all the letters perceived on one fixation as excitation values in some sort of visual word form detector or *logogen* and then get the information from the remaining letters that are now near the second (or third) fixation point to further the excitation of the logogen. However, such an account skims over certain important questions, such as how to align the letter information coming in on successive fixations (which would be made more difficult if certain letters are improperly encoded on the prior fixation). Thus, if a word is fixated twice (or more), one has to consider how the orthographic information is combined on the various fixations and whether one is tacitly introducing subword units (that might include morphemes) into the process to help with the alignment process (among other things). If so, one might not really be contrasting a one-step process of direct access with a constructive morphemic process, but instead be contrasting two different multistep processes.

The above discussion suggests that a key variable in morphemic processing may be word length. That is, if you were God designing a word-identification module, and if a multimorphemic word like *runs* is short enough, you might conclude that the best way to identify it is to go directly to the lexical entry for the whole word and then read off from this entry the meaning (which includes the fact that it is the third-person singular form of *run*). This process is plausibly less time-consuming than trying to compute this meaning directly from parsing the word into its morphemes, identifying them, and then computing the meaning from them. In contrast, for long words, using such a direct-access strategy is less obviously the more efficient encoding strategy and may run into difficulties such as keeping everything straight across fixations that a componential process may not run into.

The length of the word relative to length of the component morphemes is another factor that is plausibly related to whether identifying a word through its morphemic components is worth the effort. For example, for a relatively long word like *strengths*, the root morpheme *strength* is only one letter shorter, so one may not buy that much in trying to decompose it, because by the time you have perceptually encoded *strength*, you might as well have encoded *strengths*. However, the factor of relative length may be qualified by the positioning of the relevant morphemes. For example, for a prefixed word like *decompose*, the whole word is not much longer than the root, but if the initial fixation on the word tends to be toward the beginning of the word, it may be quite hard to process the whole word on the first fixation, and if the second fixation is somewhere in the middle of the root morpheme *compose*, that might help processing of the root and make a compositional process easier and/or faster than a direct access process. (Note that the above discussion tacitly assumes that, in a componential process, identifying the root morpheme is the key.) This suggests another variable that may influence how a complex word is processed: where the eyes land. To take an extreme case, if the eyes land just a bit to the left of the beginning of a word (even though attention is directed at that word), it may be a lot more difficult to encode all the letter information than if the first fixation is in the middle of the word.

A final "surface" aspect of morphemically complex words that plausibly would influence whether morphemic decomposition is important in encoding is the orthographic and/or phonological transparency of the component morphemes. Virtually all the examples so far have been orthographically transparent (as are almost all compound words), but many other polymorphemic words are not. Orthographic opaqueness may range from minor, such as (in English) the relatively rule-governed opaqueness that results from deleting silent *e* or doubling final consonants when adding *ing*, to greater opaqueness for something like *strength*, to completely opaque morphemic relationships like *go–went*. (We will discuss semantic opaqueness later; however, a pretty large majority of multimorphemic words are fairly semantically transparent.)

So far, by focusing on relatively low-level perceptual factors, we have avoided speculating both on the processing costs of putting the components together and about the mechanism by which composition is accomplished. However, this discussion of low-level factors has raised a point about compositional processing that should be considered seriously. That is, because many multimorphemic words are likely to be fixated more than once, some compositional process is necessary to put together the information accessed from the two (or more) fixations on the word. Thus, we think the real arena for discussion should be whether involving morphemes in this compositional process is a plus or minus, and if so, why it helps or hinders processing.

Integration across saccades

It has been clearly documented that integration of information across fixations in reading (Rayner, 1975; Rayner & Pollatsek, 1989) or object recognition (Pollatsek, Rayner, & Collins, 1984) is not a "visual" integration process, but instead occurs at a more abstract level. Perhaps the best evidence is that changing the case of all letters from one fixation to the next has virtually no effect on reading speed or identification time for a single word (Rayner, McConkie, & Zola, 1980). Thus, as a starting point, it is clear that the integration is at the level of abstract letter identities (or higher levels). The next key question that needs to be answered, obviously, is how the order of the letters is coded and/or maintained. Initially, most models of word recognition assumed that the order was somehow magically encoded, so that when one saw *work*, not only did one encode that there was a *w, o, r*, and *k*, but also one knew exactly which letter positions (or *slots*) these letters were in. This idea has been challenged in the last 10 years or so by two main factors. The first is the plausibility argument. That is, although it is not implausible that such a "slot model" might work for a four-letter word, it seems quite implausible that one would be able to reliably code veridically that *i* is the sixth letter of *plausibility*. The second is that there are now a significant number of data indicating that there is uncertainty in the letter positional coding system, so that one can get facilitation from primes or previews in which letter positions are reversed (for example, one gets a significantly bigger "preview benefit" (see below) on the target word *judge* from a preview of *jugde* than from a preview of *jupte*; Johnson, Perea, & Rayner, submitted, 2006).

Various models have sprung up to deal with these problems with a slot model (Davis, 1999; *Davis*, this volume; Grainger & Van Heuven, 2004; Perea, Gomez, & Ratcliff, 2003). They generally include one of two mechanisms. The first is that the position of a letter in a word is not explicitly coded, but, instead, a word is encoded as a constellation of letter bigrams, trigrams, and the like. Thus, *work* is possibly encoded as the individual letters plus the collection {#w, wo, or, rk, k#, #wo, wor, rok, ok#}, and *plausibility* is encoded as the individual letters plus {#p, pl, la, au, . . ., ty; or y#, #pl, pla, lau, . . . ity, ty#, ...}. (The hash sign, #, in the preceding notation stands for a space.) This type of mechanism seems like a promising step to understanding how letter order is coded in longer words, as it does not require explicit coding of letter position in extended sequences—only explicit coding of relative position in short sequences of letters. The second type of mechanism is that letter position is encoded explicitly, but with error or variability. The second type of mechanism is better at handling the letter-transposition effects discussed above (see *Davis*, this volume).

Subword units

As indicated above, many models of word recognition have been generous in positing subword units such as letter bigrams, trigrams, or even such phonologically relevant units as onset and body. However, they have often been loath to posit that there are morphemic subword units, or when they admit them, they have no special status: morphemes are just common letter strings (especially prefixes and suffixes). Although one can understand wanting to keep one's model as parsimonious as possible, this seems overparsimonious. That is, because we assume the reader had no problem in the last sentence encoding and understanding *overparsimonious* (even though the two-volume Webster dictionary we consulted did not list it among the almost 1000 prefixed words beginning with *over*), it seems clear that recognition of letter strings by morphemic decomposition is both possible and not overly time-consuming. Of course, it is still possible that the time demands of skilled reading still are such that one can afford to do such decomposition only when there is no lexical entry in one's own mental dictionary. However, it would seem strange if there were a hard and fast rule on this. That is, with many polymorphemic words, we are not really sure either whether they are in the dictionary or whether we have seen them before. Moreover, and this point is worth emphasizing, most polymorphemic words are not very high frequency at all. Thus, because the encoding of (even relatively short, monomorphemic) low-frequency words is not that rapid, it is not at all clear that "direct lexical access" is likely to be all that efficient for reasonably long, morphemically complex words. Other factors, of course, would enter in here, such as the frequency of the components (and hence their ease of identification), and, what may be as relevant for prefixed and suffixed words, the productivity of a morpheme (that is, the number of different words in which it appears as a morphemic component). Again, we would argue that it is perhaps better to ask, especially for longer words, which decompositional process is used rather than whether a decompositional process is used.

Access of meaning

So far, our discussion has focused on something fairly close to identification of the orthographic string represented by the multimorphemic word, perhaps articulated by the morphemic boundary. Of course, in reading, one has to go beyond identifying the orthographic string and identify the meaning of the word. For example, does the semantic transparency of the word make a difference? For example, are compounds that have a semantically opaque component, such as *butterfly*, more difficult to identify than compounds that are semantically transparent? The answer to this question should give clues as to the level at which compositional processes are occurring. Another type of issue is the structure of the multimorphemic word. For example, is a *French schoolteacher* a {French [schoolteacher]} (i.e. a schoolteacher who happens to be French) or a {[French school] teacher} (i.e. a teacher at a French school)? Similarly, is *unlockable* {[unlock]able} (i.e. something that can be unlocked) or {un[lockable]} (i.e. something that can not be locked)? These examples point to the fact that a complex word is more than a string of morphemes, but that there is an internal structure as well. This, of course, raises the question of whether this structure merely comes from accessing it from the lexical entry for the morphemically complex word, or whether it is constructed from the components. And if it is constructed from its components, how is this done? This latter question is beyond the scope of this chapter and is discussed in depth in the chapter by *Libben* (this volume).

The data we will focus on

As indicated by our title, the data we will consider in this chapter are virtually all from experiments in which multimorphemic words are read in sentence context, and eye-movement measures are used to infer how these words are encoded. We do so for several reasons. First, practically, an adequate discussion of these data easily fills a chapter of this length. Second, our bias is that we want to understand encoding of words in the most ecologically valid context, and we think using eye movements while people read material without having to do a task other than understanding the text is a close approximation to normal reading. Moreover, we are afraid that with other techniques, such as lexical decision, there is a danger, especially for polymorphemic words, that one will mistake decision processes and decision strategies peculiar to the task for normal encoding processes. It is also possible that some of the morphological complexity effects are the result of presenting words in isolation; this may be particularly the case for case-inflected words (e.g. *hers*) that typically appear in context (see Hyönä, Vainio, & Laine, 2002). A second restriction is that the studies we consider largely involve manipulating the frequency of constituent morphemic units. Another major paradigm that has been employed is priming, in which a complex word is primed with a morphemic constituent or vice versa. We think the story that can be told from this literature is not simple, partly because there are contradictory findings. We will comment only a bit on this literature at the end of the chapter.

Component-frequency and word-frequency effects on encoding time

Finnish: Robust component-frequency effects for longer compounds, but not for shorter compounds

To examine compositional processing in the identification of Finnish compound words, we manipulated the frequency with which the components appear in the language as separate words. (In Finnish, compound words are obligatorily written without spaces between the constituents.) In all of these studies, unless otherwise noted, the paradigm is the following. Two words that differ on a particular characteristic are inserted into a sentence frame that is identical, at least up to the target word. Various eye-movement measures are used to assess the encoding of the target word, including the *gaze duration* (the sum of the fixation durations on the word, but not including regressions back to the word) and measures of earlier processing on the word, such as the duration of the first and second fixations on the word. In this and the following section, we will tacitly assume a dual-route framework (that is, that people potentially have a whole-word look-up process and a componential process available in parallel for encoding complex words). Within that framework, an effect of component frequency is an indication that the componential route is part of the ultimate identification process, and an effect of whole-word frequency is an indication that the direct look-up route is part of the ultimate identification process. In the last section of the chapter, we will consider other possible interpretations of these results.

In the first study that examined constituent-frequency effects in reading, Hyönä and Pollatsek (1998, experiment 2) manipulated the frequency of the first constituent of long (12–14 letters) Finnish compound words (keeping the frequency of the second constituent and the frequency of the whole-word form constant). We observed a large constituent-frequency effect (about 90 ms) on *gaze duration* (Table 12.1). As 12–14-letter compounds are almost always read with more than a single fixation, it was also possible to examine the timing of the constituent frequency effect. The effect proved to be partially an early effect, as it was already apparent in the duration of first fixation made on the word; however, much of the effect was later, largely reflected by increased numbers of refixations in the low-frequency condition. Similarly,

Table 12.1 Effects of constituent-frequency and whole-word-frequency differences on fixation-duration differences for compound words

Study	*Language*	*Word length (letters)*	*Frequency manipulated*	*Gaze-duration difference*	*First-fixation difference*
Hyönä & Pollatsek (1998)	Finnish	12+	First constituent	*87 ms	*9 ms
Pollatsek, Hyönä, & Bertram (2000)	Finnish	12+	Second constituent	*95 ms	1 ms
Pollatsek, Hyönä, & Bertram (2000)	Finnish	12+	Whole word	*82 ms	†5 ms
Bertram & Hyönä (2003)	Finnish	12+	First constituent	*70 ms	*16 ms
Bertram & Hyönä (2003)	Finnish	12+	Whole word	*79 ms	†4 ms
Bertram & Hyönä (2003)	Finnish	7.5	First constituent	†11 ms	–3 ms
Bertram & Hyönä (2003)	Finnish	7.5	Whole word	*52 ms	*10 ms
Pollatsek & Hyönä (2005), experiment 1	Finnish	12+	First constituent	*47 ms	2 ms
Andrews, Miller, & Rayner (2004)	English	8.5	First constituent	†21 ms †27 ms	†8 ms †7 ms
Andrews, Miller, & Rayner (2004)	English	8.5	Second constituent	†15 ms	4 ms
Juhasz, Starr, Inhoff, & Placke (2003)	English	9	First constituent	10 ms	†11 ms
Juhasz, Starr, Inhoff, & Placke (2003)	English	9	Second constituent	*27 ms	8 ms

*Significant; †either $.05 < p_{1,2} < .1$, or p_1 or $p_2 > .1$.

Pollatsek, Hyönä, and Bertram (2000) varied the frequency of the second constituent for long compounds (experiment 1) while keeping constant the frequency of the first constituent and that of the whole-word form. Again, an equally large constituent-frequency effect was observed on gaze duration, but the effect was somewhat later, as frequency effects appeared only beginning at the second fixation (Table 12.1).

Taken together, these two studies are consistent with the view that long, two-constituent compounds are identified via their constituents: access of the first constituent is attempted followed by an access of the second constituent. However, the data of experiment 2 of Pollatsek et al. (2000) indicated that a direct access of the whole-word form was involved in accessing these long Finnish compound words as well. In this experiment, whole-word frequency was manipulated with the constituent frequencies equated. There was again a very large frequency effect on gaze duration, and the effect of whole-word frequency started to emerge at about the same time as the effect of second-constituent frequency (i.e. from the second fixation onward). The data from these three experiments are compatible with a dual-route theory of compound-word processing (Pollatsek et al., 2000), in which a decompositional process and a holistic process operate in parallel, but the effects of the holistic route take a bit longer to influence the eye-movement pattern.

Bertram and Hyönä (2003) examined whether the same pattern of results would be observed for shorter (7–9 letters) two-constituent compounds. They reasoned that if compound word processing is governed solely by structural principles, the identification process should be similar for short and long two-constituent compounds, but if visual acuity modulated processing, the holistic route may dominate the identification of shorter compounds, because the whole-word form is readily available in foveal vision when a short compound word is fixated. Their evidence supported the visual constraint hypothesis. For longer compounds, as can be seen in Table 12.1, they replicated Hyönä and Pollatsek (1998) and Pollatsek et al. (2000). They found a large first-constituent-frequency effect on gaze duration that was significant even for the first-fixation duration and a somewhat smaller whole-word-frequency effect that was not significant on the first fixation. In contrast, for the shorter compound words, there was only a small, nonsignificant first-constituent-frequency effect even on gaze duration, whereas the word-frequency effect was large and was even significant for first-fixation duration.

In sum, the above evidence suggests that componential processing may be important only for longer compound words. For these words, the whole-word route is delayed due to visual acuity constraints, and so early control of eye movements is dominated by componential processing. For the shorter compound words, a holistic process may dominate and is in control of even early eye movements. Whether this means that componential processing is irrelevant for these words is an open question.

Smaller constituent-frequency effects in English, possibly due to word length

There are reasons to think that componential effects in Finnish may be exaggerated. That is, compounding in Finnish is quite productive, and because Finnish requires all compounds to be written without a space, a Finnish reader is likely to be often presented with an unspaced compound word that cannot be accessed in the lexicon. In contrast, in a language like English, unspaced compounds are rarely, if ever, nonlexicalized, so that readers in such a language may adopt a different strategy of reading. Thus, it is of interest to examine the compound word data in other languages, and the one most studied has been English. The compounds studied in English have been a little longer than the short compounds of Bertram and Hyönä (2003) but shorter than the long compounds of Bertram and Hyönä (2003), Hyönä and Pollatsek (1998), and Pollatsek et al. (2000). The compounds used by Andrews, Miller, and Rayner (2004) were 6–11 letters, while those used by Juhasz, Starr, Inhoff, and Placke (2003) were nine letters. Andrews et al. (2004) manipulated both first-constituent and second-constituent frequency and got marginally significant effects of both on gaze duration, and a marginal first-constituent-frequency effect on first-fixation duration (Table 12.1). (Regression analyses indicated that word frequency also had an effect.) Juhasz et al. (2003) employed essentially the same manipulations and observed a significant effect of second-constituent frequency on gaze duration but only a marginal, 11-ms effect of first-constituent frequency on first-fixation duration.

The studies of compound-word identification in English thus provide evidence for compositional processing, but the evidence is not as convincing as for long Finnish compounds. However, as can be seen from Table 12.1, the sizes of the effects for the English compounds on first-constituent frequency are, if anything, larger than for the shorter compound words employed by Bertram and Hyönä (2003), and the second-constituent-frequency effects are roughly the same size as the first-constituent effects. (There are no experiments with shorter Finnish compounds in which second-constituent frequency was manipulated to compare them to.) Thus, although, a priori, there are reasons to suspect different patterns of processing in Finnish and English, the best construal of the pattern of results is as follows:

(1) There are no inherent language differences and strong constituent-frequency effects will emerge in any language if the words are long enough.
(2) The visual constraint hypothesis is correct, and constituent-frequency effects become attenuated for shorter compounds.

Reliable effects of root frequency on longer affixed words in English (and French)

Converging evidence in support of the mediating role of word length in the identification of morphologically complex words in reading sentences has been provided by Niswander-Klement and Pollatsek (in press). They examined the effects of word frequency and root frequency on English prefixed words (e.g. *remove*, whose root is *move*) that were equated on other indices but differed on either root-morpheme frequency or word frequency. In experiment 1, in which the length of the words was 5–14 letters, they found a significant root-morpheme-frequency effect on gaze duration, but only a marginal word-frequency effect (see the top two rows of Table 12.2). However, post hoc regression analyses indicated that word length influenced both effects: with increasing length, word-frequency effects on gaze duration significantly decreased, and root-frequency effects on gaze duration significantly increased. In experiment 2 (see the next four rows of Table 12.2), word length was explicitly manipulated, and for gaze duration: (1) there was a significant root-frequency effect for longer prefixed words, but no effect for shorter prefixed words; and (2) there was a significant word-frequency effect on gaze duration for shorter prefixed words, and a smaller, nonsignificant effect for longer prefixed words. There was no clear evidence for a root-frequency effect on first-fixation duration in either experiment, but in experiment 2, there was clear evidence for a word-frequency effect on first fixation for the shorter prefixed words.

The overall pattern of results is thus similar to that of Bertram and Hyönä (2003) and supports the visual constraint hypothesis proposed above. That is, shorter words are more likely to be accessed holistically, while compositional processing is likely to be important in processing longer words. The only difference in the pattern is that root frequency has no clear effect on early processing for either long or short prefixed words; however, for prefixed words, the root is not at the word beginning and thus would not be expected to be processed particularly early.

To our knowledge, the study of Niswander-Klement and Pollatsek (in press) is the only one where word length has been explicitly manipulated for prefixed or suffixed words. However, there is also suggestive evidence for the importance of word length in the processing of suffixed words. In English, Niswander, Pollatsek, and Rayner (2000) observed an early root-frequency effect (i.e. on first-fixation duration) for relatively long, derived words (an average of 9.2 letters), whereas the inflected words that were somewhat shorter (an average of 6.8 letters) showed only a reliable whole-word-frequency effect (Table 12.2).

In French, there are two studies in which the encoding of affixed words was examined in a task in which the target word was presented in isolation. Using lexical decision latency as the dependent measure, Colé, Beauvillain, and Segui (1989) obtained a root-frequency effect for suffixed, but not for prefixed

Table 12.2 Effects of constituent-frequency and whole-word-frequency differences on fixation-duration differences for affixed words

Study	*Language and type of word*	*Word length*[1] *(letters)*	*Frequency manipulated*	*Gaze-duration difference*	*First-fixation difference*
Niswander-Klement & Pollatsek (in press)	English prefixed	8.0	Root	*54 ms	6 ms
Niswander-Klement & Pollatsek (in press)	English prefixed	7.6	Whole word	†19 ms	6 ms
Niswander-Klement & Pollatsek (in press)	English prefixed	≤ 7	Root	–5 ms	1 ms
Niswander-Klement & Pollatsek (in press)	English prefixed	≤ 7	Whole word	*38 ms	*19 ms
Niswander-Klement & Pollatsek (in press)	English prefixed	≤ 8	Root	*52 ms	–5 ms
Niswander-Klement & Pollatsek (in press)	English prefixed	≤ 8	Whole word	†28 ms	†10 ms
Niswander, Pollatsek, & Rayner (2000)	English derived	9.2	Root	20 ms	*17 ms
Niswander, Pollatsek, & Rayner (2000)	English derived	9.8	Whole word	*37 ms	5 ms
Niswander, Pollatsek, & Rayner (2000)	English inflected	6.8	Root	9 ms	1 ms
Niswander, Pollatsek, & Rayner (2000)	English inflected	6.8	Whole word	†17 ms	*16 ms
Beauvillain,[1] experiment 2 (1996)	French prefixed	10	Root	*33 ms	5 ms
Beauvillain,[1] experiment 2 (1996)	French suffixed	10	Root	–6 ms	*30 ms

*significant; †either $.05 < p_{1,2} < .1$, or p_1 or $p_2 > .1$.

1. These words were not in sentences. Instead, the task was to compare the meaning of two words presented next to each other.

French words, a result that was taken to suggest that suffixed, but not prefixed, words are accessed via the decomposition route. However, a closer inspection of their materials reveals that the suffixed words were somewhat longer (an average of about 9.5 letters) than prefixed words (an average of about eight letters). Thus, one is tempted to offer an alternative explanation based on the visual acuity principle: Due to the length, longer suffixed words are accessed by the decomposition route, while shorter prefixed words are accessed holistically. In line with this reasoning, Beauvillain (1996) reported a stem-frequency effect for both French prefixed and suffixed words that were 10 or more letters long. In her eye-movement study, she observed an early effect (indexed by first-fixation duration) of root frequency for suffixed words and a later effect (indexed by second-fixation duration and gaze duration) of root frequency for prefixed words (Table 12.2). This latter finding becomes understandable if we consider that in suffixed words the root is located in the beginning of the words, whereas in prefixed words it is further in the word.

In sum, the evidence reviewed above suggests that word length also modulates the type of processing that occurs for affixed words: shorter words are more likely to be accessed via the holistic route, whereas the identification of longer affixed words is dominated by the decomposition route. It is curious that the effects of root frequency are so weak for English inflections (that were all orthographically and semantically transparent), even though the words were no shorter than the prefixed words that showed substantial root-frequency effects. That is, one might expect the strongest effects for inflections in English because they are so semantically transparent (unlike compounds). This pattern of results suggests that the relative length of the root and word may also play a role. That is, as the inflected words that were studied were only one or two letters longer than the root, it may be that encoding the word is virtually as easy as encoding the root, and thus evidence of root processing never surfaces.

Parsing compounds in Finnish, German, and English: Effects of vowel harmony, consonant type, and spacing

A successful application of the decomposition route requires the reader to parse a word into its morphological components. Many factors probably contribute to the relative ease of determining the boundary between the constituents or morphemes (Schreuder & Baayen, 1995). Morpheme frequency is one likely factor: a high-frequency morpheme is recognized with ease, and this may then more or less automatically delineate the other morpheme(s) and lead to a fast parsing. In addition, words may include orthographic cues that mark the morphemic boundary. A hyphen is a very clear visual cue that delineates the morphemic structure of a word (e.g. *co-pilot, fast-growing*), like spaces for compound words. There may also be more subtle segmentation cues, such as a "bigram trough" (a low-frequency bigram spanning the morphemic boundary).

Bertram, Pollatsek, and Hyönä (2004) examined the effects of two possible segmentation cues on the ease of identifying long Finnish compound words: (1) *vowel harmony*, and (2) the *morphological ambiguity of the consonant* at the constituent boundary. Vowel harmony refers to a feature of Finnish, where back vowels (*a, o, u*; pronounced toward the back of the mouth) and front vowels (*ä, ö, y*; pronounced toward the front of the mouth) cannot appear in the same lexeme (that is, within the same compound-word constituent), whereas vowels of different quality can appear across the constituents. Thus, when two vowels of different quality appear next to each other as in *selk**äo**ngelma* ("back problem"), there is a clear cue for a constituent boundary: the front vowel *ä* must be the end of the first constituent and the back vowel *o* must be the beginning of the second constituent. Experiment 1 compared *different vowel-quality* compounds, such as *selk**äo**ngelma*, with *same vowel-quality* compounds, such as *ryöst**öy**ritys* ("robbery attempt"), that have two vowels of the same quality (*ö* and *y*) at the constituent boundary and thus no orthographic cue indicating where the constituent boundary is. The two sets of compounds were matched on frequency and other relevant indices, and the same paradigm was employed as in the prior section (that is, the two words appeared after the same sentence beginning). The different vowel-quality compounds had significantly shorter gaze durations, but post hoc regression analyses indicated that the effect was modulated by the length of the first constituent. This hypothesis was confirmed in experiment 2, where the length of the first constituent was also manipulated while keeping the length of the whole-word constant; there was a 114-ms vowel-harmony effect on gaze duration for the compounds with a long (7–9 letters) first constituent but only a 2-ms difference for compounds with a short (3–5 letters) first constituent. The most plausible explanation for this pattern of results is the following. When the first constituent is short, its identification is rapid, and this identification is sufficient to parse the compound word, whereas with longer first constituents, the identification of the first constituent is slower, and the boundary cue in the different vowel-quality condition helps the parsing process and thus helps to identify the initial constituent.

Experiment 3 of Bertram et al. (2004) examined the effect of vowel harmony when the (dis)harmonious vowels were not adjacent but separated by a consonant (e.g. *kylpyl**äho**telli* versus *suihk**umo**ottori* = "spa hotel" versus "jet engine"). It also examined whether the type of consonant beginning the second constituent could function as a parsing cue as well. Two types of consonants were contrasted: (1) *unambiguous*—the consonant beginning the second constituent cannot end a first constituent; (2) *ambiguous*—the consonant can either be the last letter of a first constituent or the first letter of a second constituent. Thus, in (1) the constituent boundary is marked by the consonant if the boundary is assumed to be somewhere adjacent to the consonant, whereas in (2) it is not. There was a significant 60-ms effect of vowel harmony on gaze duration (about half the size of the effect obtained in experiment 2), and there was also a significant 52-ms effect of consonant ambiguity on gaze duration (the ambiguous consonant condition was slower than the unambiguous consonant condition), and the two effects were almost perfectly additive. This is interesting, because the orthography only unambiguously marks the exact location of the constituent boundary in the different quality vowel, unambiguous consonant condition. Thus, even cues that point to the approximate location of the boundary provide appreciable processing benefit (about 50–60 ms in this case).

In contrast, a study of Inhoff, Radach, and Heller (2000) failed to find evidence for bigram frequency serving as an effective segmentation cue in reading three-constituent German compound words. On the face of it, this appears to contradict the vowel-harmony results. However, there are many differences between the studies besides the difference in language. First, bigram frequency is not a particularly reliable marker of a morpheme boundary; it is more of a marker of a syllable boundary. (We should point out in this regard that bigram frequency differences did not predict the consonant ambiguity differences obtained in Bertram et al., 2004.) Another possibility is that vowel harmony is not limited to a single bigram in the middle of the word, and it often extends over the whole word; thus, it might be easier to pick up than a low-frequency bigram. Related to this, a single bigram may not have stood out in the target words of Inhoff et al. (2000); they were quite long (15–25 characters) and were three-constituent compounds (which would require finding two distinctive bigrams).

On the other hand, Inhoff et al. (2000) found significant effects of introducing spacing between the constituents of compound words. That is, their target words were long, three-constituent German compounds (presented in sentence context) that appeared either in their (legal) unspaced format or in an illegal format that had spaces between the constituents. In spite of the illegality of the spaced format, spacing had facilitative effects, as indexed by shorter gaze durations and total viewing times for spaced compounds than for unspaced compounds. On the other hand, spacing produced interference effects, as there were longer third- and fourth-fixation durations on the target word as well as longer fixation durations on the next word. The pattern of data suggests that spacing facilitated decomposition and component access, but may have interfered with meaning computation, as the grammatical relation of the constituents to each other is obscured by the spacing.

Juhasz, Inhoff, and Rayner (2005) recently provided further converging evidence from English to support the view that spacing facilitates the decomposition of compound words. Their target words were either unspaced (e.g. *bookcase*) or spaced (e.g. *rush hour*) two-constituent English compound words that could each appear either in their "correct" form (as above) or an "incorrect" form (*book case* versus *rushhour*). (In English, as there is no grammatical rule for deciding whether a compound is spaced or not, "correctness" was defined by typical usage.) They found that the first fixation on a compound was shorter if the compound was shown with a space, irrespective of whether the compound was supposed to be spaced or not—a finding consistent with the notion that providing a space between the constituents aids decomposition. The effects on gaze duration were less straightforward. Inserting a space for normally unspaced compounds lengthened the gaze duration, whereas deleting the space for normally spaced compounds did not affect gaze duration on the region. These data indicate that later processing is facilitated by removal of the space, and were taken by Juhasz et al. (2005) to support the view that the holistic route, and thus the access to the meaning of the compound word, benefits from concatenation of the constituents.

In sum, spacing, perhaps the most visually salient orthographic cue, has been shown to facilitate the working of the decomposition route in compound-word processing, but may possibly delay the initiation of the holistic route. (No work has been done to date on hyphens as a "parsing" cue.) In addition, in Finnish, two orthographic-phonological cues that are unique to marking morphemic (as opposed to syllabic) properties are also capable of facilitating the processing of compound words. Whether this latter finding is unique to these two cues in Finnish or is more general remains to be seen.

Is part of the constructive process constructing the meaning of the word from its component morphemes?

So far, we have shown that the processing of many morphemically complex words in reading involves the identification of the component morphemes. But what sort of involvement is it? Arguably, a major reason for having morphemes in a language is that one can construct new words out of old parts rather than having to coin new words for each new meaning that pops into a writer's or speaker's mind. Moreover, we would argue that this construction process is quite common, with new polymorphemic words being constructed every day. In a language like Finnish or German, this is clear for compound words, because they are written without a space, and one can consult corpuses of text for words not in "the dictionary". In English, however, a novel compound would stand out less, as novel compounds would almost always be written with a space, so it is less clear whether compounds such as *decomposition route* are novel or not. This productivity is not limited to compounds, as it is easy to construct novel prefixed words such as *misargued, overcalibrated*, and *unbewitch*, and novel suffixed words by adding suffixes like *-ize* to hundreds of words. Yet, it seems likely that readers and listeners would have little problem computing the meaning of such words and would often be unaware that they had probably not encountered them before.

Thus, if readers do have little trouble identifying the intended meaning of such words, even without much supporting prior context, it would imply that they can not only identify the component morphemes but also put the meanings of these morphemes together to construct the meaning of the word. Furthermore, if the dividing line between existing and novel complex words is blurry (for example, what may be a novel compound for one person may not be a novel compound for another person), this would lead to the expectation that the identification of existing polymorphemic words (especially longer ones, for which there is clearer evidence for componential processing) would involve, as a relatively important component, the attempted construction of the meaning of the word from the meanings of the components. However, the data we discuss below appear to argue the opposite: that construction of a word's meaning from its components plays little or no role in identifying existing morphemically complex words.

Most of the work on this topic has investigated whether semantic transparency plays a role in the time to identify compound words. Pollatsek and Hyönä (2005) examined this question in three experiments using Finnish two-constituent compound words. In each experiment, there were four sets of long target words that were defined by two factorial manipulations: (1) the target words were either semantically transparent or semantically opaque; (2) the first constituent was either frequent or infrequent. (The target words were equated on other variables such as word length and word frequency.) In all three experiments, the frequency of the first constituent affected gaze duration on the target word,[2] indicating that there was processing of the first constituent, but the transparency effects in the normal reading conditions in the three experiments were 1, 11, and –8, respectively. (In experiment 3, there was also a display change condition, and the transparency effect there was –5 ms.) Moreover, there was no hint of a transparency effect in any other eye-movement measure related to processing the compound word.

There are admittedly some problems with the definition of transparency. (To keep things simple, we will restrict our discussion to two-constituent compounds.) First, a compound word is defined as transparent if the meanings of the components are transparently related to the meaning of the compound word. However, it is rarely the case that the meaning of the compound can unambiguously be constructed from the components. Even in the case of *vaniljakastike* = *vanilla sauce*, one of the transparent compounds used in Pollatsek and Hyönä (2005), it could mean a sauce made of vanilla or a sauce to put on vanilla. Although the latter meaning might seem far-fetched, and thus the ambiguity questionable, for many words usually classified as transparent, such as *cowboy*, the construction of the meaning for someone who did not know what the word meant a priori would be quite difficult. Second, some authors have argued (Libben, 1998; Libben, Gibson, Yoon, & Sandra, 2003) that the type of opaqueness matters. They claimed that, because the second constituent is the head of the compound in English, it is more important to determine whether the second constituent is opaque than whether the first constituent is. That is, they argued that although *straw* is an opaque component of *strawberry*, it would have minimal effects on comprehension, because we know that this is some kind of berry, which may be sufficient for understanding in many contexts. In contrast, for a compound word like *doughnut* or *nightmare*, the opaqueness is more important because a doughnut is not a type of nut, nor is a nightmare a type of animal. They also argued that a word in which both constituents were opaque would be hardest to process.

Frisson, Niswander-Klement, and Pollatsek (submitted, 2006) examined whether transparency affected the processing of English two-constituent compounds in sentence context, and furthermore tested whether the type of opaqueness mattered. They had three sets of opaque compounds—OT (opaque–transparent), TO (transparent–opaque), and OO (opaque–opaque)—and, for each set, there was a set of matched transparent words. Sentence frames were constructed so that either an opaque or transparent word would fit into the same position (essentially the same design as Pollatsek & Hyönä, 2005, except for the three types of opaque words). The finding, however, was the same as with the Finnish compounds. The transparency effects were 0, –7 ms, and 15 ms, for the OO, TO, and OT conditions, respectively, an average of 3 ms overall. None of these differences were close to significant in either the participant or item analysis. Moreover, the pattern was the opposite of what Libben et al. (2003) would predict, as the only suggestion of a transparency effect was when the head was transparent. These results are consistent with lexical priming studies, which have observed comparable lexical priming for transparent and opaque compounds when the compound word is primed by its constituent (Jarema, Busson, Nikolova, Tsapkini & Libben, 1999; Libben et al., 2003; Monsell, 1984). The pattern of results from semantic priming studies, however, is somewhat different. The meaning of a constituent was primed with either a transparent (TT), partially opaque (OT or TO), or fully opaque (OO) compound (Zwitserlood, 1994), or the meaning of a constituent was primed by a semantically associated word (Sandra, 1990), and the priming effect is reduced when the compound word is partially or completely opaque. However, this is also consistent with the reading data (which show no interference for opacity), as it indicates that the constituent meanings of fully opaque compounds either are not activated or are quickly suppressed by the compound word meaning.

As far as we know, there are no studies in reading where the transparency of affixed words has been systematically manipulated. However, Niswander-Klement and Pollatsek (in press) did a post hoc analysis of the items from their second experiment and found no systematic effect of semantic transparency in the processing of prefixed words.

The data seem quite clear—but also quite hard to explain. That is, even though semantic composition is presumably necessary for novel complex words that we encounter relatively frequently, it apparently plays no role in existing compounds. Perhaps this is because existing compounds are processed so much faster than novel compounds that this semantic composition process never comes into play. This is possible, but we doubt that there is a big difference between the time to process novel compounds and the time to process existing compounds.

Theoretical implications

As indicated earlier, we used a "dual-route" framework to interpret the results. This framework assumed that there are two routes to encoding polymorphemic words. The first, the compositional route, involves accessing the morphemic components and then putting them together somehow. The second, the holistic route, involves accessing the word as a whole. However, we should make clear that our use of the term "holistic route" does not imply that we assume that the word is accessed as a visual template—there is a huge literature that makes such a notion grossly implausible. Instead, we assume that the inputs to both routes can include not only letter detectors and phoneme detectors, but possibly higher-order units such as bigram detectors and syllable detectors. The key assumption about the holistic route is that the inputs are not morphemes.

The pattern of data we presented largely makes sense in terms of such a model. In particular, as we argued repeatedly, the modulating effects of length are easily understandable in terms of such a model. That is, for shorter words, a holistic route may be reasonably efficient, as the whole word falls reasonably within the fovea on a fixation, and such a process is plausibly more efficient than (1) first trying to decide where the component boundary is, (2) encoding each component, and then (3) recombining the components. In contrast, for longer words, where holistic processing may become much less efficient because letter information has to combine over two or more fixations, a componential process involving morphemes may be a more efficient way to encode the word. Moreover, such a model does not require a central executive to decide which route to choose. The routes plausibly operate in parallel, although the success on one may inhibit the other. We will return to the issue of the routes interacting below.

Are there other models of complex word recognition that could give an equally good account of the data? We think that there are two models, which could be viewed as the "extremes", that clearly cannot work without a lot of reinterpretation. One is a "direct access" account (Butterworth, 1983), which is similar to a "supralexical" account of morphemes (Giraudo & Grainger, 2000). In this view, multimorphemic words are accessed solely through their whole-word representation and any morphemic decomposition that takes place occurs afterward. This view appears to be incompatible with virtually all the morpheme-frequency effects we have reported, especially those that occur as early as on the first fixation on a word in the absence of whole-word frequency effects on the same measures. The way that this position could possibly be maintained is by claiming that these morphemic effects are not "true" morphemic effects, but occur merely because morphemes are frequently appearing letter sequences. At our present state of knowledge, this position is defensible, but perhaps not helpful. That is, on some level, that is the point of morphemes: they are subword units that make some sense and can be (and are) frequently combined with other subword units. Thus, using them as units even when they are not being combined as morphemes at a deeper linguistic level may still be helpful. The other extreme position is that decomposition is an obligatory component of processing multimorphemic words in the sense that all components are individually accessed and always play a role in identifying these words (Taft, 2004). We think that the evidence that whole-word frequency effects can occur early—on first-fixation duration for shorter Finnish compounds and for shorter English prefixed words—rules out this view unless there is some way to explain why the effect of the components is at the same time marginal for gaze duration.

A different kind of componential model (Taft & Forster, 1975, 1976), however, makes predictions that are fairly similar to a dual-route model. In this type of model, the first constituent (or sometimes the root in the case of prefixed words) is accessed, and then the other constituents are accessed contingent on this initial access. The original metaphor was Taft and Forster's "file drawer": access of the first constituent was like accessing a file drawer, and then access of the word was like a file in the file drawer. The Taft and Forster model viewed the access of the file drawer as being dependent on the frequency of the initial (or root) morpheme and then search for the entry as being dependent on a word-frequency-ordered serial search through the file drawer. Virtually the same predictions come from variants of this model, such as the satellite model, in which the search is in parallel—but still frequency dependent (Lukatela, Gligorijevic, Kostic, & Turvey, 1980; see also Caramazza et al., 1988).

This type of componential model nicely predicts first-constituent (or root) frequency effects because the speed of access to the file drawer is dependent on the frequency of that constituent, and it predicts whole-word-frequency effects because the second stage of access is dependent on whole-word frequency. In addition, it would explain the lack of semantic transparency effects we have reported, because access of the initial component and then access of the word do not involve composition of meaning. However, we think this model would have some trouble predicting second-constituent frequency effects (with first-constituent frequency and whole-word frequency held constant), as there is no reason to think that this frequency would be correlated with position in the file drawer. However, the biggest problem with this model for the data we have presented is its insensitivity to length effects. That is, it should predict that one should first always observe first-constituent frequency or root-frequency effects (reflecting the first stage of lexical access) followed by whole-word-frequency effects (reflecting the second stage of lexical access). Instead, as indicated above, whether the component-frequency effects or whole-word-frequency effects appear early (if at all) depends on the length of the morphologically complex word. Thus, such a model would have to be revised substantially to account for the data in reading. A similar argument probably applies to the morphological race model of Schreuder and Baayen (1995).

Thus, we think the evidence is strongly in favour of a dual-route theory of the type we are advocating. (An alternative is the quite complex model advocated by *Taft* in this volume; however, we are not sure whether it is really different from the approach below or not.) However, we realize that this theory is vague in several ways, and it may have one big problem; that is, explaining why there appear to be no semantic transparency effects even when there is clear evidence of compositional processing. One way out of that would be to posit a compositional route that is something like the Taft and Forster two-stage process that operates in parallel with a direct-access route—and preserving our assumption that the relative efficiency of the routes is influenced by word length and perhaps length of the first constituent. Such a model, however, would have problems explaining second-constituent-frequency results. More deeply, however, it seems unsatisfying when one wants to explain how novel, morphemically complex words are processed. It seems quite unparsimonious to posit a process in which (1) "normal" lexical access is deemed to fail and then (2) a special, novel word process is called into play. We think, intuitively, that this is unlikely to be how these words are processed and that the processing of such words is on a continuum with existing morphemically complex words. However, this is just conjecture on our part at this point. But we think that studying the processing of such novel complex words is necessary and should shed light on how the meaning of existing morphemically complex words is arrived at. We are in the process of designing experiments to study such novel words in both Finnish and English.

Acknowledgements

The first author was supported by Grants HD17246 and HD26765 from the US National Institutes of Health, and the second author acknowledges the support of Suomen Akatemia (the Academy of Finland).

References

Alegre, M., & Gordon, P. (1999). Frequency effects and the representational status of regular inflections. *Journal of Memory and Language*, *40*, 41–61.

Andrews, S., Miller, B., & Rayner, K. (2004). Eye movements and morphological segmentation of compound words: There is a mouse in the mousetrap. *European Journal of Cognitive Psychology*, *16*, 285–311.

Baayen, R. H., Piepenbrock, R., & Gulikers, L. (1995). *The CELEX Lexical Database* [CD-ROM]. Philadelphia: Linguistic Data Consortium, University of Pennsylvania.

Beauvillain, C. (1996). The integration of morphological and whole-word form information during eye fixation on prefixed and suffixed words. *Journal of Memory and Language*, *35*, 801–820.

Bertram, R., & Hyönä, J. (2003). The length of a complex word modifies the role of morphological structure: Evidence from eye movements when reading short and long Finnish compounds. *Journal of Memory and Language*, *48*, 615–634.

Bertram, R., Pollatsek, A., & Hyona, J. (2004). Morphological parsing and the use of segmentation cues in reading Finnish compounds. *Journal of Memory and Language*, *51*, 325–345.

Butterworth, B. (1983). Lexical representations. In B. Butterworth (Ed.), *Language production* (Vol. 2), pp. 257–294). London: Academic Press.

Caramazza, A., Laudanna, A., & Romani, C. (1988). Lexical access and inflectional morphology. *Cognition*, *28*, 297–332.

Cole, P., Beauvillain, C., & Segui, J. (1989). On the representation and processing of prefixed and suffixed derived words: A differential frequency effect. *Journal of Memory and Language*, *28*, 1–13.

Davis, C. J. (1999). *The Self-Organizing Lexical Acquisition and Recognition (SOLAR) model of visual word recognition*. Doctoral dissertation, University of New South Wales, Australia.

Deutsch, A. F., Frost, R., & Forster, K. I. (1998). Verbs and nouns are organized and accessed differently in the mental lexicon: Evidence from Hebrew. *Journal of Experimental Psychology: Learning, Memory, and Cognition*, *24*, 1238–1255.

Francis, W. N., & Kučera, H. (1982). *Frequency analysis of English usage: Lexicon and grammar*. Boston: Houghton Mifflin.

Frisson, S., Niswander-Klement, E., & Pollatsek, A. (submitted, 2006). *The role of semantic transparency in the processing of English compound words*.

Giraudo, H., & Grainger, J. (2000). Effects of prime word frequency and cumulative root frequency in masked morphological priming. *Language and Cognitive Processes*, *15*, 421–444.

Grainger, J., & Van Heuven, W. (2004). Modeling letter position coding in printed word perception. In P. Bonin (Ed.), *The mental lexicon* (pp. 1–23). New York: Nova Science.

Hyönä, J., & Pollatsek, A. (1998). Reading Finnish compound words: Eye fixations are affected by component morphemes. *Journal of Experimental Psychology: Human Perception and Performance*, *24*, 1612–1627.

Hyönä, J., Bertram, R., & Pollatsek, A. (2004). Are long compound words identified serially via their constituents? Evidence from an eye-movement contingent display change study. *Memory and Cognition*, *32*, 523–532.

Hyönä, J., Vainio, S., & Laine, M. (2002). A morphological effect obtains for isolated words but not for words in sentence context. *European Journal of Cognitive Psychology*, *14*, 417–433.

Inhoff, A. W., Radach, R., & Heller, D. (2000). Complex compounds in German: Interword spaces facilitate segmentation but hinder assignment of meaning. *Journal of Memory and Language*, *42*, 23–50.

Jarema, G., Busson, C., Nikolova, R., Tsapkini, K., & Libben, G. (1999). Processing compounds: A cross-linguistic study. *Brain and Language*, *68*, 362–369.

Johnson, R. L., Perea, M., & Rayner, K. (in press). Transposed-letter effects in reading: Evidence from eye movements and parafoveal preview. *Journal of Experimental Psychology: Human Perception and Performance.*

Juhasz, B. J., Inhoff, A. W., & Rayner, K. (2005). The role of interword spaces in the processing of English compound words. *Language and Cognitive Processes*, *20*, 291–316.

Juhasz, B. J., Starr, M. S., Inhoff, A. W., & Placke, L. (2003). The effects of morphology on the processing of compound words: Evidence from naming, lexical decision, and eye fixations. *British Journal of Psychology*, *94*, 223–244.

Kambe, G. (2004). Parafoveal processing of prefixed words during eye fixations in reading: Evidence against morphological influences on parafoveal preprocessing. *Perception and Psychophysics*, *66*, 279–292.

Libben, G. (1998). Semantic transparency in the processing of compounds: Consequences for representation, processing, and impairment. *Brain and Language*, *61*, 30–44.

Libben, G., Gibson, M., Yoon, Y. B., & Sandra, D. (2003). Compound fracture: The role of semantic transparency and morphological headedness. *Brain and Language*, *84*, 50–64.

Lukatela, G., Gligorijevic, B., Kostic, A., & Turvey, M. T. (1980). Representation of inflected nouns in the internal lexicon. *Memory and Cognition*, *8*, 415–423.

Monsell, S. (1984). Repetition and the lexicon. In A. W. Ellis (Ed.), *Progress in the psychology of language* (Vol. 2), pp. 147–195. Hove, UK: Lawrence Erlbaum Associates Ltd.

Niswander, E., Pollatsek. A., & Rayner, K. (2000). The processing of derived and inflected words during reading. *Language and Cognitive Processes*, *15*, 389–420.

Niswander-Klement, E., & Pollatsek, A. (in press). The effects of root-frequency, word frequency, and length on the processing of prefixed English words during reading. *Memory and Cognition*.

Perea, M., Gomez, P., & Ratcliff, R. (2003). A model of encoding letter positions: The overlap model. *Proceedings of the XIIth Congress of the European Society for Cognitive Psychology*, Granada, Spain.

Pollatsek, A., & Hyönä, J. (2005). The role of semantic transparency in the processing of Finnish compound words. *Language and Cognitive Processes*, *20*, 261–290.

Pollatsek, A., Hyönä, J., & Bertram, R. (2000). The role of morphological constituents in reading Finnish compound words. *Journal of Experimental Psychology: Human Perception and Performance*, *26*, 820–833.

Pollatsek, A., Reichle, E., & Rayner, K. (2003). Modeling eye movements in reading. In J. Hyönä, R. Radach, & H. Deubel (Eds.), *The mind's eyes: Cognitive and applied aspects of eye movement research* (pp. 361–390). Amsterdam: Elsevier.

Pollatsek, A., Rayner, K., & Collins, W. E. (1984). Integrating pictorial information across eye movements. *Journal of Experimental Psychology: General*, *113*, 426–442.

Rayner, K. (1975). The perceptual span and peripheral cues in reading. *Cognitive Psychology*, *7*, 65–81.

Rayner, K. (1998). Eye movements in reading and information processing: 20 years of research. *Psychological Bulletin*, *124*, 372–422.

Rayner, K., McConkie, G. W., & Zola, D. (1980). Integrating information across eye movements. *Cognitive Psychology*, *12*, 206–226.

Rayner, K., & Pollatsek, A. (1989). *The psychology of reading*. Englewood Cliffs, NJ: Prentice-Hall.

Sandra, D. (1990). On the representation and processing of compound words: Automatic access to constituent morphemes does not occur. *Quarterly Journal of Experimental Psychology*, *42A*, 529–567.

Schreuder, R., & Baayen, R. H. (1995). Modeling morphological processing. In L. B. Feldman (Ed.), *Morphological aspects of language processing* (pp. 131–154). Hillsdale, NJ: Lawrence Erlbaum Associates, Inc.

Seidenberg, M. S., & McClelland, J. L. (1989). A distributed, developmental model of word recognition and naming. *Psychological Review*, *96*, 523–568.

Taft, M. (1979). Recognition of affixed words and the word frequency effect. *Memory and Cognition*, *7*, 263–272.

Taft, M. (2004). Morphological decomposition and the reverse base frequency effect. *Quarterly Journal of Experimental Psychology*, *57A*, 745–765.

Taft, M., & Forster, K. I. (1975). Lexical storage and retrieval of prefixed words. *Journal of Verbal Learning and Verbal Behavior*, *14*, 638–647.

Taft, M., & Forster, K. I. (1976). Lexical storage and retrieval of polymorphemic and polysyllabic words. *Journal of Verbal Learning and Verbal Behavior*, *15*, 607–620.

Zwitserlood, P. (1994). The role of semantic transparency in the processing and representation of Dutch compounds. *Language and Cognitive Processes*, *9*, 341–368.

Notes

1 We have evidence that both unspaced and spaced compounds are treated differently than two adjacent words in a sentence. Whereas the benefit of a parafoveal preview of a word in a sentence is typically about 30–40 ms, the preview benefit for a Finnish (unspaced) compound word is about 100 ms (Hyönä, Bertram, & Pollatsek, 2004; Pollatsek & Hyönä, 2005), and the preview benefit for both spaced English compounds is about 90 and over 100 ms for unspaced compounds (Pollatsek, Hyönä, Juhasz, & Rayner, in preparation).

2 However, the first-constituent-frequency effect was not significant in experiment 2, largely because it was a between-item variable: the sentence frames were different in the high- and low-frequency conditions.

13 Sweet nothings: Narrative speech in semantic dementia

Karalyn Patterson
Medical Research Council, Cognition and Brain Sciences Unit, Cambridge, UK

Maryellen C. MacDonald
Department of Psychology, University of Wisconsin, Madison, USA

This chapter is rather different from most in this volume. First of all, with one small and rather amusing exception, it does not concern word recognition or reading. Second, unusually (though not uniquely; see the chapter by *Balota & Yap*), it concerns abnormal rather than normal language. Third (though again not quite uniquely; here, see chapters by *Andrews*, by *Pollatsek & Hyönä*, and by *Rayner, Reichle & Pollatsek*), it treats connected speech/language rather than single-word processing. Despite these deviations from the central tendency, the chapter should be germane to the themes of the book in the sense that it concerns issues of lexical retrieval, of the relationship between language and conceptual knowledge/processing, and of the modularity or otherwise of different aspects of language processing.

The specific focus of the chapter is the consequences for speech production of degraded conceptual knowledge, as seen in the neurodegenerative condition known as semantic dementia (SD) (Hodges, Patterson, Oxbury, & Funnell, 1992; Snowden, Goulding, & Neary, 1989). Almost every publication on SD describes the patients' speech as largely normal in phonology and syntax and notably abnormal only in the lexical component of language. That is, SD patients are said to speak fluently, in well-formed grammatical sentences consisting of correctly articulated words; they are just profoundly anomic, producing a limited number of lexical terms that are strongly biased toward high-frequency general words like "thing" and "do". Here, for example, is the attempt by a typical SD patient to describe his daughter's profession: "When people come into hospital, they take their clothes off and lie down, and someone does something to them; and that's what she does, she's the one who closes them off." Listening to this fluently produced utterance, one is struck only by the patient's failure to find the word *anaesthetist* and detects no phonological or syntactic abnormalities of note. In other words, at least at an impressionistic level, the standard characterization of SD speech is a completely adequate and accurate description. As a research topic begins to mature, however, its practitioners often wonder whether their adequate impressionistic descriptions would still hold if the phenomena were subjected to more stringent scrutiny. Accordingly, the goal of this chapter is to ask whether SD speech is as phonologically and syntactically normal as it appears on informed but casual observation. Somewhat more challengingly, we can ask whether current understanding of language function should lead us to expect independence or interdependence of these different aspects of speech production.

There are reasons, both intuitive and from existing models of speech production, to anticipate both a degree of independence and a degree of interdependence between lexical and syntactic processes. For independence: more or less the same conceptual message can be expressed in the same syntactic frame with different lexical items (for example, "Mr B said to the doctor that he was having trouble talking" ≈ "Mr B told the neurologist that he was having difficulty speaking"). Likewise, more or less the same message can be expressed in a different syntactic frame using the same lexical items (for example, "The neurologist was told by Mr B about his speech difficulties"). By contrast, for interdependence: different lexical items, even within the same syntactic class, afford different syntactic structures. For example, both the verbs *give* and *donate* can be used equally well in the sentence, *The woman gave/donated her collection of teacups to the museum*; but if the sentence is uttered as a "double object" structure in which the recipient (the museum) precedes the thing being transferred (the teacups), then only *give* can be used, as in, *The woman gave the museum her collection of teacups*. Substituting *donate* for *give* here yields something that most English speakers do not consider acceptable English: *The woman donated the museum her collection of teacups*.

Thus, a key part of lexical knowledge concerns how particular words may be used in sentence structures; and this correlation between meaning and syntactic possibilities suggests that deficits in semantic knowledge should have consequences for syntactic production. If a person starts to express a conceptual message in a given syntactic frame that assumes the availability of a given lexical item that is then unavailable and is therefore replaced by one with a different structure, the resulting utterance will be at least syntactically odd if not frankly incorrect. Mr B above is, in fact, one of the SD patients seen recently in our clinic in Cambridge; when the neurologist (Professor John Hodges) asked him a question, Mr B replied, "I want to say you right now that this is what's wrong." We attribute this syntactic error to unavailability of Mr B's target verb (*tell*) which was then replaced by the word *say*, but used with the argument structure appropriate to the missing target *tell*.

These issues concerning the degree of independence of syntactic and semantic performance have previously been investigated in patients with probable Alzheimer's disease (AD), a group with well-known semantic deficits. Early investigations obtained no evidence for impaired syntactic abilities in AD patients, even those with significant semantic degradation (e.g. Kempler, Curtiss, & Jackson, 1987), which would argue for the independence of syntactic and semantic knowledge. Several, more recent studies, however, have reported that when syntactic performance is scrutinized very carefully, AD patients do show abnormalities. Some of these studies found greater rates of syntactic speech errors in the patients than in controls (Altmann, Kempler, & Andersen, 2001), while others observed declines in the range of syntactic constructions produced. In particular, AD patients are less likely than controls to produce lower-frequency or more complex syntactic structures when discourse conditions demand them (Bates, Harris, Marchman, & Wulfeck, 1995; Kemper, LaBarge, Ferraro, Cheung, Cheung, & Storandt, 1993; Lyons, Kemper, LaBarge, Ferraro, Balota, & Storandt, 1994). Given the availability of several alternative syntactic structures to convey a message, the syntactic deficits in AD patients tend to appear as a general decrease in syntactic complexity and utterance length rather than in frank syntactic errors.

There is little experimental evidence on the issue of the phonological and syntactic status of SD speech. To the extent that researchers have examined the processing of connected speech, or even sentences, as opposed to single words in SD, they have concentrated almost entirely on comprehension rather than production (see Breedin & Saffran, 1999; Rochon, Kavé, Cupit, Jokel, & Winocur, 2004; Tyler, Moss, Patterson, & Hodges, 1997, for studies of SD comprehension beyond the single-word level). These studies therefore address syntactic but not phonological issues, and address only receptive language abilities. The few investigations of production beyond the single word have been largely in the domain of verbal working memory, in which patients are asked to perform immediate serial recall of strings of unrelated words (e.g. Jefferies, Patterson, Jones, Bateman, & Lambon Ralph, 2004; Knott, Patterson, & Hodges, 2000; Patterson, Graham, & Hodges, 1994; Warrington, 1975). These studies therefore address phonological, but not syntactic, issues.

We are aware of only two publications that investigated connected speech production in SD. One, a narrative picture description study (Bird, Lambon Ralph, Patterson, & Hodges, 2000), was concerned with the nature of the lexical deficit, in particular whether the patients produce normal ratios of nouns to verbs and how the items in these two major word classes differ in word frequency and imageability; the article scarcely mentions phonology or syntax. The other paper (Benedet, Patterson, Gomez-Pastor, & Garcia de la Rocha, 2006) did, in one experiment, have a specifically syntactic focus. An SD patient and some normal controls were asked to generate a sentence to describe each of 25 pictured events; across trials, the participants were instructed to use a variety of syntactic structures specified in terms of previously practised markers. For example, if a picture of a goat kicking a cow was to be described in passive rather than active form, both the goat and the cow were marked by arrows indicating that they must both be mentioned; and a dot by the cow further indicated that the participant should start by referring to the cow. Of considerable interest, the patient had impoverished ability to produce the required range of syntactic structures, especially the less typical ones.

The data to be considered here come from short samples of narrative speech generated by SD patients and normal controls in a picture description task: the widely used cookie theft picture from Goodglass and Kaplan (1983), reproduced in Figure 13.1. This task, like any other that one might choose, has both advantages and drawbacks. As the test designers themselves noted, in spontaneous speech that is part of a free conversation, anomic patients are often skilled at avoiding difficult words; by contrast, picture description has the advantage that "The vocabulary constraints of the picture bring out word-finding difficulty more sharply" (Goodglass & Kaplan, 1983, p. 30). This is indeed a good feature, and it was part of our reason for choosing this task; but its disadvantages include the facts (1) that an adequate description of the picture does not require all that much speech; and, in particular, (2) that there is no demand to use anything other than present-tense, active-voice, single-clause declarative constructions. It is therefore not an ideal context in which to investigate the range of SD patients' productive syntax. But one must start somewhere.

The empirical component of the chapter is organized into three sections. First, we report on the lexical/semantic content of the patients' descriptions relative to those of normal speakers. In one sense, the outcome of this section is not news: the key feature of SD is semantic impairment, and its consequences for lexical production (i.e. anomia) have been pretty thoroughly documented. On the other hand, the impoverished nature of the patients'

Figure 13.1 The cookie theft picture (reprinted from Goodglass & Kaplan, 1983).

lexical/semantic production (1) is too dramatic to ignore; (2) has never, to our knowledge, been analyzed in quite the fashion that we have used here; and (3) is responsible for the title of our chapter: the patients' descriptions of the cookie theft picture are so empty that "sweet nothings" seems a distressingly apt characterization. The remaining sections report our attempts to establish whether, on closer inspection, the SD patients' speech contains any phonological (section 2) or syntactic (section 3) abnormalities.

Methods

Participants

Two subgroups of SD patients and controls, n=21 each, participated in the experiment. Some of the basic characteristics of the patient sample are listed in Table 13.1, along with equivalent values/scores for normal speakers. The age mean/range of the controls in Table 13.1 is for the actual sample of control subjects whose cookie theft descriptions will be compared to those of the SD patients; but these subjects were not given the basic neuropsychological tests listed in Table 13.1. These test scores come from control participants in other studies of SD patients by the Cambridge research group (e.g. Bozeat, Lambon Ralph, Patterson, Garrard, & Hodges, 2000). Table 13.1 demonstrates that the SD cases included the entire spectrum from very mildly to severely impaired.

Procedure

Each patient or control, tested alone, was given the cookie theft picture and told, "Tell me everything that you can about what is happening in this

Table 13.1 Basic characteristics of patient and control samples. Age is self-explanatory. The MMSE (Mini-Mental State Examination) (Folstein et al., 1975) is the standard used worldwide to assess patients with dementia or other neurodegenerative conditions. The Addenbrooke Cognitive Examination (ACE) (Mathuranath et al., 2000), is an extended test designed to give more information about language and conceptual knowledge than the MMSE. PPT pictures is the all-picture version of a test to evaluate associative knowledge about objects. Both the WPM (Word-Picture Matching) and Naming tests come from the Cambridge semantic battery (see Bozeat et al., 2000)

	Patient mean	*Patient range*	*Control mean*	*Control* S.D.
Age	63.9	56–72	67.5	Range 57–75
MMSE (30)	22.8	12–26	29.1	0.8
ACE (100)	54.0	18–90	93.8	3.5
PPT pictures (52)	37.9	24–48	51.1	1.1
WPM (64)	42.8	8–64	63.7	0.5
Naming (64)	22.1	0–62	62.3	1.6

picture." No further instruction or assistance was provided; if a participant stopped after producing very little, the experimenter merely said, "Can you tell me any more?" or "Is there anything else happening?" The experimenter wrote a verbatim version of the speech output while the person was speaking; in most cases (19/21 SD patients, 12/21 controls), the descriptions were also tape-recorded for later checking of the transcription.

Results: Section 1

Table 13.2 presents information on number of words produced (both total and separately for content and function words), amount of time taken to produce the whole narrative, and rate of speaking for patients and controls. The number-of-words measures apply to all 21 participants in each group, but, because tape recordings were not available for every subject, the timed measures apply to only the specified Ns. The results in Table 13.2 support two conclusions. First of all, relative to normal language users, SD patients, on average, produced somewhat fewer words in their picture descriptions but also spoke for somewhat less total time, with the result that the rate of speech measure is very similar in the two groups. This result confirms the clinical impression that—apart from the inevitable occasions on which SD patients pause because of difficulty in word-finding—their speech emerges effortlessly and with reasonably normal fluency. Secondly, with respect to the word-class composition of speech, the two groups produced very similar numbers of function words; the fact that control narratives contained more words than those of the patients is entirely attributable to greater usage of content words in the control group. This result is not surprising given these patients' semantic deficit and anomia, and we next report on the nature of their sparse use of content words in describing specific events in the pictures.

As can be ascertained in Figure 13.1, there are two events in the cookie theft picture (and of course the oddity of the scene derives in large part from the lack of interaction between these two events). Table 13.3 lists the main content-word vocabulary that applies to each of the two events and gives the numbers of controls and patients who used each of these terms in their

Table 13.2 Quantity and rate of speech in the cookie theft narratives. Values for the first three rows (the number-of-words measures) are based on n=21 for each group; the last two rows (time/rate measures) are based on n=19 semantic dementia patients and n=12 controls

	Patients: mean [range]	*Controls: mean [range]*
Total number of words	93.9 [17–224]	107.9 [36–223]
Content words	38.3 [8–101]	51.8 [17–119]
Function words	55.4 [9–136]	56.7 [19–104]
Time taken (seconds)	69.6 [38–177]	90.8 [39–135]
Words/minute	88.0 [30–189]	83.9 [49–156]

Table 13.3 Numbers of controls and of semantic dementia patients (each out of 21) producing particular content words in describing each of the two events in the picture

	Controls	*Patients*
Cookie event		
Stool	19	0
Cookie/biscuit	19	5
Cupboard	13	3
Fall (off)	17	14
Steal/pinch/raid	9	1
Stand (on)	7	7
Sink event		
Sink	18	3
Plate(s) and/or cup(s)	17	6
Water	14	18
Floor	12	6
Feet	4	4
Overflow	17	2
Dry (up)	13	5
Wash (up)	12	9
Stand (in)	5	3

descriptions. Note that, for verbs, the table lists only the stem form (e.g. *fall*); numbers of instances indicated for each stem include any form of the verb used (e.g. the boy *is falling*, the boy is about *to fall*).

In describing the cookie event, most control subjects use at least three main nouns—*stool, cookies* (or *biscuits* as they are more typically called in the UK), and *cupboard*—and one main verb (*fall* or *fall off*); nearly half also use the verb *steal* or its equivalent. Of these lexical terms, only one, *fall*, was used as commonly by the patients as by the normal speakers. *Fall* is, by some substantial margin, the most frequent of these words, and its occurrence in the patients' narratives therefore fits with known facts about the massive impact of frequency on the availability of vocabulary in SD (Bird et al., 2000; Lambon Ralph, Graham, Ellis, & Hodges, 1998).

The sink event produces a slightly larger typical vocabulary, with more than half of the control speakers using four main nouns: *sink, plates* and/or *cups, water*, and *floor*, and three main verbs: *overflow, wash*, and *dry* (or the more typical UK alternatives for the last two when it is crockery/cutlery that is being washed/dried, namely, *wash up* and *dry up*). Only two of these terms, *water* and *wash(up)*, were common in the SD narratives: again, highly frequent words. Interestingly, *water* was the only substantive lexical term used more frequently by patients than controls; in addition to its high frequency, this may reflect the fact that normal speakers can—and almost always do—say that the *sink is overflowing*, rendering superfluous any explicit reference to *water*. Only a tiny minority of patients produced either *sink* or *overflow*, and therefore—provided that they understood and were trying to convey what is actually happening in the sink event—there was reason to mention *water*.

Table 13.4 indicates the range of verbs used, and how commonly each was produced in describing the two main actions, that is, the water overflowing and the cookies being stolen. As can be seen, the patients managed to find a variety of alternatives, mostly of higher word frequency, with *coming out/down* the most common replacement for *overflow*, and *getting* the most common for *steal*. A few of their alternatives are rather odd (as in the water is *dropping off* or *overflooding*), though the term used by one control (*boiling over*) is also odd for an overflowing sink. Of more interest are the two phenomena in some patient descriptions that are truly abnormal: (1) 3/21 patients used no verb at all to refer to the movement of the water and 6/21 used no verb to describe the cookies being stolen or fetched; and (2) two patients incorrectly used the term *water* as a verb to describe what is happening at the sink (DV: "The water is running over, *watering*"; PF: "Mummy has done *watering*").

Finally in this section, we try to address in a limited way the issue of whether the patients' severe disorder of expressive (and for that matter, receptive) vocabulary is a lexical or a semantic deficit. Consider the fact that so few SD patients say that the boy is stealing cookies. This could arise because,

Table 13.4 Range of verbs used, and numbers of controls/patients producing each, to describe the two principal actions

	Controls	*Patients*
***Overflow* alternatives**		
Overflow	17	2
Come out/down	0	7
Run out/over	1	3
Flood/overflood	0	2
Pour out/down	1	1
Go out/down	1	0
Fall	0	1
Boil over	1	0
Drop off	0	1
Flush out	0	1
No verb	0	3
* *Water*	0	2
***Steal* alternatives**		
Steal/pinch/raid/nick	9	1
Get	5	8
Take (out)	5	2
Pick up	0	3
Reach	2	0
Pull out	0	1
No verb	0	6

* Used as verb.

despite understanding that a cookie theft is taking place, they cannot retrieve the words to say so; or it could arise because they have degraded understanding of the event. To probe this issue a little, we devised something that we called a "cookie knowledge" (CK) score.

Of the 21 patients, five said some version of "He is getting cookies (biscuits)"; this seems to indicate good comprehension of the event, and we therefore assigned it a CK score = 4. Three patients said, "He is getting something to eat", which at least indicates some understanding of what cookies are for, and this was given a CK score = 3. Seven patients said only that "He is getting something"; since *eat* is such a common activity and word, it seems unlikely that patients would be completely unable to express this concept if they grasped it; so this was treated as CK = 2. The remaining six patients did not mention anyone getting anything: CK = 1. Even when a patient said (or rather read aloud) the term *cookie jar*, as 12/21 of them did, the rest of his or her comment on this aspect of the picture often failed to reflect much cookie knowledge. For example, TW: "He's pulling things out of the cookie jar", or AB: "The boy has got up to get some cookie jar." Sometimes a patient's narrative seemed explicitly to tell us that he or she did not understand the cookie theft event, as in RS: "He's picking up something; I don't know what these are." It is of course possible that "I don't know what these are" means "I don't know their name"; but, on the other hand, when anomic patients (including those with SD) feel that their difficulty is just in finding the word, they tend to say so, often with intense frustration: "I know what it is but I can't *say* it!" We are therefore more inclined to interpret RS's comment as genuinely meaning that he had no idea what the boy was picking up.

On the basis of this simple analysis, as well as much other research on SD over the last decade or so (e.g. Lambon Ralph, McClelland, Patterson, Galton, & Hodges, 2001), we postulate that the emptiness of the patients' speech reflects semantic degradation rather than a lexical deficit—or, if this seems a preferable formulation, a lexical deficit as a direct consequence of the semantic degradation. If this is so, then the CK score derived from the patients' speech should correlate with other measures of their semantic status. Figure 13.2 displays the relationship of each patient's CK score to his or her naming of the 64 common picture items in the Cambridge Semantic Battery naming test; Figure 13.3 does the same with respect to the patients' scores for name-to-picture matching on the same 64 items (means and ranges of scores on these two tests are listed in Table 13.1). The orderliness of these scatter plots seems to support our postulate. It is true that Figure 13.2 represents the relationship between two speech-production tasks, which might be expected to correlate; but they are very different tasks: the CK score is not a simple measure of object-name production. In both Figures 13.2 and 13.3, we claim that the basis of the correlation is the degree of deterioration of the patients' amodal conceptual knowledge.

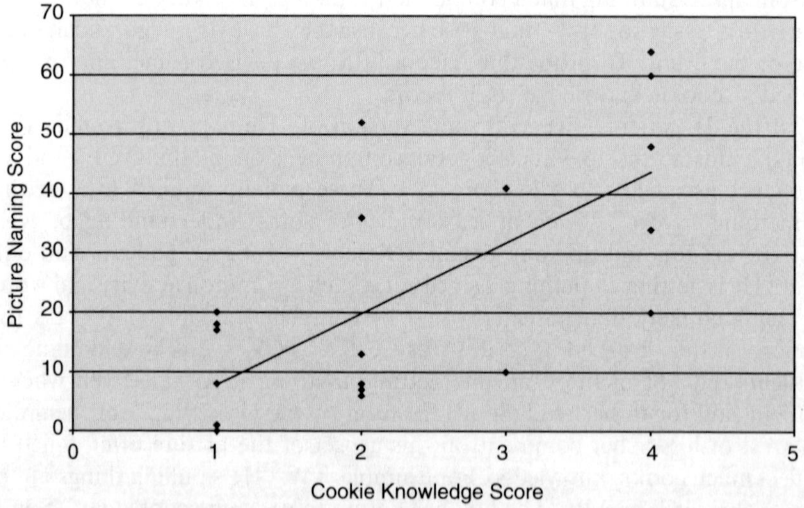

Figure 13.2 The relationship between each patient's cookie knowledge score and his or her score in naming 64 line drawings from the Cambridge Semantic Battery. Note that there are fewer than 21 data points because a few locations in the scatter plot are occupied by more than one patient.

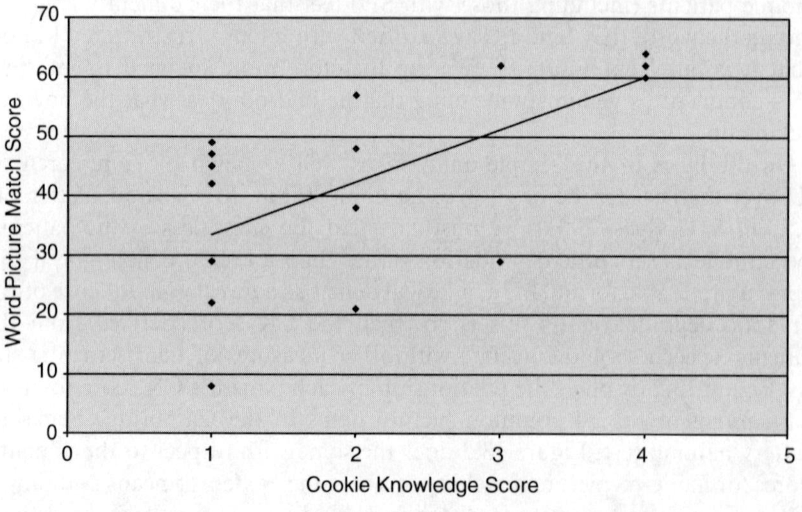

Figure 13.3 The relationship between each patient's cookie knowledge score and his or her score in comprehending 64 concrete concepts from the Cambridge Semantic Battery, as measured by name–picture matching. Note that there are fewer than 21 data points because a few locations in the scatter plot are occupied by more than one patient.

Results: Section 2

With 21 patients producing an average of about 100 words each in their narratives, we have a sample of upward of 2000 words to examine with respect to the question of whether self-generated SD speech is phonologically intact. The answer to this question is an unambiguous yes. Ignoring false starts (e.g. "She's tr——trying to clean"), of which there were a few examples in both control and patient narratives, we detected a total of three frank phonological errors in the 2000+ words produced by the 21 SD patients. Even more striking perhaps is the fact that all three of these errors, rather than suggesting any phonological disruption/distortion in self-generated speech, can be explained in terms of "external" factors. Two of the patients who read or attempted to read aloud the label on the cookie jar made a phonological error on the word "cookie" (recall that "cookie" is a low-frequency word in British English); this is the one small and amusing example in this chapter, mentioned in the introduction, that concerns word recognition/reading. And one patient produced a blend error of the sort that is common enough in normal speakers: AN said "What's that in her hand that she's trying to clean . . . a /kleit/" which is almost certainly a blend of *clean* and *plate*. Other research (e.g. Graham, Patterson, Powis, Drake, & Hodges, 2002; Graham, Patterson, Pratt, & Hodges, 1999; Jefferies et al., 2004; Majerus, Norris, & Patterson, 2006; Patterson et al., 1994) has established that SD patients make phonological errors, especially blends of phonological components of two words, at a much higher than normal rate when they are "reciting"—from short-term or longer-term rote memory—real words whose meanings are degraded for them. We interpret this as a consequence of reduced semantic (or again, lexical deriving from semantic) constraints on speech production when the speech is not generated on the basis of a conceptual message. Our analysis here, of the largest corpus of spontaneous (well, narrative) speech ever examined in SD, supports the view (1) that SD patients use very few lexical terms because of their semantic memory deficit, but (2) that whatever speech their conceptual knowledge does allow them to produce is phonologically intact.

Results: Section 3

We turn now to the main focus of this chapter: the putative interaction between lexical/semantic and syntactic processing in speech production. We began with a very simple approach: we selected any instance of syntactic abnormality that we could find in the 21 cookie theft descriptions by SD patients, and then asked whether or not there was a comparable oddity in a description produced by one of the 21 normal speakers. Examples of these are given in Table 13.5, and the conclusion was that this simple approach was insufficient to answer the question. Syntactically odd utterances were relatively rare in both groups, and some of these "errors", such as listing a series

Table 13.5 Examples of syntactic oddities in semantic dementia (SD) and control narratives

Type of oddity	*SD example*	*Control example*
List of nouns	"The woman, boy, a girl, the water coming out . . ."	"Two cups and a plate, house, bushes, path . . .
Omission of obligatory grammatical morpheme	"That looks like it [it's] falling down"	"Unfortunately, she [she's] not really with us"
Self-interruption to sentence structure	"Bubbles in the, no doubt she's using washing-up liquid"	"Outside of the window we can, which is open, we can see into the garden"
Conjunction of two unrelated clauses	"He's about to fall over and the window's open"	"Hopefully, his sister is going to get a cookie and there are two cups and a plate"

of objects without a verb, can plausibly be attributed to the particular discourse demands to describe a picture that is jointly viewed by the participant and the experimenter.

We next investigated whether the SD narratives were characterized by less complex syntax than the control narratives. We have already observed that the SD patients produced slightly fewer words; here we examine whether the two groups produced similar numbers of coherent clauses (essentially utterance units with both nouns and verbs) versus verb-less fragments. We chose "clause" as a unit of coherent speech, rather than "sentence", because it can be coded more objectively; sentence boundaries in spoken narratives are often subjective judgements of a transcriber. Table 13.6 shows little difference in clause and fragment usage in the two groups and a very low incidence of fragments overall. Within the clauses, we coded the number of simple clauses versus those that contain a clause embedded [shown here with brackets] inside another clause, as in the following statements by SD patients. AC said, "His sister is hoping [he'll give something to her]"; DV said, "The mother doesn't have many things [to wash and dry]." The table shows slightly more embedding in the control narratives than in the SD narratives. Overall, there is a low use of embedding by both groups, probably reflecting how little demand

Table 13.6 Clauses in semantic dementia and control narratives

	Patients: mean [range]	*Controls: mean [range]*
Verb-less fragments	0.88 [0–4]	1.24 [0–12]
Complete clauses	11.48 [0–25]	12.67 [5–23]
Simple clauses	9.57 [1–18]	10.33 [4–20]
Clauses with embedding	1.62 [0–5]	2.05 [0–6]
Noun phrases after verb	0.83 [0–3]	1.08 [0–7]

there is for such constructions in both this picture and this task. Similarly, the picture-description task does not encourage the use of passive structures or other lower-frequency syntactic constructions; and so a metric of variety of syntactic structures, on which AD patients and controls do differ (Bates et al., 1995; Kemper et al., 1993), cannot be sensibly applied here.

Given the limitations of our short narratives for examining syntactic variety and degree of embedding, we looked elsewhere for syntactic differences between the groups. Clauses can vary a great deal in the number of nouns following the verb, and we counted the number of nouns within the verb phrase as a measure of syntactic complexity and the amount of information conveyed in a clause. Because of the relatively small number of clauses available for analysis, we counted all nouns within the verb phrase equally and did not distinguish between direct objects, indirect objects, prepositional objects, and other forms. We also did not distinguish between informative nouns, such as "cookie", vague noun expressions such as "something", and pronouns such as "it". Thus, "giving the cookie to the girl" would be coded as having two nouns in the verb phrase (cookie and girl), as would "giving something to her" (something and her). Our coding therefore focused on the number of noun phrases of any sort in the verb phrase, independent of the richness of the semantics of these noun phrases. Table 13.6 shows the mean number of noun phrases per clause in each group. The overall numbers are not large, reflecting the fact that many events in the picture can be expressed very adequately without any noun phrases following the verb, as in "the sink's overflowing" and "she's washing up". The control narratives did, however, have more noun phrases following verbs than the SD narratives, $t(40) = 2.39$, $p < .05$. Thus, even when we ignore the semantic richness of the noun phrases, the controls produced more complex verb phrases than did the patients.

Correct pronoun usage requires integrating pragmatic knowledge (knowing when it is appropriate to use a pronoun versus a full noun phrase such as "the boy"), and morphosyntactic knowledge (knowing which syntactic positions require "he" versus "him" versus "his"). Pronoun usage is one area where it is reasonable to expect differences between SD patients and controls, as reduced ability to produce object names could lead to increased pronoun usage in the SD narratives, including vague uses such as *it* without establishing a clear referent. Table 13.7 shows slightly greater pronoun usage in the SD narratives than in the control narratives. We assigned each pronoun usage to one of two categories. Correct usages were those in which the pronoun

Table 13.7 Pronoun usage in semantic dementia and control narratives

	Patients: mean [range]	*Controls: mean [range]*
Total pronouns	8.23 [1–22]	7.38 [1–20]
Correct usage	5.19 [0–16]	7.05 [1–20]
Probable errors	3.64 [0–12]	0.33 [0–2]

referred to a noun or pronoun antecedent that had been recently mentioned and where there had been no topic shifts between mention of the antecedent and the pronoun (such intervening topic shifts would make pronoun usage infelicitous). Probable errors were those in which a pronoun was used with no prior mention of an antecedent, and those pronouns for which the antecedent was mentioned much earlier in the narrative, followed by topic shifts. We classified these usages as only "probable" but not certain errors, because in the context of picture description, it is possible for the participant to gesture to the picture and indicate the referent while saying only a pronoun. Table 13.7 shows that the control participants' pronouns were almost entirely correct; they virtually never used a pronoun without previously establishing its referent with a noun phrase such as "the woman", even though gesturing might have allowed them to do so. By contrast, nearly a third of the SD patients' pronoun usages were probable errors.

In sum, the SD narratives were less elaborate than control narratives in every metric of syntactic complexity that we could measure: They were shorter in number of words and number of clauses, had slightly fewer embedded clauses, had significantly fewer noun phrases following verbs, and contained considerably more vague pronoun references than control narratives. Some of these measures, such as pronoun usage, have a clear semantic and discourse component in addition to a syntactic component; but even the purely syntactic measure of number of noun phrases after the verb, independent of their semantic richness, distinguishes the two groups. This pattern of results is similar to that reported in AD patients: it appears that the syntactic consequences of both AD and SD, rather than being marked by frank grammatical errors, are mainly revealed in a decline in the length, variety, specificity, and complexity of the structures that are produced.

Concluding remarks

This chapter has addressed, in a modest fashion, the complex question of the modularity (or otherwise) of different aspects of language. In particular, we have tried to enquire whether a substantially degraded conceptual message has significant consequences for two aspects of the "carrier" of the message in narrative speech: its phonology and its syntax. Even bearing in mind the caveats regarding the relative paucity of data yielded by this simple picture description task, our analyses seem to provide relatively clear answers to these two questions: patients with SD, who have markedly impoverished lexical/semantic abilities, speak with normal phonology but with somewhat abnormal syntax. Both of these outcomes seem plausible if indeed not predictable.

First, with respect to phonology, it is perhaps worth specifying that we refer here not to prosody, which of course spans many words, and not to articulation, which can span at least two adjacent words due to phenomena like assimilation, but to phonological form; and the scope of this domain of phonological form is essentially the single word. If a language deficit can truly be localized to impoverished semantic knowledge, with resulting unavailability of many substantive lexical choices, then it seems sensible that the sufferer from this deficit will produce a small range of content words but will pronounce them correctly. As mentioned in section 2 of the Results, SD patients make copious phonological errors in the task of immediate serial recall (ISR) of strings of words, particularly when the words have been selected as those with degraded meaning for the particular patients (e.g. Jefferies et al., 2004). Frequently, a patient's response on a given trial of this task will contain most if not every phonological segment of the stimulus string, but with the bits rearranged to form phonologically plausible neologisms (Patterson et al., 1994). This pattern of responding is more or less identical to what happens when normal speakers perform ISR on nonwords. And although we certainly do not claim that real words with degraded semantic representations have become the exact equivalent of nonwords to the patients (for example, their ISR success is characterized by "known" words > degraded words > nonwords), it is clear that the patients' ISR is achieved with little of the lexical/semantic support that aids word ISR in normal speakers (Jefferies, Frankish, & Lambon Ralph, 2006). By contrast, the words that SD patients produce in spontaneous or narrative speech are, of necessity, only words whose production begins with a conceptual representation sufficient to activate the corresponding phonology. The conceptual representation is often vague and general, resulting in many uses of words like *thing* instead of *stool*, or *getting* instead of *stealing*. But whatever information is available from the conceptual level appears to activate a set of essentially intact phonological forms for speech production.

Correct grammatical form has a very different scope from phonological form. Syntax must operate over at least two words (as in number agreement between adjacent noun and verb; for example, *the child steals* versus *the children steal*) and typically over whole clauses or sentences. In most accounts of sentence production, the choice of a syntactic structure, and the ease with which it is constructed, appear to be affected by two major factors. First, the process is guided by the speaker's intended conceptual message and the activated lexical items, and the resulting structure typically allows the most highly activated noun to appear first in the sentence (Bock & Levelt, 1994). Given a picture of a lightning bolt and a church, for example, someone who initially focused on the lightning in the picture might choose to describe it as "The lightning is striking the church", whereas someone who initially paid more attention to the church would tend to put that object first, saying, "The church is being struck by lightning" (Bock, 1986). Second, the syntactic operations that follow from a syntactic structure choice, such as assigning a particular noun to be the sentence subject and computing verb agreement with this subject noun, are influenced by frequency. Higher-frequency syntactic structures, such as simple active sentences, are developed more rapidly and easily than lower-frequency structures, such as passives (Bock & Griffin, 2000).

Both of these conceptual and structural frequency factors appear to affect syntactic production in SD. A spontaneous utterance by an SD patient is likely to be based on an impoverished conceptual representation, and the resulting utterance will tend to be short, as there is not much information to convey. To the extent that lexical items (even rather empty ones) become activated during sentence planning, however, they will often be sufficient to generate a simple grammatical sentence structure, because even minimal semantic information can usefully direct syntactic planning. For example, the semantic distinction between "thing" (or "person") and "event" is at the heart of the grammatical distinction between nouns and verbs; and even an SD patient with considerable degradation of the fine-grained semantic knowledge that distinguishes between similar sorts of things may still have sufficient information to drive the most basic syntactic planning.

In other words, a simple or vague message may often be produced in an utterance with correct grammatical form; but this is not to say that a semantic deficit has no impact on syntactic planning during production. In particular, different speaking situations stress the planning process to varying degrees. At one end of the spectrum, when patients are in free conversation and choose to speak about something for which they still have reasonable conceptual representations, the resulting sentences are likely to be well formed, though largely limited to common and simple syntactic structures. At the other end of the spectrum, if patients are participating in a language study in which the experimenter both selects the topic and constrains the syntactic structure, the patients would be expected to make errors when they are forced to use low-frequency syntactic structures, as reported in Benedet et al. (2006). The situation of picture description is intermediate between the previous two: The topic is specified for the patients, but they are free to determine their own speech structure. What we observed under these circumstances was (1) that the clauses produced by the SD patients were shorter and less complex than those of the normal speakers, and (2) that certain grammatical constraints which should operate over the scope of several clauses were violated by SD speakers. For example, to describe the little girl in the cookie theft picture by saying *she is hoping to get something* is not wrong; but as there are two "*she*"s in the picture (woman and girl), this utterance essentially demands that there will have been very recent mention of the *girl* as the antecedent for the pronoun *she*. The normal speakers in our sample hardly ever infringed this requirement, but SD patients often did. Anecdotally, we can report that this problem gets even worse with disease progression: Several of the very severely affected patients seen in our clinic have not only referred to people by pronoun without first mentioning them by name (e.g. *Bill*) or label (e.g. *my husband*), but have also used the wrong pronoun. Patient PP's husband Bill brought her to the interview room and then went back to the waiting room in the hospital; sometime later, PP asked us, "When is she coming back?"

It goes without saying that more evidence regarding the syntactic structure of SD speech would be valuable, particularly from tasks that either encourage or indeed attempt to coerce the use of a much greater variety of syntactic structures than those generated in the cookie theft description. The data presented here, however, suggest that further evidence on this topic will uncover only more extensive syntactic abnormalities or at least limitations. At least as an interim conclusion, then, we suggest that syntactic ability in speech production is disrupted by semantic degradation.

Finally, it is worth just a brief mention that the least surprising aspect of our data remains the most dramatic, that is, the emptiness to which SD speech is reduced as a result of the patients' degraded knowledge of objects and actions and scenarios. Consider JT's narrative: *Water's coming out of the sink. Kid's going off that one he's on that's going down. He's getting something out of the jar there, and the little kid's looking*. This patient does seem to understand that water is overflowing, though she makes no comment on it (most controls comment on the oddity of the fact that the woman seems unaware of the flood that she is creating/allowing to happen). JT also seems to understand that the boy is falling off whatever it is he is on, and that he is getting something. There is no indication that she understands what he and his presumed sister are actually doing, nor that their mother is unaware not only of the flood but also of what they are up to. There are only four specific nouns in JT's narrative (*water*, *sink*, *kid*, and *jar*); *kid* is used to refer to both the boy and the girl without any differentiation; and recall that the *cookie jar* has a printed label on it, so that JT is probably reading rather than naming it. The only verbs (*coming out*, *going off*, *going down*, *getting*, and *looking*) are extremely general and high-frequency ones. In summary: what SD patients know and hence can say is sadly well characterized as sweet nothings.

Acknowledgements

This work is supported by an NIMH Interdisciplinary Behavioural Science Center grant (MH64445). We are grateful to John Hodges for permission to publish data from these cases, and to Sally Andrews and Anne Castles for comments on the first version of the chapter.

References

Altmann, L. J. P., Kempler, D., & Andersen, E. S. (2001). Speech errors in Alzheimer's disease: Reevaluating morphosyntactic preservation. *Journal of Speech, Language, and Hearing Research*, *44*, 1069–1082.

Bates, E., Harris, C., Marchman, V., & Wulfeck, B. (1995). Production of complex syntax in normal ageing and Alzheimer's disease. *Language and Cognitive Processes*, *10*, 487–539.

Benedet, M., Patterson, K., Gomez-Pastor, I., & Garcia de la Rocha, M. L. (2006). "Non-semantic" aspects of language in semantic dementia: As normal as they're said to be? *Neurocase*, *12*, 15–26.

Bird, H., Lambon Ralph, M. A., Patterson, K., & Hodges, J. R. (2000). The rise and fall of frequency and imageability: Noun and verb production in semantic dementia. *Brain and Language*, *73*, 17–49.

Bock, J. K. (1986). Syntactic persistence in language production. *Cognitive Psychology*, *18*, 355–387.

Bock, K., & Griffin, Z. (2000). The persistence of structural priming: Transient activation or implicit learning? *Journal of Experimental Psychology: General*, *129*, 177–192.

Bock, K., & Levelt, W. (1994). Language production: Grammatical encoding. In M. A. Gernsbacher (Ed.), *Handbook of psycholinguistics* (pp. 945–983). San Diego, CA: Academic Press.

Bozeat, S., Lambon Ralph, M. A., Patterson, K., Garrard, P., & Hodges, J. R. (2000). Nonverbal semantic impairment in semantic dementia. *Neuropsychologia*, *38*, 1207–1215.

Breedin, S. D., & Saffran, E. M. (1999). Sentence processing in the face of semantic loss: A case study. *Journal of Experimental Psychology: General*, *128*, 547–562.

Folstein, M. F., Folstein, S. E., & McHugh, P. R. (1975). Mini-mental state: A practical method for grading the cognitive state of patients for the clinician. *Journal of Psychiatric Research*, *12*, 189–198.

Goodglass, H., & Kaplan, E. (1983). *The assessment of aphasia and related disorders* (2nd ed.). Philadelphia: Lea & Febiger.

Graham, K. S., Patterson, K., Powis, J., Drake, J., & Hodges, J. R. (2002). Multiple inputs to episodic memory: Words tell another story. *Neuropsychology*, *16*, 380–389.

Graham, K. S., Patterson, K., Pratt, K. H., & Hodges, J. R. (1999). Re-learning and subsequent forgetting of semantic category exemplars in a case of semantic dementia. *Neuropsychology*, *13*, 359–380.

Hodges, J. R., Patterson, K., Oxbury, S., & Funnell, E. (1992). Semantic dementia: progressive fluent aphasia with temporal lobe atrophy. *Brain*, *115*, 1783–1806.

Jefferies, E., Frankish, C. R., & Lambon Ralph, M. A. (2006). Lexical and semantic binding in verbal short-term memory. *Journal of Memory and Language*, *54*, 81–98.

Jefferies, E., Patterson, K., Jones, R. W., Bateman, D., & Lambon Ralph, M. A. (2004). A category-specific advantage for numbers in verbal short-term memory: Evidence from semantic dementia. *Neuropsychologia*, *42*, 639–660.

Kempler, D., Curtiss, S., & Jackson, C. (1987). Syntactic preservation in Alzheimer's disease. *Journal of Speech and Hearing Research*, *30*, 343–350.

Kemper, S., LaBarge, E., Ferraro, F. R., Cheung, H., Cheung, H., & Storandt, M. (1993). On the preservation of syntax in Alzheimer's disease: Evidence from written sentences. *Archives of Neurology*, *50*, 81–86.

Knott, R., Patterson, K., & Hodges, J. R. (2000). The role of speech production in auditory-verbal short-term memory. *Neuropsychologia*, *38*, 125–142.

Lambon Ralph, M. A., Graham, K. S., Ellis, A. W., & Hodges, J. R. (1998). Naming in semantic dementia: What matters? *Neuropsychologia*, *36*, 775–784.

Lambon Ralph, M. A., McClelland, J. L., Patterson, K., Galton, C. J., & Hodges, J. R. (2001). No right to speak? The relationship between object naming and semantic impairment: Neuropsychological evidence and a computational model. *Journal of Cognitive Neuroscience*, *13*, 341–356.

Lyons, K., Kemper, S., LaBarge, E., Ferraro, F. R., Balota, D., & Storandt, M. (1994). Oral language and Alzheimer's disease: A reduction in syntactic complexity. *Aging, Neuropsychology, and Cognition*, *1*, 271–281.

Majerus, S., Norris, D., & Patterson, K. (2006, under review). *What does a patient with semantic dementia remember in verbal short-term memory? Order and sound but not words.*

Mathuranath, P. S., Nestor, P. J., Berrios, G. E., Rakowicz, W., & Hodges, J. R. (2000). A brief cognitive test battery to differentiate Alzheimer's disease and frontotemporal dementia. *Neurology*, *55*, 1613–1620.

Patterson, K., Graham, N., & Hodges, J. R. (1994). The impact of semantic memory loss on phonological representations. *Journal of Cognitive Neuroscience*, *6*, 57–69.

Rochon, E., Kavé, G., Cupit, J., Jokel, R., & Winocur, G. (2004). Sentence comprehension in semantic dementia: A longitudinal case study. *Cognitive Neuropsychology*, *21*, 317–330.

Snowden, J. S., Goulding, P. J., & Neary, D. (1989). Semantic dementia: A form of circumscribed cerebral atrophy. *Behavioural Neurology*, *2*, 111–138.

Tyler, L. K., Moss, H. E., Patterson, K., & Hodges, J. R. (1997). The gradual deterioration of syntax and semantics in a patient with progressive aphasia. *Brain and Language*, *56*, 426–476.

Warrington, E. K. (1975). Selective impairment of semantic memory. *Quarterly Journal of Experimental Psychology*, *27*, 635–657.

14 All about words: A lexicalist perspective on reading

Sally Andrews
School of Psychology, University of Sydney, Australia

The linking theme between the chapters in this book is that they all focus on words, and most of them are concerned solely with visual word recognition. The authors present a variety of different views about how words are represented and processed and use a wide range of methods to illustrate and substantiate their claims. But few of them feel the need to justify conducting a research programme focused entirely on the processing of written words. Literacy is crucially important in modern societies, and it is taken as self-evident that identification of written words is fundamental to literacy. In this chapter, I want to stand back from the detailed accounts of visual word recognition discussed in other chapters and focus on a more functional level of analysis.

My goal is to elaborate and illustrate a *lexicalist* account of reading—an account of *why* and *how* words contribute to effective reading that is grounded in consideration of the psychological mechanisms required for the task and the constraints imposed by the structure of written language. From this perspective, the critical questions are not about the form of lexical knowledge, but about what it is for: what is the function of lexical processing in reading?

At one level, the answer to this question is obvious—words are important for reading because texts are constructed from words. But this is a far from uncontroversial claim. It is only at the surface level that texts are constructed from words—their meanings are derived from larger units of text and depend on both syntax and context (e.g. *Libben; Patterson & MacDonald*, this volume). This is one of the reasons that whole-language approaches to reading instruction emphasize the need to focus children's attention on the level of meaning rather than on lexical or sublexical units in order to achieve the goal of reading: comprehension of meaning (e.g. Goodman, 1976; Smith, 1973). More extreme practitioners of such views advise against exposing children to words in isolation, let alone focusing on sublexical relationships between written and spoken words, because it will interfere with children's orientation to meaning. In stark contrast, cognitive psychologists advocate decoding approaches to early reading instruction that recognize the importance of phonological awareness in triggering "alphabetic insight" (Byrne

& Fielding-Barnsley, 1990) and encourage the development of an "expert lexicon" (Perfetti, 1992) in which orthographic word forms are amalgamated with their phonological codes (Ehri, 1992). Although many believe it is possible to reconcile these two approaches to reading instruction, the differences between them remain a source of controversy among researchers, teachers, and educational policy makers because they are entangled with a range of deep, philosophical differences relating to both pedagogy and research methodology (see Rayner, Foorman, Perfetti, Pesetsky, & Seidenberg, 2001).

A functional level of description details what the parts of the system do—the functional role they play—rather than what the parts are built out of (Dawson, 1998). The lexicalist position argues that words have a special status, in written language processing, but is agnostic about the precise form of lexical knowledge. In particular, it is not the same as the distinction between localist versus distributed lexical representations (see *Rastle & Coltheart; Seidenberg & Plaut*, this volume). My claim is that, whatever the "grain size" of linguistic knowledge in general, there is a functional level of description at which lexical knowledge acts in a "localist" manner. There *is* a word level of processing, defined functionally—at both the conceptual and algorithmic levels of Marr's (1982) framework—whether or not it is instantiated at the implementational level. This is because words serve as an interface or "pivot" for reading comprehension.

As far as I am aware, the metaphor of a pivot has not been applied in this domain, but it provides a particularly apt summary of the role that words play in reading. Dictionary definitions of the term include both the concrete meaning of "the end of a shaft . . . supporting something that turns" and the more abstract reference, "a thing upon which progress depends" (*Collins English Dictionary*, 1979), both of which are relevant to my current claims. Words are the things on which comprehension depends because they are the end point, or resolution, of perceptual processing, and because they provide the impetus for conceptual processing. Lexical forms are *functionally* unitized because they mediate between perception and comprehension of text.

In some senses, the lexical pivot analogy is simply a restatement of the frequently stated claim that the lexical system is "modularized" from the higher-level processes responsible for comprehension (e.g. Forster, 1989; see also *Davis & Kim*, this volume). However, as elaborated in the first section of the chapter, it implicates a temporal rather than a spatial or structural view of modularity (Fodor, 1983) that provides new ways of thinking about challenges to the modular framework (e.g. *Balota & Yap; Davis & Kim*, this volume) and about the processes contributing to lexical classification (see *Rastle & Coltheart*, this volume). In the second section of the chapter, I turn to the other side of the lexical pivot: the claim that words are the input to conceptual processing. Investigating the independence of lexical and comprehension processes clearly requires paradigms that go beyond the single-word level. I report some outcomes of an empirical research programme that uses repetition blindness effects in sentences presented in rapid serial visual presentation (RSVP) to investigate the modularity of lexical and sentence level processing.

Modules and magic moments

What is the right level at which to carve reading up in order to understand this highly complex skill? The distinction between localist and distributed representations has dominated empirical research on lexical retrieval over the 1990s. With the availability of computational implementations of the major theoretical frameworks, model simulation data are becoming an essential component of any theoretical evaluation (see Andrews, 1982, by contrast with Andrews & Scarratt, 1998; Andrews, Woollams, & Bond, 2005). Without denying the virtues of such apparently definitive tests of theoretical predictions (but see *Seidenberg & Plaut*, this volume), we can ask whether it really *matters* to know whether representations are localist or distributed at the implementational level—or at least when it matters.

What level of grain size matters?

The availability of large-scale computational models of conceptually distinct theoretical frameworks has certainly not provided the definitive resolution to the theoretical debate that might have been expected. The DRC and PDP models rely on qualitatively different assumptions about exactly how the lexical system is carved up and the form of the representations it contains. But despite the robust debates between the proponents of different theoretical views reflected in the early chapters of this volume, in many contexts they yield identical predictions—although often for different reasons (for example, whether the difficulty in processing words with atypical spelling-sound correspondences is due to regularity or consistency). Even with respect to apparently fundamental differences in underpinning assumptions, like the serial/parallel distinction discussed by *Rastle and Coltheart* (this volume), discrimination is very difficult because a parallel activation system that is sensitive to the frequency and consistency of a variety of sublexical associations often produces effects similar to those predicted by serial mechanisms (e.g. Zorzi, 2000; but see Roberts, Rastle, Coltheart, & Besner, 2003). The difficulty in empirically disentangling the two classes of model suggests that the detailed internal wiring of the lexical system may be of little relevance to understanding task performance in many contexts.

This is not to say that the theoretical distinctions between the models are not important. Questions about the grain size of lexical knowledge are clearly critical to issues about learning and the development of reading skill (see *Castles & Nation; C. J. Davis*, this volume). Until relatively recently, proponents of distributed models could claim the high moral ground on the question of learning because localist modellers had not addressed the question of how people acquire the local representations built into the structure of their models. This is no longer true. Self-organizing approaches to learning (e.g. Page, 2000) provide an explicit account of how localist representations can be acquired through experience that has been effectively implemented for the domain of visual word recognition (Davis, 1999). It remains to be seen whether large-scale computational implementations of this approach will prove capable of simulating the range of empirical phenomena that have been addressed by DRC and PDP models.

Further, as discussed by *Rastle and Coltheart* (this volume), all current PDP models employ structured, localist input and output codes, in part because of the poor generalization shown by Seidenberg and McClelland's (1989) original simulation, which deliberately avoided this degree of a priori structure. The use of such codes is sometimes an implementational decision designed to reduce computational demands or to focus on a particular component of the model (see *Seidenberg & Plaut*). However, while it remains the case that PDP implementations typically employ localist input and output codes, questions can be raised about the relevance of assumptions about distributed representations for understanding the functional outcome of lexical processes in the context of skilled reading. To put it simply, if the lexical module has localist inputs (e.g. letters) and outputs (e.g. words), the form of the "internal wiring" may have little impact on on-line reading.

In this context, the most important assertion of the PDP framework is that there is no localist form of lexical representation (see *Rastle & Coltheart; Seidenberg & Plaut*, this volume). As discussed in detail below, a localist lexical representation is not a necessary entailment of the lexicalist position, although such a representation obviously provides the most straightforward way of conceptualizing—and certainly discussing—the pivotal role of lexical unitization in reading.

Lexicalism versus localism

My lexicalist proposal does not require the assumption of localist lexical *structures*. What it does assume is that there is a lexical *state*, a point in time at which the lexical system reaches a state of "closure" in response to presentation of a particular word. This state can equally well be identified with threshold activation of a localist lexical node or with stabilization of an attractor. Moreover, stabilization of the attractor may rely on interactions between a number of distributed networks rather than depending only on activity in the orthographic network (Van Orden & Goldinger, 1994), which might include episodic instances of words rather than abstract codes (Masson & Bodner, 2003). The critical point is that this state is relatively invariant across different presentation occasions and formats of the same word. In that sense, I am claiming that the "magic moment" hypothesis of lexical access criticized by Balota (1990)—and others, including me (Andrews & Heathcote, 2001)—is valid, but does not need to be identified with threshold activation of an abstract, localist lexical code that occurs "when a reader recognizes a word but does not yet know its meaning" (see *Balota & Yap*, this volume, p. 229). Rather, it describes a functional state—the point at which an episode of perceptual processing achieves closure and triggers the processes required to act on that state to achieve current goals—the pivot between perceptual and conceptual processing. Usually, the conceptual mechanisms engaged are the integrative processes required for comprehension, but word-recognition researchers frequently require participants to achieve less practised or natural goals, such as deciding whether the stimulus is a word or a member of some defined semantic category.

The claim that lexical processing is resolved before conceptual processing is initiated does not necessarily mean that lexical resolution is completely unaffected by semantic or contextual information. Such "top-down" knowledge may contribute to lexical resolution either through interactive feedback between localist representations, as in the interactive activation model (McClelland & Rumelhart, 1981) and *Taft*'s (this volume) localist-cum-distributed model, or through reverberating activity within networks of distributed information within a "triangle" architecture (e.g. Plaut, McClelland, Seidenberg, & Patterson, 1996), or through the convergent activation of instances of previous encounters with the word (Goldinger, 1998; Masson & Bodner, 2003). However, my claim is that, to the degree that "higher-level" sources influence early processing, they contribute to lexical closure, which, in turn, provides the impetus for the integrative processes required for comprehension. In this sense, even though higher levels of knowledge may have contributed to lexical closure, processing is not fully interactive because all that ultimately drives the comprehension system is the output of lexical processing.[1]

There are a number of important differences between this notion of temporal modularity and the conventional view of structural modularity (Fodor, 1983). Most importantly, the temporal view does not necessitate the structural encapsulation that is central to the standard account. There remains a sense of encapsulation, but it is temporal, not spatial: the early processing that culminates in lexical closure is encapsulated from the subsequent processes that act on its outcomes. This view allows for task- and context-specific influences on the processing that leads to lexical closure and addresses some of the tensions discussed by *Davis and Kim* and by *Balota and Yap* (this volume). Even if lexical processing is primarily stimulus-driven, as assumed by traditional modular theories (e.g. Forster, 1989), participants' goals and intentions, as determined by task context and instructions, may influence exactly how they process the stimulus and therefore the particular processes and representations that contribute to achieving lexical closure. Task-specific goals may also influence the outcomes of lexical processing—the mechanisms that are engaged at the pivot of lexical closure. Depending on the precision of the experimental tools being used, performance measures may fail to capture lexical closure per se and reflect some combination of the processes leading to and following the "magic moment" (*Balota & Yap*, this volume).

In the context of reading comprehension, the usual goal of written word processing, the notion of temporal modularity is of particular functional significance because effective comprehension, at least in word-order dependent languages like English, requires information about the sequence in which words occurred in the text (for example, "*the run home was exciting*" means something quite different from "*the home run was exciting*"—see *Rayner, Reichle, & Pollatsek*, this volume). Thus, at some level, the spatial activity that defines each of the lexical units in a text has to be both distinguished from that generated by other lexical units and coded in a manner that preserves information about its temporal order in the processing sequence. As *Forster* (this volume) points out, the question of how multiple words are simultaneously processed remains a critical challenge for both localist and distributed parallel activation models. It has, however, been a major focus of mathematical models of eye-movement control in reading (see *Pollatsek & Hyönä; Rayner et al.*).

E-Z Reader: Lexicalist account of eye movements

The assumption of temporal modularity underpins the E-Z Reader model of eye movements during reading (*Rayner et al.*, this volume). E-Z Reader assumes that "attention is allocated serially: to only one word at a time" (*Rayner et al.*, this volume, p. 126), and that the later stage of processing each word (L_2 in the E-Z Reader model) is mandatory and needs to be completed before attention (but not eye fixation) shifts to the next word. They argue that serial processing is crucial because comprehension of text depends on "get-[ting] the word order straight" (p. 140) not only in English, in which word order conveys critical syntactic information, but also in highly inflected languages like German, Finnish, Hungarian, and Turkish, where word order contributes to nuances of meaning or to information about discourse status such as topic focus and given–new distinctions.

It is possible that the mechanisms underlying serial processing of words in text do not generalize to single-word tasks. The requirement to move the eyes to a new location may necessitate the "packaging" of previous processing in a manner that is not necessary to process a single word. However, given that reading is the usual context in which word identification occurs, it is plausible that the processing of isolated words co-opts the processes used to identify words in text whether or not they are the only way in which the single-word task could be achieved. This seems particularly likely in the light of the processing mechanisms of E-Z Reader, which is essentially driven by computations of lexical closure. Saccades are triggered by the completion of an early stage of lexical processing—initially called a "familiarity check" (Reichle et al., 1998) but now labelled more "agnostically" as L_1—that involves "a rapid estimate of whether or not the completion of lexical access is imminent" (*Rayner et al.*, this volume, p. 128). The subsequent L_2 stage continues until the "completion of lexical access" and triggers the shifting of attention to the next word. *Rayner et al.* (this volume) acknowledge that considerable ambiguity remains about exactly how the distinction between L_1 and L_2 should be conceptualized within models of lexical retrieval (Andrews, 2003) and that the distinction may not be as discrete as the current E-Z Reader implementation assumes.

For the moment, the point I want to draw from E-Z Reader is that the rationale for assuming that words play a crucial role in reading does not come only from conceptual views about representational organization. E-Z Reader is motivated primarily by evidence about the patterns of eye movements during reading and the available information about the timing of the neural processes such as the "eye-to-brain" lag and saccadic programming. To accommodate these constraints and predict a variety of eye-movement data, it proves very effective to assume that processing occurs word-by-word and that the processing of one word is resolved before attention is directed to the next. Moreover, the model clearly implicates a notion of some overall index of probability or proximity of lexical closure in its implementation of L_1 and L_2. Thus, there are a variety of functional considerations about the reading process at the level of eye-movement control that are consistent with the lexicalist claim that lexical resolution plays a pivotal role in reading.

Familiarity: Task-specific artifact or signal of lexical closure?

There is another implication of the lexicalist position that is relevant to a number of current models of visual word recognition and that is highlighted by the E-Z Reader model. This concerns effects of "familiarity" on performance in word-recognition tasks. This term has frequently been invoked in models of lexical retrieval, perhaps most notably by Balota and Chumbley (1984) and Grainger and Jacobs (1996). On the face of it, these models are very different, but the functional role of familiarity is ultimately quite similar.

Balota and Chumbley adapted Atkinson and Shiffrin's (1968) general model of memory retrieval to the lexical domain by assuming a two-stage process in which the first stage relies on an index of the item's "familiarity/meaningfulness (F/M)". Extreme F/M values allow fast classifications of common words and unusual nonwords in lexical decision task (LDT) tasks, but items with intermediate values—most low-frequency words—require further processing and therefore yield slower performance. Balota and Spieler (1998) have recently developed an extended and revised mathematical version of this model to simulate the effects of frequency and repetition on response time (RT) distributions.

Grainger and Jacobs (1996) also instantiated a notion of "familiarity" in their multiple read out model (MROM) implementation but identified it with the overall similarity of a stimulus to items in memory—"global activation". However, functionally, the consequences are the same as in the Balota and

Chumbley model because high levels of overall activation early in processing allow fast lexical classification via a mechanism that is different from that underlying responses to more slowly classified items. In MROM, this depends on threshold activation of an individual localist word node rather than the "verification" process assumed by Balota and Chumbley (1984).

It might be thought that both of these models are consistent with E-Z Reader's assumptions about L_1, but there is a crucial difference: in E-Z Reader, the "familiarity" parameter that governs completion of L_1 is a reflection on ongoing lexical retrieval—an index of the system's proximity to lexical closure. In both MROM and the Balota models, it is assumed to be a task-specific computation that is used only in the LDT—an "artifact" of decision processes deemed to be irrelevant to "true" word identification, which relies on a completely independent process. This is most critically so for MROM because the global activation mechanism was added to the model to accommodate the fact that LDT tasks show facilitatory effects of neighbourhood size (Andrews, 1989, 1997). This evidence is contrary to the predictions that arise from models like interactive activation and MROM, which use lateral inhibition between localist word representations to achieve selection between lexical representations (Andrews, 1997). For the same reason, Coltheart et al. (2001) added the global activity mechanism to the lexical system of their DRC model. Within both models, "true" lexical retrieval is defined as threshold activation of an individual word node, and the global activity index is regarded as a short-cut strategy or "cheat" that is specifically recruited for the purpose of making lexical decisions.

This is not the only way of conceiving of the role of a global measure of current lexical activity. More than 15 years ago, Monsell, Doyle, and Haggard (1989) pointed out that, rather than assuming a familiarity or global activation mechanism that is independent of unique lexical activation, a "decision process [could derive] its familiarity estimate by monitoring the ongoing identification process" (p. 48). Such a possibility gains plausibility from E-Z Reader's proposal about the role that such an index may play in "normal reading". Recognition of the functional role of such a computation also provides a way of conceptualizing Ratcliff, Gomez, and McKoon's (2004) recent application of the diffusion model to the LDT.

The diffusion model is a general mathematical account of the decision process underlying binary choice tasks that has been shown to successfully simulate performance in tasks involving a wide range of stimuli. Ratcliff et al. (2004) reported that the diffusion model effectively simulated data obtained in a number of LDT experiments that varied the frequency of word items and the "wordlikeness" of nonword items. The model predicted not just correct RT distributions, but also the pattern of accuracy data and the relative speed of correct and error responses for words and nonwords. Ratcliff et al. (2004) argued that the success of their simulation shows that performance in the LDT can be fully explained by decision processes and that the task "may have nothing to say about lexical representations or about processes such as lexical access" (pp. 159–160). They also argued that the vast accumulation of factorial investigations of the effects of stimulus attributes, such as word frequency, length, repetition, concreteness, regularity, and consistency, do not necessarily provide evidence about the lexical structures or processing pathways they have been designed to investigate. According to the diffusion model, all these variables do is "alter the amount and kind of information contributing to the degree of wordness that drives the decision process and nothing more" (p. 176). The RT and accuracy data obtained in the LDT simply reflect "a single value of the degree of match of a stimulus to the lexicon"; the complicated architectures and processing assumptions proposed in current models are irrelevant "unless these models can ultimately provide a single value of goodness of match" (p. 181).

The preceding discussion about the possible functional role of a global index of ongoing retrieval suggests that Ratcliff et al.'s (2004) conceptualization of the LDT may not be as damning for standard models as they claim. The diffusion model relies on a stationary measure of "goodness of match" that conceptually corresponds to the output of a lexical process. However, a number of related "accumulator" models of memory (e.g. Brown & Heathcote, 2005; Usher & McClelland, 2001) identify the evidence-accumulation process with a dynamic index of ongoing memory retrieval rather than with its output. This notion is compatible with PDP accounts, which do not obviously allow the distinction between "global" lexical activity and activity specific to the particular item that characterizes localist models like DRC and MROM. In distributed models, the output of the lexical system can be conceived of as a measure of "match" or "resonance" of the item with the contents of lexical memory that gradually increases as the pattern of activation converges on the target word attractor (Van Orden & Goldinger, 1994)—a measure of proximity to lexical closure. From this perspective, the effects of measures of lexical similarity, such as neighbourhood density, are not necessarily artifacts of a decision-specific strategy (Grainger & Jacobs, 1996) but may reflect variations in the shape of the activation function generated across the time course of lexical identification for items that vary in their similarity to other words in the vocabulary (Andrews, 2003). That is, in contrast to Ratcliff et al.'s claim that their analysis demonstrates that the LDT does not provide a window on lexical retrieval processes, it might be possible to use diffusion-style frameworks to explore the temporal dynamics of lexical retrieval.

There is a broader sense in which decision-based approaches, such as the diffusion model, relate to the lexicalist perspective, as exemplified in E-Z Reader. Essentially, E-Z Reader conceptualizes reading as a series of decision processes in which various indices of the retrieval process trigger decisions to program a new saccade, shift attention, abort a saccade, and so on. From this perspective, the mechanics of the reading process are driven by words—word identification is "the forward 'driving engine' in reading" (Morrison, 1984, p. 12)—for reasons related to both perceptual and conceptual processing.

Word-by-word processing affords efficient and effective control of the eye movements and attention that provide the basis for effective interactions between foveal and parafoveal processing, and the sequential nature of this process "keeps words in order" for subsequent comprehension processes. Thus, E-Z Reader provides a concrete instantiation of the pivot metaphor of the lexicalist approach.

Lexical retrieval and reading comprehension

The preceding section has been concerned with the "shaft" side of the lexical pivot analogy: elaboration and implications of my claim that a functional state of lexical closure is the outcome of word processing, whether or not it is identified with a localist lexical code. My goal in this section is to elaborate and evaluate the second component of the pivot analogy—the role of lexical retrieval in "turning" the mechanisms responsible for comprehension. To draw out this issue, I will summarize the outcomes of some recent research projects conducted in my laboratory that are part of a more general programme investigating the interface between lexical retrieval and sentence comprehension.

The research draws upon work of Molly Potter and her students and colleagues over the last 30 years and, like much of her work, uses the rapid serial visual presentation (RSVP) procedure (Forster, 1970), in which word lists or sentences are presented rapidly (100–300 ms/word), usually one word at a time. This is obviously a very unusual mode of reading. At the fast rates employed in my experiments (~100 ms/word), the time that each word is available is less than the average fixation time on a word in normal reading (~200–250 ms/word). However, as *Rayner et al.*'s (this volume) summary makes clear, this value overestimates the time required to extract sufficient information to allow lexical retrieval. It takes about 50 ms for information to be transmitted from the retina to visual processing areas, and, because of the time required for saccadic programming, the eyes often remain fixated on a word after attention has shifted. Eye-movement measures obtained in "disappearing text" studies confirm that "reading proceeds quite smoothly when the fixated word disappears after 60 ms" (p. 136) and shows a standard frequency effect on fixation time, suggesting that lexical retrieval is not disrupted. Thus, 100 ms/word may be sufficient to support the processes required for comprehension. Consistent with the view that comprehension is quite effective at these RSVP rates, Potter (1975) found that university student readers could recall a sentence presented at rates as fast as 85 ms/word with high accuracy (87%), and more accurately than when the whole sentence was presented for an equivalent time (75%). She argued that the paradigm is useful because it "allows the investigator to control the timing of words in a sentence or text . . . at rates equivalent to or faster than normal reading" while avoiding the problems associated with the response requirements of self-paced reading tasks. More generally, it allows us to "push reading to its temporal limits" (Potter, 1975, p. 115). It is this feature of the method that is exploited in the present research programme, which uses evidence about how lexical processing breaks down under RSVP conditions to provide insight into the relationship between lexical retrieval and comprehension.

Repetition blindness (RB) as evidence of the independence of lexical processing

The particular breakdown I have focused on is the phenomenon known as "repetition blindness" (RB), which refers to the failure to recall the second of two identical items in an RSVP sequence of 100–300 ms/item (Kanwisher, 1987). The RB effect has been observed for pictures, letters, digits, unrelated words, and sentences, even when visual format changes dramatically across repetitions (e.g. *nine/9;* pictures/words; see V. Coltheart, 1999, for reviews). Further evidence that stimuli do not need to be physically identical to yield RB is provided by RB effects for phonologically similar stimuli such as homophones (Bavelier, 1994). But it does not appear to occur for semantically or conceptually related words (e.g. "couch-sofa") (Kanwisher & Potter, 1990). Thus, the recall deficit appears to depend on "representations of visual entities, not their meanings" (Potter, 1999, p. 24).

The dominant theoretical account of RB effects attributes them to problems in "token individuation" or "type-token binding" (Kanwisher, 1987). Recognition of complex stimuli is assumed to involve two basic processes: activation of an abstract "type" node, reflecting a match between sensory input and a stored pattern in long-term memory (LTM), and instantiation and individuation of a "token" or specific representation of the object or event. RB is attributed to "the inability to instantiate a second new token from a perceptual code that has just been involved in individuation" (Bavelier, 1999, p. 154). The precise mechanisms underlying this difficulty remain unclear, but they are assumed to reflect conflict between the representational demands of the two types of representation or a problem in detecting similar signals of unknown time of arrival and duration (Bavelier, 1999; Bavelier & Jordan, 1992). However, RB effects in the full-recall tasks used in most research could also reflect output processes such as memory interference or response bias (e.g. Fagot & Pashler, 1995). Consistent with perceptual accounts of RB, it occurs in tasks with minimal memory demands (e.g. Luo & Caramazza, 1996). However, the relative contribution of perceptual and memory-related processes to RB remains a source of controversy (e.g. Whittlesea & Masson, 2005).

The goal of my use of RB is to explore how words contribute to comprehension, so I have focused on RB effects for sentence materials. RB effects in sentences were first reported by Kanwisher (1987) and Kanwisher and Potter (1990), who found that a sentence like "*Nancy spilled the ink and there was ink all over*" was often recalled as "*Nancy spilled the ink and there was all over*" despite the ungrammaticality of the output. The robustness of the RB effect for repeated items in sentences has subsequently been confirmed and shown to be independent of the semantic and morphological relationship between the repeated items: For example, Potter (1999) describes the consternation of her participants when they experienced RB for the second occurrence of *hot* in the sentence, "*Unless they are hot enough, hotdogs don't taste good.*" Like RB effects for word lists, sentences also show RB effects for homophones (for example, *He was the first one who won a prize*), but these are usually smaller than for repetitions (Bavelier & Potter, 1992). Kanwisher (1987) attributed the recall deficit for the second occurrence of a word to a failure to set up a token for it in the representation of the sentence constructed for the purpose of recall. This could arise from either a failure to reactivate the lexical type or a problem in the processes involved in creating or stabilizing it as a memory token, or both (Bavelier, 1999).

From the lexicalist perspective, RB appears to provide very concrete evidence of a distinction between lexical codes and the processes that operate on them. Whatever precise mechanism underlies the failure to differentiate the second occurrences of a repeated word, its selective omission from subsequent report implies that it was not available to the comprehension system. When the lexical process fails to provide an output within the appropriate temporal window—when lexical closure is not achieved in time—the word's "slot" remains unfilled in the developing sentence representation. This suggests that the lexical and comprehension systems are at least temporally encapsulated. Further, the fact that the repeated word is often completely omitted suggests a further level of encapsulation because the comprehension system does not appear to have access to the partial products of lexical processing. However, as Park and Kanwisher (1994) reported, participants are sometimes aware of the word's absence, leading to what have been called "something" errors (for example, *Nancy spilled the ink and the something ran everywhere*).

Is RB specific to RSVP conditions?

Claire Marnane, an honours student working in my laboratory, was responsible for our first investigation of RB effects in sentence recall. The aim of her research was to establish whether RB effects are specific to RSVP conditions by comparing visual and auditory presentations of the same sentences. Previous evidence about whether repetition deficits occur for auditory materials is ambiguous. Downing, Kanwisher, and Potter (cited in Potter, 1999) failed to find evidence of "repetition deafness" effects, but Miller and Mackay (1994, 1996) reported such effects for word lists, but not sentences. The attentional blink, a processing deficit obtained in RSVP conditions that has some similarities to the RB effect (Chun, 1997), appears to be restricted to the visual modality. This led Potter, Chun, Banks, and Muckenhoupt (1998) to speculate that the auditory system may have evolved to deal more effectively with rapid sequences of stimuli than the visual system. Differences between the mechanisms underlying rapid processing in the visual and auditory modality may also arise from the specific functional requirements of reading by comparison with listening. In addition to carrying out the integrative processes required for comprehension, reading requires management of the complex combination of cognitive and motor processes required to acquire the sequential "snapshots" of information provided by eye fixations. This may impose very different demands and constraints from those required to retain recent speech in some form of auditory buffer. It may be reading-specific constraints that suffer under the temporal pressure imposed by RSVP.

To investigate these questions, Marnane compared two visual and two auditory conditions. The visual conditions compared RSVP (stimulus onset asynchrony (SOA) of 117 ms between words) with a whole-sentence condition in which the complete sentence was presented for the same total duration as the RSVP total for the same sentence (e.g. a 10-word sentence presented for 1170 ms). The average duration of spoken words (200–250 ms/syllable) is longer than the RSVP duration. To reduce the discrepancy between the presentation rates for the two modalities, the auditory recordings of each sentence were compressed by half. In a second auditory condition, these compressed recordings were "flattened" in their intonational structure by setting all F0 data points to a uniform value of 210 Hz.[2] The purpose in including this condition was to evaluate whether prosodic cues might provide a basis for individuating the two occurrences of a word, as suggested by Miller and MacKay (1996).

The critical stimulus materials consisted of 80 sentence pairs: the repeated condition contained repeated words at lags of 1–3 words (for example, *Cleaning the coat makes my old coat look better*); in control conditions, the first presentation was replaced with a word of similar length and frequency (for example, *Cleaning the shoes makes my old coat look better*). Auditory versions of each sentence were recorded by a female speaker and subjected to the compression and flattening procedures described above. Separate groups of 24 and 26 participants completed the visual and auditory version of the task. Counterbalanced lists were constructed that rotated repeated and control versions of each sentence across each pair of visual and auditory conditions, resulting in 40 sentences, 20 repeated and 20 control, in each sublist. A set of 10 "incongruous sentences", constructed by removing a single word from a plausible sentence, was added to each sublist to encourage report of ungrammatical sentences. Participants were instructed to read or listen to each sentence and then attempt to repeat exactly what they saw or heard. A set of practice examples was presented that included examples of incongruous sentences that were used to remind participants to report exactly what they saw or heard. In the RSVP condition, the first three practice examples were presented at longer rates (300, 200, and 250 ms) to allow participants to accustom themselves to the task.

Table 14.1 Proportion of correctly recalled critical items as a function of position (W1 versus W2) and mode of presentation. A negative repetition effect indicates that a repeated word was less likely to be recalled than its corresponding nonrepeated control word.

	Visual				*Auditory*			
	RSVP		*Whole sentence*		*Compressed*		*Compressed and flattened*	
	W1	*W2*	*W1*	*W2*	*W1*	*W2*	*W1*	*W2*
Repeated	.89	.35	.91	.58	.86	.86	.78	.74
Control	.84	.64	.90	.56	.80	.74	.74	.69
Repetition effect	.05	−.29	.01	.02	.06	.12	.04	.05

Overall sentence recall, excluding the critical words, was more accurate in the auditory conditions (79% words recalled) than the visual conditions (69%). Table 14.1 presents the average proportion of correct recalls of the first and second critical words (W1 and W2) from repeated and control sentences in each condition. These data clearly show an RB effect that is completely confined to the visual RSVP condition. All conditions showed poorer recall average recall of W2 than W1 ($F(1,48) = 46.05$), presumably reflecting poorer recall of the later part of the sentence. The RSVP condition alone shows the selective recall deficit for repeated words that defines RB, $F(1,23) = 27.60$. This effect was enhanced when W2 performance was conditionalized on correct report of W1, $F(1,23) = 44.05$, as would be expected if the failure to report W2 was contingent on identification of W1. In all other conditions, recall is somewhat better for repeated than control words, and the facilitatory effect of repetition is significant in the conditionalized W2 report data for both auditory conditions, $F(1,25) = 29.81, 21.84$.

Thus, these data replicate the RB effect for sentence materials reported by Kanwisher and others and show that it appears to be specific to the RSVP procedures. Indeed, brief sequential presentation of auditory material showed a benefit from repetition. Facilitatory priming is, of course, a common consequence of repetition and may occur here because of the relative degradation of the auditory material consequent on compression and F0 flattening. Recent identification of the same word may have helped resolve an otherwise ambiguous word, either implicitly or explicitly. This is consistent with Potter et al.'s (1998a) suggestion that the auditory system is better prepared to deal with stimuli that disappear rapidly. Information in the auditory buffer may remain available to support strategic use of repetition, as reflected in facilitatory effects of repetition. The effects of repetition in the auditory domain may therefore reflect the reconstructive memory effects that have been suggested by many researchers (e.g. Armstrong & Mewhort, 1995; Fagot & Pashler, 1995).

There was also no evidence of RB when whole sentences were presented briefly. This condition required participants to modify their eye movements to allow fixation on the end of the sentence before it disappeared, presumably accounting for their overall poor performance for the W2 words later in the sentence. However, there was no evidence of selectively poor recall of the critical repeated words.

Only the RSVP condition showed RB, and the effect was substantial—only 35% of repeated words were recalled compared to 64% of control words. Thus, fast, sequential visual presentation, at least at the rates used here, selectively disrupts report of repeated words. The reduced performance for recently presented words observed in RSVP conditions is particularly striking in the light of the facilitation observed for the same words in auditory sentences, and it suggests that the effect reflects a severe encoding failure that could not be corrected by the strategies that were employed for auditory material. This is consistent with the type-token account's assumption that, under the temporal pressure of RSVP, the type node of the second occurrence of the word is not available to the system responsible for constructing a representation of the sentence.

From the lexicalist perspective, RB seems to provide strong evidence for an independent lexical process that provides the building blocks for subsequent comprehension processes. It also implicates a temporal definition of this process in the sense that it emerges under conditions of time pressure. However, RSVP does not only "push temporal processing to its limits". It also deprives the reader of the normal spatial array of text. Such information may contribute to the individuation of repeated words.

What factors reduce RB?

This question has been addressed in a second strand of our work on RB which has focused on determining the boundaries on RB effects in RSVP sentences (Andrews & Borgwaldt, 2006). A series of experiments has compared RB effects for the same sentences in variants of the RSVP paradigm that manipulate the availability of sources of information that might contribute to individuating the occurrences of the repeated word. The baseline condition was a standard RSVP task in which words were presented at 117 ms/word. In the "case change" version, two words in the sentence, one of which was either W1 or W2, were presented in upper case. In the "spatial" version, instead of presenting each word of the sentence in the same location, words were presented one at a time in the spatially sequential positions they would occupy if the whole sentence were presented on the screen.

The sentences were a different set from those used by Marnane. They were constructed to allow comparison of the effects of repeated words with pairs of one-letter-different word "neighbours" (Andrews, 1997). Details of stimuli and procedure are provided by Andrews and Borgwaldt (2006), who also report the results for neighbour pairs, which are not discussed here, where the focus is on repeated words. Each list of sentences contained 15 repeated sentences and 15 matched control sentences, as well as 30 sentences containing neighbour pairs or their controls, and 15 incongruous sentences from which a word had been deleted to create a sentence similar to those resulting from deletion of one of the critical words. Separate groups of 28–32 participants completed each condition. They were all instructed to recall the sentence verbatim, and it was stressed that they should report exactly what they saw, even if it did not make a sensible sentence. Practice trials reinforced this instruction, and began with five sentences presented at slower rates than the experimental trials.

Overall recall accuracy was high in all conditions: average recall for noncritical words was 87%, 73%, and 80% in the standard, case-change, and spatial conditions, respectively. As shown in Table 14.2, all three versions of the task produced RB indexed by lower recall for the second word in repeated compared to control sentences—standard: $F(1,27) = 135.67$; case change: $F(1,31) = 75.54$; spatial: $F(1,31) = 6.33$. The size of the effect observed in the case-change condition was smaller than the standard condition, $F(1,89) = 3.81$, $p = .054$, but still substantial. The RB effect in the spatial condition, although significant, was considerably smaller than the other two conditions, $F(1,89) = 43.06$. This suggests that the spatial information provided by the sentence array contributes to individuating the separate occurrences of the repeated word and therefore reduces the probability of repetition blindness.

There is, however, another difference between the standard and spatial RSVP conditions that could account for why RB is reduced in the spatial condition. When words are presented in a single location, as in standard RSVP, each word is potentially subject to masking from the words that appear before and after it. Two new RSVP conditions were created to investigate the contribution of masking to RB effects. Each condition was a variant of the spatial procedure described above, in which each word of the sentence appeared in its sentence-appropriate position for 112 ms/word. In the forward-masked RSVP, a template of the sentence, consisting of sets of hash marks corresponding to each word, appeared for 112 ms (e.g. #### ###### ### ###

Table 14.2 Proportion of correctly recalled critical items as a function of position (W1 versus W2) and mode of presentation. A negative repetition effect indicates that a repeated word was less likely to be recalled than its corresponding nonrepeated control word

	Standard RSVP		*Case-change RSVP*		*Spatial RSVP*	
	W1	*W2*	*W1*	*W2*	*W1*	*W2*
Repeated	.92	.38	.87	.45	.89	.74
Control	.83	.69	.81	.70	.86	.79
Repetition effect	.09	–.31	.06	–.25	.03	–.05

########), and the words of the sentence sequentially replaced their slot in the template (e.g. Many ###### ### . . .) and were erased after 112 ms. Thus, each word was forward masked by the hash mask. In the backward-masked RSVP, the reverse procedure was used: each word appeared for 112 ms and was then replaced by a hash mask, so that by the end of the sentence the complete sentence template was presented.

These conditions produced substantially lower levels of overall recall than the spatial RSVP condition (forward masked: 61.4%; backward masked: 51.2%). As summarized in Table 14.3, both conditions also showed a significant RB effect—forward: $F(1,31)= 17.18$; backward: $F(1,31)=18.04$—which was more than twice as big as that observed in the spatial condition. This suggests that the masking contributes to the difficulty in individuating W2 and therefore increases the RB effect relative to the unmasked spatial condition. However, the fact that the RB effects are considerably smaller than those observed in the standard RSVP condition suggests that spatially distributing the words overcomes some of the problems suffered by briefly presented repeated words, even when they are subject to masking.

The complete set of results provides strong evidence for an encapsulated lexical system that feeds the processes required to construct a sentence representation that can support verbatim recall. Temporal pressure, particularly when combined with impoverished information about the spatial array of text, can prevent the lexical system from either registering, or fully resolving, the lexical processing of words repeated in close succession. Perceptual information that distinguishes the two occurrences, such as a change in case, reduces RB a little, but, consistent with evidence that RB effects in lists survive dramatic changes in physical format (e.g. Bavelier, 1994), the effect is still substantial. The most sizeable reduction in RB comes from individuating the words spatially by presenting them in sentence locations. This is partly because such presentation eliminates the masking that occurs in standard RSVP, because RB effects are larger in conditions that provide spatial individuating information but include forward or backward masks.

There are at least three reasons to believe that the observed RB effects are

Table 14.3 Proportion of correctly recalled critical items as a function of position (W1 versus W2) and mode of presentation. A negative repetition effect indicates that a repeated word was less likely to be recalled than its corresponding nonrepeated control word

	Forward masked		*Backward masked*	
	W1	*W2*	*W1*	*W2*
Repeated	.64	.38	.57	.31
Control	.58	.52	.52	.43
Repetition effect	.06	–.13	.05	–.12

due to deficits in lexical processing rather than to reconstructive processes occurring at the time of memory retrieval, as suggested by a number of researchers (e.g. Armstrong & Mewhort, 1995; Fagot & Pashler, 1995; Whittlesea & Masson, 2005).

The first reason is the lack of relationship between the level of RB observed and overall recall. The largest and smallest levels of significant RB (.31 and .05) were observed in the standard and spatial RSVP conditions respectively, which had the highest levels of overall recall (89% and 80%). The two masking conditions produced much lower levels of overall recall (61% and 52% for forward and backward masking, respectively) but yielded equivalent, intermediate RB effects (.13 and .12). If RB effects reflect memory-retrieval strategies or biases that are invoked when participants cannot reliably retrieve or select the correct word (Armstrong & Mewhort, 1995), they should be greater in conditions that yield poorer recall. This is clearly not the case.

The second reason for preferring a lexical account of the present RB effects is that they are clearly sensitive to perceptual manipulations that would be expected to influence the process of lexical retrieval. Each of the variants on visual RSVP that was investigated increased the difficulty of sentence recall as indexed by overall accuracy, but independent of the extent of overall recall, each manipulation also influenced RB in a direction consistent with the manipulation's likely effect on lexical individuation. Changing the case of words reduced RB only slightly, consistent with the view that lexical processing operates on case-independent letter codes. Presenting each word in a different location considerably reduced RB. Not only does this manipulation provide individuating information, but it is exactly the information that is usually available for separate words in text. But this procedure also eliminates the masking that occurs in single-position RSVP tasks. Consistent with the possibility that masking contributes to RB effects in the standard RSVP paradigm, RB effects increased when masks were presented either before or after the word, even in the spatial display.

A third reason for arguing that the RB effects are not due to memory strategies is that the most obvious outcome of the application of reconstructive memory strategies to sentence materials is that observed for the auditory sentences in Marnane's experiment described earlier: facilitation for repeated words reflecting the use of the previous episode to interpret the degraded or ambiguous sensory information extracted from its second occurrence. Following Potter et al. (1998a), I suggested that information in the auditory buffer may remain available long enough to support such a strategy. The significant recall deficits observed in all conditions reported here imply that there is no equivalent visual buffer, or at least that it is not established under RSVP conditions.

Rejecting an interpretation in terms of retrieval strategies is not intended to imply that RB effects are "purely perceptual". Rather, as Bavelier (1999) emphasizes, they reflect the interface between perception and memory.

Within the lexicalist perspective, they reflect failures at the point of the lexical pivot—occasions on which a lexical output is not delivered within the required time frame. The RSVP procedure does not provide the opportunity to increase the time window, or make a regressive eye movement, and the lexical system therefore fails to deliver a token to the comprehension process.

According to Potter (1999), comprehension begins in conceptual short-term memory (CSTM), a system that transiently holds the semantic information activated by the stimuli being processed.[3] The "rapidly activated and equally rapidly forgotten representations [in CSTM] are the raw material for identification and comprehension of words, pictures and sequences such as sentences" (Potter, 1999, p. 13), and they account for the ease with which we normally understand the world. Although much of the information in CSTM is transient, "well-connected structures" can become available to articulatory rehearsal processes (Baddeley, 1990) to support recall and lead to consolidation in long-term memory. Potter argued that the structures created in CSTM are "copies or tokens of the activated [lexical] types" and their relationships, and that RB prevents the type node for the repeated word from being "tokenized" in CSTM (1999, p. 24).

Thus, RB effects reflect a breakdown in the normal interface between lexical and comprehension processes. This breakdown is partly due to time constraints, which are exacerbated by masking, but can be reduced by spatially individuating information. This suggests that RB may be due to disruptions in the processes that map the output of the lexical process onto the structure being developed in CSTM. Spatial information may play a particularly useful role in that mapping or "binding" process.

RB effects could also arise from problems in the tokenization process. Bavelier (1999) suggests that this is a dynamic process involving a number of different levels of word code that may be processed at different rates. RB effects for visually distinct items that share other identity-relevant codes (e.g. words/pictures, homophones) may arise from problems in stabilizing two overlapping codes within the same token rather than from a failure in delivering the type node. Such stabilization effects are usually smaller than the deficits observed for identical items (Bavelier, 1999). In apparent contradiction to this view, we have found virtually identical recall deficits for neighbour pairs and for repeated words (Andrews & Borgwaldt, 2005). That is, previous presentation of a similar word causes just as much disruption of sentence recall as repetition: recall deficits for *sale* are just as strong for sentences like *I noticed they had salt for sale this morning* as for *When you notice a sale the sale is already over*. This is true across all the RSVP variations reported above, demonstrating that "neighbour blindness" is modulated by exactly the same factors as RB (Andrews & Borgwaldt, 2005). This is inconsistent with type-token accounts, which most obviously predict smaller effects for nonidentical items (Bavelier et al., 1994; Kanwisher & Potter, 1990). Although this is the usual finding for similar items in unrelated word lists (e.g. Bavelier et al., 1994; Harris & Morris, 2000), our data, in combination with earlier studies comparing RB effects for similar and identical words in sentences (Chialant & Caramazza, 1997; Harris & Morris, 2001), indicate that repetition deficits for neighbours presented in sentences are equivalent to those for repeated words.

A possible explanation of equivalent RB effects for identical and similar words within the lexicalist perspective is that the lexical system may sometimes fail to distinguish between similar lexical candidates. Using a double-word version of the RSVP paradigm that required participants to select the contextually appropriate word, Potter, Stiefbold, and Moryadas (1998b) found evidence for a "modular interactive" model which assumes that the lexical process outputs a set of lexical candidates rather than a single word. They define the model as modular because the candidates' output by the lexical system is defined orthographically rather than by context or semantics. There is substantial evidence from single-word paradigms that orthographic neighbours are activated in the course of identifying a word (Andrews, 1997). If RB occurs because prior activation of the target lexical representation makes it difficult to detect a temporally proximal reactivation (Bavelier & Jordan, 1992), it could result from prior presentation of a similar word just as it does for a repetition. We are currently combining Potter et al.'s double-word paradigm with repetition to try to disentangle the relative contributions of perceptual processes and the contextually driven reconstruction processes discussed by Whittlesea and Masson (2005) to RB effects (Bond & Andrews, 2005).

Clearly, a number of issues remain to be resolved about the basis of RB effects on sentence recall and, particularly, to substantiate the claim that they reflect early, perceptual/lexical processes rather than later, reconstructive, or "attributional" processes (Whittlesea & Masson, 2005). My purpose in providing this overview of my research with this paradigm is not to provide a definitive answer to this question but to demonstrate a method of investigating the interface between lexical and conceptual processing that underpins the pivot metaphor of the lexicalist framework.

Conclusions

The aim of this chapter has been to elaborate a "lexicalist" perspective that ascribes a central functional role to word processing in reading. I have argued that words serve as the pivot of the reading process because they are the end point of perceptual processing and the input to comprehension processes. This view reiterates the importance of modularity in language processing, but does not identify modularity with representational structures. Rather, I have argued for a temporal notion of modularity that relies on a state of lexical closure rather than a lexical node.

I have gone to some lengths to dissociate the lexicalist stance from debate about localist versus distributed representations because I do not think that lexical structures are a necessary entailment of the lexicalist position, and because I want to avoid confusing it with the "standard" localist view. However, I think there are a variety of reasons for believing that there *is* a localist level of representation that underpins the pivotal contribution of lexical retrieval to comprehension.

Proponents of PDP models have rejected the notion of lexical codes (e.g. Plaut, 1997) because they violate the general principles of their framework (*Seidenberg & Plaut*, this volume). But arguing for distributed rather than localist knowledge structures at all levels of a system may be "throwing the baby away with the bathwater". There is nothing in the PDP framework that inherently precludes modularity. The fact that the network is initially an undifferentiated set of connections does not preclude the development of a modular organisation: "There is a huge difference between *starting* modular and *becoming* modular" (Elman et al., 1996, p. 101). Apparently modular behaviours have been simulated by connectionist networks in which functional modularity emerged within the system as a function of the different patterns of correlations between input and output patterns (Hinton & Shallice, 1991; Plaut & Shallice, 1993; Plunkett & Marchman, 1991). In contrast to nativist assumptions about the principles underlying modular organization (e.g. Chomsky, 1965), PDP frameworks predict *functional* specialization. Networks will develop a functionally modular architecture if such an organization facilitates the distinctions between input and output patterns that are required to achieve effective performance. A "horizontally modular" architecture in which perceptual processes are functionally encapsulated from higher-level processes—as assumed by the lexicalist framework—will emerge if it facilitates effective performance.

Despite PDP theorists' emphasis on the lack of lexical codes, there are few computational data that really address the issue at the level relevant to this discussion. Current large-scale implementations of the PDP framework have restricted their focus to lexical processing with little consideration of how it is translated into performance. The models' performance is often assessed by general measures of network activity (e.g. cross-entropy; semantic or orthographic stress) that bear little direct relationship to the particular dependent measure being modelled (e.g. reaction time versus errors). Thus, the question of how the outcomes of lexical processing feed into higher-level processes has rarely been directly addressed. Even if lexical knowledge is distributed, it is still possible that the product of that processing is transmitted to other networks only when activity within the lexical network has been resolved such that the outcome of lexical processing is, at least functionally, a discrete unit of information: a localist lexical code. Indeed, Plaut (1999) pointed out that it is more "neurobiologically plausible" to assume "a procedure that need only access unit states" than one that has explicit access to the weights among units (p. 351).[4]

As discussed above, the development of localist representations is compatible with the principles outlined by *Seidenberg and Plaut* (this volume) because functionally modular architectures can arise through learning if they provide the best solution to the particular set of mapping problems presented to the network (Elman et al., 1996)—if it is the best way of managing the task of reading. I have argued that the E-Z Reader model (*Rayner et al.*, this volume) exemplifies one set of functional demands on the reading process that depend crucially on the notion of discrete states of lexical retrieval. Another set of functional demands that implicate words arise from issues about the learning process discussed by *Kello* (this volume).

Kello's junction model, like Harm and Seidenberg's (2004) PDP model, explicitly acknowledges the fact that children approach the task of identifying written words with a well-established repertoire of spoken words. Thus, connections between phonology and semantics (P–S connections) already exist when children begin to read. Kello (p. 53) argued that orthographic knowledge may "interfaced with the representations that mediate between sound and meaning"—a level that he suggests may be morphologically structured. This contrasts with the distinct O–P and O–S connections that are typical of the "triangle model". Kello implements the representations that link orthographic patterns to the mediating P–S level as localist lexical codes. At this stage of model development, this decision is principally one of computational convenience. However, he argues that the theoretical assumptions of his single-route architecture implicate "a lexicon of sorts . . . regardless of whether . . . [it] comprises lexical nodes or more distributed representations" (p. 64), and he implies that further developments of the model may rely on self-organizing principles (Davis, 1999; Page, 2000), based on adaptive resonance theory (Grossberg, 1980), to develop localist lexical units. Critically, such localist systems allow activation of a node to be graded as a function of its similarity to a given input pattern preserving the PDP principle that supports effective generalization (Kello, Sibley, & Plaut, 2005).

Thus, a hybrid system containing both localist and distributed codes is perfectly compatible with the principles on which PDP models are based (*Seidenberg & Plaut*, this volume). The notion of lexical codes is also consistent with recent evidence about the neural bases of word identification—satisfying a second principle critical to the PDP approach. A convergent body of evidence provided by cognitive neuroimaging data (e.g. Price et al., 1994), and electrophysiological (Posner & McCandliss, 1999) and cognitive neuropsychological studies (e.g. Warrington & Shallice, 1980) has been taken to demonstrate an isolable system in the left prestriate cortex that is selectively activated by written words and well-structured nonwords, but not by nonlinguistic or poorly structured linguistic stimuli.

This visual word form system (VWFS) is argued to serve as the "primary gateway" between the visual system and core components of the pre-existing language apparatus (Carr, 1999). Carr and Posner (1995) suggest that the VWFS can be identified either with the lexical level of localist interactive activation models, or with the orthographic layer of PDP models. They also argue that this system would be expected to emerge in the course of reading development and to be distinguishable from a more biologically constrained process underlying phonological processing. This hypothesis is supported by neuroimaging comparisons of readers at different skill levels, which have shown that the VWFS appears to play a greater role in the processing of competent readers than disabled readers. Pugh et al.'s (2001) review of available neuroimaging evidence led them to conclude that successful reading relies on two consolidated left-hemisphere posterior systems: the temporoparietal area, which "performs the function of learning to decode print for normally developing young readers", and the extrastriatal VWFS region, which "develops with reading experience into a system that recognizes printed words in a fast, automatic manner" (Pugh et al., 2001, pp. 246–247). Convergent evidence from event-related potential (ERP) procedures suggests that activity in this area distinguishes between words and nonwords within at least 200 ms after stimulus onset and across a variety of tasks requiring word identification. Carr (1999) argues that the accumulating evidence about the VWFS is consistent with the gateway hypothesis, which implies that "orthographic encoding gets the ball rolling . . . and hence should be found early and often" (p. 479), and he speculates that development of this system reflects "a critical step in learning to read [that] involves mastering the perceptual properties of written language so that the visual system can talk effectively to the language system" (p. 476).

From the perspective of the lexicalist framework, the existence of the VWFS and its association with individual differences in reading skill provides converging evidence for a brain state, localized in this region, that is activated in a manner consistent with the role I have attributed to "lexical codes". The question of whether the representations of word forms in this system are spatially localist or distributed is relatively immaterial—what is important is that this system appears to be the gateway, or pivot, for subsequent higher-order processing.

There are two major implications of identifying the activity in the VWFS with the lexical codes or states discussed in the first section of this chapter. First, it does appear to implicate a "magic moment", defined as "when a reader recognizes a word but does not yet know its meaning" (*Balota & Yap*, this volume, p. 229) because the VWFS is activated by orthographic properties and activated early, consistent with the gateway metaphor. However, this area transmits visual codes for word forms to a number of different brain regions involved in further linguistic processing (Carr & Posner, 1995). Further evidence about the timing of activation in the various cortical systems involved in reading and its relationships to reading skill is required to fully understand the role this area plays in lexical processing and reading.[5]

The second implication of linking VWFS to the lexicalist argument follows from the parallel between the specificity of this area of the extrastriate cortex to *visual* word forms and the apparent specificity of RB effects to the visual modality. There are at least two reasons why orthographic word forms may play a specific role in reading that is not fully paralleled in spoken-language processing. The first derives from the late acquisition of reading by comparison with speech. Orthographic word forms are "grafted on" to an existing spoken-language system and therefore have the potential to both capitalize on—and shape—spoken-word representations (Taft, 2001; this volume). Secondly, the mechanics of the reading process—the need to control the eye movements across text while maintaining a sequential record of what was read—may rely on segmenting the text into words. These properties of reading by comparison with listening may combine with other differences between the modalities. Because of its temporal demands, the auditory system may have a more durable memory buffer that is not available to the visual system. Alternatively, RSVP procedures may interfere with the visual buffering system, as suggested by the reduced RB obtained in conditions that maintain spatial information.

Finally, to return to the issue posed at the beginning of the chapter of "what level of grain size matters", my argument is that the critical issues for understanding skilled on-line reading lie at a more macro-level of cognitive architecture that may be relatively independent of assumptions about the "distributedness" of the representations within the different modules of the network. In addition to their assumptions about representational grain size, all computational models also build in assumptions about this level of cognitive architecture instantiated in the interconnections between orthographic (O), phonological (P), and semantic (S) networks and the hidden units mediating between them. *Kello*'s (this volume) "junction model" exemplifies how such differences in cognitive architecture affect the PDP framework's account of empirical phenomena assumed to demonstrate lexical and sublexical processes. Similarly, Harm and Seidenberg's (2004) model demonstrates how changes in the sequence in which particular connections are trained influence the division of labour between different modules of the lexical network. At least some of the critical questions about lexical architecture—about exactly how the O, P, and S systems of the triangle framework are linked—may be relatively independent of issues about the grain size of the representations within these systems. Certainly, it is important to clearly distinguish issues about broad functional architecture from issues about whether knowledge is implemented in a localist or a distributed manner.

It is also important to move beyond the level of the single word and evaluate how the lexical system interfaces with higher cognitive processes in order to address such questions. Eye-movement methodologies provide one approach to this goal (e.g. *Pollatsek & Hyönä; Rayner et al.*, this volume), and the systematic examination of the comprehension and discourse of brain-injured patients in structured contexts like those investigated by *Patterson and MacDonald* (this volume) provide insight into the functional architecture supporting language comprehension and production through its pattern of breakdown. The empirical section of this chapter showed how RSVP procedures, which impose temporal constraints on reading, can be used to explore the interaction between lexical retrieval and sentence comprehension in skilled readers. The lexicalist perspective argues that reading is all about words, but this does not justify focusing entirely on word-level processing. We need to understand how words are *used* in the service of comprehension to fully evaluate the validity of theories of how words are represented and retrieved from lexical memory.

The functional account of why words are important to reading provided by the lexicalist approach may also provide a basis for reconciliation in the debate between "whole language" and "phonics" approaches to reading instruction (e.g. Rayner et al., 2001) referred to at the beginning of this chapter. The lexicalist position implies that early methods of reading instruction need to focus on words because words are the building blocks of comprehension. Drawing children's attention to sublexical structure is not a goal in its own right, but a means to an end. Children need to extract systematic sublexical relationships in order to develop precise, redundant lexical representations that support efficient, effective comprehension (Perfetti, 1992). This is particularly true for deep orthographies like English (*Castles & Nation*, this volume). Thus, decoding-based instruction directly contributes to the functional goal of reading—achieving effective comprehension. The functional role of this form of instruction is not to teach children about sublexical structure per se, but to allow them to structure what they know about the words of their language in a manner that will support effective reading comprehension.

Acknowledgements

This research was supported by the Australian Research Council. I am grateful to Susanne Borgwaldt and Anna Woollams for their invaluable assistance in preparing and conducting the experiments.

References

Andrews, S. (1982). Phonological recoding: Is the regularity effect consistent? *Memory and Cognition*, *10*, 565–575.

Andrews, S. (1989). Frequency and neighbourhood effects on lexical access: Activation or search? *Journal of Experimental Psychology: Learning, Memory, and Cognition*, *15*, 802–814.

Andrews, S. (1997). The role of orthographic similarity in lexical retrieval: resolving neighborhood conflicts. *Psychonomic Bulletin and Review*, *4*, 439–461.

Andrews, S. (2003). E-Z Reader's assumptions about lexical processing: Not so easy to define the two stage of lexical access? *Behavioral and Brain Sciences*, *26*, 477–478.

Andrews, S., & Borgwaldt, S. (2005). *Repetition blindness in sentences: Turn a blind eye?* Paper presented at the 15th Australian Language and Speech Conference, Macquarie University, Australia, December 2005.

Andrews, S., & Heathcote, A. (2001). Distinguishing common and task-specific processes in lexical retrieval: A matter of some moment? *Journal of Experimental Psychology: Learning, Memory, and Cognition*, *27*, 514–544.

Andrews, S., & Scarratt, D. (1998). Rule and analogy mechanisms in reading nonwords: Hough dou peapel rede gnew wirds? *Journal of Experimental Psychology: Human Perception and Performance*, *24*, 1052–1086.

Andrews, S., Woollams, A., & Bond, R. (2005). Spelling-sound typicality only affects words with digraphs: Further qualifications to the generality of the regularity effect on word naming. *Journal of Memory and Language*, *53*, 567–593.

Armstrong, I. T., & Mewhort, D. J. K. (1995). Repetition deficit in rapid-serial-visual-presentation displays: Encoding failure or retrieval failure? *Journal of Experimental Psychology: Human Perception and Performance*, *21*, 1044–1052.

Atkinson, R. C., & Shiffrin, R. M. (1968). Human memory: A proposed system and its control processes. In K. W. Spence & J. T. Spence (Eds.), *The psychology of learning and motivation: Advances in research and theory* (Vol. 2, pp. 89–195). Oxford: Academic Press.

Baddeley, A. (1990). *Human memory: Theory and practice*. Hove, UK: Lawrence Erlbaum Associates Ltd.

Balota, D. A. (1990). The role of meaning in word recognition. In D. A. Balota, G. B. Flores d'Arcais, & K. Rayner (Eds.), *Comprehension processing in reading* (pp. 9–32). Hillsdale, NJ: Lawrence Erlbaum Associates, Inc.

Balota, D. A., & Chumbley, J. I. (1984). Are lexical decisions a good measure of lexical access? The role of word frequency in the neglected decision stage. *Journal of Experimental Psychology: Human Perception and Performance*, *10*, 340–357.

Balota, D. A., & Spieler, D. H. (1998). The utility of item-level analyses in model evaluation: A reply to Seidenberg and Plaut. *Psychological Science*, *9*, 38–40.

Bavelier, D. (1994). Repetition blindness between visually different items: The case of pictures and words. *Cognition*, *51*, 199–236.

Bavelier, D. (1999). Role and nature of object representations in perceiving and acting. In V. Coltheart (Ed.), *Fleeting memories: Cognition of brief visual stimuli* (pp. 151–179). Cambridge, MA: MIT Press.

Bavelier, D., & Jordan, M. I. (1992). A dynamic model of word recognition. In C. L. Giles, S. J. Hanson, & J. D. Cowan (Eds.), *Advances in neural information processing systems* (Vol. 5, pp. 879–886). San Mateo, CA: Morgan Kaufman.

Bavelier, D., & Potter, M. C. (1992). Visual and phonological codes in repetition blindness. *Journal of Experimental Psychology: Human Perception and Performance*, *18*, 134–147.

Bavelier, D., Prasada, S., & Segui, J. (1994) Repetition blindness between words: nature of the orthographic and phonological representations involved. *Journal of Experimental Psychology: Learning, Memory, and Cognition*, *20*, 1437–1455.

Besner, D., & Smith, M. C. (1992). Models of visual word recognition: When obscuring the stimulus yields a clearer view. *Journal of Experimental Psychology: Learning, Memory, and Cognition*, *18*, 468–482.

Bond, R., & Andrews, S. (2005). *Repetition blindness in context*. Paper presented at Australian Language and Speech Conference, Macquarie University, Sydney.

Brown, S., & Heathcote, A. (2005). A ballistic model of choice response time. *Psychological Review*, *112*, 117–128.

Byrne, B., & Fielding-Barnsley, R. (1990). Acquiring the alphabetic principle: A case for teaching recognition of phoneme identity. *Journal of Educational Psychology*, *82*, 805–812.

Carr, T. H. (1999). Trying to understand dyslexia: Mental chronometry, individual differences, cognitive neuroscience and the impact of instruction as converging sources of evidence. In R. M. Klein & P. A. McMullen (Eds.), *Converging methods for understanding reading and dyslexia*. Cambridge, MA: MIT Press.

Carr, T. H., & Posner, M. I. (1995). The impact of learning to read on the functional anatomy of language processing. In B. de Gelder & J. Morais (Eds.), *Speech and reading: A comparative approach*. Hove, UK: Lawrence Erlbaum Associates Ltd.

Chialant, D., & Caramazza, A. Q. (1997). Identity and similarity factors in repetition blindness: Implications for lexical processing. *Cognition*, *63*, 79–119.

Chun, M. M. (1997). Types and tokens in visual processing: A double dissociation between the attentional blink and repetition blindness. *Journal of Experimental Psychology: Human Perception and Performance*, *23*, 738–755.

Collins dictionary of the English language: An extensive coverage of contemporary international and Australian English (1979). Sydney: Collins.

Chomsky, N. (1965). *Aspects of the theory of syntax*. Cambridge, MA: MIT Press.

Coltheart, M., Atkins, P., & Haller, M. (1993). Models of reading aloud: Dual-route and parallel-distributed-processing approaches. *Psychological Review*, *100*, 589–608.

Coltheart, M., Rastle, K., Perry, C., Langdon, R., & Ziegler, J. C. (2001). DRC: A dual route cascaded model of visual word recognition and reading aloud. *Psychological Review*, *108*, 204–256.

Coltheart, V. Ed. (1999). *Fleeting memories: Cognition of brief visual stimuli*. Cambridge, MA: MIT Press.

Davis, C. J. (1999). The self-organising lexical acquisition and recognition (SOLAR) model of visual word recognition (doctoral dissertation, University of New South Wales, 1999). *Dissertation Abstracts International, 62(1-B)*, 594 (www.maccs.mq.edu.au/~colin).

Dawson, M. W. (1998). *Understanding cognitive science*. Malden, MA: Blackwell.

Ehri, L. C. (1992). Reconceptualising the development of sight word reading and its relationship to decoding. In P. B. Gough, L. C. Ehri, & R. Treiman (Eds.), *Reading acquisition* (pp. 107–143). Hillsdale NJ: Lawrence Erlbaum Associates, Inc.

Elman, J. L., Bates, E. A., Johnson, M. H., Karmiloff-Smith, A., & Plunkett, K. (1996). *Rethinking innateness: A connectionist perspective on development*. Cambridge, MA: MIT Press.

Fagot, C., & Pashler, H. (1995). Repetition blindness: Perception or memory failure? *Journal of Experimental Psychology: Human Perception and Performance*, *21*, 275–292.

Fodor, J. A. (1983). *Modularity of mind*. Cambridge, MA: MIT Press.

Forster, K. I. (1970). Visual perception of rapidly presented word sequences of varying complexity. *Perception and Psychophysics*, *8*, 215–221.

Forster, K. I. (1989). Basic issues in lexical processing. In W. Marslen-Wilson (Ed.), *Lexical representation and process* (pp. 75–107). Cambridge, MA: MIT Press.

Gillund, G., & Shiffrin, R. M. (1984). A retrieval model for both recognition and recall. *Psychological Review*, *91*, 1–67.

Goldinger, S. D. (1998). Echoes of echoes? An episodic theory of lexical access. *Psychological Review*, *105*, 251–279.

Goodman, K. 1976. Reading: A psycholinguistic guessing game. In H. Singer & R. B. Ruddel (Eds.), *Theoretical models and process of reading* (2nd ed.). Newark, DE: International Reading Association.

Grainger, J., & Jacobs, A. M. (1996). Orthographic processing in visual word recognition: A multiple read-out model. *Psychological Review*, *103*, 518–565.

Grossberg, S. (1980). How does a brain build a cognitive code? *Psychological Review*, *8*, 1–51.

Harm, M. W., & Seidenberg, M. S. (2004). Computing the meanings of words in reading: Cooperative division of labor between visual and phonological processes. *Psychological Review*, *111*, 662–720.

Harris, C. L., & Morris, A. L. (2000). Orthographic repetition blindness. *Quarterly Journal of Experimental Psychology*, *53A*, 1039–1060.

Harris, C. L., & Morris, A. L. (2001). Identity and similarity in repetition blindness: No cross-over interaction. *Cognition*, *81*, 1–40.

Hinton, G. E., & Shallice, T. (1991). Lesioning an attractor network: Investigations of acquired dyslexia. *Psychological Review*, *98*, 74–95.

Kanwisher, N. G. (1987). Repetition blindness: Type recognition without token individuation. *Cognition*, *27*, 117–143.

Kanwisher, N. G., & Potter, M. C. (1990). Repetition blindness: Levels of processing. *Journal of Experimental Psychology: Human Perception and Performance*, *16*, 30–47.

Kello, C. T., Sibley, D. E., & Plaut, D. C. (2005). Dissociations in performance on novel versus irregular items: Single-route demonstrations with input gain in localist and distributed models. *Cognitive Science*, *29*, 627–654.

Luo, C. R., & Caramazza, A. (1996). Temporal and spatial repetition blindness: Effects of presentation mode and repetition lag on the perception of repeated items. *Journal of Experimental Psychology: Human Perception and Performance*, *22*, 95–113.

Marr, D. (1982). *Vision*. San Francisco: W. H. Freeman.

Masson, M. E. J., & Bodner, G. E. (2003). A retrospective view of masked priming: Toward a unified account of masked and long-term repetition priming. In S. Kinoshita & S. J. Lupker (Eds.), *Masked priming: The state of the art* (pp. 57–94). New York: Psychology Press.

McClelland, J. L., & Rumelhart, D. E. (1981). An interactive activation model of context effects in letter perception. I. An account of basic findings. *Psychological Review*, *88*, 375–407.

Miller, M. D., & MacKay, D. G. (1994). Repetition deafness: Repeated words in computer-compressed speech are difficult to encode and recall. *Psychological Science*, *5*, 47–51.

Miller, M. D., & MacKay, D. G. (1996). Relations between language and memory: The case of repetition deafness. *Psychological Science*, *7*, 347–351.

Monsell, S., Doyle, M. C., & Haggard, P. N. (1989). Effects of frequency on visual word recognition tasks: Where are they? *Journal of Experimental Psychology: General*, *118*, 43–71.

Morrison, R. E. (1984). Manipulation of stimulus onset delay in reading: Evidence for parallel programming of saccades. *Journal of Experimental Psychology: Human Perception and Performance*, *10*, 667–682.

Page, M. (2000). Connectionist modelling in psychology: A localist manifesto. *Behavioral and Brain Sciences*, *23*, 443–512.

Park, J. & Kanwisher, N. (1994). Determinants of repetition blindness. *Journal of Experimental Psychology: Human Perception and Performance*, *20*, 500–519.

Perfetti, C. A. (1992). The representation problem in reading acquisition. In P. B. Gough, L. C. Ehri, & R. Treiman (Eds.), *Reading acquisition* (pp. 145–174). Hillsdale, NJ: Lawrence Erlbaum Associates, Inc.

Plaut, D. C. (1997). Structure and function in the lexical system: Insights from distributed models of word reading and lexical decision. *Language and Cognitive Processes*, *12*, 767–808.

Plaut, D. C. (1999). Computational modeling of word reading, acquired dyslexia and remediation. In R. M. Klein & P. A. McMullen (Eds.), *Converging methods for understanding reading and dyslexia*. Cambridge, MA: MIT Press.

Plaut, D. C., McClelland, J. L., Seidenberg, M. S., & Patterson, K. E. (1996). Understanding normal and impaired word reading: Computational principles in quasi-regular domains. *Psychological Review*, *103*, 56–115.

Plaut, D. C., & Shallice, T. (1993). Deep dyslexia: A case study of connectionist neuropsychology. *Cognitive Neuropsychology*, *10*, 377–500.

Plunkett, K., & Marchman, V. (1991). U-shaped learning and frequency effects in a multi-layered perceptron: Implications for child language acquisition. *Cognition*, *38*, 43–102.

Posner, M. I., & McCandliss, B. D. (1999). Brain circuitry during reading. In R. E. Klein & P. A. McMullen (Eds.), *Converging methods for understanding reading and dyslexia*. Cambridge, MA: MIT Press.

Potter, M. C. (1975). Meaning in visual search. *Science*, *187*, 965–966.

Potter, M. C. (1999). Understanding sentences and scenes: The role of conceptual short-term memory. In V. Coltheart (Ed.), *Fleeting memories: Cognition of brief visual stimuli* (pp. 13–46). Cambridge, MA: MIT Press.

Potter, M. C., Chun, M. M., Banks, B. S., & Muckenhoupt, M. (1998a). Two attentional deficits in serial target search: The visual attentional blink and an amodal task-switch deficit. *Journal of Experimental Psychology: Learning, Memory, and Cognition*, *24*, 979–992.

Potter, M. C., Stiefbold, D., & Moryadas, A. (1998b). Word selection in reading sentences: Preceding versus following contexts. *Journal of Experimental Psychology: Learning, Memory, and Cognition*, *24*, 979–992.

Price, C., Wise, R., Watson, J. D. G., Patterson, K., Howard, D., & Frackowiak, R. (1994). Brain activity during reading: The effects of exposure duration and task. *Brain*, *117*, 1255–1269.

Pugh, K. R., Mencl, W. E., Jenner, A. R., Katz, L., Frost, S. J., Lee, J. R. et al. (2001). Neurobiological studies of reading and reading disability. *Journal of Communication Disorders*, *34*, 479–492.

Ratcliff, R., Gomez, P., & McKoon, G. (2004). A diffusion model account of the lexical decision task. *Psychological Review*, *111*, 159–182.

Rayner, K., Foorman, B. R., Perfetti, C. A., Pesetsky, D., & Seidenberg, M. S. (2001). How psychological science informs the teaching of reading. *Psychological Science in the Public Interest*, *2*, 31–74.

Rayner, K., Foorman, B. R., Perfetti, C. A., Pesetsky, D., & Seidenberg, M. S. (2002). How should reading be taught? *Scientific American*, *286*, 84–91.

Reichle, E. D., Pollatsek, A., Fisher, D. L., & Rayner, K. (1998). Toward a model of eye movement control in reading. *Psychological Review*, *105*, 125–157.

Roberts, M., Rastle, K., Coltheart, M., & Besner, D. (2003). When parallel processing in visual word recognition is not enough: New evidence from naming. *Psychonomic Bulletin and Review*, *12*, 405–414.

Seidenberg, M. S., & McClelland, J. L. (1989). A distributed, developmental model of word recognition and naming. *Psychological Review*, *96*, 523–568.

Smith, F. (1973). *Psycholinguistics and reading*. New York: Holt, Rinehart & Winston.

Taft, M. (2001). Processing of orthographic structure by adults of different reading ability. *Language and Speech*, *44*, 351–376.

Usher, M., & McClelland, J. L. (2001). The time course of perceptual choice: The leaky, competing accumulator model. *Psychological Review*, *108*, 550–592.

Van Orden, G. C., & Goldinger, S. D. (1994). Interdependence of form and function in cognitive systems explains perception of printed words. *Journal of Experimental Psychology: Human Perception and Performance*, *20*, 1269–1291.

Warrington, E. K., & Shallice, T. (1980). Word-form dyslexia. *Brain*, *103*, 99–112.

Whittlesea, B. W. A., & Masson, M. E. J. (2005). Repetition blindness in rapid lists: Activation and inhibition versus construction and attribution. *Journal of Experimental Psychology: Learning, Memory, and Cognition*, *31*, 54–67.

Zorzi, M. (2000). Serial processes in reading aloud: No challenge for a parallel model. *Journal of Experimental Psychology: Human Perception and Performance*, *26*, 847–856.

Notes

1 The lexicalist position is also compatible with the cascaded processing assumptions that characterize DRC and PDP models as long it is restricted to interactions within the lexical system.

2 I am grateful to MARCS Auditory Laboratories at the University of Western Sydney, and particularly to Caroline Jones and Michael Tyler, for assistance in collecting and modifying the auditory materials, and to Dr Hideki Kawahara for use of his Straight program to create the compressed and flattened versions.

3 CSTM differs from theories of short-term or working memory (Baddeley, 1990) on three grounds: the speed with which "postcategorical meaning-level" information becomes available, the rapid structuring of this information, and "the lack of awareness (or immediate forgetting) of information that is not structured or otherwise consolidated" (Potter, 1999, p. 13).

4 Plaut did not intend to implicate localist representations, but rather to justify a measure of "stress" over measures based on the differences in "energy of words versus nonwords" (Plaut, 1999, p. 251). However, it is worth noting that the implementation in which he applied this used binary-coded semantic representations—localist codes.

5 Chertkow et al. 1990 (cited in Carr & Posner, 1995) proposed an alternative hypothesis about the role of the VWFS that assumed it is responsible for the "preparatory processing" that precedes access to lexical representations in the inferior temporal cortex rather than "instantiating the visual word forms themselves" (Carr & Posner, 1995, p. 275), but Carr and Posner suggest that Chertkow et al.'s results might reflect contributions from short-term memory processes. Alternatively, the state of lexical closure could be identified with a neural circuit involving both the VWFS and temporal areas. The interaction between these systems may be critical to distinguishing words from well-structured nonwords that also yield activity in the VWFS.

Author index

Subject index

P 326.5 .P75 F76 2006
From inkmarks to ideas
08-2176